HELPING FRIENDS AND HARMING ENEMIES

A STUDY IN SOPHOCLES AND GREEK ETHICS

HELPING FRIENDS AND HARMING ENEMIES

A STUDY IN SOPHOCLES AND GREEK ETHICS

MARY WHITLOCK BLUNDELL

Assistant Professor of Classics
University of Washington, Seattle

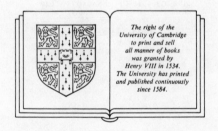

The right of the
University of Cambridge
to print and sell
all manner of books
was granted by
Henry VIII in 1534.
The University has printed
and published continuously
since 1584.

CAMBRIDGE UNIVERSITY PRESS

CAMBRIDGE

NEW YORK · NEW ROCHELLE · MELBOURNE · SYDNEY

PA
4417
.B54
1989

Published by the Press Syndicate of the University of Cambridge
The Pitt Building, Trumpington Street, Cambridge CB2 1RP
32 East 57th Street, New York, NY 10022, USA
10 Stamford Road, Oakleigh, Melbourne 3166, Australia

© Cambridge University Press 1989

First published 1989

Printed in Great Britain at
The Bath Press, Avon

British Library cataloguing in publication data
Blundell, Mary Whitlock
Helping friends and harming enemies: a
study in Sophocles and Greek ethics.
1. Drama in Greek. Sophocles – Critical
studies
1. Title
882'.01

Library of Congress cataloguing in publication data
Blundell, Mary Whitlock.
Helping friends and harming enemies: a study in Sophocles and
Greek ethics/Mary Whitlock Blundell.
p.   cm.
Revision of thesis (Ph. D.) – University of California at Berkeley. 1984
Bibliography: p.
Includes index.
1. Sophocles – Ethics.   2. Ethics in literature.   3. Ethics –
Greece – History.   1. Title.
PA4417.B54   1989
882'.01 – dc 19   88-15971   CIP

ISBN 0 521 35116 2

NIAGARA UNIVERSITY LIBRARY

EA

To Stephen

οὐ μὲν γὰρ τοῦ γε κρεῖσσον καὶ ἄρειον,
ἢ ὅθ' ὁμοφρονέοντε νοήμασιν οἶκον ἔχητον
ἀνὴρ ἠδὲ γυνή· πόλλ' ἄλγεα δυσμενέεσσι,
χάρματα δ' εὐμενέτῃσι· μάλιστα δέ τ' ἔκλυον αὐτοί.

CONTENTS

PREFACE

Anyone who ventures a further contribution to the current profusion of Sophoclean criticism must do so with due humility, trusting that the inexhaustible richness of the original plays justifies such imprudence. It is not my intention to add to the many general books on Sophocles that have appeared in recent years. But I believe there remains a place for a work of more limited scope on the ethical content of his plays. As Schadewaldt well expressed it in a related context, 'However polyphonous the symphony may be, it aids understanding and need not detract from the whole if one pays attention to the basic themes and makes some of them audible.' I have pursued some of these basic themes in five tragedies, omitting the two to which they are less central. Since I have no chronological axes to grind, the plays are treated in the most generally accepted order.

In the hope that the book will find some readers other than classicists, I have kept Greek out of the text, with the exception of certain words whose full significance might otherwise be lost, which I have transliterated. These are translated or explained at their first occurrence and are listed in a glossary at the beginning of the book. Greek has been used sparingly in the footnotes for textual or linguistic points. All translations are my own unless otherwise indicated, and are designed to be functional rather than elegant. I have used Pearson's Oxford Classical Text except where otherwise specified. Assuming that any Greekless readers will have plenty to grapple with, I have with some reluctance used the Latinised versions of Greek proper names, since these are still used in ordinary speech and are more familiar to most readers than more accurate transliterations.

    This book is the product of several years' intermittent labour,
so I have many to thank. Large portions of it started life as a Ph.D.
dissertation at the University of California at Berkeley, completed in
1984. I am grateful for the help and encouragement of many friends
and colleagues at Berkeley, Harvard, the University of Washington
and elsewhere, not all of whom can be mentioned by name. Above
all I am permanently indebted to my thesis director, Tony Long, for
his tactful criticism and warm moral support. I also owe a special
debt of affection and gratitude to Gregory Vlastos, who was the first
to take an interest in this project and agreed to serve on my thesis
committee despite the numerous pressing calls upon his time. Special
thanks are also due to the following: Mark Griffith, for friendly
advice on the dissertation; Martha Nussbaum, for comments on
chapters 1 and 4; Seth Schein, for valuable help with the first two
chapters; Nick Smith, for useful remarks on the first two chapters
and for helping me clarify my thoughts on *Antigone*; Richard
Buxton who provided invaluable advice on transforming a cumber-
some dissertation into a more manageable book; Christopher Gill
and Alan Sommerstein, who read the typescript for the press and en-
abled me to improve it in a number of ways; my colleagues Michael
Halleran and James J. Clauss, for reading and commenting usefully
on the entire typescript. They and all my friends at the University of
Washington provided a congenial atmosphere for the completion of
the work. I am also grateful to the Woodrow Wilson Foundation
for a Newcombe Dissertation Fellowship in 1983–4, which gave me
a free year to work on the dissertation. Most of all I thank Stephen
Sharpe, to whom this book is dedicated, for the years of love and
moral support that made it possible.

GLOSSARY

The following Greek words are used in transliteration.
Note: Most words ending in *-os* have plurals in *-oi*.

agathos   brave, excellent, good (opposite of *kakos*)

aidos   respect, shame

aischros   ugly, disgraceful, shameful (opposite of *kalos*)

aischune   disgrace, sense of shame

arete   courage, excellence, goodness

aristos   most excellent, best (superlative of *agathos*)

charis   favour, gratitude

chrestos   worthwhile, good

deinos   awesome, terrible, wonderful

dianoia   thought, intellect

dike   judgement, lawsuit, justice

dolos   craft, cunning, deception

dusmenes   hostile

echthistos   most hostile, most hated, greatest enemy (superlative of *echthros*)

echthros   hated, hostile, enemy

eros   passionate desire, passion (plural *erotes*)

esthlos   brave, noble, good

ethos   moral character

eugeneia   good birth, nobility

eugenes   well-born, noble

gennaios   true to one's birth, noble

gnome   judgement, general moral statement (plural *gnomai*)

hubris   outrage, insolence

homonoia   unanimity, concord

kakistos   most cowardly, most base, worst (superlative of *kakos*)

kakos   cowardly, base, bad (opposite of *agathos*)

kalos   beautiful, fine, honourable (opposite of *aischros*)

kalôs   well, finely, nobly (adverb from *kalos*)

kerdos   profit, gain

nike   victory

nomos   custom, law

panourgos   villainous

xi

panourgia	villainy	*soteria*	salvation, preservation
philos	dear, beloved, loving, friend, relative	*summachos*	ally (sometimes of subordinate status)
philtatos	dearest, greatest friend (superlative of *philos*)	*sun* or *xun*	preposition or prefix meaning 'with'
phusis	nature	*thumos*	passionate spirit,
polemios	enemy in war		temper
polis	city-state	*turannos*	monarch, tyrant
prohairesis	purposeful moral choice	*xenia*	guest-friendship
		xenos	stranger, host, guest-friend
sophos	skilful, clever, wise		
sophrosune	self-restraint		

I

Introduction

Let us add to the philosophers a most learned man, and indeed a
divine poet: Sophocles.

Cicero, De Divinatione

Tragedy and ethics

According to Aristotle, character or *ethos* in tragedy is 'that which
reveals what the moral choice is like' (*Po.* 50b8f.). Although I did not
come to this study by way of Aristotle, this kind of *ethos* is what I
wish to explore in Sophocles, by examining five tragedies in which
moral choice is central to the course of the drama. These choices are
made within the context of traditional Greek morality, which,
amongst other things, expected one to help one's friends and harm
one's enemies (abbreviated hereafter as 'Help Friends/Harm
Enemies' or 'Help Friends' and 'Harm Enemies'). Closely allied to
these principles, as we shall see, is the conception of justice as retaliation. I have chosen to focus my discussion around this nexus of
principles, since they provide a pervasive ethical background to most
of Greek literature and are of special significance for tragedy. They
are also connected with broader ethical questions, such as the nature
of pleasure and advantage. In particular, both Help Friends/Harm
Enemies and retaliatory justice are rooted in passion, and therefore
raise profound questions about the rationality of moral action and
the relationship of moral justification to the emotions. In the next
chapter I shall outline the salient features of Help Friends/Harm
Enemies, in order to illustrate its scope as a moral code and provide a
context in which to assess Sophocles' handling of such issues. I shall
go on to argue that they are fundamental to the plays under discussion, not merely as an unthinking reflection of popular attitudes, but

as an integral part of each drama.[1] First, however, some preliminary questions must be addressed.

To begin with, can we expect an intellectually serious presentation of ethical issues from a dramatist such as Sophocles? Critics have not hesitated to approach Greek tragedy in such a spirit, in the hope of determining the playwrights' moral and religious thought. Although Sophocles has often suffered in comparison to his fellow tragedians in this regard,[2] he has had his share of such investigations.[3] But these discussions tend to be vague and subjective, seeking the 'philosophy of Sophocles' in a very broad sense: a sweeping metaphysical scheme into which all the surviving plays can be fitted.[4] In their concern to discover the dramatist's own views, none of these writers examines the way in which moral issues are explored within the plays through the ethical language and argument used by the various characters.[5] Moreover the search for Sophocles' personal world-view or general moral and religious stance must ultimately be a subjective exercise.[6]

[1] So too Winnington-Ingram 312–16 and passim, and most recently Goldhill 85–106. Others have noted the importance of the talio and Help Friends/Harm Enemies for Sophocles, usually assuming that he accepted them uncritically (so Hirzel 468f.; Hester, *Friends* 24f.).

[2] For more or less patronising remarks about Sophocles' intellect, often contrasting him with Aeschylus and Euripides, see e.g. Rohde 431f.; Perrotta 630; Jaeger 266f.; Norwood 177; Jones 167, 171 and cf. 181; Hester, *Unphilosophical* 46f. Many scholars seem to share a tacit assumption that if Sophocles is eulogised sufficiently for his many other excellences, then it is acceptable to neglect or even belittle the intellectual content of his work. Yet it is precisely the inextricable synthesis of thought and artistry in Sophocles which has led, through concentration on the latter, to the obscuring of the former (cf. Bowra 2; Opstelten 2f.; Torrance 270).

[3] See e.g. Webster ch. 2; Moore; Kitto, *GT* ch. 6 and *SDP*; Musurillo ch. 11.

[4] Kitto glosses 'philosopher' as someone with 'coherent thoughts about the universe' (*SDP* 2).

[5] Moore, despite his title *Sophocles and Arete*, never actually discusses Sophocles' use of the word *arete* (likewise Kieffer and Whitman). Similarly Kitto speaks of *dike* in the most general terms. (For the meaning of these and other transliterated Greek words see the glossary.) Moreover Kitto's *dike* may be an amoral force (*SDP* 47–9, *GT*[3] 135f.), and is therefore of little use for resolving problems of human justice. (Some of Kitto's admirers have been less careful to distinguish between human morality and universal *dike*.) For criticism of such approaches see Torrance 271f.; Vickers 23–9.

[6] Bowra's interpretation depends on his own dubious criteria for determining which passages are being used by Sophocles to 'show us what to think' (11). The same problem arises with Webster ch. 2 and Musurillo ch. 11. Cf. also Opstelten 141–8.

Such discussions of Sophocles' 'philosophy' usually focus on his view of the gods and their relation to mortals, often succumbing to the anachronistic temptation to tie morality too closely to religion. Much criticism has been coloured by the Judaeo-Christian tradition in which morality (how people relate to each other) and religion (how they relate to their gods) are linked far more consistently than they are in Greek thought. So Bowra tells us of *Electra*, 'The gods and his dead father work with Orestes. They approve, demand and further his vengeance. We need no other proof that Sophocles thinks the vengeance right' (Bowra 226f.). But the role of the gods in human morality (do they enforce it, share it, ignore it?) is a persistent problem for the Greeks, and one which is solved, if at all, in a variety of ways.[7] The attempt to ascertain Sophocles' religious and metaphysical views is no substitute for examining those questions of human choice and action that constitute the stuff of moral theory.[8]

The last several decades have seen some more promising approaches to the ethical content of Sophocles' plays.[9] One strand of criticism has studied human morality in Sophocles from the perspective of the protagonist or 'hero' and the choices that he or she faces. 'Human responsibility now fills both foreground and background', declared Whitman in 1951 (Whitman 39). He departed radically from earlier interpretations, announcing a new approach to the Sophoclean hero: 'The real moral nature of his position must be judged only by his own standard as he reveals it in the play, and by the moral choices open to him in the action' (Whitman 16). Yet Whitman did not carry out the careful analysis of Sophocles' handling of ethical issues which this programmatic statement might sug-

---

[7] Cf. Kitto, *FMD* 74, *SDP* 44–6; Adkins, *Tragedy* 96f.; Dover 246–61. For the multiplicity of religious attitudes to be found in Sophocles' plays see Kirkwood 269–72. On religious anachronism see the salutary warning of Hester, *Unphilosophical* 41–6.

8 The words 'moral' and 'morality' themselves risk anachronism (cf. the unfortunate and by now notorious remark of Adkins 2 that 'we are all Kantians now'). I shall use such language in the broadest sense, for values that provide a guide for conduct in situations affecting the well-being of others, thus imposing constraints on what one may do in pursuit of personal gain (cf. the definitions of Dover 1; Vlastos, *Justice* 301). For a recent discussion of these terms see Williams ch. 1.

[9] At the same time there has been a growing number of attempts to place the dramatist more adequately within his intellectual milieu. See Webster ch. 1; Finley, *Three* passim; Long; Rose.

gest. The approach he championed necessarily touches on ethical issues, and may provide considerable insight into the hero's moral psychology, as it has done most notably in the hands of Bernard Knox in his book *The Heroic Temper*. Its focus, however, is the character of the protagonist rather than the ethical concepts articulated through the dramatic characters.

Philosophical writers have also been showing an increasing interest in the moral content of Greek literature. Much discussion has been provoked by Adkins' *Merit and Responsibility*, which uses Greek literature as evidence for the development of ethical concepts before the advent of formal moral philosophy. Adkins distinguishes two sets of values which he calls 'competitive' and 'cooperative' or 'quiet', and argues that the former were traditionally the dominant values of Greek culture, while the task of moral philosophy was to gain acceptance for the latter.[10] There has been considerable criticism both of this basic dichotomy and of its application to particular authors.[11] But with respect to fifth-century non-philosophical authors like Sophocles, the most general charge of which Adkins is guilty is question-begging.[12] Adopting a narrowly lexical approach, he assumes that any occurrence of a word such as *agathos* always refers to the 'competitive' values inherited from the Homeric tradition. When such words appear in a context which ties them unequivocally to one of the 'quiet' values, he treats them as exceptions, characterised as 'abortive moralism' (Adkins 246).[13] But given the acknowledged 'turmoil of values' of the period (Adkins 232), he is not entitled to dismiss such cases in this way. It is this assumption of what he intends to prove which leads him to conclude, for example, that 'Sophocles does not employ *agathos* or *arete* in a quiet moral sense' (Adkins 193). In fact *agathos* and its cognates and synonyms

---

[10] This is the central thesis of *Merit and Responsibility*, reaffirmed by Adkins in a series of subsequent articles.

[11] See Robinson's review in *Philosophy* 37 (1962) 277–9; Long, *Morals*; Lloyd-Jones ch. 1; Creed; Dover, *Evaluation*. For Sophocles see Freis (to whom I am grateful for making her dissertation available to me). For recent contributions to the continuing debate on Homer see Rowe; Morris 115–20.

[12] Cf. Creed 218; Freis 93.

[13] Similarly in his treatment of Homer any passage that does not fit his scheme is discounted as a 'persuasive definition' (38–40).

do have significant areas of overlap with the 'quiet' virtues in Sophocles.[14]

Another limitation in Adkins' treatment of tragedy is his use of individual scenes or brief passages without considering the overall dramatic context or the place of moral debate in each play as a whole.[15] On *Philoctetes* 119f., for example, he notes that Sophocles is making use of the 'confusion of values' which is 'part of the moral scene at this period' (Adkins 189). Again, he observes that line 1248 'indicates that there has been a change of linguistic habits in at least a section of society' (Adkins 183). But such passages, within the context of the entire drama, may contribute to a more complex exploration of moral issues than Adkins suggests. In a work as wide-ranging as *Merit and Responsibility* it would be impractical to cover complete plays in any depth. But the decision to treat only select passages leads Adkins to represent Sophocles as merely reflecting a contemporary 'confusion of values', without asking whether the dramatist is articulating such confusions into a constructive ethical debate. Despite these shortcomings, however, Adkins has helped to stimulate the currently burgeoning interest in the relationship between Greek literature and moral philosophy.[16]

Such interest is entirely appropriate, since the two, until at least the time of Aristotle, are inextricably linked. Homer is the wellspring of all Greek culture, including both tragedy and moral philosophy, and many of the issues that will later come under the scrutiny of ethics receive their first articulation in epic.[17] Poets generally were regarded by the Greeks as repositories of wisdom on all kinds

[14] This is demonstrated by Freis, employing the criteria for synonymity outlined in Dover 62–4.

[15] Cf. Dover, *Evaluation* 36–44. Ironically, Adkins makes the same criticism of Dover's *Greek Popular Morality* (*Problems* 157f.), also with some justification. But Dover is scrupulously careful in his choice of sources and makes little use of tragedy. Pearson's *PE* does look at whole plays, but the treatment of Sophocles is brief and superficial.

[16] Nussbaum, *Consequences* is an explicit reaction to Adkins. On the relationship between literature and ethics see also Schadewaldt 100; Raphael, *Paradox* 71–4, 94–111 and *Literature*; Redfield 80–2; Putnam 488f.; Barbour ch. 7; Nussbaum 12–16. Nussbaum's recent substantial contribution is influenced by the work of Bernard Williams, whose interest in the ethical implications of tragedy goes back many years (cf. *ML* 30 n. 2, *PS* 173).

[17] See especially Lloyd-Jones chs. 1 and 2.

of matters, especially morality. The conception of the poet as a
'teacher' was applied not only to avowedly didactic poets like
Hesiod,[18] but to every kind of poetry, even lyric.[19] Tragedy, like
the 'dramatic' portions of epic, was thought to 'teach' through the
mouths of its characters. The conventions of old comedy allowed
even a comic poet like Aristophanes to claim humorously for his
chorus the role of political adviser (e.g. *Frogs* 686–8).

Only gradually does philosophy come to be conceived of as a
distinct activity in its own right. Early thinkers as well as rival poets
assert their claims in opposition to the received wisdom of the
dominant poetic tradition (represented principally by Homer and
Hesiod).[20] When Socrates quarrels with the poets (Pl. *Ap.* 22abc),
and Plato treats them as fundamental enemies of philosophy (*Rep.*
607bc), they are not only reacting against a deeply ingrained traditional attitude, but acknowledging poetry as a serious competitor.[21]
And despite Plato's assault on the poets' claim to knowledge (e.g. *Ion*
536d–42b, *Rep.* 598d–600e), he is not above appealing to their
authority, especially Homer's, when it suits him (e.g. *Rep.* 404bc,
407e–408a, 468c–469a; *Leg.* 706d–7a). Many early philosophers
(notably Parmenides and Empedocles) wrote in verse, which was
not only a memorable form of expression but the most natural way
of claiming their place in the tradition, enabling them to dignify
their rival brand of wisdom with the cloak of poetic authority.[22]
Nor did prose writers necessarily eschew the 'literary' qualities of
poetry. Heraclitus' ornate and riddling prose and Plato's dialogue
form are each in their own way essential to the author's philosophical purpose.

Philosophers, dramatists, rhetoricians and even historians used
the dramatic technique of opposing speeches and sometimes dialogue to articulate the moral debates which formed part of their
common intellectual inheritance. Any writer could grasp the opportunity to air various sides of an issue in the mouths of different

[18] See Hes. *WD* passim and cf. Solon 4.30 (West); Theogn. 769–72. For a discussion of the purpose of Hesiod's poems see Heath, *Hesiod*.

[19] For the evidence see Heath 39–44. See further below, p. 12–16.

[20] Cf. Xenoph. DK 21 B 1.21–3, 10–12, 14–16; Heracl. DK 22 B 57, 104; Solon 29
(West); Plut. *Solon* 29.4f. On rival claims to truth and the question of poetic
truth and falsehood see Heath 39f.

[21] Cf. Havelock, *Preface* 27–31; Raphael, *Paradox* 74–9; Nussbaum 123f.

[22] This is especially apparent in Parmenides' proem. See Fränkel, *Parmenides* 1–6.

speakers. The *agon* ('contest' or 'debate') was a fundamental feature of Athenian life, manifested variously in the assembly and the law-courts, in tragedy, comedy and the philosophical dialogue:

> In understanding each of these as a manifestation of the *agon*, we ought to recognize that the categories *political, dramatic, philosophical* were much more intimately related in the Athenian world than in our own. Politics and philosophy were shaped by dramatic form, the preoccupations of drama were philosophical and political, philosophy had to make its claims in the arena of the political and the dramatic.
>
> (MacIntyre 129)

Drama and dialectic

Many extant Greek tragedies revolve around the questions of human choice and action that provide the raw material of ethics. Hence tragedy frequently dramatises particular cases of the kind of problem that moral philosophy attempts to solve, and in doing so may help to shed light on such issues by placing them in a new perspective.[23] It offers us a concrete, particular and urgent enactment of a crisis, encouraging us to identify with the subjective viewpoint of particular figures, without preventing us from judging them. At the same time it is free to avoid the kind of trivial particular that may blur the dilemmas of real life, thus prompting reflections extending beyond the specific situation. Literature has the capacity to suggest that the persons it portrays exemplify universal human predicaments. In Greek tragedy this capacity owes much to the resources of poetry, most clearly visible in the choral lyrics whose significance often extends well beyond their immediate dramatic reference.[24]

Many of the ethical issues dramatically presented in tragedy are also important to Plato. Like tragedy, his dialogues scrutinise the nature of justice and revenge, the relationship of the individual to friends, family, state and gods. But the philosophical dialogue typically dramatises not the problem itself but its discussion in theoretical

---

[23] See especially Raphael, *Literature*.

[24] This does not mean, however, that the chorus may not be viewed as a reasonably coherent character. I shall follow Aristotle (*Po.* 56a25–7) and recent critics such as Burton and Gardiner in treating them this way. See also Kirkwood 180–6; Vickers 10–17 (who interestingly ascribes to Sophocles' chorus the role of the Socratic victim, and brings out well the thought-provoking quality of Sophoclean ethical debate).

terms. It must therefore, like non-dramatic philosophical discourse, introduce specific cases into the discussion in order to test the validity of its general claims. Unlike drama, such cases are elaborated only so far as is necessary for their philosophical purpose. Accumulated detail is rarely required, and may either confuse the issue or over-clarify it, 'dissolving' the dilemma so that it is no longer useful.[25] Moreover since a dialogue does not enact the problems it aims to solve, it will tend to suffer from a lack of immediacy in comparison with the urgently presented dilemmas of tragedy.

Plato does his best to minimise this disadvantage. In the *Euthyphro* he constructs an elaborate example to test various notions of piety and justice and the relationships between them: Euthyphro is prosecuting his own father for murder because he negligently allowed a labourer, himself an arrested killer, to die (4cd). Plato deliberately 'dissolves' the potential dilemma by accumulating the kind of detail that would make the case seem absolutely clear cut to any ordinary Greek. As a test case it is tailor made for the purpose at hand. But in order to give it serious reality, Plato introduces it not hypothetically, but as the real situation that has generated Socrates' chance meeting with Euthyphro and is soon to be decided in court. Moreover Euthyphro was probably a historical figure, like most of Plato's named characters.[26] This use of real persons as participants is an important way in which Plato gives immediacy to his dramatised discussions. Their reality is both reinforced and exploited for philosophical purposes through the requirement that they say only what they really believe (e.g. *Gorg.* 495a, 500b, *Rep.* 350e), which is an essential ingredient of the Socratic method.[27]

Euthyphro is rather a comic figure (cf. 3c), his case has an artificial air, and he is undertaking no serious personal risk by his extraordinary behaviour. We therefore do not feel the anxious concern for his situation that we do for the great figures of tragedy. His role is more closely analogous to those lesser tragic characters who help to shed light on the protagonist. Plato's tragic hero was, of course, Socrates. The encounter on the courtroom steps has implications

[25] The latter observation is drawn from Williams 180.
[26] See Burnet 85f. I make no claims about the historicity of Euthyphro's lawsuit. There is no external evidence, and the elaborate detail of the case can be used to argue either way.
[27] See Vlastos, *Elenchus* 35–8.

whose profound seriousness overshadows Euthyphro's mild absurdity. Socrates' impending trial for impiety gives far greater depth and urgency to the question that emerges from the discussion of Euthyphro's case, namely the true nature of piety. This kind of use of the dramatic setting and circumstances is more fully developed by Plato in the *Apology* and *Crito*. In each the dramatic situation arises from certain moral choices made by Socrates prior to the action. Both works reenact such choices and demonstrate their consequences. In both the issue, as so often in tragedy, is one of life or death for the central character, with broader implications for his friends and the community as a whole. The *Crito* even resembles a Sophoclean tragedy in its structure, with the hero resisting persuasion, even from a well-meaning friend, to abandon his principles and save himself.[28]

Other dialogues do not have this special unity of moral dilemma and dramatic circumstances, nor do they concern specific matters of life or death. But Plato continues to use the figure of Socrates to generate a comparable sense of urgency for the subject of his enquiry. In the *Phaedo* the prison setting and the moving narrative description of Socrates' death both illustrate the practical consequences of his refusal to compromise his principles and give special significance to the discussion of the immortality of the soul. In the *Meno* and especially the *Gorgias* Plato uses Socrates' death to similar effect, by foreshadowing it in the veiled threats of his interlocutors (e.g. *Meno* 94e, *Gorg.* 485e–86d). By such means Plato tries to give philosophical and above all ethical issues an urgency and relevance which a purely theoretical discourse might seem to lack. He exploits dramatic form to convey the vital significance of what he sees as the central question of human life:

> And do not take what I say as if I were playing, for you see that the subject of our discussion is – and about what subject should someone with even a little sense be more serious than this? – what way one should live.
>
> (*Gorg.* 500c)[29]

---

[28] Knox 58 ascribes to Socrates the 'heroic temper' which he sees in the Sophoclean hero. Individual Sophoclean heroes have often been compared to Socrates. The prototype for all of them is Achilles (see especially Wolff 36–40). On Plato and drama see Kuhn (1) 5–11; Egermann 34–48; Tarrant, *Plato*; Friedländer 167; Raphael, *Paradox* 79–89, *Literature* 2–4; Nussbaum, interlude 1.

[29] Cf. *Gorg.* 487e; *Lach.* 187e–8a; *Rep.* 352d, 578c, 608b.

A special virtue of dramatic form is the opportunity it provides for the persuasive presentation of various points of view without obliging the author to commit himself to any of them or provide any systematic answers. In an early aporetic dialogue like the *Euthyphro* it enables Plato to conduct an inconclusive debate while raising many suggestive points in the process. Later he canvassed a range of viewpoints in the mouths of some of his most famous characters, such as Callicles, Protagoras and Thrasymachus. The dramatic form enables him to present such views with uninhibited rhetorical power, giving them full value as dangerous forces to be reckoned with, but without having to subscribe to them himself.

The tension of competing personal perspectives contributes to the authentically dramatic feel of many of the earlier dialogues. But this kind of drama is potentially inimical to constructive dialectical argument. The complacent but well-meaning Euthyphro may end up merely bewildered,[30] but in many cases the argument degenerates into hostile confrontation. As Socrates himself says in Plato's *Apology*, his conversations earned him 'many most harsh and severe enmities' (23a). If dialectical argument promotes conflict rather than cooperation, it becomes self-defeating. This is vividly illustrated by the sulks and ill-tempered outbursts of a Socratic victim like Thrasymachus, who is beaten in argument but remains far from convinced.[31] Thrasymachus also illustrates how Plato, like anyone working with dramatic form, can and does use characterisation to direct the audience's sympathies. The skilful delineation of personality may enhance or undermine the credibility of a speaker's arguments, as it does with Thrasymachus and often with Socrates. Or Plato may lead us to a sympathetic understanding of a character's viewpoint while simultaneously exposing its inadequacy (Crito, Protagoras, Alcibiades). These vivid portraits make an intrinsic contribution to a dialectic that exploits not only a speaker's views, but the personality and way of life in which those views are rooted.[32] But this dramatic form of dialectic operates in Plato's hands with an inbuilt bias, for he was searching for answers and was fundamentally hostile to ethical plurality and conflict.

---

[30] It is a moot point whether Euthyphro's departure at the end of the dialogue (15e) shows that his encounter with Socrates has taught him to think again about prosecuting his father.

[31] Cf. Annas 55–7.

[32] On the ad hominem character of the Socratic method see Kahn; Stokes.

Although the dialectical spirit remains important to Plato, he turns increasingly to a more sustained and constructive form of argument. At the beginning of *Republic* 2 Glaucon and Adeimantus, Socrates' allies in the pursuit of truth, restate at some length the views of the obnoxious Thrasymachus. Plato pulls out all his rhetorical stops to give their words a powerful emotional appeal and thus convey the vital importance of combating them. As Socrates remarks, 'There must be some divine element in you, if you are not convinced that injustice is better than justice, when you are able to make such an eloquent case for it' (368a). Such arguments in the mouths of Socrates' willing accomplices illustrate the changing character of Plato's dialectic. The silencing of Thrasymachus makes possible a sustained exploration of positive ideas quite contrary to the confrontational spirit in which the first book ended. As the stranger says near the beginning of Plato's *Sophist*, 'When the other party to the conversation is tractable and gives no trouble, to address him is the easier course; otherwise, to speak by oneself' (217d, trans. Cornford). Moreover Glaucon and Adeimantus' restatement makes it clear that the implications of Socrates' arguments extend beyond the ad hominem discomfiture of an unpleasant sophist. The brothers can feel the power of the opposing viewpoint, but since they are not committed to it, Socrates' arguments do not assault their convictions, their lives or themselves. It is therefore no accident that their personalities are at best shadowy and remain virtually indistinguishable. The development of a constructive argument need not exclude drama or lively characterisation, but it does make them less integral to Plato's purpose. Hence the dramatic personality of his speakers tends to dwindle, and with it the dramatic force of his dialectic.

Moral conflict was not a notion congenial to Plato or most Greek philosophers, but it is the life blood of tragedy. The playwright, like Plato the dramatist, is free to make some characters more sympathetic than others and to suggest a preference for certain views. But a simple 'right answer' to the complex ethical issues central to many Greek tragedies risks reducing the plays to melodrama. The essence of the tragedy in such cases is often precisely that moral conflict is insoluble or soluble only at enormous cost. This kind of tragic conflict tends to arise from the clashing ethical perspectives of different characters, making moral confrontation integral to the drama. A tragic outcome is inevitable as long as the characters cannot agree on criteria for resolving disputes. While most do share the same set of terms for expressing approval and disapproval, conflict is frequently generated by the varying content which two or more speakers ascribe to the same value term.[33] Such conflict can only be resolved by persuasion, which may induce one of the disputants to alter or even abandon a decision or moral principle. Speeches of persuasion therefore play a substantial part in the drama, as the disputants and others try to avert the disaster that threatens to result if all persist in adhering to their original positions.[34] These speeches rarely succeed, usually because of the intransigence of one or more central characters. Such doomed attempts at persuasion are a characteristically Sophoclean means of effecting tragic pathos and suspense, and at the same time provide a forum for the revelation of moral character and the airing of ethical issues.

This dialectical picture of tragedy does not correspond to the way in which the Greeks themselves commonly viewed their poets as 'teachers'. On the contrary, they often treat poetry as a source of factual or categorical wisdom. Isocrates considers the poets an influence making ordinary people 'better', for they bequeath 'precepts on how one should live' (2.3).[35] Such precepts might be harvested and evaluated independently of their context or poetic purpose (cf. e.g. Demos. 19.247; Arist. Rhet. 1416a28–35). Poets were also thought to exert a moral influence through the active example of their characters. Protagoras in Plato's dialogue tells us that teachers make children memorise poetry full of worthy sentiments and eulogies of good men, 'so that the child may emulate and imitate them, and exert himself to become such a one' (Prot. 326a). This view of the educational function of poetry may be implicit in the judgement attributed to Eudicus' father, that the Iliad is a finer poem than the Odyssey to the extent that Achilles is 'better' than Odysseus (Pl. Hipp. Min. 363b).[36] It certainly underlies the moral debate between

---

[33] See MacIntyre 125–8; Vickers 26–9; Segal, Praise 47f.; Vernant, GT 279–83, Tensions 31–6. Cf. also Eur. Phoen. 499–502; Havelock, Dikaiosune 67; Stevenson 333, 344–50.

[34] On persuasion and its importance in tragedy see Buxton.

[35] The wording recalls the practical ethical concern of Plato's Socrates (above, p. 9). Cf. also Aeschin. 3.135.

[36] Homer was the 'educational' poet par excellence. Cf. Pl. Hipp. Min. 364b–65b, Alc. 1 112b; Xen. Symp. 3.5; Isoc. 4.159; and see Verdenius 5–19; King 78f. On the role of poetry, especially Homer, in Greek education see also Beck 117–22.

Aeschylus and Euripides in Aristophanes' *Frogs*.[37] Aeschylus claims to have improved the citizenry by writing the *Seven against Thebes*, since 'after seeing it any man would have desired to be warlike' (1021f.). Later he says he portrayed the exploits of Homeric heroes 'so as to rouse each male citizen to strain to equal them' (1041f.). When Euripides asks what harm his Stheneboeas have done, Aeschylus answers that (by their example), they induced many noble Athenian women to commit suicide (1050f.).[38] According to the orator Lycurgus, one reason Euripides is a good poet is that he portrayed patriotic behaviour as a model to which the citizens might look, and so accustom their souls to love their country; similarly Homer is worthy of praise for portraying fine deeds, which inspired his audience's ancestors to emulate and surpass them at Marathon (*Leocr.* 100–4).[39]

This naive view of the didactic function of poetry does not do justice to extant Greek tragedy, and a strong case can be made for the view that although poetry was used in this way, the poets' own aims were not didactic in any such simple sense.[40] Apart from anything else, if they aimed to provide their audience with models of virtue, they undoubtedly failed a great deal of the time. It was partly the manifest inadequacy of tragic characters as uplifting moral exemplars which led Plato to banish them from his ideal state. But the underlying view of the relationship between art and life has various interesting implications, explored in different ways by Plato and Aristotle, which point towards a more sophisticated understanding of the moral content of tragedy. Although this more complex view is not to be found in our ancient sources, it is one that can be developed from various elements in ancient views of tragedy, and so does not seem to me alien in principle to the spirit of ancient literary theory.

[37] Taplin, *Trugedy* argues that the notion of the poet as teacher is also presupposed in other plays of Aristophanes.

[38] The 'bad example' tradition is said to go back to Solon, who objected to Thespis' 'lies' because of their anticipated corrupting influence (Plut. *Solon* 29.4f.; cf. also Pl. *Rep.* 424d).

[39] He adds that Tyrtaeus' elegies 'educate' the Spartans in courage; all their soldiers are obliged to listen to them before battle, in order to make them more willing to die for their country (*Leocr.* 106f.). For further examples from the orators see Heath 44.

[40] Cf. Rosenmeyer, *Gorgias* 238f.; Gomme, *Attitude* 5of.; and most recently Heath ch. 2.

First of all, why is it that we are supposed to reproduce in our own lives the behaviour of dramatic characters? Isocrates and Plato's *Protagoras* both speak of 'emulation' and 'desire' (Isoc. 4.159; *Prot.* 306a; cf. also Isoc. 1.51); Aristophanes' Aeschylus of 'stirring up' men (*Frogs* 1041), so that they will 'passionately desire' to be brave (*Frogs* 1022); Lycurgus of 'habituation in the soul', 'persuasion', and 'emulation' (*Leocr.* 100, 102, 104). Aeschines tells us that Homer's depiction of Achilles and Patroclus is enough to make one weep and emulate their excellence and love (*arete* and *philia*) (1.146). Aristophanes' Aeschylus claims that Euripides 'persuaded' the women of the audience to commit suicide, supposedly because they felt the same shame as the tragic heroine whose behaviour they were imitating (*Frogs* 1050f.). This kind of language suggests that the means by which poetry influences us to imitate dramatic characters is the arousal of emotional sympathy with their point of view.[41] This accords well with various Greek views on the effects of poetry.[42] Plato's Socrates suggests to Ion that when he is reciting, 'you go outside yourself and your soul thinks it is present at the events which you narrate under inspiration' (*Ion* 535bc). The soul is envisaged as a sort of invisible bystander 'in Ithaca or at Troy', sharing the emotions of the principal characters (a role analogous to that of the theatrical audience). Ion warmly concurs: 'When I recite something pitiful, my eyes fill with tears, and when I say something fearful or terrible, my hair stands on end with fear and my heart leaps.' The passage strikingly recalls Gorgias' discussion of poetry: 'Into the listeners comes fearful shuddering and tearful pity and mournful longing, and through words the soul experiences emotions of its own at the successes and failures of the persons and affairs of others' (*Helen* 9).[43] This is the Gorgianic 'deception' which signifies the emotional hold of the poet over his audience, their involvement in the emotions of his characters.[44] As Aristotle puts it, 'the hearer always shares in the

---

[41] For the avoidance of the word 'identification' in such contexts cf. Heath 15 and see Harding 141f. Harding finds it too vague to be useful, since it may indicate 'empathy, imitation, admiration, or recognition of similarities' (141). As the ancient examples show, at least the first three are relevant here, as is the further element of the onlooker's emotional response *to* the characters (e.g. pity), on which see Harding 145–7.

[42] See Heath 5–10.

[43] For the influence of Gorgias on Plato's *Ion* see Flashar 68–73.

[44] Cf. Gorg. DK 82 B 23 with Rosenmeyer, *Gorgias* 227–33; Heath 40. Cf. also Untersteiner 108–14; Lanata 193f.

same emotions as the one speaking emotionally' (*Rhet.* 1408a23f.; *Pol.* 1340a12f.). There is also some evidence for the view that a drama will benefit from the poet's own emotional involvement with his characters.[45]

The view that poetry influences the audience by accustoming them to feeling the emotions of others is shared by Plato, who sees sympathetic involvement as one mechanism whereby poetry exerts its pernicious influence.[46] It can corrupt 'even good men', he says, for when we listen to Homer or a tragedian, 'you know that we enjoy it and giving ourselves up we follow along sharing in the emotions' (*Rep.* 605cd).[47] The damaging effect of this sympathetic engagement, which swamps our rational judgement and habituates us to emotional indulgence, is one reason for Plato's great fear of 'imitation' (cf. *Rep.* 387d–88d, 606ab). But he is not just concerned about the dangers of empathy with an inferior character. There is also the fragmenting effect of empathy with a variety of characters of any kind. His guardians are to be specialists, and their single-mindedness will be impaired by 'imitating' many models (*Rep.* 394e–5b). Plato mistrusts the poets not merely as 'teachers' of a rival brand of categorical wisdom, but as purveyors of a plurality of viewpoints with which the performer and audience are induced to sympathise.[48]

Yet the idea that the poet teaches through the example of his characters also presupposes that these characters may be evaluated as models of behaviour, and hence may legitimately be subjected to moral scrutiny. The plays themselves invite us to locate their characters within such an evaluative framework, not only through the kind of action that they represent, but through the characters' frequent deployment of moral language and argument. As we saw with Plato, the resources of poetry and rhetoric may be used to rein-

---

[45] See Ar. *Ach.* 410–13; *Thesm.* 146–72 (the main point here is that the play as a whole will reflect the character of the poet, but the application of this theory to the characters seems assumed e.g. at 153); Arist. *Po.* 1455a29–32 (note γάρ in the second sentence; the passage is correctly interpreted by Bywater ad loc.; Jones 34f.; Gill, *Ethos* 152f.; cf. also Lucas ad loc.; Brink 182f.). For a related idea cf. Eur. *Supp.* 180–3.
[46] Cf. Havelock, *Preface* 44f. Most interpretations of Aristotle's defence of mimesis through catharsis also imply sympathetic involvement on the part of the audience (cf. von Fritz xiii).
[47] For the treatment of Homer as a tragedian by Plato and others see Heath 4.
[48] See Annas 96–8 and cf. MacIntyre 132f.

force moral judgement by arousing the audience's sympathy or
revulsion towards various characters. Conversely, our moral judgements will undoubtedly influence the nature and degree of our
emotional responses. But these judgements may also come into conflict with the emotional sympathy that encourages us to understand a
character's behaviour from his or her own point of view.[49] In particular, we may respond sympathetically to characters of whom we
disapprove. Plato thinks that in such cases emotion will overwhelm
and corrupt the capacity for moral judgement, but the situation is
not so simple. The poet controls both kinds of response, and may
play them off against each other using a range of dialectical techniques. He is free both to pit one moral standpoint against another,
with or without resolving the resulting conflict, and to bias us in
various ways both ethically and emotionally. We may be asked to
sympathise with several characters in turn or simultaneously. If the
moral viewpoints of such characters are in conflict, we must either
choose between them or conclude that some moral conflicts are incapable of resolution. It does not follow in drama or life that *just*
because someone evokes sympathy, we will either lose our capacity
for judgement or be driven to grant our approval. Nor are arguments used by an unsympathetic character necessarily to be spurned.
Such an oversimplified view obliterates the potential complexities of
competing sympathies and judgements by reducing them to a clear-
cut right and wrong. There is a tension inherent in multiple
emotional sympathies, which a dramatist can avoid only by eschewing moral conflict between sympathetic characters. This serious limitation would exclude both the sense that two sympathetic
viewpoints are tragically irreconcilable, and the powerful tragic
effect that may be generated by the tension between sympathy and
judgement.[50]

Ethos and *dianoia*
The method followed in this book depends on the hypothesis that
Sophoclean stage figures may be treated as bearers of a broadly con-

---

[49] For these two perspectives on character and the tension between them see Gill,
   Character. Cf. also Heath 80–8.
[50] On this kind of mixed response see Vickers 57 and cf. Black 73f.

sistent Aristotelian *ethos*, or moral and intellectual character.[51] Plot is fundamental for Aristotle, because he sees it as logically prior to the other qualitative parts of tragedy (50a20–5). But he is more interested in dramatic *ethos* than is sometimes allowed. It is the only serious contender with plot for primacy, remains an easy second of the six 'parts' of tragedy (50a39), receives detailed treatment in its own right, and is inextricably involved in the discussion of plot and action.[52] 'They do not act in order to represent their characters, but they include the characters for the sake of their actions' (50a20–2). Thus despite the logical priority of action over *ethos*, the two are intimately related. Not only does *ethos* help to generate action, but action also reveals *ethos*.[53] This I take to be the implication of another crucial passage: 'The action is performed by people doing it, who must *necessarily* be of a certain kind with respect to both *ethos* and intellect, *for* it is through these that we also say that actions are of a certain kind' (49b36–50a1). 'Necessarily' and 'for' show that it is precisely because we characterise actions in this way that the agents must also have the appropriate qualities. Thus the presumed moral and intellectual character of the agent will generate the *ethos* of the action, but at the same time particular actions and speeches will reveal these aspects of the agent.

Ethos and action are inextricably linked for Aristotle. And in Sophocles they are even more closely knit.[54] The *ethos* of a figure like Odysseus in *Philoctetes* does not merely generate the action, nor

---

[51] I shall say more on 'intellect' as an aspect of *ethos* below. Aristotle's *ethos* does include personal traits such as walking and talking at the same time (*Rhet.* 1417a22–4), but for him these are indicative of moral character (cf. also *EN* 1125a2–16).

[52] Moral terms pervade these parts of the *Poetics* (see especially 49b36–50a1, 52b30–53a17).

[53] The usual translation of διά as 'for the sake of' is supported by the teleological colouring of the passage (ὅπως 20; τέλος 22, 23). Pearson suggests 'as a result of their actions are certain moral qualities' (*Poetics* 83). The idea that Aristotle means *ethos* is revealed through action in the course of the play is attractive, but Pearson's stronger conclusion, that Aristotle means character is actually formed in the course of the play by the relevant actions, is dubious. This may be true of life (*EN* 1103b1, cited by Pearson, *Poetics* 80), but it is implausible for the limited timespan of drama.

[54] Cf. Dale, *Electra* 221f. Sophocles himself is said to have described his own third stage as 'most full of *ethos* and best' (Plut. *Mor.* 79b). The ancient life of Sophocles praises his ability to delineate the *ethos* of an entire character with 'a little half-line or a single word' (Pearson xxi.21).

is it just revealed in passing by his deeds. For his moral character
could have been quite different without significantly affecting the
development of the plot, while the same actions, performed from
different motives or principles, could have displayed a different *ethos*.
As Sophocles portrays him, he could be open to Aristotle's charge of
being worse than is 'necessary' for the plot (54a28f.). But this particular version of his *ethos* forms part of the plot as Sophocles conceived it.

Aristotle requires dramatic *ethos* to be consistent or 'consistently inconsistent' (54a26–8). The stringency of this demand is
shown by his objection to Iphigeneia's about-face in Euripides' *Iphigeneia at Aulis* (54a32), which some have found insensitive or perverse.[55] Paradoxically, tragedy may require a greater degree of
consistency than we may expect in real life, for only then can the
universal patterns of human behaviour be clarified and understood.[56] Like most of us, however, Aristotle could overlook minor
discrepancies (at least he never seems perturbed by the kind of
minute inconsistencies discovered by diligent modern analysts). He
takes exception only to what he apparently considers an abrupt or
poorly motivated character change.[57]

Iphigeneia's inconsistency evidently violates 'probability', for
the portrayal of *ethos*, like other aspects of tragic construction, must
follow either probability or necessity (54a16–36).[58] Aristotle's criterion accords naturally with the demands of a drama that achieves its
effects through the representation of persons. A reasonable coherence and plausibility of character are necessary both to prevent the
audience from being distracted or confused,[59] and to provide an
effective personal focus for emotional engagement.[60] Consequently
'human behaviour is portrayed – through whatever artificial conventions or whatever fantasy – as something we can understand and
identify with. And inconsistency, though exploited for dramatic

---

[55] See Lucas ad loc.
[56] Cf. Halliwell 135–7.
[57] Vahlen 61f. and Lucas ad loc. suggest that Aristotle's mention of Neoptolemus at
     EN 1151b18 shows he did not object to an adequately motivated change of char-
     acter. But Neoptolemus does not really change. He wavers, but finally confirms
     his true *ethos*.
[58] On this aspect of Aristotle's theory see Halliwell 99–106.
[59] See Easterling, *Presentation* 15.
[60] See Heath 90–7, 115–23.

purposes in all kinds of ingenious ways, is not allowed to break the illusion' (Easterling, *Presentation* 15).[61] The dramatist is assisted here by 'our overwhelming natural expectation that most figures should show some continuous identity and some approximation to a human nature' (Garton, *Characterisation* 250). He or she may also choose to subvert this expectation, but cannot disregard it. If a fundamental consistency and plausibility of character are neglected in favour of other considerations, it must either be in the hope that the inconsistency will pass unnoticed, or in a desire to draw it to our attention.

The evidence suggests that the Greeks too expected dramatic characters to display 'some continuous identity and some approximation to a human nature'. Aristotle specifies that *ethos* should be 'similar' (54a24), which probably means 'like human beings'.[62] The view of the poet as a teacher, in so far as it assumes that we can both sympathise with and evaluate the characters, offers prima facie evidence that this was a general cultural expectation. Moreover most tragic characters were thought of as historical figures.[63] Aristotle attributes the preference for characters from the past to their greater plausibility (51b15–19).[64] He also likes to use legendary examples in both the *Ethics* and *Rhetoric*, habitually referring to the situations of specific characters as presented in tragedy.[65] The epic, from which most such characters are descended, presents itself as essentially

---

[61] On inconsistencies and the ways they are disguised see Heath 111–15; cf. also Goldhill 173f.

[62] See Vahlen 60; Gomme 55 n. 8; Else, *Poetics* 460f.; Lucas ad loc. 'Likeness to truth' is used as a criterion for plausibility in fiction (cf. Hom. *Od.* 19.203; Hes. *Theog.* 27f.; Theogn. 713; *Diss. Log.* 3.10). Cf. also Heath 116 n. 45 on the attitudes of the scholia towards *ethos*.

[63] Cf. Easterling, *Presentation* 7. Aeschylus' *Persians* is thus not an exception in quite the way that is sometimes assumed.

[64] I follow the usual interpretation of τῶν γενομένων ὀνομάτων at 51b15 (see Lucas ad loc.). Cf. the use of ὁ ὢν λόγος to mean 'what really happened' (Herod. 1.95.1, 116.5; Ar. *Frogs* 1052f.).

[65] E.g. *EN* 1146a19–21, 1151b17–21 (Neoptolemus), 1150b8–10, 1135a28–30 (a clear allusion to Oedipus); *Rhet.* 1417a28–33 (Antigone). Rhetoricians also liked to debate the dilemmas of such characters. Note that neither Plato nor Aristotle has a word for a dramatic persona as opposed to a real person (cf. e.g. *Rep.* 605e4–6). In the *Poetics*, *ethos* seems to mean *dramatis persona* only once (60a10d). See Lucas ad loc.; Vahlen 316; and cf. Bywater on 1454a23 (contra Schütrumpf 93–5). πρόσωπον (originally 'face') is used in the *Poetics* for 'mask' (1449a36, b4). For its later ethical development see Pohlenz, *Führertum* 68 and cf. De Lacy 163–5.

truthful, insisting on the divinely inspired accuracy of its historical claims (e.g. *Il.* 2.484–92, *Od.* 8.487–91).[66] These figures from the legendary past are far less concrete in their historicity than many of the participants in Plato's dialogues. Some of them – Creon, for example – seem to have inherited no clearly defined personality, and could thus be characterised at the poet's convenience. But the major heroes of the past – Achilles, Odysseus, Ajax – were endowed with limited but definite character traits. Although later writers could vary these personae for their own purposes,[67] certain basic features had to be respected. Later critics might complain if a dramatist equipped traditional figures with inappropriate traits or behaviour.[68]

Aristotle also requires *ethos* to be 'fitting' or appropriate to type: it is inappropriate for a woman to be courageous or clever, and for a hero to weep (54a22–4, 30f.).[69] Plato attributes a similar concern to Ion, who boasts that the rhapsode knows 'what is fitting for a man to say, and what for a woman, what for a slave and what for a free man, what for a subject and what for a ruler' (*Ion* 540b4–6). Plato himself, like Aristotle, thinks (for example) that lamentation is womanish and unsuitable for a hero (*Rep.* 387e–88b, 605de), though his objection is of rather a different kind from Aristotle's (he disapproves of portraying any behaviour that does not befit the 'good man'). It is true that he also censures the tragic poets for pandering to the masses by portraying 'the fretful and varied *ethos*' instead of 'the wise and calm *ethos*, always consistent with itself' (*Rep.* 604e–605a). But this merely shows that he interprets variation within a dramatic character in terms of his own understanding of human charactertypes (in this case the type dominated by the passions).[70]

[66] On Greek belief in the historicity of Homeric characters see Finley, *Odysseus* 22–5; Gomme ch. 1.

[67] Cf. Lattimore, *Patterns* 58–62. We shall see such variation in Sophocles' handling of Odysseus.

[68] See Lucas on 54a24. Some of Gudeman's examples of inappropriateness from the scholia could (though they need not) refer to 'likeness to prototype' (Gudeman on 54a29). Some have also interpreted Aristotle's criterion of 'similarity' in this way (see Bywater ad loc. and cf. Lucas ad loc.; Else, *Poetics* 460).

[69] For Aristotelian character types see *Rhet.* 1388b31–91b6. These may be compared with specific characters in tragedy (e.g. the 'young man' of the *Rhetoric* with Neoptolemus in *Philoctetes*).

[70] Cf. also Arist. *EN* 1159b7–9: 'The wicked have no constancy; for they do not even remain similar to themselves.' Plato was right that tragedy favours the pas-

The characters are, of course, presented through the formal conventions of the ancient Greek tragic theatre. Heath has well observed that such conventions actually enhance our perception of continuity by 'naturalising' features of theatrical presentation that might otherwise seem highly implausible.[71] Yet he has joined others in arguing that the techniques of rhetoric may be exploited in an opportunistic way that leads to '"suspension" of *ethos*', offering evidence from Aristotle for this view.[72] But on Aristotle's view of *ethos* there is no intrinsic conflict between *ethos* and rhetoric. Rhetorical argument belongs to the 'part' of tragedy called *dianoia* or 'intellect' (*Po*. 50b4–7; cf. 56a34–7). But rather than 'suspending' *ethos*, *dianoia* is an important vehicle for its articulation.[73]

In the *Poetics*, *dianoia* as a part of tragedy (50a6f.) is derived from the need for the persons doing the action to have certain qualities of intellect (49b36–8). This implies that the stage figures' use of rhetorical argument will characterise them in respect of intellect. But intellectual character is itself an important aspect of *ethos*. Although 'ethical' and 'intellectual' virtue are distinguished in the *Ethics* (*EN* 1103a3–7), they are bridged by the intellectual virtue of practical wisdom, which is essential for a good moral choice or *prohairesis* and hence for complete virtue (*EN* 1139a22–b5, 1144a6–22, 1144b30–2). *Prohairesis*, which is what reveals *ethos* in both oratory and drama (*Rhet*. 1395b13f.; *Po*. 50b8f.),[74] thus has an essential intellectual element (*EN* 1139a33f., 1139b4f.). In the *Rhetoric* we are told that the speaker must project various desirable qualities as indicators of *ethos*

sionate *ethos*, though we might ascribe this to the demands of effective tragedy rather than to the low tastes of the audience. But for Plato the two apparently coincide. He might approve of Theseus in *OC*, but a play with only such characters would be dull indeed.

71 Heath 113f. On stylisation cf. also Vickers 54–6; Easterling, *Character* 121. Gould's interesting paper is vitiated by the idea that stylisation makes the audience *perceive* the action and stage figures as 'fragmented and discontinuous' (Gould 50).

72 Heath 130f. Heath's use of *Rhet*. 1356a8–10 is misleading. It is not the case that Aristotle 'explicitly denies that rhetorical *ethopoiia* [portrayal of *ethos*] depends on maintaining consistency with a previously established impression of character' (Heath 131). He simply says *ethos* should be achieved through the speech itself rather than a prior opinion about the speaker.

73 On the close relationship between *ethos* and *dianoia* see Dale, *Ethos*; Halliwell 154–6.

74 Cf. also *Rhet*. 1367b22–7; 1374a11–13; 1417a16–19; *Po*. 54a17–19.

(1356a4–8, 1366a23–8), including practical wisdom (1378a6–9).[75]
Similarly in the *Poetics* 'cleverness', a close relative of practical wisdom,[76] is included under *ethos* (54a23f.). Moreover in both works
one of the functions of *dianoia* is to express *gnomai*, or moral generali-
sations (*Po*. 50a6f.; cf. 50b11f.; *Rhet*. 1403a34–b1; cf. 1394a21–5). In
the *Rhetoric* we are told that these are useful for showing *prohairesis*
and hence the speaker's *ethos* (1395b12–17; cf. 1395a19–33, 1418a17–
21). Sometimes the meaning of the *gnome* will be clear, but if not,
then further explanation is needed (1394b7–34, 1395a27–9). This is
the province of the enthymeme or rhetorical syllogism, which
embraces the *gnome* and constitutes a broader branch of rhetorical
dianoia. Similarly, the reasoning behind a particular *prohairesis* must
sometimes be explained if it is to carry conviction. Aristotle illustrates this point with Antigone's famous self-justification (1417a28–
33). In such cases the techniques of argument encompassed by *dianoia*
may furnish the reasoning to explain and justify a *prohairesis*, and
thus become a vehicle for the expression of *ethos*, both moral and
intellectual.

The playwright may, when convenient, exploit the 'rhetoric of
the situation',[77] using a speech-writer's techniques to make a speaker
more persuasive and attractive and to delineate other characters,
especially the speaker's opponents (cf. *Rhet*. 1417a3–7). Like lyric or
stichomythia, this kind of rhetorical argument is an accepted formal
convention, used to some degree by all the Greek dramatists. As such
it 'naturalises' behaviour that might otherwise seem strange or
inappropriate, such as coherent and systematic argument from a
'grief-stricken old woman', or the elaborate presentations of a tragic
messenger.[78] But the techniques of rhetoric do not thereby 'suspend'
ethos, at least in the Aristotelian sense. Rather they provide the play-

---

[75] In both *Poetics* and *Rhetoric* this process is spoken of as being or appearing 'of a
certain kind' (*Po*. 49b37, 50a5f.; *Rhet*. 1377b20–8). On *ethos* in the *Poetics* and
Rhetoric cf. Gill, *Ethos* 151–5. We may note that the practice of Lysias in the fifth
century accords well with Aristotle's recommendation to present oneself as virtuous. He was to become famous for his portrayal of *ethos* (Dion. Hal. *Lysias* 8;
see Usher for discussion and bibliography).

[76] It is morally neutral, but a necessary condition for practical wisdom (*EN*
1144a23–8).

[77] Dale xxvii (who has influenced e.g. Gould, *Character* 57f.).

[78] The quoted phrase is from Heath 130, who is quoting Lee on *Hecuba* in Euripides' *Trojan Women*. On the messenger convention see Heath 153–7.

wright with a valuable dramatic resource for its articulation. For the fact that a speech is forensic or otherwise conventional in form or tone does not make it meaningless or irrelevant. The rhetorical element in tragedy reflects not just the sophist's school but the real Athenian world of the assembly and the lawcourts.[79] In these contexts the effectiveness of a speaker's rhetoric depends on his being taken seriously by his audience. The portrayal of oneself as virtuous, as Aristotle recommends, will not arouse sympathy or admiration if the audience can merely dismiss it as so much 'empty' rhetoric.[80] In drama as well as life a speaker's rhetorical arguments may enhance his or her character and credibility, or undermine them, as with the flagrant sophistry of Helen in Euripides' *Trojan Women*.[81] As in life, so in drama, an audience comfortable with such techniques may be expected to evaluate speakers according to the use they make of them.

I shall work on the assumption, then, that *dianoia* is expressive of *ethos*, and that we are entitled to approach the dramatic figures with a broad expectation of continuity and coherence of moral character. This does not mean the *ethos* of every character is always consistent. Indeed, it is only if the characters are granted a continuous moral identity that it becomes possible to ask questions about their ethical consistency or lack of it. Apparent inconsistencies in their ethical views will become data to be explained in terms of a unitary moral personality. Odysseus in *Philoctetes*, for example, is highly inconsistent in his moral language.[82] I shall assume that we may treat such inconsistencies as indicators of his *ethos*.[83] The 'rhetoric of the situation', in the hands of a skilful speech-writer, could give him a far better case. But for the playwright the situation served by the rhetoric includes the *ethos* with which he wishes to endow his

---

[79] Heath 135 reminds us that Gorgias' *Helen* is a jeu d'esprit (*Helen* 21). But Gorgias' overall rhetorical project was both serious and highly practical. For the right emphasis see Goldhill ch. 9.

[80] The rhetorical convention of denying one's own rhetorical skill (e.g. Lys. 19.1f.) is designed to preempt such reactions.

[81] On the relation of Eur. *Tro.* 914–65 to Gorgias' *Helen* see Nestle, *Euripides* 90f.; Adkins 124–7; Goldhill 236–8.

[82] I have discussed this aspect of his character in my *Odysseus*.

[83] I do not mean that during a performance the audience is constantly alert for minute verbal discrepancies, but that they respond to the overall effect to which each discrepancy contributes. On audience awareness see Taplin, *GTA* 6.

Odysseus. When Sophocles presents us with such a character he expects us to understand, in Aristotle's phrase, 'what kind of person' would use moral language in this way.

Questions about consistency may be of several different kinds. To behave in contrary ways in analogous situations may be condemned as folly or even as disgraceful.[84] A specially heinous kind of inconsistency is the failure to act on one's words, for this undermines trust and so strikes at the heart of social cooperation.[85] Equally reprehensible is the failure to hold oneself to the standards one demands of others.[86] But such breaches need not arise through the agent's planning or choice. They may be a consequence of internally inconsistent principles. If so, we must ask whether the agent can or should render his or her values coherent, or whether the conflict is inescapable. Socrates set himself the task of ironing out the inconsistencies in the convictions of his fellow Athenians.[87] Yet the removal of inconsistency may be either undesirable or impossible.[88] Even in such cases, however, one must ultimately choose a single course of action and face its consequences.

These choices and the passions and principles from which they spring, as presented by Sophocles, are the subject of this book. In order to reduce it to manageable proportions, I have centred my discussion round the Help Friends/Harm Enemies code. This choice of ethical focus is not arbitrary, for the code lies at the heart of Greek popular ethics and is fundamental to the understanding of much of Greek tragedy. Its importance does, however, vary from play to play. Although both *Oedipus Tyrannus* and *Trachiniae* could be examined from such a perspective, the code is less integral to either than to the rest of extant Sophocles. Moreover in *Trachiniae* the moral issues are further complicated by the fact that the central tragic decision is made in ignorance of a vital particular. As Aristotle would agree, actions performed in ignorance of a relevant particular are not open to moral evaluation in the same way as those that result

---

[84] For disapproval of this and other kinds of inconsistency see Dover 219f.

[85] For condemnations see e.g. Theogn. 979–82; Democr. DK 68 в 82; Ant. Soph. DK 87 в 56; Lys. 12.26. Cf. also Lys. 1.48.

[86] Cf. Pittacus DK 10.3є.4; Hyp. 3.31; Isoc. 3.49, 62; Demos. 20.135, 25.81; Plut. *Mor.* 88d–89b.

[87] For Socrates' emphasis on personal consistency see Pl. *Crito* 46bcd.

[88] This is a central argument of Nussbaum's book. On moral consistency see further her ch. 2 and Gowans. Cf. also Mackenzie 14.

from fully informed decisions (cf. *EN* 1109b30–11b3). The same, of course, applies to Oedipus' actions revealed in the course of *OT*.[89] On this play I can only echo Bowra's judgement, that 'in the dark emotions aroused by *King Oedipus* approval and disapproval have a very small place' (Bowra 8). For these reasons I shall concentrate on the five remaining extant plays of Sophocles. Before turning to them, however, I shall outline the principal features of the Help Friends/Harm Enemies code as a background for the discussion that follows.

[89] Ignorance does play an important role in other Sophoclean tragedies (notably *Electra* and *Philoctetes*), but it does not distort a central moral decision in the same way.

2

Helping friends and harming enemies

> A feud is this way. A man has a quarrel with another man, and
> kills him; then that other man's brother kills *him*; then the other
> brothers, on both sides, goes for one another; then the *cousins*
> chip in – and by-and-by everybody's killed off, and there ain't
> no more feud. But it's kind of slow, and takes a long time.
>
> Mark Twain, *Adventures of Huckleberry Finn*

Helping friends and harming enemies

Greek popular thought is pervaded by the assumption that one
should help one's friends and harm one's enemies.[1] These fundamental principles surface continually from Homer onwards and survive
well into the Roman period, and indeed to the present day,
especially in international relations. They are firmly based on observation of human nature, which yields the conclusion that most
human beings do in fact desire to help their friends and harm their
enemies, and derive satisfaction from such behaviour. Thus Xenophon's Socrates can count benefiting friends and defeating enemies
as one of the things which bring 'greatest pleasures' (*Mem.* 4.5.10).[2]

Friendship, and the desire to help our friends and protect them
from hostility, may seem to us as to the Greeks both natural[3] and

---

[1] See Earp 31–5; Dirlmeier; Ferguson ch. 4; Pearson, *PE* 15–17, 86–9; Vickers
243–5; Dover 180–4; Vlastos, *Justice* 303–7. There is also much relevant material
in Glotz and in Bolkestein ch. 2. I am indebted to these writers for some of my
references, though I have sometimes used them for different purposes.

[2] I am aware that the use of isolated references may leave me open to the kind of
criticism I have made against Adkins (above, p. 4f.). I shall try, however, to
minimise the risk of misinterpretation by avoiding sentiments that appear controversial or provocative, and that cannot be paralleled in authors of widely
varying genres or periods. I shall confine myself (with a few exceptions) to
examples from outside tragedy, emphasising Homer (as the fountainhead of all
Greek literature and thought), wisdom poets such as Hesiod and Theognis, and
prose authors, including philosophers where they help to shed light on conventional opinion. On the value of various sources for popular views, see Dover
1–45, with the criticisms of Adkins (*Problems* 144–7), and Dover's response
(*Evaluation* 47f.).

[3] Xen. *Mem.* 2.6.21; Pl. *Lys.* 221e; Arist. *EN* 1169b16–22, 1162a16–19.

pleasant.[4] But unlike most of us, they realistically acknowledged that it is also human to be pained by our enemies' success and take pleasure in their downfall. When people see an enemy's dogs or horses admired, says Plutarch, they feel pain; if his land is well worked or his garden flourishing, they groan (*Mor.* 88b). On the other hand the anger provoked by injury can, in Achilles' famous words, be 'sweeter than dripping honey' (*Il.* 18.109).[5] This in turn stimulates the desire to retaliate,[6] for 'revenge is sweet' (Arist. *Rhet.* 1370b30).[7] The death of a Homeric hero consoles his own victims and their bereaved relatives (e.g. *Il.* 13.413–16; 17.38–40, 538f.). Thucydides suggests that such pleasure was proverbial (7.68.1f.). Xenophon's Hiero is quite specific: 'the sweetest thing of all is to take from enemies against their will' (*Hiero* 1.34).[8] Nietzsche's comment still holds true, that 'close observation will spot numerous survivals of this oldest and most thorough human delight in our own culture' (*Morals* 198).[9]

This pleasure is balanced by alarm at the prospect of enemies experiencing such pleasure in one's own humiliation. Homeric warriors regularly gloat over their victims – a fate the latter are anxious to avoid (e.g. *Il.* 3.43–51, 6.82, 12.390f.). Aeschines can ask in court, 'Is it not pitiful to see the face of a mocking enemy, and to hear his reproaches in one's ears?' (2.182f.). The Platonic Socrates can assume for the sake of argument that it is neither unjust nor envious to rejoice at an enemy's misfortunes (*Phileb.* 49d). A saying of the sage Pittacus advises us to tell no one our plans, so that we cannot be mocked for failure (DK 10.3.ε.2).[10] Such mockery may be anticipated for humiliations ranging from the choice of a bad wife,[11] to the sufferings of bereavement (Lys. 2.74).

In accordance with the view that both revenge and friendship

---

[4] *Il.* 21.45; Pind. *Nem.* 8.41f.; Philemon fr. 108 (Kock); Xen. *Hiero* 3.2; Arist. *EN* 1159a25–8, 1162a7–9, 24–7.

[5] Cited e.g. by Pl. *Phileb.* 47e; Arist. *Rhet.* 1370b10–12, 1378b6f.

[6] Anger is often defined by philosophers as the desire for retaliation (e.g. Arist. *Rhet.* 1378a30, *de An.* 403a29–31, cf. *EN* 1126a13–18; *SVF* III 395–8). Democritus calls it 'insensibility' not to take revenge on an injury (DK 68 B 193).

[7] Cf. 1373a4f., 13–16, 1378b1f.; *EN* 1117a5–7, 1126a21f., 30.

[8] Cf. also *Il.* 21.423; Thuc. 3.67.4; Xen. *Hier.* 1.36; Demos. 15.5; Plut. *Mor.* 92def.

[9] For modern examples cf. Jacoby passim.

[10] For the significance of sayings attributed to the Seven Sages see Bolkestein 74f.

[11] Hes. *WD* 701; Archil. *Pap. Col.* 7511 (= *SLG* 478), 22f.; Semon. 6.73f. (West). Cf. also Sappho 15 (Voigt).

may be a source of pleasure, the complementary principles Help
Friends and Harm Enemies appear most characteristically not as a
commandment but as an expression of desire or approval. (For these
abbreviations, see above, p. 1.) In our earliest statement of the dual
theme Odysseus tells Nausicaa that nothing is better than when a
man and woman live together in harmony: this brings 'great pain to
their enemies, and joy to their well-wishers' (*Od.* 6.182–5). The sentiment often appears as a prayer: 'Zeus grant that I repay my friends
who love me, and overpower my enemies.' So Theognis prays,
adding that this would make him seem a god amongst mortals (337–
40).[12] Failure in such an enterprise is a matter for lamentation
(Theogn. 1107f.), success a matter for boasting: 'I know how to love
one who loves me, and how to hate and abuse my enemy' (Archil.
23.14f. (West)).[13] In Aristotle's *Rhetoric* (whose discussion of the virtues and emotions is largely a compendium of accepted values), Help
Friends/Harm Enemies is included amongst 'things chosen'
(1363a19–21, 33f.; cf. 1399b36f.).[14] The most positively prescriptive
references suggest that this double ideal is not merely desirable, but
admirable. 'Consider it equally shameful to be surpassed by your
enemies in doing harm and your friends in doing good' (Isoc. 1.26;
cf. *Diss Log.* 2.7). This is how both Plato's Meno (*Meno* 71e) and
Xenophon's Socrates (*Mem.* 2.6.35) define a man's 'excellence'
(*arete*), and how Polemarchus in the *Republic* defines justice (332ab;
cf. also *Clit.* 410a).

The bridge from the evident pleasure of Help Friends/Harm
Enemies to its elevation as a positive norm is the justice of the talio,
whose essense is reciprocation, repayment in kind.[15] This wide-

---

[12] Cf. Sol. 1 (West) 5f.; Sappho 5.6f. (Voigt); Xen. *Anab.* 1.9.11. Cf. also the
wishes of Theogn. 869–72; Pind. *Pyth.* 2.83–5; Xen. *Cyr.* 1.4.25.

[13] Cf. Thuc. 2.41; Xen. *Cyr.* 8.7.7; Plut. *Sulla* 38.4; *Anth. Pal.* 5.107.

[14] Other statements of general approval: Ar. *Birds* 418–21; Xen. *Mem.* 4.5.10;
Gorg. *Pal.* 25: 'madness' to harm friends and help enemies; Lys. 9.20: 'it has
been laid down' (τετάχθαι); Pittacus DK 10.3.ε.8: 'illogical' to speak badly of
friend or well of enemy; Pl. *Rep.* 362bc: one of the 'advantages' of the unjust
man; Xen. *Hier.* 2.2: one of the 'advantages' of the tyrant; Theogn. 1032f.: do
not pain a friend or gladden an enemy; Xen. *Mem.* 2.3.14: praiseworthy to anticipate friends in doing good and enemies in doing evil. Cf. also Plut. *Mor.*
807ab; Pl. *Rep.* 375c; Ev. Matt. 5.43.

[15] The name comes from the Latin legal term *talio*, 'repayment in kind' (see *OLD*
s.v. and cf. e.g. *Lex. xii* 8.2). For a wide range of examples, not confined to
Greece and Rome, see Hirzel; Dihle 13–40. Cf. also Hirzel, *Themis* 189–95;
Thomson[1] on *Cho.* 311–13.

spread and superficially plausible notion of justice assimilates both punishment for injury and the reciprocation of favours to the repayment of a debt.[16] The language of debt and repayment is pervasive in Greek discussions of both revenge and friendship.[17] The talio requires that like be paid for like, the biblical 'life for life, eye for eye, tooth for tooth, hand for hand, foot for foot, burning for burning, wound for wound, stripe for stripe' (Exod. 21.23–5).[18] Plato bears witness to the antiquity of this doctrine.[19] In early times it is applied especially to murder, and (as befits the idea of repayment) is expected to operate regardless of the intention of the offender.[20]

The talio appears at its most general in the formula 'the doer suffers', which we associate particularly with Aeschylus' *Oresteia*, but which is echoed in many other sources.[21] It is also very frequently expressed as repayment in kind, ranging from the fairly broad to the uncomfortably specific: pity is owed to the compassionate, but the pitiless deserve no pity (Demos. 21.100f.; cf. 25.84; Thuc. 3.40.3); those who fail to help others forfeit any right to assistance (Demos. 23.106); death in battle is a 'payment' for other deaths (*Il.* 14.483f.; 16.398); victims of injustice wish for their persecutors to suffer what they have inflicted (e.g. *Il.* 13.622f.; Demos. *Ep.* 3.35); Zeus demands from Hera one of her favourite cities in return for abandoning Troy (*Il.* 4.40–3); Nestor urges the Greeks not to give up until each has slept with the wife of a Trojan (in revenge for Paris' abduction of

---

[16] See Vlastos, *Justice* 304f.; Hirzel, *Themis* 191f. n. 3.

[17] Some common words: τίνω, 'pay'; ποινή, 'payment'; ἀποδίδωμι, 'pay back'; ἀμοιβή, 'exchange'; τιμή, both 'honour' as social worth and 'payment' or compensation (see Adkins, *Honour*; Mackenzie 70–81); cognates and compounds of the above; words prefixed with ἀντι- (which indicates reciprocity or exchange). Aristotle takes very seriously the model of friendship as contractual obligation analogous to a financial transaction (e.g. *EN* 1162b21, 1163b32–1164a2, contrast 1167b17–33). Plut. *Mor.* 93f. says we 'buy' friends in the 'coin' of good will, favour (*charis*) and virtue (*arete*). Cf. also ib. 96b; Xen. *Mem.* 2.5.

[18] For 'an eye for an eye' in the Greek world cf. Demos, 24.140f.; Diod. 12.17.4.

[19] In a discussion of kin-murder he refers it to the authority of 'ancient priests' (*Leg.* 872d–73a).

[20] See Glotz 48–50; Dihle 14–18.

[21] The locus classicus for this theme in Greek is Aesch. *Cho.* 306–14. On its significance in the *Oresteia* see Dodds, *Morals* 25–9. Similar wording is used at Pind. *Nem.* 4.32; Soph. fr. 223b, 962 (Radt); Eur. *Andr.* 438; Ar. *Thesm*, 519; Ant. Soph. DK 87 B 58; Pl. *Leg.* 872e; *Anth. Pal.* 12.132.13f., 16.199; Hes. fr. 286 (Merkelbach–West). Cf. also the Pythagorean doctrine discussed at Arist. *EN* 1132b21–33, *MM* 1194a28–b3.

Helen) (*Il.* 2.354–6); the Athenians justify killing Spartan prisoners
and throwing the bodies into a pit on the grounds that the Spartans
treated Athenians in the same way (Thuc. 2.67.4); as a punishment
for castrating young boys for the eunuch trade, Panionius is forced
to castrate his own sons and have them do the same to him, thus
suffering what he inflicted on the parents as well as the boys (Herod.
8.104–6). [22]

Reciprocation of benefits may also be expressed as payment in
kind,[23] though it tends to appear in broader terms than the sometimes gruesome specificity of revenge. Hesiod tells us, 'love the one
who loves, and approach the one who approaches, and give to the
one who gives, and not to the one who does not' (*WD* 353f.). When
Xenophon's Socrates tells Chaerecrates that he does not know how
to treat his brother, he replies that of course he does, 'I who know
how to speak well to the one who speaks well to me, and to treat
well the one who treats me well. But I could not speak well to or
treat well the one who tries to pain me in word and deed, nor will I
try' (*Mem.* 2.3.8; cf. Thuc. 4.63.2).

Return of both good and evil may go beyond simple reciprocation to requital of more than one has received. Hesiod recommends:
'If he starts it, either saying or doing some unpleasant thing, be sure
to pay him back twice as much' (*WD* 709–11).[24] This principle,
which Dover calls 'a head for an eye', adds an element of retribution
to the financial model of restitution.[25] The reasoning behind it
appears to be that revenge requires some satisfaction or further
punishment beyond the mere restoration of the status quo. Dover
suggests that it 'takes account ... of the injured man's feelings as a
distinct ingredient of the situation which needs to be rectified' (loc.
cit.). Athenian law both acknowledged these feelings and set limits
to their satisfaction, by allowing the prosecutor in a successful
murder trial to witness the execution but 'to do no more' (Demos.
23.69). From this perspective, simple retaliation appears not vengeful

---

[22] For other examples of repayment in kind cf. *Il.* 9.32–9; Arist. *EN* 1149b6–13;
     Anth. Pal. 5.23.1–4.
[23] Cf. Thuc. 1.42.1; Arist. *EN* 1156b33–57a6, 1157b34–58a1; Men. *Mon.* 448
     (Jäkel).
[24] Cf. *Il.* 13.445–7; Theogn, 1089f.; Ant. 4.β.2f.; Pl. *Leg.* 642e; Xen. *Anab.* 1.9.11;
     Mem. 2.6.35.
[25] Dover 184; cf. Mackenzie 18–20.

but a restraint on the impulse to revenge.[26] Hesiod also recommends that one outdo one's neighbour in generosity, if possible (*WD* 349f.).[27] Here, according to Hesiod, the idea is to return the onus of gratitude to the other person and lay up future favours for oneself (*WD* 350f.).

The precise return of like for like is often inappropriate, impossible or even absurd.[28] Lysias speaks of the impossibility of repaying the Thirty Tyrants in kind for the number or the enormity of their crimes (12.82–4). In Herodotus, Astyages kills Harpagus' son to punish him not for a similar deed but for *failing* to kill the infant Cyrus – a perverse distortion of 'payment in kind' which shows the limitations of strict reciprocity (Herod. 1.119).[29] Help Friends/Harm Enemies overcomes this kind of difficulty by declaring that one's friends and enemies are those to whom one owes benefits or harms on a more general level. There is an underlying assumption that they have either helped or harmed one in the past, and may be expected to do so in the future. So Theognis can say that no excuse is needed for paying back an enemy who falls into your hands (363f.). Similarly friends have a presumptive claim on one's benevolence. The justice of reciprocation thus imparts moral worth to both the lust for revenge and the natural desire to help a friend.

Friendship and enmity
Respect for friends could be ranked alongside reverence for gods, parents and laws (Isoc. 1.16). In other words, it was amongst the most powerful moral imperatives of Greek life. When Hesiod predicts the total moral degeneracy in which the iron age will culminate, he envisages the breakdown of the bonds of *philia* between parent and child, guest and host, friend and friend, brother and brother (*WD* 182–8; cf. 327–34).

The importance of *philia*, 'friendship', in every aspect of life was enormous. Friends are highly desirable, not just for the pleasure

---

[26] See Glotz 244f.; Hirzel 407, 410.

[27] Cf. Democr. DK 68 B 92; Herod. 3.140.4; Isoc. 1.29; Xen. *Anab.* 1.9.11; Arist. *EN* 1124b9–15; 1163a19–21.

[28] Cf. Vlastos, *Justice* 304f. Schein comments on the logical impossibility of Achilles' demand that Agamemnon 'repay' his injury at *Il.* 9.386f. (Schein 109f.; cf. also 132f.).

[29] Harpagus' son is also served up to his father for dinner, a revenge that goes beyond simple 'repayment'.

of association but for the help and support which they bring. They are a refuge in misfortune,[30] indispensable in daily life,[31] and an essential base for political ambition.[32] Like wealth, health, honour and other advantages, they are 'productive of many things' (Arist. *Rhet.* 1362b14–26). They are a treasure store (Men. *Mon.* 810 (Jäkel); cf. Isoc. 1.29), the greatest profit (Xen. *Mem.* 1.2.7), the best and most precious of possessions, which should be valued as such (Herod. 5.24.3; Xen. *Mem.* 2.4; cf. *Oec.* 1.14).[33] Abundance of friends is considered a fine (*kalos*) thing (Arist. *EN* 1155a30),[34] whereas it is shameful to have none (Isoc. 1.24; cf. Hes. *WD* 715). The friendless are liable to be victimised (Arist. *Rhet.* 1373a5). Without one good friend, life is not worth living (Democr. DK 68 B 99; cf. Arist. *EN* 1155a5f.). The corresponding significance of *philia* in ethical thought can be seen from the attention devoted to it by philosophers and moralists.[35]

Friendship involves a general requirement of reciprocal help and benefit.[36] General benevolence replaces precise payment in kind as the currency in which 'repayment' may be made, so that the obligations of friendship may be satisfied in all kinds of ways.[37] Such helping usually takes place in the area of conventionally desirable goods, such as health, wealth and power, which are assumed to bring pleasure to the recipient. It is commonly expressed in terms of preservation (*soteria*), benefit, profit (*kerdos*), favour (*charis*) and pleasure, of which *soteria* is the most pressing and *kerdos* the most

---

[30] Arist. *EN* 1155a11f.; Men. fr. 639 (Körte–Thierfelder); Philemon fr. 108 (Kock).

[31] Cf. Arist. *EN* 1155a3–16 and see Hands 32f.

[32] See e.g. Xen. *Cyr.* 8.7.13; Pl. *Ep.* 7. 325cd; Arist. *Pol.* 1284a20f.; Plut. *Aristides* 1.2.4. Plutarch calls friends the 'tools' of politicians (*Mor.* 807d). For an excellent discussion of *philia* in public life see Connor.

[33] For this way of speaking of friends see further Dirlmeier 50.

[34] Cf. also *SVF* 3.631. But moralists also advise us not to have too many friends (Hes. *WD* 715f.; Arist. *EN* 1170b20–71a20; Plut. *Mor.* 93a–97b).

[35] See Xen. *Mem.* 2.4–6; Pl. *Lys.*; Arist. *EN* bks 8 and 9, *EE* bk 7. For later treatises, see Ferguson 65–75. Fraisse also assembles much useful material, though his interpretations are often unreliable (see Long's review, *CR* 29 (1979) 80–2.

[36] For the idea that reciprocity is essential to friendship cf. Pl. *Lys.* 212cd; Arist. *EN* 1155b27–56a5, 1156b33–57a6, *Rhet.* 2.4.2; and on Aristotle, Annas, *Friendship* 532–4. For the ordinary language of reciprocal benefit see Bolkestein 159.

[37] Note that the payment model admits both this and financial compensation as substitutes for payment in kind. In Homer, for example, a murderer may literally pay for his deed (*Il.* 9.632–6, 13.659; see Glotz 103–34).

equivocal.[38] Any kind of favour or service can be given and repaid like a gift.[39] In the *Iliad*, for example, we hear of gifts of gold given in exchange for personal loyalty (11.123–5), a bride-price as payment for a woman's (sexual) *charis* (11.243), military assistance as payment for a wife (replacing the bride-price) (13.365–7), and the gift of a horse as a substitute for military aid (23.296–8). On the divine level, Hephaestus repays Thetis' *soteria* by making arms for her son Achilles (18.394–407). Various factors may influence the relative value of favours. For example, a small *charis* in need is worth as much as a greater one at other times (Democr. DK 68 B 94; Herod. 3.140.4; Thuc. 1.42.3). When no other return is possible, the recipient of a favour 'repays' it with honour, esteem and loyalty until such time as more concrete return can be made (cf. Arist. *EN* 1163b10–14).

Charis is a concept fundamental to *philia* and the personal and social relations it governs. Its original signification is of something delightful, that which arouses desire or joy.[40] It is used both for an initial favour and for its reciprocation as gratitude. 'Gratitude' is not merely a sentiment, but must if possible be expressed in a form as practical as the original favour which earned it.[41] This essential reciprocity of *charis* is brought out well by a remark of Aristotle, who thinks the public temple in Athens to the *Charites* (Graces, the plural of *charis*) signifies the importance of reciprocal *charis* in community life (*EN* 1133a3–5).

The expression of gratitude is imperative, and not merely because failure to reciprocate means you are unlikely to receive future gifts or favours (Men. *Mon.* 443 (Jäkel); Xen. *Mem.* 14). It is a form of evil not to reciprocate something good (Demos. 20.6); all agree that one should show good will towards one from whom one has received gifts (Xen. *Anab.* 7.7.46f.); no law is so unjust as to de-

---

[38] It often connotes self-interest, is potentially shameful and may be condemned as such (e.g. Chilon DK 10.3.γ.10; Periander DK 10.3.ζ.4). For common verbs of benefiting and the kinds of deed to which they refer see Bolkestein 95–102.

[39] On the exchange of gifts as the basis of social systems see Mauss. On gift giving in Greek society see Bolkestein 219–23; Finley, *Odysseus* 61–8 and passim; Hands ch. 3; and cf. Benveniste 65–70.

[40] See Scully 21–3. I am indebted to S. E. Scully for making his dissertation available to me.

[41] Hewitt discusses other expressions for gratitude in Greek, many of which are associated with reciprocation or repayment.

prive one of *charis* (Demos. 18.112); a beneficiary should remember it forever (Demos. 18.269).[42] Ingratitude is a serious reproach. Achilles sulks because Agamemnon has shown no *charis* towards those who fight for him (*Il.* 9.315–17). Theognis complains, 'You give a bad exchange to one who treats you well, nor is there any *charis* from you in return for good things; you have never benefited me at all, but I, who have often treated you well, get no respect' (1263–6).[43] Conversely it may be considered 'disgraceful' to refuse a benefit offered by a friend (Isoc. 1.18), perhaps because it shows an unwillingness to reciprocate or to become involved in a trusting relationship.

Trust is clearly crucial to the successful functioning of this system of relationships, and accordingly it receives great emphasis.[44] Treaties, which cement ties of *philia* between states, may include the provision that they are to be observed faithfully and without deceit (e.g. Tod 58, 68, 72, 157, 158).[45] We hear many a gloomy lamentation and warning on the scarcity of honest and reliable friends, especially from Theognis.[46] For trust makes us vulnerable to treachery (cf. Demos. 53.12f.; Alcmaeon DK 24 B 5). As Alcibiades coolly explains to the Spartans, his familiarity with Athens means he is peculiarly well placed to help them against his native city (Thuc. 6.92.5). Such treachery is the greatest danger of friendship: 'It is hard to deceive an enemy, but easy to deceive a friend' (Theogn. 1219f.). 'Open enmity is far better than deceptive friendship' (*Anth. Pal.* 11.390.3f.). The necessary trust arises only after long familiarity and testing (Arist. *EN* 1157a20–4, 1156b25–9), so one should be slow and cautious in making friends (Isoc. 1.24; Plut. *Mor.* 94ef.; Diog. Laert. *Solon* 1.60). For in Plutarch's inimitable words, 'as harmful and disquieting food can neither be retained without causing pain and

---

[42] Cf. also Pind. *Pyth.* 2.24; Xen. *Anab.* 7.7.23, *Hell.* 6.5.48, *Mem.* 2.2.1–3; Hyp. 3.32; Onas. *Strat.* 24; Cic. *Off.* 1.15.

[43] Cf. also *Il.* 5.650f., 17.146–8, 24.33–5; Ar. *Wealth* 1028–30; Demos. 53.3; Men. *Mon.* 243 (Jäkel).

[44] Cf. e.g. Hes. *WD* 708f.; Pind. *Pyth.* 2.83–5; Isoc. 1.22; Xen. *Anab.* 7.6.21, *Hiero* 4.1; Men. *Mon.* 649 (Jäkel); Diog. Laert. 1.54. For the close association of the language of trust with friendship see Taillardat 4–8. Cf. also Vickers 224–6; Nussbaum 507 n. 21.

[45] Cf. also Herod. 1.69.2. According to Wheeler the intention was to preclude sophistic circumvention of the terms of the treaty.

[46] Theogn. 65–8, 73f., 77–92, 95f., 115–28, 415f., 811–14, 857–60. Cf. also Xen. *Cyr.* 8.7.13; *PMG* 889; Plut. *Mor.* 97b.

injury, nor ejected in the form in which it was taken in, but only as a disgusting and repulsive mess, so an unprincipled friend either causes pain and discomfort by his continued association, or else with accompanying enmity and hostility is forcibly ejected like bile' (*Mor.* 94d, trans. Babbit).

For trust to flourish, a friend must sincerely pursue what he or she believes to be in the other friend's best interests. Friends may be both useful and pleasant, but this does not entitle us to use them simply for our own pleasure or advantage. Help Friends is not based merely on self-gratification or self-interest.[47] There are times when a friend's need or pleasure is paramount, and a true friend cares about such needs for the friend's sake rather than his or her own. This aspect of friendship is especially emphasised by Aristotle, who defines a friend as 'one who tries to accomplish for his friend's sake what he thinks is good for him' (*Rhet.* 1361b36f.; cf. also *EN* 1157b31f., 1167a15–18, *Rhet.* 1361b35–7). But Aristotle implies that he is not alone in this view when he prefaces it with an anonymous 'they say' (*EN* 1155b31). And the Democritean remark that the true giver of *charis* does not think of the return (DK 68 в 96) finds an echo not only in Aristotle (*EN* 1162b36f.; *Rhet.* 1385a17–19), but in Demosthenes (18.269) and Thucydides' Pericles (2.40.4f.). This may be one of the points on which a moralising ideal diverges furthest from ordinary practice.[48] Yet literature is not devoid of examples of self-sacrificing friendship. Achilles, despite his selfishness and its destructive consequences to all his friends, goes to meet his death not merely to win personal glory but out of remorse for failing Patroclus and the rest of the Greeks (*Il.* 18.98–106).[49] In Herodotus, Adrastus agrees to repay Croesus with the favour he requests, even though this contravenes his own wishes and best judgement (1.41f.). Such an altruistic element is essential to a trusting friendship, and it is certainly true that one who thought of friendship solely in terms of self-interest 'would have been accounted a false friend by most Greeks' (O'Brien 31 n. 18). Yet a disinterested concern for a friend's interests is not incompatible with a more general expectation of advantage from the relationship.[50] Selfless concern for a friend may be thought

[47] So rightly O'Brien 30–8 (contra Snell 168; Adkins, *Friendship* 33).
[48] So Bolkestein 169f.
[49] On Achilles' loyalty to Patroclus see O'Brien 32.
[50] Cf. Cooper 314f.

of as benefiting oneself in the long run. A selfish, unreliable or dishonest friend will damage his or her own reputation and is unlikely to gain many new friends (cf. Xen. *Anab*. 7.7.23f., *Hell*. 6.5.41).

Most ordinary people regard as a loyal friend one who helps to fulfil their desires. Yet one certainly cannot be expected *always* to give a friend's wishes precedence, especially at the expense of one's own best judgement. Indeed, one who caters to a friend's immediate whim is often condemned as no true friend but a pernicious flatterer. Most of us are susceptible to such flattery, since we enjoy the indulgence of our desires.[51] But moralists all agree that true friends will speak their minds, despite any irritation this may cause. Long-term mutual benefit must take priority over immediate gratification: 'It is a characteristic of good friends not to give such favours to their well-wishers as will bring harm to both of them, but to join in doing whatever may be beneficial to both together, and if oneself has better foresight than the other, to arrange it for the best and not value the immediate gratification (*charis*) more highly than all the time to come' (Demos. 23.134).[52]

But what if a friend remains swayed by 'immediate gratification', or evaluates the long-term advantage differently from ourselves? Parents may discipline children for their own good (Ar. *Clouds* 1409f.; Xen. *Mem*. 2.2.9; Pl. *Lys*. 207d–208e), even if the children hate them for it (Pl. *Lys*. 213a). Insanity justifies similar treatment (cf. Pl. *Rep*. 331c, 382c). But the paternalistic treatment of sane adult friends is a different matter. Force is occasionally used by sincere friends to thwart a friend's desires for that friend's own good, as in the *Iliad* when Priam's friends prevent him against his will from going out to beg for Hector's body (22.412–20). Deception may also be used in very exceptional circumstances. A stock example is the deception of one's troops in order to make them fight more bravely (Xen. *Mem*. 4.2.17; *SVF* III 513; Onas, *Strat*. 23). But both force and deception are normally treated with the greatest suspicion as hostile behaviour appropriate only to enemies.[53] Such unwelcome 'favours'

---

[51] Cf. Ant. Soph. DK 87 B 65; Isoc. 1.45; Arist. *Rhet*. 1371b18–24; Plut. *Mor*. 48f–49a.

[52] Cf. Isoc. 1.30; Pl. *Phdr*. 233bc; Arist. *EN* 1173b31–74a1; Crates 1.5 (Diehl). For further examples see Pearson, *PE* 151f., who rightly observes that 'the argument, of course, was in constant use by politicians'.

[53] Cf. *Il*. 7.142; DK 10 Bias 14; Pind. *Pyth*. 2.83–5; Lysias 2.19; Xen. *Cyr*. 8.7.13;

are unlikely to be received with gratitude, for 'ill-timed pleasures produce displeasure' (Democr. DK 68 B 71). Instead, one must try to procure agreement by persuasion. 'To force belong enmities and risks, but through persuasion the same things happen without risk and with *philia*. For the victims of force feel hatred, as though robbed, but those persuaded feel *philia*, as though they have received a favour' (Xen. *Mem.* 1.2.10; cf. 2.6.9). Xenophon's address to Seuthes gives us an example of an attempt to persuade the hearer that, despite any suspicions to the contrary, one speaks as a sincere friend (*Anab.* 7.7.43).[54]

Enmity, as the converse of friendship, may range from passionate hatred to blunt acknowledgement of conflicting interests. It may be caused by unprovoked aggression, which gives rise to self-defence (the most easily justifiable form of retaliation) or repayment in kind.[55] The question of who started a quarrel is crucial. It is common to argue that one's opponent is responsible for initiating hostilities, thus giving oneself the right to retaliate. Before Paris and Menelaus fight their duel, soldiers on both sides pray that whoever started the dispute may die (*Il.* 3.320–3; cf. 3.351–4, 4.235–9, 270f.). So too in the courts: 'I am participating in this conflict not as the initiator, but in revenge; for my opponent was the first to initiate our enmity, never having suffered any harm from me in word or deed' (Demos. 59.1).[56]

Friendship establishes a presumption of trust and tolerance, so that it should not be ruptured over petty offences or untested accusations (Theogn. 97–9, 323–8; Demos. 25.87–9; Diog. Laert. *Solon* 1.60). Kinship, which as we shall see carries a strong presumption of friendship, may be urged as a ground for restraint in court.[57] A friend who begins a quarrel should be punished with interest, but

Isoc. 8.21; and on paternalism cf. Mackenzie 56f. As some of the references in this paragraph show, the circumstances in which such treatment of friends might be justified was of some interest to philosophers. Cf. also *Diss. Log.* 3.2–4; Xen. *Mem.* 4.2.15–18; *SVF* III 513.

[54] On the relationship between force, deceit and persuasion see Buxton 58–66.

[55] Despite the essential difference between these two reactions, they are often hard to distinguish in practice. Ἀμύνομαι shades from self-defence to retaliation. See the examples in Classen on *Thuc.* 1.42.1 and cf. Dihle 16.

[56] Cf. Ant. 4.β.2f.; Demos. 59.15; Hes. *WD* 707–11; Thuc. 2.67.4; Xen. *Vect.* 5.13; Arist. *EN* 1138a20–2. In cases of assault the key question was who struck the first blow (Lys. 4.11; Isoc. 20.1; Demos. 47.47). Cf. MacDowell, *LCA* 123.

[57] For examples see Dover 61, 187, 275.

should also be welcomed back if he offers amends, for fickleness is not an admirable trait (Hes. *WD* 709–14). Nevertheless, the instability of friendship and enmity, especially the former, was commonly acknowledged. A famous maxim of the sage Bias of Priene recommended that one love as if going to hate, and hate as if going to love (Ar. *Rhet.* 1389b23–5; cf. Diog. Laert. 1.5.87).[58] Aristotle refers to the former as the conventional wisdom, though he recommends the latter as making a better impression (*Rhet.* 1395a26f.).

Enmity is not an inevitable consequence of the dissolution of friendship. When Amasis becomes convinced that Polycrates must fall, he simply breaks off their relationship in order to avoid grief at the suffering of a friend (Herod. 3.43.2). More often, however, friendship is weakened by failure to reciprocate or violated by positive injury and so turns into enmity. The worst kind of ingratitude is harm to a friend, for 'a friend who gives one pain is no different from an enemy' (Men. *Mon.* 805 (Jäkel); cf. Dio Chrys. 3.114). We resent an injury from a friend more than from an enemy, and the strongest love turns into the strongest hatred (Ar. *Pol.* 1328a1–16). A legal attack on relatives could be justified by arguing that it was they who first treated one like an enemy rather than a *philos*, thus rupturing the bond of presumptive *philia* and transforming it into hostility (Isae. 1.6f., 5.30f.). In a famous passage on homicide, Demosthenes informs us that it is not kinship but actions which create friends and enemies: 'In defence of those for whom we fight our enemies . . . [the lawgiver] allows us to kill even friends if they illegally outrage or defile them. For there is no natural family of friends and enemies, but deeds create these categories and the law allows us to punish as enemies those who do the deeds of enemies' (Demos. 23.56; cf. Democr. DK 68 B 107; Men. fr. 475 (Körte–Thierfelder)). In Thucydides, Alcibiades justifies his treachery towards Athens by claiming that he has been forced into enmity by the villainy of others, and the fatherland he once loved 'no longer exists' (6.92.2–4). But the argument is a dubious one, for one's obligations to *polis* and parents, if not absolutely inalienable, can only be violated in the most extreme circumstances without severe disapproval.

---

[58] For the sentiment cf. also Stes. *P. Lille* 76 A 204–8; Eur. *Hec.* 846–9; further parallels in Dirlmeier 53; Mühl. On the Bias maxim see Winnington-Ingram, *Sophoclea* 3.

Philoi

Help Friends/Harm Enemies expands the *talio* from a specific conception of justice into a moral code in the broadest sense, namely those values that govern our relations with other people, setting limits on what we may do in pursuit of self-interest when this conflicts with the wishes or interests of others. If this seems narrow for a general code of conduct, that is partly because we are less inclined than the ancient Greeks to divide up our world between friends and enemies. Indeed the word 'enemy' is seldom used today without hesitation, at least in personal relations.[59] But Help Friends/Harm Enemies is a much less narrow code than may at first appear. This is largely because the Greek *philos* (translated as 'friend', 'beloved' or 'dear') and *philia* (translated as 'friendship' or 'love'),[60] go well beyond our concept of friendship to cover a complex web of personal, political, business and family relationships, each of which when violated may turn to enmity. The most frequent and general word for 'enemy' is *echthros*.[61] The more specific *polemios* came into use for a strictly military enemy, but *echthros*, always the regular word for a personal enemy, remained in use alongside *polemios* for enemies in war, for example in treaties (e.g. Tod 68.18f.; Thuc. 1.44.1, 3.75.1). Conversely *polemios* is sometimes (though less often) used for personal enemies (e.g. Demos. 23.56).

There are many levels and varieties of *philia*, with degrees of closeness extending out from the self, overlapping and intersecting like ripples on a pond.[62] But for present purposes they may be discussed under three main headings. First and fundamental is the family.[63] There is a sense in which the most obvious object of kinship-*philia* is oneself. Plato alludes to a saying that oneself is

[59] Cf. Dover 181. But informal surveys of my students suggest that this inhibition may be on the wane.
[60] For the semantic range of *phil-* words see Chantraine s.v. φίλος (article by J. Taillardat). On the translation of *philia* as 'love' see Vlastos, *Love* 3f.
[61] Its etymology is uncertain, but it may originally mean 'outsider' (Chantraine s.v.). Another common word for an enemy is *dusmenes*, 'hostile one'.
[62] The Stoics used the image of concentric circles for varying degrees of relationship (see Hierocles apud Stob. 4.671–3 (Wachsmuth), and cf. Cic. *Off.* 1.53f.). On the hierarchy of relationships in Greek life see Earp 32–4; Dover 273; Rowe 26of.; and cf. Bolkestein 79–95.
[63] On kinship-*philia* see especially Dirlmeier 7–21.

'closest and dearest of all' (*Leg.* 873c; cf. Isoc. 20.1).[64] A comic fragment declares 'there is no one who is not *philos* to himself'.[65] Conversely the close tie of friendship could be expressed by the saying that a friend is a second self.[66] But the idea that one is one's own friend is something of a paradox, and parasitic upon the basic relational sense of *philia*. This can be seen from Homeric usage, where *philotes* (the Homeric predecessor of *philia*) is fundamentally a social relationship but can be used by extension for anything to which one has a close personal attachment, including parts of the body as well as friends and family members.[67] Self-love is clearly natural. Little encouragement is needed to include oneself amongst the recipients of pleasure, safety, profit and advantage. But the ethical role of *philia* is to extend this natural desire to include the well-being of others.[68]

One is tied to other family members by a presumptive bond of natural affection, arising from blood-ties and common interests. It was often observed that parental love is something human beings share with other animals. In Homeric similes both wasps and bees are said to fight in defence of their 'children' (*Il.* 12.167–70f., 16.264f.),[69] and many writers note that reproduction and care for offspring are natural to all creatures.[70] Aeschines gets considerable mileage out of Demosthenes' alleged failure to display proper grief at his daughter's death: 'The child-hater and bad father could never become a good leader of the people, nor will one who does not love the dearest and closest persons ever place great value on you who are not kin' (3.78; cf. Pl. *Lys.* 219d). The natural power of parental affection is so great that it will even tolerate maltreatment from its

---

64 According to Aristotle, one wishes a friend the greatest goods second only to oneself (*EN* 1159a10–12). The word οἰκεῖος (which I have translated as 'close') is often part of the language of *philia* (cf. Pl. *Lys.* 221e–22a). It literally means a member of one's household, and hence anything closely belonging to one.

65 Men. *Mon.* 407 (Meineke) (= 560 (Jäkel) with a slightly different text); cf. 814 (Jäkel). For other dramatic parallels see Eur. *Med.* 86 with Page ad loc, to which add *OT* 611f. Cf. also [Xen.] *Ath. Pol.* 2.20.

66 Arist. *EN* 1166a31f., 1169b6f., 1170b6f.; *MM* 1213a10–26; Men. *Mon.* 803 (Jäkel); Plut. *Mor.* 93e.

67 See Benveniste 337–53.

68 Aristotle derives *philia* from self-love (*EN* 1166a1–33; cf. *MM* 1210b33–11a5; Annas, *Friendship* 539–44).

69 Cf. also Pl. *Rep.* 467ab.

70 E.g. Democr. DK 68 B 278; Pl. *Symp.* 207ab; Arist. *EN* 1155a16–21; Plut. *Mor.* 93f–94a.

objects. Aristotle gives natural *philia* as one reason why fathers so rarely disown their sons (*EN* 1163b21–5). This is even more true of maternal love, characterised by Aristotle as the only love that can be satisfied without acknowledgement or reciprocation (*EN* 1159a27–33).[71]

Contact with close family members whom one loves is normally a source of pleasure, and it is natural that one should wish to protect their interests. It is 'madness' to harm those closest to one (Isae. 1.20). But the requirement of family loyalty is by no means based simply on benevolence prompted by natural affection. Like other forms of *philia*, family ties are sustained by relationships of mutual *charis*, of favours given and received.[72] Parents naturally love and care for their children, but they also expect to benefit from them in quite practical ways, especially through the reciprocation of nurture when the time comes.[73] One of the greatest misfortunes which could befall one was to be doomed to a childless old age. The helplessness of the bereaved parent is already a source of pathos in Homer (e.g. *Il.* 5.152–8),[74] and centuries later Lysias can ask what could be worse than to bury one's children and so be helpless and without *philoi* in old age (2.73). Procreation was an explicit object of Athenian marriage,[75] and if necessary a son might be adopted to ensure support for his aged father (Isae. 2.10; cf. *Il.* 9.492–5).

If parental love is the strongest form of natural affection, respect for parents was one of the strongest obligations in Greek society, and the greatest opprobrium was reserved for those who violated it.[76] It could be considered disgraceful even to contradict one's father (Arist. *Rhet.* 1398b33–99a1). The obligation for children to support their parents in old age, commonly expressed as a repay-

---

[71] This is based on the behaviour of mothers whose children are reared by others. For maternal partiality cf. also Lys. 31.22; Lyc. Leocr. 101; Xen. *Mem.* 2.2.13.

[72] For a humorous expression of this idea cf. Ar. *Clouds* 860–2.

[73] Cf. Xen. *Oec.* 7.12 and further examples in Bolkestein 161. Democritus contrasts humans with animals in this regard (DK 68 B 278).

[74] Cf. also Hes. *Theog.* 603–7. On Homer see Griffin 123–7.

[75] See Lacey 110f.

[76] Cf. e.g. Pl. *Euth.* 4a–e; Ar. *Clouds* 1321–1451, *Frogs* 145–51. Plato counts maltreatment of parents among the worst abuses of the tyrannical man (*Rep.* 574abc). Both Plato's Socrates and Aristotle argue that the obligation of child to parent is inalienable (Pl. *Crito* 50e–51a; Arist. *EN* 1163b18f.).

ment for birth and nurture,[77] was enshrined in Attic law.[78] Its reciprocity is brought out by the fact that under Solon's laws a son was exempt if his father had prostituted him or not had him taught a trade, or if he were a bastard (for in that case the father evidently did not reproduce to benefit his offspring but as an incidental byproduct of self-indulgence).[79] But the relationship, though reciprocal, was not evenly balanced.[80] If ingratitude against any *philos* was an offence, that against parents was the most heinous, and, in the words of Xenophon's Socrates, the only form of ingratitude punished by the state (*Mem.* 2.2.13).

The closest bond of natural *philia* unites parents and children. A special bond was also believed to exist between brothers, based on their common origins and upbringing.[81] This tie could be rationalised by the old saying that like attracts like (a proverbial truth often mentioned as a basis for friendship).[82] But the presumption of *philia* also extends beyond the immediate family to all those related by blood or marriage.[83] Its strength varies with the degree of relationship, from parenthood at one extreme to broad racial ties at the other. Historical kinship ties may be invoked to reinforce treaties or alliances, which embody *philia* between states and are regularly referred to as 'friendships' (e.g. *Il.* 3.323; Tod 118, 168).[84] Racial ties

---

77   E.g. *Il.* 4.477f. = 17.301f. Cf. also Ant. Soph. DK 87 B 66.
78   Under Solon's laws, its neglect could be punished by loss of civil rights (Diog. Laert. 1.55). At Andoc. 1.74 it is listed with such crimes as desertion and triple perjury. Cf. also Arist. *Ath. Pol.* 56. For the legal details see Glotz 359f.; Wyse 219f.; Lacey 116f. On relations between parents and children see further Bolkestein 79f.; Bowra 327f.; Harrison 70–81; Vickers 112–19; 230f.; Dover 273f.
79   Aeschin. 1.13; Plut. *Solon* 22.1, 4. Cf. also Xen. *Mem.* 2.2.4. For the reciprocity of the arrangement see Beauchet 362–7.
80   Aristotle regards the debt to parents, like that to gods and philosophy teachers, as so great that we cannot hope to repay it in full (*EN* 1164a33–b6). Cf. also *MM* 1211b18–39; Xen. *Mem.* 2.2.3.
81   Xen. *Cyr.* 8.7.14f., *Mem.* 2.3.4; Arist. *EN* 1161b27–36. Cf. also Hes. *WD* 707; Pl. *Rep.* 362d; Theogn. 97–9. For further examples see Bolkestein 80–2.
82   Though the contrary view, that opposites attract, was also held, especially by natural philosophers. See Thuc. 3.10.1; Pl. *Lys.* 214ab, *Leg.* 716c; Arist. *EN* 1155a32–b8, *Rhet.* 1371b12–17; *Mag. Mor.* 1208b7–20, 1210a6–22; Dio Chr. 3.117; Plut. *Mor.* 96de; *SVF* 3.631; and cf. Ferguson 55f. Aristotle uses 'like to like' to rationalise love for all blood relatives (*EN* 1161b16–62a4, *EE* 39b12–23; cf. *Rhet.* 1371b18–25). For brothers see references in preceding note.
83   On marriage see further below, p. 46.
84   See Glotz 135–64 and (for kinship in treaties) 141 n. 1.

may be used as a reason for support or preferential treatment (Herod. 5.49.2f., 8.22.1; Thuc. 8.28.4).[85] The kinship of the whole human race is a further step which emerged only slowly and uncertainly in Greek thought, perhaps beginning with the Sophists.[86]

Philos and the superlative *philtatos* are regularly used for relatives regardless of sentiment, though an element of affection would normally be taken for granted: 'No *philos* is more sympathetic than a blood-relative, even if the kinship is distant' (Pl. Com. fr. 192 (Kock)). In the *Iliad* Aeneas is urged to stand by his dead brother-in-law, who nurtured him when he was little, 'if you care about kinship' (13.463–6), while Apollo is abashed at the idea of fighting his uncle Poseidon (21.468f.; cf. also 14.482–5, 15.553f.). In classical Athens such feelings are echoed in court. A speaker will express embarrassment at prosecuting a relative, even when there is no love lost between them.[87] Relatives retained certain legal obligations towards one another, including avenging murder and burying the dead (Demos. 43.57f.),[88] and provision of support in old age where there was no offspring to do so (cf. Isae. 1.39.5).

The second main circle of *philoi* consists of fellow citizens, with whom one is presumed to share common interests. An orator flatters the Athenians that their natural *philanthropia* ('love of human beings') towards each other makes them live together like a family (25.87–9).[89] A comic character includes in his list of woes the fact that he will become an enemy to a fellow demesman (Ar. *Clouds* 1218f.). Lysias explains that his father helped out fellow citizens financially, 'thinking it the part of a good man to help his friends, even if no one was going to know about it' (Lys. 19.59).[90] Most ties of *philia* exist in the context of the *polis*, so that the most painful

[85] Cf. also Pl. *Rep.* 470e–471b.
[86] Baldry 39–45. Aristotle says human beings are naturally close and *philos* to each other (*EN* 1155a16–22). The Stoics extended the notion to embrace our relationship with animals (Stob. 2.120, 143 (Wachsmuth); Porph. *de Abst.* 3.25). Cf. Bolkestein 88–90, 122–8; Baldry 142–5; Pembroke 132–5.
[87] For examples see Dover 187f., 275f. Cf. also Pl. *Euth.* 4a–e.
[88] On vengeance by relatives see Glotz 76–93, 425–42.
[89] On *philanthropia* see Ferguson ch. 6; Bolkestein 110f.; Dover 201–3; and cf. Else, *Poetics* 368–70.
[90] The sentiment in the conditional may seem exceptionally altruistic, but there is no suggestion that the beneficiaries themselves should not recognise the father's generosity. The point is that he did not plan for his behaviour to be used publicly to his advantage (as it is in fact being used in court). Cf. Dover 222.

thing about exile may be identified as a lack of friends (Theogn. 209f.).

Unanimity of the citizens, *homonoia*, is defined by Aristotle (claiming to follow common usage) as political *philia* (*EN* 1167a22–b3).[91] This was a subject of great concern in Greek social and political life as it struggled to overcome the divisive loyalties of clan and class. The abstract notion of 'love of country' develops gradually in fifth-century Athens out of these more specific loyalties.[92] When it does emerge, it is reinforced by the language of family loyalty, which imparts extra emotional and moral force to patriotic exhortations. The fatherland must be cherished like a real father (Lys. 13.91), and like a parent it must be 'repaid' for the benefits of birth and nurture which it has, metaphorically, bestowed upon us (Isoc. 6.108; Lyc. *Leocr.* 53).[93] The extreme debt to this adopted 'father' outweighs the closest family feelings and obligations (cf. Lys. 2.70f., 17.9f.; Xen. *Hell.* 1.7.21; Lyc. *Leocr.* 100–1).[94] In return, the *polis* has ways of rewarding the service of its most devoted 'children' which go beyond the benefits it provides to all. A speaker may use the favours he has bestowed on the city as an argument for acquittal by his fellow citizens (e.g. Lys. 21.22–5). Service to the *polis* may be 'repaid' with *charis* and 'gifts' such as public recognition.[95] These are the classical equivalent of the concrete honours paid to Homeric heroes, such as the best food and drink and a place of honour at the feast. Heroes must earn these by their prowess, thus fulfilling the contract of noblesse oblige.[96]

The third main group of *philoi* approximates most closely to modern conceptions of a friend. These are personal friends bound by reciprocal favour and often, though not necessarily, by mutual esteem and affection. This kind of *philia* will often, of course, overlap with others. Those united by kinship or political and other more

---

[91] Cf. also *EN* 1155a22–6, *MM* 1212a14–27; Pl. *Alc.* 126c; *SVF* 1.263. See further Ferguson ch. 7 and below, p. 125f. *Homonoia* was apparently a popular subject of discourse (cf. Heracl. DK A 3b; Gorg. DK A 1, B 8; Ant. Soph. DK B 44a–71).

[92] See Connor 99–108. On patriotism see also Bolkestein 85f.

[93] Cf. also Pl. *Crito* 50d–51c and see Cameron 90–5.

[94] Even suicide could be regarded as a wrong to the *polis* (Arist. *EN* 1138a9–14; cf. also Pl. *Leg.* 873cd).

[95] See Bolkestein 163–5.

[96] The Homeric locus classicus is *Il.* 12.310–21, but cf. also 4.257–64, 338–48; 8.161–3. On noblesse oblige see Finley, *Odysseus* 95–7; Havelock, *Justice* 107–13.

formal ties may also enjoy personal friendship and affection. Thus we hear, for example, that Deiphobus was Hector's dearest brother (*Il.* 22.233f.), and Phaenops his dearest guest-friend (*Il.* 17.583f.). But when no presumptive *philia* exists, or when closer bonds are developed within a broader circle, the new relationship must be initiated on one side by a spontaneous gift or favour (cf. Thuc. 2.40.4f.).[97]

Such favours must not be bandied about indiscriminately, but should be bestowed only on one who is likely to reciprocate, if not in kind, at least with the promise of grateful and loyal support.[98] A *charis* owed by a good man is a treasure-store, but you might as well benefit the bad as feed stray dogs, which bark at their benefactors as much as anyone else they encounter (Isoc. 1.29). A curious anecdote reports that Socrates cursed someone handing out favours indiscriminately for 'prostituting the virgin Graces (*Charites*)' (Stob. III.478.8 (Wachsmuth)). A *charis* to enemies may be not just wasted, but dangerous (Arch. 6 (West)). We must therefore choose the recipients of our *charis* carefully, for fear they turn out to be of base metal and return us evil for good (Democr. DK 68 B 93).[99]

'Most people want to receive benefits, but avoid bestowing them as being unprofitable' (Arist. *EN* 1163b26f.). But an incentive to initiate good will is provided by the fact that friends are an invaluable commodity, and as Democritus remarks, someone unwilling to show *philia* is unlikely to get any from others (DK 68 B 103). Demosthenes argues that you may only request help from one you have helped yourself (23.106; cf. Xen. *Mem.* 2.2.12, 2.3.11–13). Menander's Sostratus advises his father to be generous with his money, for in the long run, friends are more valuable than wealth (*Dysc.* 805–12), and Xenophon reports how successful this strategy was for Cyrus (*Anab.* 1.9.11f.; cf. 7.6.20; *Hiero* 11.13). As a comic fragment puts it, 'Why else should one pray to be rich, if not to be able to come to one's friends' help and sow the fruit of *charis*, sweetest of the gods?' (Antiphanes fr. 228.1–4 (Kock)).[100]

---

[97] Cf. Dover 277.

[98] Hes. *WD* 354f.; Democr. DK 68 B 93; Theogn. 101–12; Xen. *Mem.* 2.6.4; Thuc. 1.32.1. Cf. also Xen. *Oec.* 7.37, *Anab.* 6.20; Bolkestein 213f.

[99] Note the coinage metaphor in κίβδηλος, often used of human fraudulence (e.g. Theogn. 117). Cf. also Theogn. 105–8.

[100] On giving in expectation of a return see also Bolkestein 156–67.

Marriage constitutes a special case of this *philia* established through the offering and repayment of favours. In Homeric times the bride is given as part of an exchange of gifts between two families who thereby become allied.[101] Enmity is ended or friendship sealed and perpetuated by the provision of a wife.[102] In classical times marriage was similarly used to ally two families for political purposes,[103] making them presumptive *philoi* as extended kin. At the heart of this relationship lies the specially intimate tie of *philia* between husband and wife. Despite the prevailing sexual double standard, Isocrates can reproach unfaithful husbands for failing to abide by the marital contract to share in the whole of life, and hence causing pain to those by whom they expect not to be pained themselves (3.40). In classical Athens the rape of a married woman was a less serious crime than adultery because it did not involve alienation of the woman's *philia* for her husband (Lys. 1.32f.; Xen. *Hiero* 3.4). Such alienation impairs the reciprocal marriage partnership, to which each spouse must contribute for the good of both (Arist. *EN* 1162a20–4; Xen. *Oec.* 7.13). Amongst the purposes of this partnership is the procreation of children, which is 'the greatest bond of *philia*' (Men. *Mon.* 809 (Jäkel)). Reproduction cements marital *philia* by creating an indirect blood tie between the partners and their families. In a successful marriage husband and wife are also united by the mutual *charis* of sexual gratification.[104] As Aristotle says, the *philia* of husband and wife is natural, useful and pleasant (*EN* 1162a16f., 24f.). This personal tie may outweigh all others: Hector tells Andromache that he cares more about her fate than that of any of the Trojans, including his own parents and brothers (*Il.* 6.450–5; cf. also 9.341f.).

Another special case is the kind of friendship which may obtain between mortals and gods. Their relationship to us as well as to each other is governed by the talio and Help Friends/Harm Enemies.[105]

---

101 On this complex subject see Lacey 39–41; Morris 105–10; Finley, *ES* 237–41. Cf. also Vernant, *MP* 139f. In classical Athens by contrast the bride was accompanied by a dowry (Lacey 107–10).

102 Cf. Glotz 130; Benveniste 345.

103 See Connor 15–18.

104 On *charis* and mutuality in marriage see Redfield, *Notes* 196–8. Cf. also Dover 210; Halperin 162.

105 For the talio between gods cf. Hes. *Theog.* 164–6, 472f. On the talio and religion see Dihle 20–30. For Help Friends/Harm Enemies cf. *Il.* 1.218; 18.394–407;

We offer them honour and sacrifices to win their favour, and if we are successful they will reciprocate. This conventional view of religion as a quid pro quo persisted despite philosophical criticism.[106] Mortals who please the gods are *philos* to them, while gods may in turn be called *philos* for their general benevolence or for the special aid they grant their favourites.[107] But the enormous difference in power which divides us from them means that the relationship, though reciprocal, is never as balanced as even the most unequal case of human *philia*.[108] In particular, the gods have the power to violate their side of the bargain with impunity (cf. e.g. *Il.* 2.419f.).

The range of Help Friends/Harm Enemies is considerably broadened by the transitivity of *philia* and enmity. If you become my *philos*, we are expected ipso facto to share in each other's friendships and enmities.[109] As a corollary I will become an enemy to my enemies' friends, in so far as they share their friends' hostility to me. In the courts, as in Homer, mutual friends might try to effect a reconciliation instead of taking sides.[110] But their position was a delicate one. When Phoenix participates in the embassy to Achilles, Achilles tells him not to bring *charis* to Agamemnon: 'You should not love him, lest you become hateful to me, who love you. It is *kalos* for you to join me in hurting whoever hurts me' (*Il.* 9.613–15; cf. Demos. 25.86).[111] Xenophon's Socrates prudently advises us to avoid making friends with someone 'who is quarrelsome and likely to provide his friends with many enemies' (*Mem.* 2.6.4). Marriage was an especially important way of extending ties through transitivity, for the *philia* between husband and wife brought with it a whole new web of family connections. Transitivity is also often written into military alliances, which may stipulate that the parties must share common friends and enemies (e.g. Tod 68, 72; Thuc. 3.75.1, 5.23.1–2).

18.362–7; 20.293–9; 24.33–5; examples from tragedy in Vickers 124–6. See also Adkins, *Gods* 11–17.

[106] See Bolkestein 157 and cf. Pl. *Euth.* 14c–15b, *Rep.* 390e.

[107] For examples of popular address to Zeus as *philos* see Cook 2.2.1167.

[108] On our relationship with the gods see Dirlmeier, *Theophilia*. Aristotle thinks it is too one-sided to qualify as *philia* (*EN* 1158b33–59a5; cf. *MM* 1208b27–35).

[109] Cf. Arist. *Rhet.* 1381a7–9, 13–17, *EN* 1171a4–6; Polyb. 1.14.

[110] Cf. *Il.* 11.793 = 15.404; Demos. 21.118, 41.1, 52.21; Isoc. 25.27.

[111] On Achilles and *philia* see Nagy 104–9; Schein 97–9, 112–20. Achilles is especially prone to this exclusivity (cf. *Il.* 11.648–50, 24.433–6).

Transitivity is at its strongest within the family, where inherited enmity leads to the family feuds of myth and history.[112] A son might think it impious to speak to the son of a man who had been at loggerheads with his father (Isae. 9.20). Aristotle includes in his list of victims of wrongdoing: 'those against whom [the aggressors] have an excuse that [the victims'] ancestors or themselves or their friends either have harmed or will harm [the aggressors] or their ancestors or those they care about' (*Rhet.* 1372b37–73a3). Legal punishment as well as revenge might extend to an offender's family, especially the children.[113] Inherited enmity between entire races may be considered 'natural' (Demos. 21.49). On the positive side, 'children should inherit their father's *philia*, like his property' (Isoc. 1.2).[114] A speaker may beg that his children as well as himself receive *charis* for his contributions to the public good (Lys. 21.25). It was also common practice to appeal in court to an ancestor's or relative's fine qualities and deeds as an extenuating factor in one's own case (cf. Demos. 25.76–8). Andocides even argues that one reason for his ancestors' admirable public service was to ensure leniency for their future descendants, in case any of them, such as himself, should run into trouble (1.141).

The breadth of the concept of *philia*, combined with its transitivity, means that the vast majority of those with whom one normally comes into contact may be classified as either friends or enemies. Help Friends/Harm Enemies therefore has a much better claim to be considered as a general moral code than may at first appear. There does remain, however, a class of 'neutrals', with whom one has no specific relationship of *philia* or enmity. To some extent, this neutrality is relative. All my fellow citizens are, or should be, my *philoi* on the civic level, but on the personal level some are likely to be my enemies, whereas those with whom I have nothing whatever to do will be neutral. But such neutrals still have a claim to *philia* in virtue of their common citizenship. A total stranger, however – a *xenos* from another city or country – is neutral in every sense (unless our cities are allies or enemies), so that my behaviour towards him is not governed by Help Friends/Harm Enemies.

---

[112] For examples see Glotz 271f.; Dover 182, Vickers 265 n. 54.
[113] See Glotz passim; Dover 303f.; Bond on Eur. *HF* 166ff.
[114] Cf. *Il.* 6.215–31; Demos. 19.193–5, *Ep.* 3.35.

This hiatus is filled by the traditional law requiring hospitality towards strangers,[115] which initiates *xenia*, 'guest-friendship', between host and guest.[116] So we hear in Homer of Axylos, who 'was a *philos* to people, for he showed friendship/hospitality to all, living as he did in a house by the road' (*Il.* 6.14–6).[117] Like other varieties of *philia*, this is a reciprocal relationship.[118] When the host welcomes and assists the stranger this places the latter under a debt of gratitude, and reciprocal *philia* is initiated. The relationship is often sealed by the exchange of gifts (e.g. *Od.* 1.306–18; Herod. 3.39.2).[119] The *xenos* may not offer any immediate recompense, but when the opportunity arises may reciprocate in any of the usual ways, such as providing a ransom (*Il.* 21.42), or performing a favour when called upon to do so (Herod. 1.41).

This kind of *philia* carried a special obligation, 'for all strangers and beggars are from Zeus' (*Od.* 6.207f. = 14.57f.). A transgression from either party risked the wrath of Zeus Xenios, protector of strangers.[120] Thus Menelaus prays to Zeus for revenge on Paris' violation of hospitality (*Il.* 3.351–4; cf. 13.620–7), and Aeschines can denounce Demosthenes for impiety because of his involvement in the torture and death of an erstwhile host (3.224). The religious sanction on the host is even more powerful if the stranger arrives as a suppliant, usually a helpless fugitive who seeks refuge and aid by specific ritual means.[121] As a result of these institutions, most 'neutrals' have in effect the rights of presumptive *philoi*, unless they forfeit them through unprovoked aggression.

---

[115] On obligation to 'neutrals' see Bolkestein 90–3, 128–33 (though it should be noted that those in question are often fellow citizens) and cf. Pearson, *PE* 213f. n. 10. Cf. also Bolkestein 69–71 on the ἀραὶ Βουζύγιοι. Kindness towards strangers could be seen as an expression of common humanity, thus making contact with the notion of the human race as a single 'family' (above, p. 43).

[116] On *xenia* see Finley, *Odysseus* 98–103; Bolkestein 214–31. On its fundamental role in Homeric *philotes* see Benveniste 337–53. *Xenos* means both 'host' and 'guest', and later also 'stranger'. See Chantraine s.v.; Benveniste 95f.; Bolkestein 87f.

[117] On the verb φιλέεσκεν see Benveniste 341f.

[118] Cf. Bolkestein 165f.

[119] See Bolkestein 166f., 219–23; Benveniste 94f.; Finley, *Odysseus* 64f.

[120] Zeus also had a title Philios ('Zeus of friendship') which dates back to the fifth century (see Cook 2.2.1160–1210) and is often associated with his function as Xenios (ib. 1177 n. 2).

[121] On supplication see Gould, *Hiketeia*; Bolkestein 91–3.

Problems with Help Friends/Harm Enemies

The multifarious ties which were the province of *philia* inevitably led to conflicting loyalties (cf. Arist. *EN* 1164b22–65a35). The tight bonds of kinship were especially likely to conflict with the demands of the *polis* (e.g. Lys. 2.70f., 17.9f., 21.23f.);[122] the claims of a personal friend might clash with those of kin (e.g. Andoc. 1.53) or country (e.g. Thuc. 2.13.1); one might be bound by conflicting loyalties towards two personal friends or relatives, and so on. The likelihood of such conflicts is further exacerbated by transitivity. Obligations to friends may also conflict with self-interest. This too can be seen as a conflict of loyalties, in so far as one is one's own best friend. But although one is in a sense one's own *philos*, the desire for self-interest is so fundamental to human nature that the main function of Help Friends, like any moral code, is to counteract it.[123] 'If you have too much *philia* towards yourself, you will not have a *philos*' (Men. *Mon.* 431 (Jäkel); cf. *MM* 1212a28–b23). On the other hand, one cannot *always* be expected to give a friend's wishes priority. How far must one go in satisfying his or her desires, which may be destructive to oneself, to the wider community of *philoi*, or even to the friend in question?

Help Friends/Harm Enemies may also clash with other moral norms. Aristophanes' Strepsiades urges his son to do wrong out of obedience to his father (*Clouds* 860f.). Gorgias mentions helping friends or harming enemies as a plausible reason why one might act unjustly (*Pal.* 18; cf. Pl. *Rep.* 364c). Aristotle includes amongst the victims of wrongdoing those whom people injure as a favour to their friends (*Rhet.* 1373a16f.).[124] An important method of helping a friend was to support him in court (e.g. Isae. 1.7; Hyp. 1.10; cf. Lys. 21.22),[125] regardless of the justice of his case (Arist. *Rhet.* 1372a11–21; Pl. *Rep.* 343e). Failure to perform such a favour may be applauded by others (e.g. Demos. 49.37f.; Lys. 26.15). But an honest judgement against a friend was likely to incur his enmity (Ant. Soph. DK 87 B 44 col. 1; Diog. Laert. 1.87; cf. Ar. *Frogs* 1411–13). A

---

[122] See Glotz, especially bk 2; and cf. Knox 76f.; Connor 47–9; Dover 301–6.

[123] Cf. Williams 11f.

[124] A speaker may boast that he did not use his connections to take vengeance on his enemies or to help his friends (Lys. 9.14). On the other hand even the moralistic Plutarch, who shuns any injustice, recommends helping one's friends get money, office and influence (*Mor.* 808b–809b).

[125] See further Dirlmeier 36f.

compromise is offered by Demosthenes, who argues that you should not denounce a friend for murder even if you think him guilty, but that you should terminate the friendship (21.117f.). A different solution is attributed to Ephialtes, who is said to have refused a large sum of money from his friends on the grounds that he would have to do some injustice as a *charis* in return, or else seem ungrateful (Ael. *Var. Hist.* 11.9). Such dilemmas remained a persistent theme for moralising (Gell. 1.3; Plut. *Mor.* 807a–808c).

A related difficulty is the alignment of Help Friends/Harm Enemies with independent moral terms. Our friends may have bad qualities, and our enemies good ones, but according to the simple formula Help Friends/Harm Enemies, such qualities are irrelevant, for all that counts is personal loyalty or hostility. Yet the possibility of friends who are bad people (as opposed to bad friends), or enemies who are good people, is an embarrassment,[126] and is only occasionally acknowledged. Pindar alludes to a saying that one should praise 'even an enemy' if he acts nobly (*Pyth.* 9.165–70).[127] But the telltale 'even' shows that such disinterested magnanimity was not the norm. Enemies are normally characterised as the lowest of the low, and loyal friends in glowing terms.[128]

This is often harmonised with the independent claims of Help Friends/Harm Enemies by the assertion that one's own friends are chosen for their fine moral characters, while one's enemies are hated for their wickedness.[129] Plato's Polemarchus, when pushed to say what he means by *philoi*, replies: 'It is likely ... that one loves those one thinks good, and hates those one thinks wicked' (*Rep.* 334c). An oratorical fragment commands us to 'flee the *philia* of the bad and the enmity of the good' (Hyp. fr. 209 (Jensen)).[130] In many cases,

---

[126] One reason for this is the old assumption that like is attracted to like (above, p. 42).

[127] Cf. Arist. *Rhet.* 1363a11–14; Diog. Laert. 1.54; Plut. *Mor.* 91ab, 809f–810a. For a striking example from drama see Eur. *Heracl.* 998f.

[128] But for acknowledgement of friends who are bad cf. Aeschin. 3.194; Isae. 5.30f.

[129] Philosophers dealt with this problem by moralising friendship. Thus for Aristotle, true and complete friendship can only exist between good men (*EN* 1156b7f.; cf. also Pl. *Lys.* 214bcd; Xen. *Mem.* 2.6.14f.; *Mag. Mor.* 1208b22–5, 1209a3–b37). For the Stoics only wise men have friendship and *homonoia*, and do so even without knowing each other (*SVF* 3.625, 630, 631, 635; the latter idea is anticipated in Eur. fr. 902 (Nauck²)).

[130] Cf. Hes. *WD* 716; Xen. *Anab.* 7.7.41f.; Arist. *Rhet.* 1381a25–8; Plut. *Mor.* 94b; Lys. 14.1; Lyc. *Leocr.* 6; Dio Chr. 3.117.

NIAGARA UNIVERSITY LIBRARY

however, the fine qualities for which friends are to be chosen are precisely those which make a desirable friend, so that the line is blurred between what it is to be a good person and to be a good friend. This is especially evident in Theognis. He repeatedly enjoins us to make friends with 'good men' and avoid 'bad' ones (e.g. 31–8, 69–72, 113f., 579), yet for him a 'bad man' is a useless friend who will not help you out, share with you or reciprocate favours; 'good men', in contrast, remember favours and reciprocate *charis* (101– 12).[131] Similarly a fourth-century moralist recommends doing favours for 'good men' because they can be relied on to reciprocate (Isoc. 1.29). There is thus a tendency for approval and condemnation based on the criteria of Help Friends/Harm Enemies to converge with independent judgements of moral character.

The problem of reconciling loyalty and hostility with other criteria of excellence is least likely to arise on the battlefield. The better my enemy is as a fighter, the more desirable it is for me to kill him, regardless of his excellence of character. It is in such military contexts, a province of political *philia*, that the Help Friends/Harm Enemies code appears in many ways at its simplest and most work- able. Few have ever denied (and no Greek would have done so) that in warfare one has an obligation to inflict maximum damage on the enemy while producing maximum advantage for one's own side.[132] For the most part, this obligation will coincide with the protection of one's personal *philoi*.[133] A military context makes, for example, the saying that it is 'most lawful and most sweet' to defeat one's enemies (*polemioi*) seem reasonable rather than vengeful (Thuc. 7.68.1). Similarly when Aristotle mentions 'the opposite of what helps enemies' as an arguable criterion of what is good, the case appears at its most plausible through his use of cowardice and cour- age as an illustration: 'That of which the opposite is bad, is good. And that of which the opposite benefits one's enemies. For example if to be cowardly most benefits one's enemies, it is clear that courage

---

[131] Theognis' value language also has political implications.

[132] Socrates, who believed one should not reciprocate harm (Pl. *Cri.* 49c), had an honourable military career (for the evidence see Guthrie, *Socrates* 59). The situ- ation in Homer is, of course, quite different from classical times. Achilles' re- fusal to fight may be an offence against *philoi* (*Il.* 9.628–32), but desertion was punishable in Athens by disfranchisement (MacDowell, *LCA* 160).

[133] Soldiers were expected to fight more bravely in the presence of personal *philoi* (cf. *Il.* 2.363 with the scholiast ad loc.; Pl. *Rep.* 467a.; Onas. *Strat.* 24).

is most beneficial to the citizens. And in general, the opposite of what one's enemies want or enjoy appears beneficial' (*Rhet.* 1362b30–5). We may note that 'citizen' and 'enemy' are quite naturally treated here as opposites, for one would expect military enemies to be coextensive with enemies of the citizen body (cf. Cleobulus DK 10.3.a.15). Conflict of interest is much less likely in warfare than in civic life, though it may still arise or be suspected (cf. e.g. Thuc. 2.13.1). Homer's Glaucus and Diomedes, ancestral guest-friends who meet as enemies upon the battlefield, manage to evade the problem, since, as Diomedes remarks, there are plenty of others for each to kill (*Il.* 6.227–9). Transitivity may still cause difficulties, and may be excluded from the terms of a treaty for precisely this reason (e.g. Thuc. 1.44.1). But although Help Friends/Harm Enemies works best in military contexts, the code does not simply apply a military model to a broader spectrum of relationships. On the contrary, military hostility may itself be presented in intensely personal terms. In the *Iliad* in particular, the killing of enemies is often an act of wrath in revenge for the death of a friend.[134]

The twin principles Help Friends and Harm Enemies have a pleasing symmetry, as the frequency with which they appear as a balanced pair attests. They are also to some extent complementary. The sage Chilon is reported to have said that friendship and enmity are inextricably linked (Gell. 1.3.31; Plut. *Mor.* 96ab). Xenophon's Cyrus tells his sons that if they benefit their friends they will also be able to punish their enemies (*Cyr.* 8.7.28; cf. *Hiero* 11.15). Again, this is most clearly the case on the battlefield,[135] but it may also apply in other contexts.[136] In practice, however, there is considerable divergence in attitudes towards Help Friends and Harm Enemies. Although requital of wrongs is approved as just, it is often expressed not in its personal form ('retaliate against your enemy') but in an impersonal form ('the doer must suffer'), which does not specify the agent of justice or assert the justice of personal revenge. In such cases implementation of the talio may be entrusted by mortals to the gods, or may be controlled and legalised in a court of law.

---

134 Cf. above all Achilles' pursuit of Hector in revenge for the death of Patroclus. But many minor cases show that Achilles is not aberrant in this respect (e.g. the sequence of killings at *Il.* 14.453–507).

135 Cf. Isoc. 9.32; Arist. *Rhet.* 1362b30–5 (quoted in the previous paragraph).

136 Cf. Theogn. 1107f. (quoted below, p. 57), where the context could be military or political or both.

The latter possibility suggests a way of approaching one of the most fundamental problems with the talio as a theory of justice, namely the dubious moral status of the injury inflicted in return.[137] The talio is characteristically expressed as the reciprocation of an equivalent evil. One meaning of 'evil for evil' may simply be that what is bad for me must be repaid by what is bad for you (cf. Hes. *WD* 265f.). I may be quite happy to classify the second 'evil' as both right and good. But this can only be accomplished by the ad hoc and one-sided imposition of the 'definitional stop', which merely stipulates that in certain cases a harm is to count as a good.[138] The unsatisfactory nature of such a solution is revealed by those cases in which, as befits the notion of 'repayment', both injury and response are described not merely as both bad (for someone), but in the same morally pejorative terms. A saying of Epicharmus, for example, recommends villainy as a useful weapon against a villain (DK 23 B 32). Yet the harm administered in the name of justice, though 'bad' for the offender, should be evaluated not as a wrong paid for a wrong, but as right.[139]

A court of law can in theory provide a disinterested arbiter with the authority to decide when such harms are right and just. Punishment – a harm inflicted by society in the name of justice – is thus distinguished from the personal retaliation of revenge. As Aristotle remarks, 'there is a difference between revenge and punishment' (*Rhet.* 1369b12).[140] Revenge is prompted by the subjective feelings of the injured party, whereas punishment is, in theory, determined impersonally by society or its representative: 'To go to the judge is to go to justice; for the judge is supposed to be like justice incarnate' (Arist. *EN* 1132a20–2). But various problems remain. For one thing, this kind of justice no longer constitutes a strict application of the talio. The exact repayment of an injustice would be an equal injustice, which contradicts the very idea of legal punishment. The talio cannot be used to justify such punishment without resorting once more to the definitional stop. Furthermore revenge

---

[137] See Vlastos, *Justice* 306f.; cf. also Winnington-Ingram 312.

[138] On this objection to the talio see Mackenzie 32. For the expression see Hart 5f.

[139] On the difference between punishment and payment see Mackenzie 10.

[140] In Aristotle's view, as he goes on to explain, punishment is aimed at the offender, whereas revenge is to give the victim satisfaction. See also Mackenzie 11f.

and justice are not so easily distinguished in practice. In Greek culture they remained persistently linked. Not only are enmity and revenge accepted as natural motives for a lawsuit, but language of revenge came to be used for legal punishment, while litigation is often treated as legalised revenge.[141] This attitude is not always commended,[142] but it may be endowed with unimpeachable respectability by claiming that it will benefit the *polis* (Demos. 24.8), or that one is seeking vengeance on the city's behalf as well as one's own (Lys. 1.47, 13.1–3; cf. 13.92).

When Harm Enemies in the form of personal revenge is applauded, it is often in terms of manly honour. 'To have revenge on one's enemies and not to make terms is finer (more *kalos*). For to retaliate is just, and what is just is *kalos*, and not to be defeated is a sign of manliness' (*Rhet.* 1367a20–23; cf. *EN* 1132b21–33a5). Antiphon imagines a murderer thinking along similar lines: 'Even if he were to be convicted, it seemed more *kalos* to him to suffer after having his revenge than to be destroyed by the indictment in an unmanly way after doing nothing in retaliation' (Ant. 2.a.8). Failure to exact revenge may correspondingly be a matter for reproach, whether in Homer (*Od.* 24.433–6), or in the fourth century, when an orator can claim that 'everyone' urged him to take revenge, reproaching him as 'most unmanly' not to do so (Demos. 59.12).[143]

Yet there are limits to the acceptable ill treatment of enemies, especially after their death. The gods are angered by Achilles' treatment of the dead Hector at the end of the *Iliad* (24.113–15). Odysseus

---

[141] E.g. Ant. 2.a.5–7, 6.6; Lys. 1.4, 7.20, 12.2, 14.2; Demos. 21.28, 22.3, 53.1, 15, 59.1, 15; *Rhet. ad Alex.* 1442b13f.

[142] Cf. Isoc. 15.27; Demos. 18.278; Lys. 9.7, 31.2.

[143] Cf. also Glotz 58f. At *Diss. Log.* 2.7 benefiting one's enemies is said to be *aischros*. But the strongest statement of disapproval for neglecting Harm Enemies is attributed to none other than Socrates, who allegedly 'said it was *hubris* to be unable to reciprocate good treatment, just as also with bad' (Arist. *Rhet.* 1398a24–6; cf. Diog. Laert. 2.25, Xen. *Ap.* 17). If this is the correct interpretation (Jebb, *Rhetoric* translates 'just as it is to requite them with evil'), it seems absurdly inappropriate to Socrates (see below). Moreover the language is extraordinarily strong. Often the recipient of a favour can make no return but loyalty and benevolence, and the inability to respond exactly in kind could scarcely be called *hubris*. Further, *hubris* is ordinarily used for aggressive behaviour and is thus not appropriate for *failing* to reciprocate harm (on *hubris* see below, p. 61 n. 6, and for its strangeness here cf. Cope and Sandys ad loc.). Could this be an authentic Socratic utterance, ironically questioning the authority of the talio?

reproves Eurycleia for crowing over the dead suitors, telling her to rejoice in her heart and not gloat aloud, for the latter is 'impious' (*Od.* 22.411f.). Lysias applauds the view that 'good men' should take vengeance on their living enemies, but not display their valour over corpses (Lys. 2.8; cf. Ar. *Clouds* 549f.). We also encounter disapproval of gloating at anyone's misfortune (Democr. DK 68 B 293; cf. Pittacus DK 10.3.ε.5.), and excessive revenge against the living may be presented as abhorrent and subject to divine disapproval (e.g. Herod. 4.205; Paus. 9.17.6). In classical Athens, recourse to law could be regarded as a proper substitute for escalating violence in a personal quarrel (Demos. 54.17–19).[144] Moreover a failure to exact revenge at all may be positively commended, especially when personal hostilities are sacrificed to the interests of the community as a whole. So Andocides flatters the Athenians as 'most excellent and prudent' for placing the *soteria* and unity of the citizens before revenge (1.140).[145] In these cases enmity is sacrificed to a stronger imperative. Active disapproval of Harm Enemies per se is not found before Socrates, who argued that one should harm no one, even in retaliation (Pl. *Crito* 49bc; cf. Xen. *Mem.* 4.8.11).[146]

Harm Enemies, then, tends to be commended in terms of personal honour, and infractions of it, though often reproached in such terms, may also be commended on other grounds. Approval of Help Friends, by contrast, knows virtually no bounds, and the strongest disapproval is directed towards those who fail to abide by it. This

---

[144] Cited by MacDowell, *LCA* 123.

[145] Cf. also Protagoras' enlightened view of punishment (Pl. *Prot.* 324b). More examples of 'magnanimity' may be found in Dover 190–5, though not all are quite as magnanimous as he suggests. E.g. in Demos. 15.16, before urging his audience not to bear grudges, Demosthenes professes to rejoice at the Rhodians' misfortunes, which serve them right, and only recommends helping them because it will benefit Athens.

[146] See Vlastos, *Justice* and cf. Dihle 61–6. Diogenes Laertius cites Pythagoras (8.23) and Cleobulus (1.91–3; cf. DK 10.3.α.14) for the view that we should make our enemies into friends (giving in the latter case a prudential justification). He also attributes to Pittacus the view that forgiveness is better than revenge (1.76) and to Solon the claim that none of his enemies had suffered at his hands (1.54). See Dihle 45–8 for other possible antecedents to Socrates. For evidence of sophistic support for the talio and Help Friends/Harm Enemies see Dihle 101 (though, pace Dihle, Pl. *Meno* 71e cannot be used as evidence for Gorgias' views, as 71d shows; but cf. Gorg. *Pal.* 25). Later moralists attach great importance to friendship but ignore Harm Enemies (as Aristotle does) or reject it (see e.g. Cic. *Off.* 1.25.88, 1.14.43; Plut. *Mor.* 90f.; Diog. Laert. 8.23).

difference in attitude emerges clearly from a comparison of two passages. First a couplet from Theognis, who laments that he has violated both principles simultaneously: 'Alas, wretch that I am! I was both a source of joy to my enemies, and of toil for my friends in my wretchedness' (1107f.). Here humiliation before enemies is placed on an equal footing with the shame of letting down friends. But the situation is clearly one in which the two principles are fully complementary – it was a single event that delighted Theognis' enemies and brought pain to his friends. Harm Enemies is not pursued simply for its own sake. As in warfare, it is the principal means by which the speaker may help both his friends and himself.

Contrast a passage from the speech against Andocides. The speaker says sneeringly that his opponent, 'has this skilled ability, to do his enemies no harm, but his friends whatever harm he can' (Lys. 6.7). The context is Andocides' treachery as a friend, not his meekness as an enemy, for the speaker has just asserted that only one of his associates was never deceived by him. The gratuitous mention of enemies produces a neat reversal of the traditional code. Nevertheless, the speaker does not go so far as to claim that Andocides positively benefits his enemies. This evidently would not be an insult on a par with the charge of betraying friends. Perhaps it would be no insult at all, or even a compliment. So he suggests instead that Andocides is as *incompetent* an enemy (note the sarcastic use of 'skill') as he is an unreliable friend. Like Theognis, this speaker deplores a failure to help friends. Theognis can also decry his own failure to harm enemies, in a context where this is essential to helping friends. But such failure in others apparently carries no weight as a gratuitous insult.

We may express the difference in attitude by saying that Harm Enemies tends more towards the descriptive, and Help Friends to the prescriptive. That is, it is generally taken for granted that everyone desires revenge on enemies, and that most people pursue it, but its violation is condemned primarily in terms of personal honour, and may even be praised. Help Friends, on the other hand, is less descriptive, since incentives to violate it in pursuit of self-interest easily arise and may be very powerful.[147] To counteract such temptations,

---

[147] Misfortunes, which put a strain on our friends' loyalty, therefore become a test of true friendship (cf. Theogn. 299f.; Democr. DK 68 B 101; Lys. 2.74; Isoc.

it acquires a more powerful prescriptive force backed by strong social disapproval of its violation.

Reasons for this difference are not hard to find. Transgression of Help Friends may cause serious hardship to the abandoned friend, and threatens to undermine an entire system of social relations. Violation of Harm Enemies, on the other hand, will rarely interfere with the well-being of others and may actually have beneficial consequences. Not that enmity is entirely without value. Shared enmity may enhance the solidarity of a group by excluding outsiders and encouraging unity against a common foe. Aeschylus' Furies link unanimous hatred with unanimous love, alongside reciprocal joy and the rejection of reciprocal bloodshed, as antithetical to civil strife and 'a cure for many ills' (*Eum.* 976–87). Even Plutarch, who argues vehemently for the control of hatred, suggests that any residual strife, envy and contentiousness should be vented on enemies (*Mor.* 92ab). Enmity directed towards outsiders may thus promote a kind of social cohesion whose value may be seen most clearly in military contexts. Even hostility within the group may be of use, by performing a policing function. Isocrates praises the 'educational' value of freedom of speech and 'the privilege which is openly granted to friends to rebuke and to enemies to attack each other's faults' (Isoc. 2.3, trans. Norlin).[148] In the absence of a system of legal redress, personal or familial revenge on enemies may also serve as a form of summary justice.[149] With the advent of a working legal system, however, it not only loses this function, but creates friction by competing with codified justice. It may also be actively destructive when the pursuit of personal enmities produces divisive or conflicting loyalties.

The bonds of *philia*, on the other hand, are clearly of great importance for the cohesion of any social group. They too may be divisive, in so far as they perpetuate clannish enmities and promote the development of competing loyalties. But the cultivation of friendship per se should enhance rather than diminish the well-being and

1.25f., 8.21; Diog. Laert. 1.70, 98). The absence of friends in times of hardship is a favourite theme of Euripides (for examples see Pearson, *Fragments* on his fr. 733).

[148] Poetry of blame fulfilled this function in early times (see Nagy ch. 12).

[149] Plato in his hostility to litigation encourages self-help in his ideal state (*Rep.* 464e).

harmony of the citizen body. Moreover friends are not only desirable but indispensable, whereas despite the pleasure and alleged justice of harming enemies, it remains preferable to have no enemies to harm. 'Is it pleasant to have many enemies? No, it is not even safe!' (Demos. 19.221; cf. Isoc. 1.20). Lack of enemies, quite unlike lack of friends, may be something to be proud of (Lys. 12.20).[150] For these kinds of reasons society has a greater stake in enforcing Help Friends than Harm Enemies.

Most of the points made in this chapter could be documented with numerous references to tragedy, which is often deeply concerned with the dilemmas of retaliation, friendship and enmity.[151] I now turn to Sophocles, in an effort to show how these ideas and their implications are worked out in some of his plays.

[150] Cf. Dover 203.
[151] As Aristotle says, the best tragic plots take place 'amongst friends' (Po. 1453b15–22). His examples show that he is thinking of close kinship ties (cf. Else, Poetics 349–51).

3

Ajax

He who accepts benefits, and denies a return of them when needed, inflicts a real hurt, by disappointing one of the most natural and reasonable of expectations, and one which he must at least tacitly have encouraged, otherwise the benefits would seldom have been conferred. The important rank, among human evils and wrongs, of the disappointment of expectation, is shown in the fact that it constitutes the principal criminality of two such highly immoral acts as a breach of friendship and a breach of promise. Few hurts which human beings can sustain are greater, and none wound more, than when that on which they habitually and with full assurance relied, fails them in the hour of need; and few wrongs are greater than this mere with-holding of good; none excite more resentment, either in the person suffering, or in a sympathising spectator.

J. S. Mill, *Utilitarianism*

Ajax and his enemies

The opening lines of *Ajax* are spoken by the goddess Athena, who addresses her favourite, Odysseus, as an adherent of Harm Enemies: he is tracking down an enemy as usual, in a manner worthy of his traditionally tricky persona (1–8).[1] She is the dearest of gods to him, and they enjoy a solidarity inherited from the *Odyssey* (14–19).[2] He places himself in her hands, as he has always done in the past (34f.). But despite the bond between them, a conflict of values emerges. When Odysseus is reluctant to view the mad Ajax Athena scolds him as a coward (74f.).[3] She implies that any kind of fear or 'reluct-ance' (81) constitutes cowardice. Odysseus picks up her term in his reply, tacitly accepting the charge, but with an important qualifica-tion: 'I would not have avoided him from reluctance were he sane'

---

[1] See Kamerbeek on line 2 and cf. Heath 167. For the tricky implications of hunt-ing see Detienne and Vernant ch. 2. The hunting metaphor is picked up in 19 (see the editors ad loc. and cf. Detienne and Vernant 42).

[2] But for contrasts with the *Odyssey* see Bowra 37; Guthrie, *Odysseus* 115–19; Kirkwood, *Homer* 66–8.

[3] Stanford on 74–5 compares Athena's rebuke to Diomedes at *Il.* 5.812. But Dio-medes denies feeling fear or 'reluctance' (817) – he hung back by Athena's own command. On Odysseus' 'cowardice' see Perrotta 136f.; Stanford, *UT* 104f.

(82).[4] Ajax's abnormal condition excites abnormal responses: his divine affliction inspires fear in the brave, and, as we shall see, pity even in an enemy.

Odysseus' admission of 'reluctance' aligns him with the fearful Tecmessa (531, 587, 593) and the faint-hearted chorus, who enter declaring their fear and 'reluctance' (139), and repeatedly return to the theme (227, 253, 583, 1211–13; cf. 164–71). They form a contrast both with the uninhibited boldness of Ajax and with Teucer and the Atreidae, who see courage as the imposition of one's will through brute force.[5] But there is also a point of contact between Odysseus and the Atreidae. Although the kings will not admit that on occasion they can (and should) yield without loss of face, they expect such compliance from their subordinates. Odysseus too tacitly acknowledges the importance of respect for authority, when he allows his awe for Athena to overcome his natural fear of the insane Ajax. He finally subordinates his wishes to hers (88), displaying not only piety but *sophrosune* – the self-discipline which, amongst other things, enables one to place the desires of a *philos* above one's own.[6] This virtue is essential if Help Friends/Harm Enemies is effectively to constrain self-interest. Menelaus is right when he calls for *sophrosune* in an army, though he characteristically sees it not as internal, but as external discipline, to be induced by fear (1075f. cf. 1259). For Odysseus in his encounter with the goddess such conduct might seem only common sense, since, as Athena tells us, the gods love the

---

[4] The suggestion that true courage is not indiscriminate fearlessness but a prudent judgement of which dangers to face recalls philosophical definitions of courage as knowledge of what should and should not be feared (cf. Pl. *Lach.* 195, *Prot.* 360d, *Rep.* 429c, 442c; Arist. *EN* iii.6).

[5] For Ajax's view of courage see 319f., 364–6, 455f., 545–7 and cf. 46. The only thing he cannot face is his father's reproaches (466), so he must die to prove his courage (470–2, cf. 650, 1004). For Teucer and the Atreidae cf. 1014, 1109f., 1314f., 1334f., 1362.

[6] For a general discussion of this virtue see North, who notes that it came to be especially associated with Odysseus (North 8). The noun does not appear in Sophocles, but its cognates are more prominent in *Ajax* than any other extant play (North 58–61; Stanford on 132f.). The play is often interpreted in terms of *sophrosune* and *hubris* (see e.g. Grossmann 72–80). It contains more occurrences of *hubris* and cognates than any other Greek play (MacDowell, *Hybris* 21), though despite the statement of countless critics (e.g. Lesky, *GT* 99; Sicherl 93), Ajax's defiance of Athena is never characterised in such terms. On *hubris* generally cf. Demos, 21.71f. and see especially MacDowell, *Hybris*; Fisher; cf. also Vickers 29–32; Lattimore, *Patterns* 23–6.

self-disciplined and hate the *kakoi* (132f.). Superficially, this sounds
like a claim that the gods enforce human morality by dispensing
their *philia* and hatred accordingly. But in the context Athena seems
less interested in mortals' treatment of each other than in their maintaining a properly respectful attitude towards the gods (cf. *Phil.*
1440–3). For her as for the Atreidae (1071f., 1075, 1259) and for Ajax
himself (586, 677), 'self-disciplined' and *kakos* connote 'compliant'
and 'recalcitrant' respectively.[7]

The goddess has rightly discerned that Odysseus is pursuing an
enemy, and challenges him with a harsh application of the traditional code: 'Is not laughing at enemies the sweetest laughter?' (79).[8]
Help Friends/Harm Enemies expects and justifies (though it does not
necessitate) such gloating pleasure in an enemy's misfortune, and this
aspect is particularly prominent in *Ajax*.[9] This pleasure is taken for
granted both by tormentors expressing their glee and by victims
complaining of it. When Ajax is mad he enjoys torturing his enemies
(105, 303; cf. 52, 114, 272); when sane he dreads their mockery (367,
382, 454). The chorus, Tecmessa and Teucer all assume that their
enemies gloat in this way, and the words and actions of the Atreidae
seem to confirm them.[10]

Odysseus, however, is different. Being both pious and eminently tactful, he does not directly contradict Athena, but answers
evasively, in implicit disagreement, 'It is enough for me if he stays
inside' (80). This could merely reflect his prudent desire to avoid a

---

[7] Many critics find *kakos* a surprising word to apply to a hero like Ajax, even by
implication (cf. Winnington-Ingram 55f.; Adkins 172; Linforth, *Ajax* 4–6;
Scodel 19). In heroic terms this is certainly true (contrast Ajax's own usage at
319, 456, 551), but *kakos* is a broad term, used here in opposition to 'self-
disciplined' (see Heath 169 n. 8).

[8] Jebb and others think she is 'testing' Odysseus, but there is no sign of this. Her
question expects an affirmative answer (cf. 1348 and see Denniston 431 for the
force of οὔκουν).

[9] Cf. Grossmann 80–3; Pearson, *Ajax* 125. Stanford on 79 notes that γέλως,
'laughter', and cognates are used more than four times more often for mockery
than for merriment in Sophocles. On Help Friends/Harm Enemies in *Ajax* see
also Knox, *Ajax* 3–10.

[10] Chorus: 151–3, 196–9, 955–60, 1042f.; Tecmessa: 961f., 969; cf. 500–3; Teucer:
988f. There are no explicit references to the laughter of the Atreidae, but several
to the humiliating treatment and *hubris* associated with this kind of glee (e.g.
1348f., 1087f.; cf. 1151). For gloating as the verbal expression of *hubris* cf. 151–
3, 196–9, 367 and see MacDowell, *Hybris* 20f. For the close association of *hubris*
with shame and honour see Fisher.

mad enemy, but a reluctance to gloat becomes apparent when Ajax does emerge (121–6). Contrary to the general assumption, he feels no pleasure at this particular enemy's humiliation. Other characters will describe a deceitful, cunning and vengeful Odysseus, endowed with his traditional traits at their least attractive (cf. 148–50, 188f., 379–82, 388f., 445, 955–9, 971). But the prologue establishes a persistent irony, which challenges us to examine the versatility and prudence of Athena's favourite with a fresh eye.[11]

When Athena observes that Odysseus is pursuing an enemy, he acknowledges it, but changes her word 'enemy' (*echthros* 2) to 'hostile' (*dusmenes* 18). Though the two are often used interchangeably, the latter strictly refers to just one side of the relationship, suggesting that it was Ajax who initiated their enmity (cf. 1336f.).[12] This is only a hint (mutual hatred would naturally be assumed), but it is developed when Odysseus responds to the mad Ajax not with hatred, but with compassion: 'I pity him, the wretch, even though he is hostile to me, because he is yoked to an evil doom. [I say this] looking at my own fate as much as his. For I see that all we who live are nothing more than phantoms or an insubstantial shadow' (121–6).[13] Here enmity is significantly, and emphatically, distinguished from the total indulgence of hatred.[14] Pity, based on shared humanity, is proposed as an alternative response to an unfortunate enemy – at least in some circumstances. Odysseus belies Athena's remark in the first line of the play that he 'always' hunts down his enemies.[15] He does not say one should *never* hate an enemy, only that in this in-

---

[11] For the history of Odysseus' ambiguous persona see Stanford, *UT*. On Sophocles' development of his character from the Homeric Odysseus see Kirkwood, *Homer* 63–6.

[12] Note that Odysseus refrains from hasty accusation (21–3), although he has volunteered to investigate (24), and the evidence against Ajax is so damning that 'everyone' is blaming him (28–31). The hostility of Ajax towards Odysseus was famous from their Homeric encounter in the underworld, where Ajax turns aside from Odysseus' friendly overtures (*Od.* 11.543–64).

[13] For human transience cf. especially Herod. 1.32 and see Fränkel, *Ephemeros*; North 56 n. 53. A related theme in the prologue is the contrast between divine and human knowledge (cf. 13, 23, 32f., 36).

[14] The dramatic context makes this particularly striking, since Ajax has just departed to inflict gruesome torture on an imaginary Odysseus (101–16). Note especially the echo of δύστηνον, 'wretch' (109, 111) at 122. Note also the dramatic irony of the rare word ἐνστάτην (104) for 'adversary', which also suggests 'Odysseus who is present'.

[15] On ἀεί ('always') here and throughout the play see Knox, *Ajax* 18–20.

stance his enmity is tempered by pity for Ajax's terrible fate. Nor does he explicitly condemn the attitude which Athena shares with other human characters, or argue for his own. But his appeal to the common lot of humanity does have normative implications. Athena, who harms her enemies with impunity, can conclude from human transience that mortals must respect the gods (127–33). This lesson is inescapable, for when it comes to permanence and sheer power, human beings can never compete with immortals. But like Odysseus we can draw different conclusions for our relations with our fellow humans. If we are all mere shadows, subject to divine whim and mortal transience, the relentless pursuit of bitter hostilities becomes petty, destructive and ultimately futile.

The mad Ajax represents the greatest possible contrast to the piety, *sophrosune* and caution that we have observed in Odysseus. Besides a complete absence of fear or 'reluctance', he subscribes whole-heartedly to the Harm Enemies ethic, echoing Athena when he calls the captivity of Odysseus 'sweetest' or 'most pleasant' (105; cf. 79). His language shows that he thinks his personal revenge not merely 'sweet' but also justified: Odysseus must 'pay the penalty' (113) of a savage and humiliating whipping, described by Athena as an 'outrage' (111).[16] He brusquely disregards Athena's appeal on behalf of 'Odysseus' and insists on doing what he pleases, or as Athena puts it, what gives him 'delight' (114). He does promise the goddess rewards for her 'help' (92f.), grants her the respectful title of 'mistress' (105; cf. 774), and patronisingly declares that she can have her way in all other respects (112). But he is devoid of Odysseus' self-discipline and respect for Athena's wishes. He treats her as an equal or even a subordinate, urging her to remain his loyal 'ally' (*summachos* 117),[17] and addressing her in the peremptory tone of a commander.[18]

---

[16] On the verb in 111 see below, n. 25.

[17] Cf. Athena's ironic use of the same word (90). Knox, *Ajax* 8 notes that it was used by the Athenians for their subject allies, but it is also often used for divine helpers, especially in prayers (e.g. *Ant.* 923; Sappho 1.28 (Voigt); Aesch. *Cho.* 2, 19; Eur. *Ba.* 1343; for further examples see Burnett 257 n. 80). Nevertheless, Ajax's tone is not that of a pious appeal for aid, and later the word is used to imply subordination (1053, 1098).

[18] Note the repetition of ἐφίεμαι, 'I order' (112, 116). The command is Ajax's characteristic mode of address. Cf. 527f., 566f., 991 and the numerous imperatives that fill his speeches (e.g. 578–86, 684–92). Heath 173f. rightly rebuts the

Both Athena and Ajax indiscriminately involve innocent associates of their enemies in their revenge. Athena ruins Ajax without
regard for the harm she is doing to his pious and blameless dependants. Her wrath against him outweighs any independent claims that
they may have.[19] Ajax equals and even surpasses her in his undisciplined application of a private 'justice'.[20] Not content with attacking
those he thinks have personally wronged him, he explicitly embraces
the entire army in his dying curse (843f.).[21] He also resembles Athena in the 'weight' of his wrath (41, 656; cf. 757, 776f., 951), his
pleasure and gloating laughter at the humiliation of his enemies (79,
105, 303), his scorn for cowardice (75, 319f., 455f., 545–7), and his
brusque treatment of subordinate *philoi*.[22] These two are the only
characters addressed by their affectionate friends with the superlative
philtatos (14, 977, 996, 1015). Both are also called 'master' or 'mistress' by inferiors.[23] Both are erroneously treated as subordinate
'allies' by those who should honour and depend on them (90, 117,
1053, 1098). They share the epithets 'mighty' (402, 1319) and 'awesome' (205, 366, 952; cf. 312, 773),[24] and the same verb is used for
the way both torment their enemies (65, 111, 300, 402).[25] Finally, a
more tenuous resemblance lies in the way Athena deludes Ajax and
he misleads his friends.

Besides this dangerous resemblance to his own nemesis, there
are other hints of divine stature in Ajax. Tecmessa attributes her enslavement to 'the will of the gods and, most of all, your hand'
(489f.). He is twice described by the chorus as 'raging Ajax' (212,
1213), an epithet also used of Ares in this play (612f.), and which

---

view that Ajax's attitude towards Athena in the prologue is a product of his
madness.

[19] Cf. Aphrodite's explicit statement of priority at Eur. *Hipp.* 47–50.
[20] Cf. Knox, *Ajax* 8.
[21] Jebb compares Apollo's punishment of the whole army in *Iliad* 1 (*Introduction*
§13).
[22] Athena's repeated command to Odysseus to be silent (75, 87) will be echoed by
Ajax to Tecmessa (293; cf. 592).
[23] δέσποτα (368, 485, 585); δέσποινα (38, 105). Cf. ἄναξ (e.g. 593); ἄνασσα (774).
[24] ἄλκιμος and δεινός. The latter is also used of the natural phenomena to which
Ajax assimilates himself in the deception speech (649f., 669, 674). Where possible I have translated it as 'awesome' in an attempt to capture a word that
shades from 'terrible' to 'wonderful'. See Schlesinger, Δεινότης.
[25] This verb (αἰκίζω) can be used for torture (LSJ s.v.). Cf. Ajax's treatment of the
sheep (including 'Odysseus'), which involves abuse said to have been 'taught'
him by a divinity (235–44).

recalls the Homeric 'raging Ares' (e.g. *Il.* 5.30, 15.127).[26] When the chorus speculate on the possible causes of divine wrath against him, the motives they attribute to the gods are strikingly similar to Ajax's own reason for the rage which causes his downfall. Perhaps Artemis, they suggest, drove him mad for his lack of gratitude (*charis*) for some victory (176),[27] or because she was 'cheated of glorious spoils' (177) – a phrase which could just as well refer to the arms of Achilles. Or perhaps Ares or the war god Enyalius 'was wroth for dishonour to his aiding spear, and took vengeance by nightly wiles' (179–81, trans. Jebb) – a description that could be directly transferred to Ajax himself.[28] In their lust for honour and vengeance these gods, in Homeric style, bear a fundamental resemblance to passionate human heroes.

The difference, as Athena reminds Odysseus, is that the gods are immeasurably more powerful even than an Ajax, and so cannot be crossed with impunity.[29] Ajax was 'dauntless' (365) only until he met the 'unconquerable' (450) goddess.[30] He has disdained the friendship of the gods, which every human needs to ensure lasting success. Ironically, it is only once he is mad that he promises Athena gifts in gratitude (*charis*) for her 'help' (92f.). This self-sufficiency, as we learn from Athena herself and more fully from the messenger, is the direct cause of his humiliation (127–33, 758–77). Athena warned in the prologue against saying any 'excessive' word to the gods (127). But Ajax, against the specific advice of his father, boasted that he could reap renown without divine help, and then 'said an awesome and unspeakable word' to Athena, rejecting her help as she encouraged him on the battlefield (762–75).[31] Moreover he refuses

---

[26] Ares is the only person (divine or human) of whom the epithet is used in the *Iliad*. Note that θοῦρον Ἄρηα and θούριος Αἴας have the same metrical quantity.

[27] *Charis* is used here in an idiom meaning 'for the sake of', but in this context it retains the connotation of reciprocal favour.

[28] For the retention of ἤ in 179 see Kamerbeek and Stanford ad loc.

[29] See especially Guthrie, *Odysseus* 117–19 and cf. the scholiast on 79.

[30] ἄτρεστον (365); ἀδάματος (450) (or ἀδάμαστος; see Kamerbeek and Stanford ad loc.).

[31] Cf. his boast at 96, Knox, *Ajax* 31 n. 39 compares 774 with 112. Cf. also Achilles' parting from his father (*Il.* 9.252–9, with Winnington-Ingram 40 n. 89), and note the greater emphasis in *Ajax* on the role of the gods. Cf. also the boast of the lesser Ajax at *Od.* 4.502–4 (discussed by Dawe, *Ate* 115; Scodel 18). On the messenger speech see especially Winnington-Ingram 39–43.

to be humbled by her revenge. In the midst of his humiliation, after the chorus have nervously warned him not to say anything 'big' (386), he declares, 'I shall say a big word' (422f.). When Tecmessa supplicates him by the gods, he answers, 'Don't you know that I no longer owe the gods any service?' (589f.). In his suicide soliloquy he prays to Zeus, Hermes, the Erinyes, the sun and death (824–58), calling on the power of the gods only now that events have moved beyond his own control.[32] And this prayer is no humble appeal for help, but an imperious claim of his due.[33] He remains 'one born of mortal nature with thoughts not proper to a mortal' (760f.; cf. 770).[34]

The bond between mortal and immortal is a friendship of unequals. In such a relationship, says Aristotle, the one who is inferior in power or merit must offer a proportionately greater share of devotion in exchange for the favour of the more powerful *philos* (*EN* 1158b11–28).[35] Telamon warned his son 'always to conquer with the gods', to which Ajax scornfully replied that even a 'nothing' can win that way, whereas *he* is confident that he can reap glory without divine support (765–9). He has forfeited the friendship of the gods by failing to acknowledge his dependence. They too subscribe to Help Friends/Harm Enemies.[36] Like mortals, they give *charis*, *soteria* and laughter to those they love, but lamentation to those they hate.[37] Any merely human ability to harm an enemy pales in comparison with theirs. 'Do you see', says Athena after ex-

---

[32] Cf. Gellie 21f.

[33] Burial is to be his 'prize of honour' (γέρας 825). Cf. Perrotta 158f.

[34] This is compatible with the view that his words display 'a high heroic spirit' (Linforth, *Ajax* 26; cf. Adams 35). Compare Achilles' rebuke to Apollo (*Il.* 22.15–20). But Winnington-Ingram 18 reminds us that the rejection of divine help is *not* characteristic of the Homeric hero (cf. also Willcock 4).

[35] Aristotle himself thinks there cannot be *philia* between mortals and gods, but see above, p. 46f.

[36] Knox, *Ajax* 9 claims that Help Friends/Harm Enemies is legitimate for the gods, who act on it in accordance with justice. But the internal difficulties with the code apply equally to gods and mortals. And as Knox acknowledges, the issue is presented in terms of Athena's personal enmity (ib. 7f.; cf. also Heath 170f.). There is no suggestion that Ajax's fate is a divine punishment for attempted murder.

[37] Like victory, *soteria*, laughter and lamentation are all said to come 'with a god' (σὺν θεῷ 383, 765, 779; cf. 180, 705, 950). For the 'cooperative' use of *sun* ('with') see below, n. 67 and p. 103f.). For the gods' *charis* cf. 952f. and for their love and hatred 132f., 457f.

hibiting Ajax's terrible fate, 'how great is the power of the gods?' (118).

Pleasure and principle

Ajax's ruthless indulgence of his own desires, exhibited in the pro-logue, matches his portrayal throughout the play as a man who pur-sues personal gratification to the exclusion of the claims of all *philoi*, whether friends, relatives, allies, dependants or gods. His inclinations seem unconstrained by principles that might curtail the selfish pur-suit of pleasure. When Tecmessa supplicates him by his child and the gods not to abandon them, he silences her by declaring that she is causing him too much pain (589). More drastically, he appears to elevate 'delight' into a supreme goal, when he declares that it is 'dis-graceful' to prolong a life without it and contemptible to live on 'empty hopes' (473–8). In another remarkable passage he envies his young son's ignorance of misfortune, 'for the sweetest life is to have no sense' (554f.).[38] Although Ajax does not claim that pleasure is the only or the greatest good, he ranks the ignorant bliss of childhood above adult rationality with both its joy and its pain.[39] Such a senti-ment, even uttered at a moment of acute anguish, has implications which extend beyond the innocence of childhood to the mindless-ness of the insane Ajax. Ajax's madness led to his disastrous error of reason (447–9; cf. 40, 51f.), but it also made him, like his son, oblivi-ous of misfortune (cf. Eur. *Ba* 1259–62), and even brought him pleasure (105, cf. 114).[40] Tecmessa explains to the chorus that Ajax's restoration to his senses is an evil (259–62, 265–77), but this bewilders them, for it violates the common sense view that madness is itself an evil, and its departure an improvement (264, 278–80; cf. 635). Their uneasiness suggests that pleasure as such is an inadequate goal for a

---

[38] 554b (omitted by Stobaeus) dilutes the claim by adding that lack of reason is none the less an evil, though a painless one. It may be an interpolation, perhaps designed to clarify the thought by making explicit the distinction between pain and evil which Ajax otherwise ignores. It is deleted by most editors (see Jebb and Stanford ad loc.) but defended by Kamerbeek and Winnington-Ingram 31 n. 62.

[39] Judging from frag. 577 (Radt) the theme of pleasure was resumed in Sophocles' *Teucer*.

[40] On Ajax's mental state see especially Winnington-Ingram ch. 2. Cf. also Biggs 224–7.

rational animal. But it is in keeping with the monstrous, savage Ajax to scorn the life of reason.[41] He is god-like but also bestial.[42]

Ajax's emphasis on gratifying his own desires does not make him a conventional hedonist. In a nostalgic ode, the chorus provide a list of typical Athenian 'delights' (1185–1222):[43] garlands, deep wine-cups, company, sweet flute music, the night-long pleasures of sleep and love.[44] These are the joys of civilised and peaceful human social life, which the chorus contrast with the physical discomforts of warfare. But despite his preoccupation with 'delight', Ajax is not concerned with such pleasures.[45] He ignores Tecmessa's reminder of the sexual 'delight' she has given him (521). While the chorus' reaction to trouble is to wish that they could run away (245–50; cf. 900), leaving the misery of Troy for the delights of home, his desires harmonise with more lofty considerations of honour and justice.

Ajax's view of justice is simple: he is the greatest warrior at Troy, and is therefore owed the greatest honour.[46] When the Greek army denies him the arms of Achilles,[47] leaving him dishonoured (440; cf. 98, 426f.), it forfeits all claims on him. He is filled with hostile wrath towards the erstwhile friends who have violated the law of

[41] Odysseus agrees with Athena that before his madness there was no one with greater foresight (προνούστερος 119). But there is a sense in which he was 'mindless' (ἄνους 763) and deficient in 'sense' even before the onset of madness (761, 766, 777).

[42] In this he resembles the Homeric Achilles at the height of his fury (cf. Schein ch. 5; King 13–28). Cf. also Aristotle's famous remark that the self-sufficient apolitical man is 'either a beast or a god' (Pol. 1253a27–9). On Ajax as irrational and animal see Knox 42f.; id. Ajax 21; Rosenmeyer, Masks 178f.; Segal 127–31, 139. He is particularly characterised by the word ὠμός, 'savage' (205, 548, 885, 930; on its implications see Linforth, Antigone 471, 196f.). He is also described as 'fiery' (221, 1088), a bull (322) and a 'great eagle' (169 with Stanford ad loc.; cf. also Easterling, Notes 56f.). Agamemnon scornfully calls him a 'great ox' (1253) – a dumb animal, like the 'stupid beasts' he slaughtered and amongst whom he is still lying when we first see him (324f., 407; cf. 611, 614f. with Stanford's notes). In the myth of Er he chooses the life of a lion, shunning human life because of the judgement of the arms (Pl. Rep. 620b).

[43] τέρψις ('delight') appears three times (1201, 1204, 1216). Cf. Burton 36f.

[44] For interpretation of 1203–6 see Stanford ad loc.

[45] Cf. Segal 145.

[46] Others consider him the greatest after Achilles, but Ajax himself actually boasts (it is his 'great word') that he is like no other who ever came to Troy (422–6). Lawall 294 n. 3 aptly compares the claim of Achilles at Il. 18.105. Cf. also Trach. 811f. and see Winnington-Ingram 14f.

[47] Note that he calls them 'my' arms (100) – a fine touch rightly commended by the scholiast.

friendship (928–32; cf. 349f., 619f.), and craves the vengeance sanctioned by the talio.[48] He regards the allocation of the arms as an act of *hubris*, which he attempted to repay with interest (304),[49] trying in heroic fashion to exact revenge well beyond the limits of strict retaliation.[50] When this misfires he realises that he is now hated by both gods and mortals (457–9) and can expect no help from either (397–400). He justifiably foresees relentless hatred and persecution from his enemies (829f.).[51] He still longs to destroy his enemies, but evidently rules this out as impossible (387–91; cf. 403–9). He rejects the idea of going home, since he could not show his face to his father. Telamon, one of the great heroes of the previous generation, 'will not endure to look on' him if he returns without the prize of the greatest hero, the *aristos* (462–5; cf. 434–40).[52] To return home under such circumstances is 'unendurable' (466).[53] He rejects the

[48] Simpson 92 argues that Ajax's madness is the product of the clash between Help Friends and Harm Enemies, and thus 'symbolizes the potential for chaos within the heroic world'. But Ajax shows no difficulty with the fact that his enemies were his former friends (except to resent it). There is no sign that he was faced with 'an unbearable contradiction'. His shift in allegiance follows the usual pattern for the breakdown of friendship.

[49] Stanford ad loc. attractively interprets the *hubris* here as reciprocal. This is supported by the verb ἐκτίνω, 'repay'.

[50] On the extremity of Ajax's attempted revenge cf. Perrotta 159. At *Il.* 1.188–205 Achilles is on the point of killing Agamemnon when Athena redirects him (more favourably, of course, than she does Ajax). Many have seen his self-restraint in obedience to Athena as an important difference between him and Ajax (e.g. Kirkwood 174, Winnington-Ingram 17), though Achilles' 'restraint' will still result in terrible suffering for the whole army and greater honour for himself. Other significant differences include the fact that Achilles' attack was not surreptitious, and that he will eventually regret his excessive wrath.

[51] And further retaliation from 'the whole army', if Lobeck's τίσις is adopted with Pearson in 406. But this is an implausible solution to a difficult passage (see the editors ad loc.; Johansen 176; Stinton (2) 127f.).

[52] The expressions used in 462–5 denote strong feelings of shame in both father and son. For the association of eyes and looking with a sense of shame cf. *Phil.* 110, 929, 1354, *OT* 1371; Eur. *IA* 851f., *Med.* 469–72; Arist. *Rhet.* 1384a33–84b1; further parallels in Jebb and Kamerbeek ad loc. Ajax shows no sign of filial affection, or of fear such as Teucer will express as he foresees Telamon's wrath at his failure to preserve Ajax's life (1008–20). Each son thus anticipates the paternal reaction least favourable to himself. For the sequel in Sophocles' *Teucer*, see below, n. 100.

[53] Kamerbeek on 460 compares *Il.* 9.356–63, but for Achilles to leave Troy would be not a retreat but a form of revenge. Flight is the only alternative to suicide which is seriously considered in the play. It is canvassed by both Ajax and the chorus, and later (for himself) by Teucer. Other possibilities, such as fighting to

idea of dying in battle against the Trojans, doing 'some worthwhile deed', since this would bring pleasure to the hated Atreidae (466–9). Within the limits he has set himself, there is no alternative to suicide. But he still regards himself as the victim of *hubris* (304, 367),[54] still prays for vengeance, blames the Atreidae for his death, and calls on the Erinyes, goddesses of vengeance, to destroy his enemies and the entire army as completely and as horribly as he himself is destroyed (387–91, 835–44).[55] This is his conception of justice – direct personal retaliation, with no holds barred.

The fact that Ajax considers himself a victim of injustice does not diminish the disgrace of going home dishonoured. In this respect he adheres to Adkins' Homeric success-ethic.[56] Failure to rescue his honour is shameful per se, despite the 'justice' of his cause. And honour is paramount – it outweighs personal safety and even life. The 'noble man' (*eugenes*) must either live or die nobly (*kalôs*) (479f.).[57] To live on, enduring unrelieved misery, is disgraceful (*aischros*) (473f.).[58] For Ajax such misery is caused not by physical deprivation but by a dishonoured life, such as he faces if he runs away from Troy or stays to face further humiliation from his

the death (and enduring a humiliating defeat), or reconciliation, or (even less plausible!) standing trial, are never raised. One function of the messenger speech is to justify the fears of Ajax and the chorus that the entire army is against them, and indicate the kind of treatment they may expect.

[54] Cf. also 550 where he blames his troubles on bad luck. Critics emphasise his preoccupation with shame rather than guilt (e.g. Jones 178–80; Gellie 20). But guilt is not an issue for one who thinks his actions utterly justified.

[55] Most editors (though not Dain or Stanford) agree that at least part of 841f. is interpolated; see the editors and Dawe, *Studies* ad loc.; Pearson 26f. Delcourt 159f. defends the lines, but see contra Knox's review of Stanford's edition (*WA* 163f.). For the savagery of Ajax's dying curse cf. *Il.* 16.98f., *Phil.* 1200–2 and see Winnington-Ingram 45. Suicide is itself a form of revenge (see Delcourt; Glotz 64–6; Seidensticker 139f.). It carries a special pollution (Parker 41f.) and increased cursing power (ib. 198 n. 48), and may therefore be used as a weapon of last resort by suppliants (ib. 185). At Athens, suicides had their right hand cut off, 'presumably to ... render the spirit of the deceased harmless' (Garland 98).

[56] Adkins ch. 1 and passim.

[57] For this cardinal point of the aristocratic code cf. 1310f., *Ant.* 72, *El.* 989, 1320f. Cf. also Achilles' choice of a short glorious life over a long quiet one, and the Aristotelian version at *EN* 1169a22–5. Ajax's decision is sometimes compared to that of Socrates, but they make strange bedfellows. On *eugenes* in Sophocles see especially Kirkwood 177–9. Id. *Homer* 61f. compares *Il.* 15.511–13.

[58] *Aischros* is the opposite of *kalos* (cf. *El.* 593f. where it is implicitly equated with non-*kalos*; Adkins 44f. denies this equivalence for Homer, but see contra Long, *Morals* 128).

enemies. He must die not only because this is the only honourable way out of his original disgrace, but also because he would be further shamed by staying alive. These considerations prompt his last desire, a passionate longing for death.[59] As only Tecmessa realises, suicide is 'sweet' to him and brings 'delight' (966–8; cf. 583, 812). Like other tragic figures, his action is prompted by pleasure and self-interest as well as principle.[60] As we shall see in other cases, however, these are not self-interest and pleasure of a conventional kind.

Ajax and his *philoi*

Ajax is motivated by pleasure in that he indulges to the full the desires to which his conceptions of justice, honour and *eugeneia* give rise. But he is not willing to acknowledge that other values, or justice, honour and *eugeneia* in a different guise, may conflict with these personal desires. He is surrounded by loyal and affectionate *philoi* whom he has thrown into crisis. When they rally round he withdraws into a heroic isolation of his own making, and persists in indulging the desire for death.[61] His attitude is encapsulated by Tecmessa's description of his madness: 'grieving his friends, while enjoying pleasure himself' (266; cf. 272f.).

He praises the chorus as his only *philoi* still abiding by the 'upright law' of loyalty (349f.; cf. 359f., 406), but acknowledges a need for them only in commanding them to kill him (359–61) – a suggestion which, from their perspective, would only compound disaster (362f.). He does not consider his own responsibility to them as a *philos* or the consequences of his death for them.[62] They, however, are acutely aware of their position as subordinate *philoi*. The opening anapaests of the parodos emphasise both affection and dependence.[63] The chorus' first words identify their interests closely with those of their master: 'When you are well off I rejoice', but

---

[59] Indicated by the verb ἐρῶ (686, 967), used for passionate and especially erotic love. On the hero's desire for death see Knox 34–6.

[60] For this complexity of motivation cf. Long, *Fratricide*.

[61] On this isolation see Stanford on 614–15; Knox 32–4; Gellie 13–15; Biggs 225; Weinstock 46–8; and below p. 84. Ajax's neglect of his *philoi* is emphasised by Gardiner 74–6.

[62] Only at 349f. and 406 does Ajax call another character *philos*. His supporters, by contrast, constantly identify themselves as his *philoi* (330, 483, 615, 910, 917, 920, 1413), and him as their *philos* (941, 977, 996, 1015).

[63] Cf. Burton 10f.; Davidson 163–77.

when disaster strikes you, 'I have great fear and am terrified. So now ...' (136–41). They go on to expound an ideal of *philia* between unequals. The 'small' are wholly dependent on the 'great', who are a 'tower of defence' (158–60),[64] protecting them from fear as Ajax used to do (1211–13; cf. 167–71). But the great also need the small, who keep them 'upright' (161).[65] The details of this reciprocal benefit are not spelled out, but dependants presumably provide their patron with prestige as well as advice and support, both moral and physical, in military and personal conflicts.[66] Those who cannot comprehend this mutual need are 'senseless' (162f.). The theme is resumed when the chorus implicitly criticise Ajax for skulking in his tent instead of coming out to defend his reputation. His passivity brings grief to them as well as himself (200), for they are helpless without him.

This emphasis on their dependence is maintained throughout the play. The rumour of Ajax's slaughter of the cattle brings shame to them as well as him (174), though he acknowledges only a personal disgrace. If he is sane, they feel fortunate (263). They are his 'fellow sufferers' (283), fearing to suffer death with him (255).[67] Tecmessa addresses them as friends (315, 328) who are jointly concerned: 'Lamentation is ours, we who care for the house of Telamon far away' (203f.).[68] As 'sharers' in the whole affair they have the right to hear her story (284).[69] She asks for their help, since 'people in this state are won by the words of friends' (329f.).[70] They will respond

---

[64] On πύργου ῥῦμα (159) see Kamerbeek and Stanford ad loc.

[65] Or 'straight' (ὀρθοῖτο 161; for the metaphor cf. 350, 1254). On the frequency of the word 'great' (μέγας) in this passage see Stanford xxvii n. 37 and Winnington-Ingram 22.

[66] Sailors perform a particularly essential function, since the captain is immobile without them. Tecmessa and Ajax both address the chorus as 'defenders' of his ship (201, 357). Pace Burton 6 they are also soldiers (cf. 565). On their status see Davidson 163–5; Gardiner 52.

[67] Τοῖς συναλγοῦσιν (283); ξυναλγεῖν (255). The verb carries the *sun-/xun-* prefix, meaning 'with', which is often used to suggest the cooperation of *philoi* (cf. Arist. *EN* 1171b32–72a8; Dirlmeier 53f.; Ferguson 22f., 61; Griffith on *PV* 162). The chorus use it to call themselves Ajax's 'fellow sailors' at the very moment they discover he has deceived them (συνναύταν 902). See also below, p. 103f.

[68] Her word (κηδόμενοι) suggests the affection and concern of relatives (cf. below, p. 122).

[69] Cf. also 267 with Stanford's note ad loc. and Winnington-Ingram 24 n. 42.

[70] Both Stanford and Kamerbeek retain the ms. reading φίλοι (rather than λόγοις) in 330, but see contra Knox, *WA* 163. The essential point is not affected.

with an appeal to Ajax to let friends overrule his purpose (483f.). But Ajax ignores them. They long to steal away and set sail (245–50). But he rejects that option without reference to them, the crew he would need to make his escape.[71] After deciding to die, he orders them to perform a 'favour' (*charis*) for him by sharing Teucer's responsibility for Eurysaces (566). He commends them too to Teucer's good will, but his final words are a command to 'honour' his wishes and obey his instructions, in the hope that he himself may end up 'saved' (687–92).

The sailors' joy at Ajax's apparent conversion is expressed with extraordinary passion (693–705), and with his death they are plunged into despair: 'Alas for my homecoming! Alas, lord, you have killed your fellow sailor!' (900–2). They lament that he died in solitude, unprotected by *philoi* (910) – he has not allowed them to fulfil their side of the reciprocal relationship. Later they sing sadly of all they have lost through the death of the master who was their 'bulwark against nightly fear and missiles' (1211–16). Their unheroic distaste for 'shared warfare' (1196) reminds us that they came to Troy in a subordinate role, leaving everyday pleasures to support their leader in his pursuit of glory. But they now see the Trojan war as a 'wretched reproach to the Greeks' (1191).[72] Ajax has indeed 'turned out to be a great grief to his *philoi*' (615f.).

Tecmessa is even more vulnerable. Like the chorus, her first words express involvement in Ajax's troubles, with a reminder of how far they all are from home (201–4). To her, Ajax's madness is 'equal to death' (215), and his death means her own, for her life is not worth living without him (392f.). Her dependence on him is total, since he has destroyed her country (515).[73] He is now her only home, her wealth and her salvation (518f.). He is her master (368, 485, 585), and she his slave (489).[74] As such she has no formal claim on him, but she appeals beyond this relationship to the ties of intim-

---

[71] At 412–15 he seems to adopt the choral perspective, declaring that it is time to leave Troy, but the next line makes it clear that he is referring to the departure of death.

[72] For a similar view of this ode see Gardiner 71.

[73] And perhaps implicitly her parents, as in later versions (see Roscher s.v. *Tekmessa* and cf. Kamerbeek on 516). But the text of 516 is problematic (see Dawe, *Studies* and the editors ad loc.).

[74] She is often inaccurately referred to as Ajax's wife (e.g. by Stanford on 211–12 and passim). For the right emphasis cf. Easterling, *Homer* 3.

acy and mutual affection. Although he acquired her by force, she has accepted her fate and become attached to his interests (490f.).[75] We see her affectionate, obedient and eager to please (294, 529, 537). She addresses and even 'scolds' Ajax with a colloquial familiarity (288f.).[76] The chorus assume that as the 'spear-won partner of his bed' she has an intimate knowledge of his actions (211f.). She supplicates him not to 'betray' them, 'by the gods and your child' (587f.) and by 'Zeus of the hearth' (492) – Zeus as protector of the values of family solidarity which Ajax is violating. She also beseeches him 'by your bed, in which you had intercourse with me', not to abandon her to his enemies (493–5).[77] She has given him pleasure, which puts him under an obligation: 'If a man experiences some delight, he should be mindful of it' (520f.). She appeals to the principle of reciprocal favour, which she expresses as a universal truth: 'for it is *charis* which ever gives birth to *charis*' (522).[78] She reinforces this principle with a strong claim: anyone who is not properly 'mindful' of kind treatment cannot qualify as 'noble' (*eugenes*) (523f.). Like her reference to 'delight', this is a challenge to Ajax's conception of *eugeneia* (479f.)[79] He used such language to justify the indulgence of his desire for death, but Tecmessa dwells on a different aspect: to be *eugenes* requires the reciprocation of pleasure or favours, and hence a concern for the interests of *philoi* as well as oneself.

She also begs Ajax to pity their son, who will grow up fatherless, in the hands of 'unfriendly guardians' (510–12; cf. *Il.* 6.407f., 431f.). 'Think how great an evil you will be assigning to him and me' (512f.). Her verb emphasises Ajax's responsibility for their fate, and 'unfriendly' (512) is not just a euphemism for 'hostile' but a

<hr />

[75] Note her concern for the house of Telamon (203f.). Cf. Eur. *Med.* 54f. and especially Herod. 1.89.1.

[76] For the colloquialism of τί χρῆμα (288) see Stevens, *Euripides* 190f.

[77] Her verb (συνηλλάχθης 493) is a euphemism for sexual intercourse, but also carries connotations of reciprocal exchange, reconciliation and contractual obligation (see LSJ s.v. and cf. Gardiner 75 n. 40). Her use of the *sun*- prefix echoes 491 (cf. Winnington-Ingram 30). Note also that Ajax is the subject of the clause. Tecmessa's language always centres on him rather than herself. Besides numerous second person verbs, her speech includes an extraordinary number of second person pronouns and possessive adjectives.

[78] On the *charis* theme see Segal 136–8.

[79] For the symmetry of their speeches see Reinhardt 19; Finley, *Three* 78. For a good discussion of Tecmessa's speech see Easterling, *Homer*; cf. also Heath 181f.

reminder of Ajax's own obligations as a *philos* to his son.[80] The pity she calls for is an obligation to be fulfilled in action. The chorus are stirred by pity, but are helpless to act except by urging Ajax to share their feelings. If he did so, they claim, he would approve her words (525f.). But he replies that she will gain his approval only by obeying orders (527f.). He makes it clear that he has no time for the 'feminine' emotion of pity, and the lamentation to which it gives rise.[81] But the play associates pity not only with women (cf. 629, 895), but with the male chorus (525f.) and with Odysseus (121).[82]

Given Ajax's anxiety for paternal approval, Tecmessa should be on strong ground when she reminds him of his parents. She suggests that he should feel shame (*aidos*) at leaving them to a miserable old age (506–9), thus violating the bond of filial piety.[83] At the end of the scene the chorus will picture the distress of Ajax's mother, 'nurtured' by old age instead of her son, when she hears of his 'sickness' (621–34). They also invoke the 'wretched father' who must hear of his son's uniquely terrible fate (641–5). This scene of mourning from a remote place and time adds a further dimension to Tecmessa's picture of the dire consequences of Ajax's death. Before he dies, Ajax will re-echo the theme, referring to his father's advanced age and acknowledging his mother's pain at his death (848–51).[84] He calls her his 'nurse' (849), echoing the chorus' 'nurture' and suggesting once again the obligation to reciprocate parental care. But he dismisses such regrets as futile (852). They cannot impede the course he has chosen, which 'must be speedily begun' (853). Tecmessa's variety of *aidos* is overruled by his own desire to redeem himself in his

---

[80] With μὴ φίλων, 'unfriendly' (512), compare the chorus' use of ἄφιλα, 'non-*philos*' in 620.

[81] He calls women φιλοίκτιστον (580), which is usually derived from οἰκτίζομαι, 'lament' (so Stanford, Jebb). But this in turn derives from οἶκτος, 'pity' (and hence 'lamentation'). Hence LSJ gloss φιλοίκτιστον as φιλοικτίρμων, 'prone to pity'.

[82] The femininity of pity/lamentation was a commonplace (see Dover 101 and cf. *Trach.* 1070–5; Pl. *Rep.* 387de; Arist. *Hist. An.* 608b; other parallels in Jebb on *Aj.* 580). But pity was highly valued in democratic Athens (see Glotz 423f.; Bolkestein 112–14, 141–3; Dover 195–201). Democritus associates it with a harmonious social order (DK 68 B 255).

[83] On *aidos* see further below, p. 242. For its association with Ajax in Homer see Stanford xxxiii.

[84] For Telamon's age cf. 1017. Tecmessa's and Ajax's lines are closely parallel. Both mention first the aged father, then the mother, who receives two further lines. Ajax's words also echo the sense and structure of the choral passage.

father's eyes. Telamon will doubtless be grieved at Ajax's suicide, but less than he would be at his son's disgrace, and this outweighs a mother's anguish. Tecmessa dwells on Ajax's mother and the 'feminine' emotion of pity, but he himself is anxious not to betray his father's masculine honour.[85]

But Tecmessa also enlists Ajax's family honour on her own side. She claims that if she and Eurysaces suffer the 'nurture' of slavery (499), the mockery they must endure will bring disgrace on Ajax himself and his whole line (505). Tecmessa is already a slave, but the threat of painful servitude, echoing the scene between Hector and Andromache in the *Iliad*, helps to suggest the stronger claim of a free wife.[86] It also prompts comparison between Hector and Ajax. Both reject a woman's appeals, but Hector is not only going forth to defend his family (*Il.* 6.464f.) but acting out of *aidos* for the Trojans, men and women (443), and the prospect of renown for both himself and his father (446). He is motivated by honour, but this honour will be won in the service of others. Similarly Tecmessa's conception of 'disgrace', like her 'nobility', demands sensitivity to the needs of others. To Ajax it is disgraceful to stay alive (473). But the glory or shame of the individual reflects on the family, as Ajax himself implies by the reaction he expects from Telamon. If Tecmessa˙ and Eurysaces suffer ignominy, his honour will be clouded. More significant, however, is the suggestion that by abandoning them to enemies (495), Ajax has failed in his duties as a *philos*, and that *this* is a cause of disgrace.[87] Despite his isolated stance, his personal honour remains bound up with his treatment of *philoi*.

The appeal to honour is Tecmessa's strongest card, but like the rest of her speech, Ajax ignores it. The chorus has told us that he reciprocated her devotion by being 'constant in his affection', or at least by tolerating her (212).[88] She herself will imply that before the

---

[85] Contrast *Il.* 24.485–516 (Achilles is moved to *aidos* and pity by the thought of his aged father).

[86] Cf. *Il.* 6.399–465. The two scenes have many points of contact (see especially Kirkwood, *Homer* 56–9; Easterling, *Homer*; cf. also Perrotta 144–7; Reinhardt 20–2; Winnington-Ingram 16).

[87] Note that they are in the first instance his enemies: any hostility Tecmessa and her son suffer will be by association with him. He is therefore doubly responsible for their fate.

[88] The quotation is Jebb's translation of στέρξας ἀνέχει, but στέργω can mean anything from positive love to mere acquiescence (compare e.g. *OC* 7 and 1529;

disaster she used to enjoy his favour (*charis* 808). But within the play he is brusque with her. Before he appears, she reports how he made 'awesome threats' to her (312). His first words to her on stage are 'get out of the way' (369). He repeats the cliché that silence is an ornament to women (292f.),[89] recommends the virtues of obedience (527f.) and self-restraint (586), which he will not adopt himself, tells her to ask no questions (586) and declares that she pains him, he is not listening to her, she talks too much and she is stupid (589–94). His final command to her is typically egocentric: 'Go inside, woman, and pray to the gods to fulfil completely what my heart passionately desires' (685f.).

When she hears the words of the messenger, Tecmessa sees the approach of 'inescapable chance' (803), which struck her once before at the hand of Ajax (485). She realises that he has broken that bond of mutual favour to which she appealed: 'I understand that I have been deceived by the man, and cast out of former *charis*' (808). When she finds him dead she laments her own ruin, expressed in a crescendo of three verbs of destruction addressed to her equally helpless *philoi*, the chorus (896). His corpse is a sight that no *philos* could bear to look on (917). She and their child are now destined for the yoke of slavery (944f.). His death is as bitter for her as it is sweet for his enemies, and (paradoxically) 'delightful' for himself (966f.).[90] His legacy to her is pain and lamentation (972f.).[91]

Ajax has already preempted several of Tecmessa's arguments in his rhetorical survey of the options open to him. By placing that speech (430–80) *before* her attempt to dissuade him, the poet allows Ajax to defend his decision while leaving him totally unresponsive to her appeal. He obliquely answers other points, again without

for more examples see Stanford, *Emotions* 39); ἀνέχει is taken by commentators as 'support constantly' or 'honour' (for parallels see Schneidewin–Nauck ad loc.), but it could mean no more than 'put up with' (the question is begged e.g. by Stanford xxix).

[89] For parallels see Jebb ad loc.; Bowra 23f.; Heath 183f. Contrast the futile attempts of Tecmessa and the chorus to silence Ajax (362, 591).

[90] Both text and interpretation of these lines are controversial. Most editors retain the manuscripts' ἤ in 966, meaning 'or', but this is anomalous (see Jebb, Stanford and Dawe, *Studies* ad loc., and Jebb's appendix). Pearson prints and defends (*Glosses* 122–4) Schneidewin's ᾗ. Pace Stanford, this does not give 'a feebler or looser construction', but neatly captures a paradox.

[91] For λείπω as 'bequeath' see LSJ s.v. A.1.2. The word order of 972 strongly contrasts Tecmessa's fate with Ajax's own.

addressing her, in the speech to his son. Eurysaces is the only *philos* besides Telamon for whom Ajax shows a strong concern. His first words on recovering from his madness, after a repeated cry of lamentation for his own fate (333, 336), are a call for his son (339).[92] Later he will address to Eurysaces an extended farewell (545–77). But even this long speech contains no word of affection, and remains self-centred in its treatment of the son as an extension of the father. The desire for a child to resemble oneself is not unnatural (cf. Eur. *Ba.* 1252f.; Arist. *Pol.* 1252a28–30), but Ajax sees his son exclusively in such terms. Eurysaces will not flinch at the sight of fresh blood, if he is 'justly' his father's son; he must be 'broken in' from the start to his father's harsh ways and made to resemble him in nature; if he is like him in everything but ill fortune, then he will not be *kakos* (545–51).[93] When he reaches the proper age, he must avenge his father by 'proving amongst your father's enemies what kind of son you are of what kind of father' (556f.). The only moment of tenderness is the command to 'feed till then on insubstantial breezes, nourishing your young spirit, a joy to your mother here' (558f.).[94] Ajax makes on his son the same demands that he expects Telamon to make on him.[95] The son is to live up to his father, whether by winning equal glory or by avenging paternal disgrace on his inherited enemies. In order to ensure such a future for Eurysaces, Ajax commends him to the absent Teucer, certain that his brother will ward off the *hubris* and ill-treatment of the Achaians (560–4). He orders Teucer and the chorus to take the child home to his grandparents so that he may fill Ajax's role by supporting them in their old age (565–71). Here is his implicit response to Tecmessa's pathetic picture of the future. Although he expresses no concern for Tecmessa herself, he does tacitly admit a responsibility for his son and his parents.

But he lives up to it only by shifting the burden onto his

---

92 The echo of 333 and 336 helps to suggest the close identification of father and son.

93 Contrast Hector's desire for his son to turn out 'far better' than himself (*Il.* 6.479).

94 This is his only allusion to the future of Tecmessa, whom Ajax never mentions by name. Both his language and his disregard for her probable fate recall the unjustified optimism of Hector (*Il.* 6.481).

95 Kamberbeek on 1010 remarks that there is a family likeness between Ajax and his father (though he is inaccurate in suggesting that Teucer actually says this). Cf. the reference to Telamon's evil and quarrelsome temper (1017f.).

brother, without consultation and with a confidence which events
will prove unwarranted. After the first cry for his son he calls im-
patiently for Teucer (342f.), assuming that his brother will be able to
do everything necessary to protect his dependants (560–4, 688f.).
Ajax also mentions Teucer in his final soliloquy, but only to pray
that his brother may find his body and protect it from his enemies
(826–30).[96] He treats him merely as a useful supporter, and leaves
him in an impossible position as a result of his death. The two
brothers never meet within the play. There is no scene of confrontation, no attempt by Teucer to dissuade his brother from dying, or by
Ajax to extract an assurance of loyalty from Teucer (contrast *OT*
1503–14, *OC* 1629–35). Teucer enters only after Ajax is dead. But
when he does eventually arrive, back from 'hunting down enemies'
(564; cf. 342f.),[97] he immediately sees his responsibility. His first
reaction is grief for 'dearest Ajax, my beloved brother' (977; cf. 996,
1015).[98] His second is 'What of his child? Where on earth is he?'
(983f.). And when he hears that Eurysaces has been left alone by the
tents, he sends for him at once, to protect him from Ajax's enemies
(985–7). It is only then that the chorus relays his brother's command
to act just as he is already doing (990f.).

Ajax bequeaths to his brother the crisis that he himself died
rather than face. The parallel is brought out by the way in which
Teucer's deliberations echo Ajax's own. Both start with a rhetorical
question, explained by the straits the speaker is in: 'What must I do, I
who am hated by gods and mortals?' (457–9); 'Where can I go, to
what people, I who did not help you in your troubles?' (1006f.).
Both first reject the idea of going home (460–6, 1008–21), then go
on to consider the difficulty of staying at Troy, where Ajax spurns
the idea of doing any good to his enemies while for Teucer there are

---

[96] The first part of this prayer will be answered (cf. 998f., pace Winnington-
Ingram 44 n. 100). Perhaps it already has been, by the friendly cooperation of
Calchas. But the second part goes unanswered. Kitto, *FMD* 192 argues that the
gods work through Odysseus, but if so they do not give Ajax what he prayed
for.

[97] This is perhaps more than a dramatic convenience. It contrasts with Ajax's
night exploit and echoes Odysseus' hunting of Ajax in the prologue (5–8, 12–
20). It shows us a Teucer loyal to the Greeks, not yet involved in his brother's
quarrel, and provides a glimpse of life before the disaster – a paradigm of Help
Friends/Harm Enemies in a military context.

[98] On the untranslatable ξύναιμον ὄμμ' ἐμοί (977) see Stanford ad loc.; Long 124f.

'many enemies and few benefits' (466–70, 1021f.).[99] Particularly striking is the way both dwell on the hostile reception they expect from the redoubtable Telamon (462–5, 1008–20). As a result even Teucer, whom Ajax designated as his son's 'unshrinking' guardian and protector (562f.), expects to be reduced to slavery (1019f.; cf. 1235, 1259f.).[100] In this he echoes both Tecmessa's fears for the future (496–9) and the fate she has already endured. She was the daughter of a free and wealthy man, but is now Ajax's spear-captive and slave (485–90; cf. 211, 894). Her fate also reproduces that of Teucer's mother (the spear-captive of Telamon), while her child Eurysaces is in the same precarious position as Teucer himself, the bastard 'spear-captive's son' (1213). These parallel fates declare that free birth and slavery are gifts of fortune and not legitimate criteria for the judging of human worth. As Tecmessa tells Ajax, 'There is no greater evil for mortals than inescapable chance' (485f.). But for both her and Teucer the instrument of 'chance' is Ajax.[101]

Teucer's words formally emphasise Ajax's responsibility through ring composition. He prefaces his deliberations by exclaiming, 'What sorrows you have sown for me by dying...', and concludes them with, 'All this have I acquired through your death' (1005, 1023).[102] He ends where Ajax began, with the question so often used in tragedy to pinpoint a practical crisis or moral dilemma: 'Alas, what shall I do?' (1024). He echoes Tecmessa's repeated use of the same phrase (809, 920), as well as Ajax's firmer version, 'What must I do?' (457). Ajax's answer to this question obliges them in turn to face it. Teucer answers it implicitly, as he turns to care for his brother's body (1024–6). Faced with responsibility for Ajax's corpse and dependants, he does not abandon them. Instead, the scene seems set for him to die in their defence (cf. 1310f.).

---

[99] Note the rhythmic echo in the transitional lines 466 and 1021. In each a strong pause falls at the same point before the speaker moves on to the Trojan option.

[100] In Aesch. *Salaminiae*, Soph. *Teucer* and probably also *Eurysaces*, he was exiled but not enslaved (see Jebb *Introduction* §7, §18; Radt 431–3; Sutton 49–56).

[101] As the scholiast on 1005 aptly remarks, Ajax is Teucer's ἀρχὴ κακῶν, his 'beginning of evils'.

[102] Cf. the more delicate way that Tecmessa mentions Ajax's responsibility near the start of her speech (489f.) and reiterates it towards the end (515). It has been pointed out that reproaching the dead is a conventional feature of the funeral dirge (Heath 199; cf. Garland 30f.; Alexiou 182–4). But unlike most people Ajax chose his own death, and left his survivors in an unusually pressing predicament.

Friendship and deception

When Ajax emerges from his tent for the second time, he claims to
have been won over by Tecmessa, who he says has 'feminised' him
(651).[103] Although he expresses this apparent change of heart in
terms of yielding rather than cooperation, his language echoes values
of Odysseus, Tecmessa and the chorus for which he elsewhere shows
nothing but scorn: the alteration of the human mind with time
(648f.; 594f., 1361), pity (652; cf. 121, 510, 525, 580),[104] softening
under the influence of friends (650–2; cf. 330, 594f., 1353),[105] yielding to the gods (655f., 666f.; cf. 112f., 589f., 766–75). Particularly
striking are the lines where he dwells on the mutability of friendship:

> For I have learned today to hate a foe
> So far, that he may yet become a friend,
> And so far I resolve to serve a friend
> Remembering he may yet become a foe.
>
> (678–82, trans. Kitto, *FMD* 190)

'For', he adds, 'comradeship is an untrustworthy harbour for most
mortals' (682f.).[106] Still more surprisingly, he appears to concur
with the arguments from discipline which we shall hear from the
Atreidae, concluding that he too should learn *sophrosune*, the virtue
of the disciplined subordinate (666–77; cf. 1071–6, 1352).[107] But a
hundred lines later he re-enters and kills himself, without a word of
further explanation.

Tecmessa and the chorus are taken in (807, 911f.),[108] and there

---

103 This phrase is ambiguous between the literal 'feminised in mouth' and the
metaphorical 'softened in edge' (see the editors ad loc.). For its pejorative implications see Hester, *Distemper* 251f.; cf. also Knox, *Ajax* 15.

104 In particular, 652 closely echoes Odysseus at 121 (cf. also *Il.* 6.431f.). Most interpreters agree that whatever else Ajax may be up to, his pity for Tecmessa is sincere (exceptions are Sicherl 74; Dale, *Electra* 223). But if the speech is a
deception, then the entire ruse is predicated on the speaker's alleged pity, which
suggests that the pity itself is a lie. Further, pity is one of a complex of values
accepted by others but rejected elsewhere by Ajax. Why should it be the only
sincere element in the speech?

105 Ironically in *Il.* 9 it is Ajax himself who – as Odysseus' partner in the embassy –
tries to sway Achilles with an appeal to friendship (cf. Gardiner 63).

106 These lines echo a famous maxim of Bias of Priene (see Winnington-Ingram,
Sophoclea 3). For other parallels see above, p. 38. On 'comradeship' (683; cf.
687) cf. Gardiner 66 n. 29.

107 The preceding and following context both suggest that *sophrosune* in 677 relates
to the Atreidae.

108 For the significance of 807 see Waldock 74 (pace Taplin, *Forethought* 129). Segal

is no good reason to doubt that Ajax means to deceive them.[109] Contrary to Sophocles' practice in three other plays, we have no advance notice of an intention to lie.[110] In this case such advance warning would ruin the impact of a totally unexpected volte-face, which is only gradually undermined by the speech's systematic ambiguities.[111] These soon become so transparent that the informed spectator must infer that Ajax is still set on suicide.

Dolos may refer to any kind of underhand behaviour, cunning, trickery or deception. It is a tool of the weaker against the stronger,[112] and hence especially a women's weapon.[113] But although it tends to meet with disapproval in Sophocles, especially when used to take advantage of the weak,[114] it is not necessarily unheroic per se even for the strong to use it against an enemy.[115] It is, however, especially associated with Odysseus, whom Ajax in our play despises, and who (as his cautious behaviour in the prologue reminds us), represents a different paradigm of heroism.[116] Moreover there are few exploits of *dolos* by non-Odyssean heroes that command unambiguous approval.[117] Ajax himself, both in his tradi-

114 thinks Tecmessa is not 'fully' deceived, but the lines he cites (787, 791) suggest the opposite. It is sometimes argued that the chorus' reaction shows self-deception, thus absolving Ajax, but 911f. need bear no such weight.

109 I speak dogmatically since this is not the place to add to the awesome and still growing number of detailed interpretations. For doxography see Errandonea 24–8; Johansen 177f.; Moore, *Ajax* 48–54; Hester, *Distemper* 247–50; Winnington-Ingram 46 n. 107; Segal 432 n. 9; Lesky, *GTP* 131.

110 *El.*, *Phil.* and *OC*. But Lichas' deception in *Trach.* is a reminder that the dramatist may enlighten us only after the event.

111 On which see especially Sicherl 77–85.

112 Cf. Detienne and Vernant 13f., 28f.

113 See Dover 100; Buxton 63f.; Stanford, *Lies* 45 and n. 15. Deianeira (cf. *Trach.* 275–9) and Clytemnestra provide notable examples, and on the positive side, Penelope. Cf. also Eur. fr. 288 (Nauck); Pl. *Laws* 781a; Arist. *Hist. An.* 608b.

114 As by Odysseus in *Phil.* and Creon in *OC*. Cf. also fr. 79 (Radt).

115 See especially Stanford, *UT* 21f., *Lies* 35–9, and cf. above, p. 36.

116 Ajax is an 'Achillean' hero (cf. below, p. 184 n. 1 and see Lawall 290–4). This difference is emphasised by von Fritz, *Aias* 242. On the contrast between Ajax and Odysseus in Homer see Kirkwood, *Homer* 69f. Kott 76f. attractively recalls their different choices in Plato's myth of Er (*Rep.* 620bcd). They remained a contrasted pair of heroic figures and ethical paradigms (cf. Cic. *Off.* 1.113).

117 'Odyssean' covers other notorious tricksters such as Autolycus, Sisyphus and Palamedes. As Stanford acknowledges, the 'conventional hero' (such as Achilles) hates 'Autolycanism' (*UT* 18; cf. *Il.* 7.242f., 9.312f.). At *Trach.* 275–9 Zeus punishes Heracles for his use of *dolos* even in a just cause. Orestes' matricide is a controversial case, discussed further in ch. 5.

tional persona and in our play outside this speech, displays a brutal honesty. His night attack on the chieftains, however, was an unequivocal deed of *dolos* (47).[118] It is therefore demonstrably false that craft per se is incompatible with Ajax's character as Sophocles conceived it in this play.[119] But although *dolos* may be used against enemies, honesty should prevail between friends. Thus Teucer expects Telamon to accuse him of cowardice, treachery and *dolos* against his brother (1014f.), and Agamemnon reproves Ajax's use of *dolos* to try and subvert justice (1245). Tecmessa couples Ajax's deception with her loss of his *charis* (807f.), a sign that she thinks she has not been treated as a friend should.[120]

Mere deception does not, however, account for the depth and substance of Ajax's speech, with its justly famous meditation on the nature of time and change.[121] We need some explanation beyond the dramatic convenience of allowing Ajax to escape by himself,[122] and beyond the functions of surprise, suspense and irony. These effects provide one level of explanation, but do not do justice to the speech's rich and complex content, including the way it systematically embraces the values that Ajax elsewhere rejects. For he gives us precisely the arguments we might have expected from some other character trying to dissuade him from suicide. It is as if a plea of Odysseus were spoken by Ajax himself. Just as the poet avoids letting Ajax answer Tecmessa's appeal, and avoids facing him with Teucer, so here we see him rejecting the values of others without confronting them or engaging in argument, which would undermine his self-sufficient isolation.[123] Since the speech is deceptive, the

---

[118] For the association of *dolos* with night (cf. 1056) see Buxton 64.

[119] Many ingenious attempts to explain away or excuse his supposed lapse of character in the deception speech are accordingly misdirected.

[120] The connection with *charis* supports the view that her word ἠπατημένη, 'deceived' (807) refers to active deceit by Ajax rather than self-deception on her own part.

[121] On these central themes see especially Knox, *Ajax*.

[122] This could easily have been engineered in some other way, e.g. by Ajax intimidating his dependants. (At 595 they think he is going into his tent to kill himself; cf. Gellie 281 n. 9; Cohen 34 n. 1; Burton 22–6.)

[123] Cf. Reinhardt 19. Ajax's first long speech is addressed to those present only in the last line (480), and gives the impression of a personal deliberation. The second is addressed to his son, who (being pre-rational) cannot respond. The third has the air of a soliloquy (see especially Knox, *Ajax* 12–14). Cf. also Gardiner 61, on his failure to address the chorus in their lyric dialogue.

case for the opposition can be made not just from Ajax's scornful perspective, but as persuasively as possible. It is 'the supreme – ironic – revelation of the mind of Ajax through the expression of its reverse'.[124] At the same time these arguments, so eloquently conveyed, seem to constitute an admission that this is the way things are in the world he spurns, adding tragic depth to his refusal to compromise.[125]

Ajax's speech is rich in irony. But the final irony is that in a sense he has indeed been overcome by the forces he despises, the mutability of the world and especially of friendship.[126] He has been laid low by that 'single day' which Athena assured us 'tilts down the scales and lifts them up again for all human fortunes' (131f., trans. Stanford ad loc.).[127] The perceived fickleness of friends induced him in turn to exchange friendship for enmity. As a result he has been reduced to *dolos*, the weapon of women and weaklings, and to a wailing which Tecmessa tells us she had never heard from him before, such as he used to say belonged to 'a heavy-hearted and *kakos* man' (317–20; cf. 410f.).[128] The chorus likewise tell us that he is not what he used to be (635–40).[129] After deciding to kill himself he declares that his character (*ethos*) is unchangeable (594f.), but paradoxically it is this very rigidity, the demand for absolute loyalty on his own terms, which has reduced him to the behaviour he formerly despised. His last speech reasserts the permanence of his hatred.[130] But the same rage at disloyalty that prompts this final curse has made him violate his own obligations to other (loyal) friends, providing them too with a single day on which everything hangs (cf. 496–9).[131] Agamemnon will speak disapprovingly of fickle friends, and Odysseus reply by defending flexibility (1358f.).[132] With a final

124 Winnington-Ingram 47 n. 109. Cf. also Perrotta 148–58.
125 Cf. Gellie 15f.; North 60f.
126 Cf. von Fritz, *Aias* 247f.
127 This I take to be the significance of Calchas' prophecy that Athena's wrath will last only this one day (753, 778, 801f.; cf. 1362). One day is enough. (See also Fraenkel, *Ephemeros* 141; Winnington-Ingram 39; Segal 112.)
128 Cf. also *Trach.* 1070–5. On βαρυψύχου see Jebb ad loc.
129 See Gardiner 76f.
130 See Knox, *Ajax* 27f.; Rosenmeyer, *Masks* 185f.
131 The effect of Tecmessa's words here is enhanced by Bothe's ἦ in 496 (see Stanford ad loc.).
132 On this exchange see further below, p. 98f.

twist of irony, Ajax is excused by his enemy for the very fickleness he scorns.

The suicide that brings disaster to Ajax's friends really does improve his own lot. Even the chorus, with their desperate anxiety to save him, acknowledge that in his present condition he would be better off dead (635). A wedge is thus driven between their wishes and his own, exposing the frailty of the ideal of united interests amongst *philoi*. This leads Ajax to disregard a fundamental aspect of traditional heroic values, the support and protection of dependent *philoi*. If he followed a private moral code it might be argued that conventional norms have no claim on him, and his pursuit of honour would have the virtue of consistency. But his choice of values does not entitle him to neglect the claims of others, for such claims are also a part of the code by which he lives. He expected recognition for helping his allies, thus laying himself open to Tecmessa's argument that it is disgraceful to abandon one's friends (505). Even the patrilineal solidarity that he demands of his son is challenged by his rejection of his own father's advice (763–9).

Above all, Ajax's indignation at ingratitude is undermined by his treatment of his dependants. It was the failure of *philoi* to reciprocate due honour for his help which first drove him to revenge. As the chorus lament, his exploits 'fell unloved amongst unloving friends, the wretched Atreidae' (616–20; cf. 962–5).[133] But Tecmessa's claim on him is analogous to his on the Atreidae. This emerges strikingly from parallels between her words to him and Teucer's to Agamemnon. When Tecmessa speaks of reciprocal *charis* she begs Ajax to 'remember' her too, for a man cannot be *eugenes* if 'remembrance of good treatment flows away' (520–3).[134] She also supplicates him not to 'betray' them (588). Teucer exclaims at the transience of *charis*, which 'flows away and is convicted of betrayal' (1267), for Agamemnon no longer 'remembers' Ajax and his services (1269).[135] There is a final echo, not of Tecmessa but of the chorus, when Teucer calls Agamemnon's ungrateful speech 'sense-

---

133 Translation cannot do justice to ἄφιλα/παρ' ἀφίλοις (619f.).

134 μνῆστις ('remembrance') occurs three times in this play (520, 523, 1269) but nowhere else in extant Sophocles (according to Ellendt s.v.). Cf. also cognates at 521, 1166, 1273, 1390. On the use of such language to express gratitude see Hewitt 146f. For 'remembrance' as an obligation of *philia* cf. *El.* 346.

135 Teucer also fears that Telamon will blame him for 'betraying' Ajax (1014).

less words' (1272). In the prologue the chorus declared it impossible to teach the 'senseless' that great and small both need each other (162f.). Ajax, called 'senseless' by Calchas for failing to acknowledge his need of the gods (763), has borne out the truth of their words.

The hero needs both superior and inferior *philoi*, both divine supporters and human dependants, to ensure his glory. Ajax disregards the reciprocal bond of *philia* in both directions. He fails to acknowledge his own dependence on the gods, and violates the contract of noblesse oblige with his own dependants by demanding the benefits of *philia* without its reciprocity, the privileges of authority without its responsibilities. This utter alienation from the reciprocity of *philia* is symbolised by his paradoxical relationship to Hector and his sword. In the *Iliad* the exchange of gifts between Hector and Ajax is explicitly a token of friendship (*Il.* 7.302). Yet this sword, a tribute of honour and friendship from the noblest of foes,[136] is now *echthistos*, the gift of the 'most hostile' Hector, and must be buried to end Ajax's ill fortune (657–63).[137] 'For the proverb of mortals is true, that the gifts of enemies are non-gifts and not beneficial' (664f.). This proverb, which asserts the permanence of enmity, undermines Ajax's specious submission to transience (679–84).[138] Before dying on Hector's sword, he repeats the paradox that it is the gift of 'the most hated and greatest enemy of all my stranger-friends (*xenoi*)' (817f.).[139] But since it will help him fulfil his desire to die, it

---

[136] It is presented with a speech of high praise from Hector, who extols Ajax as large, strong, wise and best spearman of the Achaians (*Il.* 7.288f.). Note also that it is Hector who initiates the gesture (299–302); Ajax says he will not stop fighting unless Hector gives up first (286). On the sword motif in *Ajax* see especially Hirzel 415–17; Kott 64–6.

[137] On Hector as enemy see Winnington–Ingram 19.

[138] For parallels to the 'proverb' see the editors ad loc. On Ajax's rejection of the mutability of friendship see especially Knox, *Ajax*; Winnington-Ingram 52f. Knox claims that the mutability of *philia* invalidates Help Friends/Harm Enemies (10) and that the play shows the code is 'a failure in practice' (4). His reason for this is that Ajax cannot exist in the world of the *polis*, since he belongs to the heroic world in which 'nothing ever changed', in particular friendship and enmity (25). But Help Friends/Harm Enemies survived into the world of the *polis* far more than Knox (21–6) allows. Conversely even in heroic society friendships and enmities do not always have the permanence suggested by Knox. *Ajax* is better seen as exploring the place of the individual in society in more general terms (see e.g. Schadewaldt 101–9; cf. also Easterling, *Notes* 53).

[139] On the ambiguity of *xenos* see above, p. 49 n. 116.

is also 'most kindly' (822), just as death itself, the ultimate *echthros*, may in the last resort become a *philos*.[140] Teucer too expatiates on the gift of Hector, which he says was 'forged by an Erinys' (1034) – a goddess of relentless retaliation. But he adds the reciprocal dimension that Ajax neglected. For Hector too received a gift, 'made by the savage craftsman, Hades' (1035), and died from it, tied by Ajax's belt to the chariot of Achilles.[141] Their attempt to escape enmity through reciprocal *philia* is purely symbolic, even in Homer – 'We shall fight again another day', says Hector (*Il.* 7.291). But in Sophocles it has turned out to symbolise the victory of hatred and mutual destruction.

Justice and excellence

If the criterion for receiving the arms of Achilles was individual martial prowess, then Ajax's claim was clearly unimpeachable.[142] The chorus refer to the 'contest for the most excellent hand' (934f.), and lament his enemies' ingratitude for 'the deeds of his hands, of the greatest excellence' (616–20).[143] He himself is obsessed by the prize of supreme excellence which he, unlike his father, was denied (463–5; cf. 434–6), and declares that Achilles himself, were he still alive, would award him the arms as such a prize (441–4). We have no reason to doubt him.[144] For Ajax and his supporters the allocation of the arms was a bitter injustice. He therefore rejects the authority of society's justice to resolve disputes and feels entitled to exact his own terrible revenge, which he expects the Erinyes to accomplish on his

---

[140] Death is 'enemy to mortals and hateful to gods' (Eur. *Alc.* 82; cf. *Aj.* 607). But for its role as *philos* cf. Bacchyl, 3.47; Eur. *Tro.* 287. Taplin notes that the enemy land of Troy also becomes Ajax's helper in death (*GTA* 87f.).

[141] Sophocles has diverged from the Homeric account in order to introduce this reciprocity. In the *Iliad* there is no mention of Ajax's belt, and Hector is already dead when Achilles ties him behind the chariot (see Jebb and Kamerbeek on 1031). In 1028 Ajax and Hector are linked with a dual (as they are at *Il.* 7.279–81). As Teucer suggests (1028), we may compare their fates (cf. Brown 118–21).

[142] See Stanford xix–xxiv, xv n. 16; Winnington-Ingram 15 n. 12.

[143] Cf. also 636f. with the editors and Dawe ad loc. Despite the uncertainty of the text, the essential meaning is clear: Ajax is 'most excellent' (*aristos*) in lineage. Throughout the play Ajax's 'hands' (the Greek χείρ includes the arm as well) represent both his violent raw strength and his personal responsibility for his actions. Odysseus, in contrast, is guided by the 'hand' of Athena (35).

[144] When Athena and Menelaus call him *kakos* (133, 1071) they are accusing him of insubordination, not casting aspersions on his fighting capacity. Agamemnon does try to belittle his accomplishments (1236–8), but cannot refute Teucer's response (see below, p. 94).

behalf when he is thwarted. The Atreidae, however, argue that Odysseus was allocated the arms through the impartial justice of a vote. According to Menelaus, 'He had this fall at the hands of the judges, not me' (1136). Agamemnon will claim that the award to Odysseus was made by a majority of judges (1243), hinting at a democratically fair procedure. Ajax's faith in an absolute, divinely sanctioned retaliatory justice is thus countered by a legalistic justice that is purely human in its authority and enforcement.[145]

This institutionalised justice should remove the matter from the area of personal vendetta. Agamemnon rightly argues that it will undermine the basis of legal justice if the losers in a lawsuit try to exact their own revenge, using violence to reverse the legal decision (1239–49).[146] Ajax wished to destroy his enemies so that they could never cast another such judgement (*dike* 449), but the fact that he disagrees with the decision does not entitle him to go beyond the legal process. His view of the justice of the case is not necessarily incompatible with Agamemnon's. A legally sound judgement by majority vote may still result in an unjust assessment of merit, just as an honest jury may convict an innocent person. But while Teucer does not deny that Odysseus won the majority of the votes, he claims that the voting was corrupt, engineered by Ajax's enemies to cheat him of the arms (1135, 1137; cf. 188).[147] The judgement was thus not merely unjust, but a fraudulent act of a kind that undermines the credibility of the merely human administrators of legal justice.[148] If he is right, Ajax is not exculpated, but his enemies' position is seriously undermined.[149] Yet we have only Teucer's word for it that

[145] Cf. Knox, *Ajax* 22f. on the legal language used to refer to the judgement. There is a striking increase in the incidence of *dike* and cognates in the final third of the play (Freis 168, table 19).

[146] He echoes his brother when he speaks of 'the establishment of law' (κατάστασις . . . νόμου 1247; cf. 1074). On κατάστασις see Long 72f.

[147] At 1285–7 Ajax's forthright courage is contrasted with various ways in which lots could be biased, thus casting doubt on the fairness of such ostensibly impartial procedures (voting and lot-taking were the two principal methods for the election of officials and other public decisions in democratic Athens).

[148] Cf. Hesiod's complaints (e.g. *WD* 221–4). But such criticisms do not necessarily constitute a challenge to the authority of the judicial system or of legal justice per se. On this problem see Mackenzie 88–90.

[149] Would even Socrates have endured a conviction fraudulently obtained? Nevertheless, there remains an important difference between merely evading punishment, or even protesting against such a decision, and exacting one's own revenge on those deemed responsible.

the judgement was corrupt as he claims. Although Ajax's admirers continued to accept this version of events,[150] the Atreidae, unpleasant as they are, belong to an alternative tradition which saw Odysseus as the rightful winner.[151] Sophocles refrains from taking sides on this point, portraying instead the incompatibility of two conceptions of justice and the pitfalls of both.

The immediate issue is whether, in the light of his attempt at murder, Ajax is entitled to burial.[152] Teucer opens by demanding to know the charge (1051).[153] Menelaus responds with a formal statement: Ajax, who came to Troy as a *philos* and ally (*summachos*), has become 'a greater enemy than the Trojans' by plotting to kill 'the entire army' (1052–6).[154] But he soon broadens his argument beyond the immediate charge, turning to general issues of authority and status.[155] Like Athena he uses *kakos* for insubordination (1071f.; cf. 133).[156] Fear is coupled with respect and shame (*aidos* and *aischune*) as the foundation for effective laws in a city, *sophrosune* in an army, and *soteria* for the individual (1073–6, 1079f.).[157] In the absence of 'timely fear', where a man can commit *hubris* and do whatever gives him pleasure with impunity, the *polis* will not stay afloat for long (1081–6).[158]

---

[150] Notably Pindar (*Nem.* 7.20–31, 8.23–38) and Socrates (Pl. *Ap.* 41ab).

[151] See Stanford xx–xxiii.

[152] Traitors could be punished both with death by stoning (cf. 254, 728, *Ant.* 36, and see Pearson, *Ajax* 130–2) and with denial of burial (MacDowell, *LCA* 176f.). Stoning was not used in classical Athens (ib. 254f.), but hurling into a pit (the βάραθρον) may have been a substitute (so Bonner and Smith 206). On the burial issue in *Aj.* see Bowra 48–50. See also below, p. 118 n. 47.

[153] On the form and language of these debates see Finley, *Three* 78–82; Nestle 145f.; Wolf 54f. On their content see Bowra 50–60. For a vigorous defence of the final scenes see Heath 197–208.

[154] The last phrase is a rhetorical exaggeration, but not unjust (cf. especially 844, and see Knox, *Polis* 10f.).

[155] Cf. Long 155f.

[156] Contrast Ajax's view of the *kakos* (319, 456, 551). Teucer, on the other hand, contrasts being *kakos* with justice (1389–92; cf. 1042f., 1175–7, 1241).

[157] Cf. especially Aesch. *Eum.* 517–21 and see de Romilly 109–14; Stanford on 1073ff.; Long 72; Edmunds, *Chance* 218f. The Spartan Menelaus is often described as an oligarch, but the parallel with Pericles (Thuc. 2.37.3) shows the sentiment is not exclusively oligarchical (cf. Knox, *Polis* 12).

[158] Freedom to do as one wished was a feature of Athenian democracy, but only within strictly circumscribed limits (see Thuc. 2.37.2). In a close parallel to Menelaus' speech, an Attic orator argues that if everyone follows his own will, the laws will be undermined and replaced by violence and *hubris* in the entire

Clearly discipline and respect for some kind of authority are essential for the survival of any social group. Moreover Menelaus accurately pinpoints several of Ajax's faults. He manifestly lacked any such 'fear' for authority, and did whatever gave him pleasure without, apparently, expecting to pay for it. He was deficient in *aidos, aischune* and *sophrosune* – language that recalls the vain appeals of the chorus and Tecmessa, as well as the ominous warning of Athena (132). But the content of Menelaus' words is vitiated by their ugly authoritarian tone. Like Ajax himself he ignores the mutual dependence of great and small, so eloquently evoked by the chorus as they lamented the ingratitude of Ajax's enemies (cf. 164). He disregards both the need of leaders for the support of their subordinates and the obligation of rulers to protect and benefit their subjects, which is the only justification for the kind of authoritarian control he demands.[159] He sees fear solely as something to use against his inferiors, not as something from which to protect them.[160] Moreover his shift to the plural ('Let us not think ...' 1085) makes his warning potentially applicable to himself. And he ends by claiming the right to 'think great thoughts' (1088) – precisely the fault for which he blames Ajax, and for which Ajax was divinely punished.[161]

Menelaus' opening sally was a blunt but accurate statement of a reasonable grievance. Teucer begins his rebuttal polemically by accusing Menelaus of failing to live up to the standards of noblesse oblige: 'I would no longer be surprised at someone who is a nothing by birth going wrong, when those who are thought to be *eugenes* by nature make such errors in their speech' (1093–6).[162] He goes on to twist the issue of *philia* into one of status, arguing that Ajax was not a

---

polis; the disobedient must therefore be punished (Demos. 25.20f.). Cf. also Ant. Soph. DK 87 B 58.6–10; Lys. 1.26.

[159] The only hint of this is in his use of the ship of state metaphor (1082f.), on which see below, p. 118 n. 46.

[160] Contrast his φόβου πρόβλημα, 'defence of fear' (1076) with the chorus' description of the old Ajax as their δείματος ... προβολά, 'defence against fear' (1212).

[161] Cf. the choral warning at 1091f., and 586 with North 61. Despite the enormous difference in heroic stature, the values of the Atreidae are essentially the same as Teucer's and Ajax's own. Cf. especially Winnington-Ingram 69f.

[162] Birth and status will feature extensively in his debate with Agamemnon (1228–31, 1235, 1257–63, 1290–1305). In defending his birth Teucer implies that *eugeneia* of blood is more important than mere legitimacy, and *eugeneia* of behaviour more important than either. He and Tecmessa show in different ways that noble birth or status need not be coextensive with noble character.

summachos, since he came to Troy as an independent agent, not under the authority of the Atreidae (1097–1108).[163] This is a sophistic quibble, for whether or not Ajax was subordinate to the Atreidae he was a participant in a cooperative endeavour, and as such was their ally and *philos*. This reciprocal relationship is implicit in Ajax's own demand for recognition from his fellow Greeks. But picking up the term *summachos*, rather than *philos*, enables Teucer to slide past the attempted murder and focus on Menelaus' claims about authority and relative status.

When Teucer repeats that justice is on his side, Menelaus responds by tacitly equating attempted with successful murder and stressing the importance of intention: 'As far as he's concerned, I'm a dead man' (1128).[164] Here he pinpoints the weakest aspect of Teucer's case, Ajax's flagrant violation of the ties of loyalty, which can be defended only by placing no limit on retaliation against a disloyal *philos*. If such excess is condoned, it is hard to deny the Atreidae the right to dishonour Ajax's corpse. But instead of trying to justify the attack, Teucer resorts to a different kind of argument: to deny burial is to dishonour the gods, to violate their laws (1129–31). This could be a general claim on behalf of all the dead, which would constrain the ruthless pursuit of enmity beyond the grave. But it is weakened as soon as Menelaus pushes him into arguing for its applicability in this instance.[165] Menelaus claims that it is not *kalos* to bury those personally hostile to one (*polemioi* 1132).[166] Instead of relying on the universal right to burial, Teucer moves to much weaker ground by questioning whether Ajax was ever Menelaus' enemy (*polemios* 1133). This implausible claim appears to rely sophistically

---

[163] Scodel 17 notes that this echoes the power structure of the *Iliad*. In Homer Agamemnon has a council of elders (e.g. *Il.* 2.53). In *Aj.* the king has a council of chieftains (749), and the elders exercise some authority (731f.).

[164] Cf. Democr. DK 68 B 89 and see Dihle 17f. On attempted homicide cf. Lys. 3.41–3 with MacDowell, *LCA* 123f. The prologue of *Aj.* provides a dramatic representation of the culpability of intention, since Ajax actually thinks he has performed and is performing such atrocities. It is clear that this intention preceded the onset of madness (44f.). Ajax's responsibility is heavily emphasised in Athena's conversation with Odysseus from 40 onwards. Cf. Knox, *Ajax* 7; Winnington-Ingram 25.

[165] At 1391f. Teucer's language suggests there could be justified cases of denial of burial.

[166] He would be on stronger ground if he forbade burial to Ajax as a public enemy (see above, n. 152, and cf. Winnington-Ingram 64 n. 20).

on the meaning of *polemios*, which strictly signifies a military opponent rather than a personal enemy. When Menelaus points to their obvious mutual hatred, Teucer shifts his ground yet again, justifying Ajax's hostility by the fact that the Atreidae 'stole' from him the arms of Achilles (1135). He has thus moved away from the more broad, humane, religious justice which demands burial of (all) the dead back to Ajax's original claim that as the first to be wronged, he was justified in seeking vengeance.

The scenes with the two Atreidae are separated by a brief interlude in which Teucer settles Eurysaces as a suppliant to protect, and be protected by, his father's body. This tableau remains in place for the rest of the play, hinting at Ajax's subsequent hero-cult (cf. especially 1166f.),[167] and reminding us what is at stake for his son as well as his corpse.[168] When Agamemnon enters upon this scene he echoes his brother in many ways.[169] He goes further, however, by belittling Ajax's military achievements, which he says were no greater than his own (1236–8), adding that a mere broad-shouldered ox of a man is less useful, for all his bulk, than those with 'good sense' (1250–4). Ajax's impressive physical size contributed to his supreme excellence on the Homeric battlefield.[170] Yet Athena tells us that previously no one showed more foresight or was 'more fit for action when occasion called' (119f., trans. Bowra 34).[171] But she also warns that those who take excessive pride in their 'weight of hand' are liable to fall (129f.). Calchas too will declare that it is 'excessive

---

[167] On the ritual significance of the scene see Burian, *Ajax*. On Ajax as a cult-hero see Jebb's *Introduction* §11; Méautis 47–9. But in contrast to *OC*, the cult is not of major importance for the play (cf. Winnington-Ingram 58 n. 2).

[168] On the impact of the tableau see Taplin, *GTA* 65, 108f. The suspense generated by the uncertain fate of Ajax's dependants has rarely been given its due in discussions of the play's 'unity' (but see now Gardiner 69f., 73f.; Heath 196). In the tableau Eurysaces holds a lock of Tecmessa's hair as well as his own and Teucer's (1174), but her location is unclear. Teucer neglects Tecmessa in favour of the boy in both the supplication (1171–81) and the exodus (1409–11) (cf. Seale 168–73). In this, as in other ways, he is an extension of his brother.

[169] On the use of both Atreidae where one might suffice cf. Wilamowitz 67f.; Rosenmeyer, *Masks* 191f. Many think the tone rises with Agamemnon, but there is little to choose between them (so also Winnington-Ingram 65).

[170] For Ajax's size see Stanford xv n. 16.

[171] For the significance of these lines see Kirkwood, *Homer* 62; cf. also Winnington-Ingram 21 n. 30. They tell us of an Ajax who fulfilled the heroic ideal encompassing excellence of judgement as well as action (*Il.* 9.438–43). Cf. *Il.* 7.289 (cited above, n. 136) and see Stanford xiii–xiv.

and useless bodies' which take the heaviest falls from the gods,
implying that Ajax's mighty bulk is not guided by the 'sense' appropriate to mortals (758–61).[172]

When Agamemnon contrasts mere brawn with brain, he is less
interested in piety than in devaluing the kind of *arete* that Ajax
represents. But he echoes Calchas in contrasting Ajax's bulk with
people of 'good sense', who 'conquer everywhere' (1252). This is the
excellence of Odysseus, who both 'thinks mortal thoughts' in relation to the gods and is prudent and disciplined in relation to his fellow mortals, and who did indeed 'conquer' in the contest so vital to
Ajax. By elevating 'sense' over strength, Agamemnon implicitly
defends Odysseus' right to the arms. Where the necessary 'sense' is
lacking, it must be replaced by externally imposed discipline, the
'little evil' that causes the downfall of a large but recalcitrant body
(1077f.), the 'little storm cloud' that extinguishes a loud shout
(1148f.), the 'little goad' that keeps the hulking bull straight or
upright on the path (1253f.; cf. also 161, *Ant.* 477f.; Herod. 7.10.ε).
This is the 'medicine' that Agamemnon sees approaching Teucer if
he does not acquire some 'sense' (1255f.). Teucer's defence of Ajax is
thus represented by the Atreidae as a fault essentially similar to his
brother's – a deed of *hubris* (1258), caused by deviance from his
proper social role.

Teucer refutes Agamemnon's denigration of Ajax with the
uncontestable facts of Ajax's epic heroism, recalling both his
unequalled exploits in defence of the ships and his courage and integrity in the lottery for the duel with Hector (1272–89).[173] He declares
that Ajax's deeds were 'just' (1282) – the service due to friend from
loyal friend – and entitled him to a gratitude which was not forthcoming (1266f.). It is now his own obligation, as Ajax's brother, to
defend his corpse and so his honour: 'Could I cast shame on my kinsman [by failing to defend him], when you are thrusting him out
unburied ... without shame at your own words?' (1304–7).[174] With

---

172 Pearson adopts the Suda's ἀνόητα ('senseless') in 758, which is thematically
   appealing (and preferred for that reason by Pohlenz, *Erläuterungen* 76), but
   should be rejected in favour of the mss. ἀνόνητα ('useless'), retained by most
   editors. For the thought cf. *Il.* 5.440–2 and further parallels in Bowra 30–2.
173 As Knox remarks, 'Where did he go or stand that I did not?' (1237) is 'a question which anyone familiar with the *Iliad* could answer at once' (*Polis* 13).
174 I follow Stanford's interpretation of 1305. The alternative, that Teucer's
   'shame' would arise from his low parentage, is preferred by Jebb and Kamerbeek, but see contra Stanford ad loc.

the first 'shame' he displays that sense of family honour which drove
Ajax to kill himself rather than face his father. With the second he
implies that the denial of burial brings shame, not on Ajax, but on
Agamemnon for even proposing it.[175] He echoes Ajax's own principle that the *eugenes* man should either live or die *kalôs*, declaring
that it would be *kalos* for him to die fighting for his brother's corpse
(1310f.; cf. 479f.). But unlike Ajax, he is facing death in the service of
others whom he has an obligation to defend.

Odysseus, Agamemnon and *philia*

Odysseus reappears in response to the uproar over what he respectfully calls 'this mighty corpse', and Agamemnon explains, accurately
enough, that he has 'heard most shameful words' (1319f.). Odysseus
replies, tactfully and non-committally, that he does not blame one
who hears abuse for returning it (1322f.). This could apply to either
disputant.[176] It shows that Odysseus does not object to retaliation
per se and reserves the right to reprove whoever started the quarrel.
Agamemnon now admits that he started it – Teucer too 'heard
shameful things' – but claims that Teucer had *done* shameful things
to deserve it (1324). This both blackens Teucer further and suggests
that Agamemnon's merely verbal response was a moderate one.
Accordingly Odysseus asks, 'What has he *done* to you to constitute
an injury?' (1325).[177] But Agamemnon's only charge is back in the
realm of words: 'He *says* he will not leave this corpse unburied, but
will bury it in defiance of me' (1326f.).

Odysseus asks if he, as a friend, may help his friend, as he has
before, by speaking the truth (1328f.).[178] The reference to past services discreetly suggests not only that Odysseus' advice is valuable,
but that his *philos* may owe him a favour. Agamemnon has so far
shown the same harshness and rigidity as Ajax himself, but now,
unlike Ajax, he responds to a friend's appeal: 'Speak. For I would be
deficient in good sense [if I did not listen], since I count you my

---

[175] His words tell against the view of Adkins 182f. that *aischros* is not used by
Sophocles for 'unjust success' before *Philoctetes*.

[176] Editors assume that it favours Teucer, but it could equally justify the 'shouting
of the Atreidae' (1319).

[177] On the legalistic overtones see Stanford ad loc.

[178] Campbell and Stanford rightly observe that *philos* in 1328 is syntactically ambiguous and could agree with either Odysseus himself or Agamemnon. The
reciprocal sense of *phil-* words lends them particularly to such ambiguities (cf.
e.g. *Ant.* 99).

greatest friend among the Argives' (1330f.). Teucer disparaged Agamemnon's ingratitude towards Ajax as 'senseless' (1272). Now Agamemnon shows he can also display 'good sense' (presumably of a
prudential kind) in relation to a tactful and loyal friend.

Odysseus strongly endorses the suggestion raised briefly by
Teucer, that justice imposes constraints on the indulgence of hatred
for an enemy. 'By no means let violence conquer you so that you
hate so much as to trample on justice' (1334f.).[179] He also reiterates
his earlier view that enmity and hatred need not be coextensive, but
with an important development. In the prologue he was overcome
by pity rather than hatred for the hostile Ajax (121f.). Now he distinguishes both enmity and hatred from the evaluation of worth and
proper distribution of honour:

> To me too he was once the greatest enemy in the army... But
> even so I would not dishonour him by failing to acknowledge
> that I saw him alone as most excellent of the Argives who came
> to Troy, except Achilles. He could not therefore with justice be
> dishonoured by you. For you would be destroying not him,
> but the laws of the gods. It is not just to harm a good (*esthlos*)
> man after death, not even if you hate him.
>
>   (1336–45)[180]

Like Ajax and Teucer, Odysseus believes in a divine justice. Unlike
Teucer, however, he does not allow the argument from justice to
become contingent upon friendship and enmity (contrast 1130–4).
Unlike Ajax, he does not think this justice permits the pursuit of
unlimited personal revenge. On the contrary, it overrules merely
human preferences, and actually limits the lengths to which such revenge may go. His justice is not simple retaliation, but the dispensa-
tion of honour according to personal worth. He thus departs both
from Ajax's anarchic and violent pursuit of an absolute justice, and
from the Atreidae's relentless insistence on law and order without regard for either divine authority or human sensibility. Moreover
when his justice is challenged, he resorts not to violence but to persuasion. His are the weapons of the courtroom, of restraint and good

---

[179] Cf. 1363 and contrast 1159f. Cf. also Winnington-Ingram 66.
[180] The construction of 1338 echoes 122. See Stanford and Dawe, *Studies* on 1339
for discussion of Bothe's attractive conjecture ἀντατιμάσαιμ' ἄν, which would
provide a reciprocal force.

sense – the values preached but not practised by the Atreidae – against the brute force of the battlefield and the autocrat.

To harm Ajax by denying him burial is an infringement of both piety and justice. But there are two important qualifications. First, Odysseus' prohibition only applies to a great or noble man – one who is *aristos* (1340; cf. 1357, 1380), *esthlos* (1345) or *gennaios* (1355). Second, it applies only after death. When Agamemnon asks 'Are *you* really standing up for *him* against *me*?' (1346),[181] Odysseus replies, 'I hated him as long as it was *kalos* to do so' (1347). For the Atreidae, Ajax's suicide merely makes it easier to triumph over him (1067–9), but for Odysseus his death brings about an even more radical change than his madness.[182] Previously weighty arguments no longer apply.[183] Ajax's life must now be evaluated as a whole. His former exploits, despite the crimes of the last few hours, now entitle him to the honour normally due to friends (1339, 1342). Odysseus is proposing that Ajax receive belatedly the recognition whose absence drove him to attempted murder and aroused the enmity of the chiefs. He thus raises the possibility not just of respecting Ajax as an enemy, but of transforming enmity back into friendship.

He must now sell this view to Agamemnon, who thinks that the proper treatment for a fallen enemy is to trample on him (1348).[184] Throughout the passage of stichomythia Odysseus keeps returning to the principles of friendship. When Agamemnon concedes that 'it is not easy for a king (*turannos*) to be pious', he does not press the point, but answers '[No], but [it *is* easy for him] to give honour to his friends when they speak well' (1350f.).[185] The honour to Ajax of acknowledging his greatness and granting burial, which Teucer demanded as an honour to the gods, is now tactfully presented as the honour owed to a friend, Odysseus. When Agamemnon continues to harp on Ajax's insubordination, Odysseus answers

---

[181] For the emphasis provided by the pronouns see Weinstock 55.

[182] The time when it was no longer *kalos* to hate Ajax could have begun with the madness, which aroused Odysseus' pity (cf. Jebb and Stanford on 1347). But the main contrast is between life and death, as Agamemnon's response (1348) shows. Only after Ajax's death can Odysseus act on his pity.

[183] Cf. Perrotta 132.

[184] For parallels see Fraenkel on *Ag.* 884f., 1394.

[185] *Turannos* can mean merely 'monarch', but in democratic Athens it acquired pejorative overtones and eventually came to mean 'tyrant' (see especially Knox, *Tyrannos*).

'Stop! You are the winner when conquered by friends' (1353).[186]
Agamemnon, who has failed to grasp the distinctions between the
proper circumstances for hatred, enmity and maltreatment, and
between enmity and nobility, tells him to remember the kind of
man to whom he is proposing to give this *charis*, and asks how he can
show *aidos* for an enemy's corpse (1354, 1356). Odysseus reiterates
his distinctions: 'He was an enemy, but *gennaios* (1355); *arete* con-
quers me more than enmity' (1357).[187] Agamemnon protests that
'such people are unstable' (1358).[188] 'Many people', Odysseus replies, 'are friends one moment and unpleasant the next' (1359).[189]
This insight into the way of the world echoes Ajax's 'Odyssean' insight in the deception speech (678–83), and provides the foundation
for a plea for tolerance. 'Then do you approve of getting such people
as friends?' asks Agamemnon (1360).[190] In reply Odysseus avoids a
direct answer – how could he approve of disloyalty? – and shifts the
emphasis to Agamemnon's own inflexibility, 'I do not love to praise
a stubborn spirit' (1361). The implication is that yes, Ajax shifted his
allegiance, but he was not the first to do so, nor will he be the last.

---

[186] He echoes the chorus' futile appeals to Ajax (330, 483f.). Contrast 1334 and cf.
(ironically) Aesch. *Ag.* 941–3 where Agamemnon yields to Clytemnestra.

[187] νικᾷ should be retained (see Stanford ad loc.; for the theme see previous note).
The line is ambiguous. It could mean that the Ajax's *arete* moves Odysseus
more than his hostility, or that his own concern for *arete* motivates him more
than personal enmity. Since Odysseus has been stressing Ajax's virtues, the context supports the former interpretation, but either way Odysseus is devaluing
enmity. Cf. Winnington-Ingram 68 n. 32.

[188] On ἔμπληκτοι see Stanford ad loc., who connects it with Odyssean flexibility
(cf. also Fraenkel, *Ephemeros* 140 n. 33). Kitto translates it as 'frantic' (*FMD*
194), a legitimate sense which makes it more applicable to Ajax than Odysseus
(see below, n. 190). Stanford's 'unstable' captures both possibilities.

[189] πικρός (literally 'sharp' or 'bitter') is used for what one wishes on an enemy (e.g.
Eur. *Tro.* 65–8), but may also mean 'unpleasant' and hence 'hateful' or 'hated'
(e.g. *Phil.* 254, 510, *OC* 615). Tecmessa uses it for the effect of Ajax's death on
her (966).

[190] The generalising 'people' in this exchange is usually thought to allude to Odysseus himself. But Winnington-Ingram (*Sophoclea* 3f.; cf. also *Sophocles* 68)
argues that the reference is to Ajax. There are two good reasons for accepting
this suggestion. First, it is more natural for the pronouns in 1358 and 1360 to
have the same reference, and if the second refers to Odysseus it must mean 'Do
you approve of getting such people as yourself as friends?', which is strained at
best. Since the issue is whether to treat Ajax as a friend, it is much more natural
if it means 'such people as him'. Second, 1359 is more appropriate to Ajax, for it
is he who moves from friendship to enmity with Agamemnon. If it refers to
Odysseus, it must be taken as a veiled threat (so Kamerbeek, Stanford).

Odysseus tactfully interprets Ajax's violent change, a product of rigidity, through his own insight into the transient nature of *philia*. Odysseus' words bring out the similarity between Agamemnon and Ajax (cf. 594f., 926 and the choral warning to Teucer at 1119). Both expect others to yield, while resisting the efforts of those who try to win them over. But Ajax resisted to the last, whereas Agamemnon is about to succumb.

In the prologue Odysseus pitied Ajax, 'looking at my own fate as much as his' (124). Now he similarly urges burial on the ground that 'I too will one day reach that need' (1365). Agamemnon is able to climb down without conceding anything to Odysseus' loftier sentiments, sulkily commenting, 'It's always the same: every man labours for himself' (1366). Odysseus accepts this interpretation (1367). But his is a very subtle variety of self-interest.[191] Ajax's burial has no direct bearing on Odysseus' own. He is self-interested only in so far as he is upholding a practice that benefits all in the long run, including himself. When Agamemnon finally permits the burial he simultaneously dissociates himself from it, declaring, 'then it will be called your deed, not mine' (1368).[192] Odysseus promises him the credit regardless, but Agamemnon's final words concede nothing: 'I would do *you* even a greater *charis* than this one, but *he*, both here and in the underworld, will remain *echthistos* to me. But you may do what is necessary' (1370–3).[193] He never acknowledges either Ajax's excellence or the justice of burial, and defiantly refuses to accept the transience of friendship and enmity. Although his behaviour accords with Odysseus' principles, he does not embrace these principles as such.

With the departure of Agamemnon, Odysseus is free to turn the *charis* (1354) he has gained for Ajax's body into positive friendship with his survivors. He formally announces, in a striking echo of Ajax's deception speech, that he will henceforth be Teucer's friend 'to the same extent' that he was formerly his enemy (1376f.; cf. 679–82). As a token of this he wants to help with the burial, reiterating

---

[191] See Weinstock 56–9; Jones 186–90; Stanford on 124–6.

[192] For the force of the verb see Stanford ad loc.

[193] Retaining the mss. χρή in 1373 with Kamerbeek and Stanford (see also Johansen 179). This need not imply that Odysseus is right, merely that there are certain requirements for burial (cf. *Ant.* 72). But Dindorf's χρῆς (adopted by many editors) has the attraction of sustaining Agamemnon's personal interpretation of Odysseus' motives.

that Ajax deserves the treatment due to an *aristos* man (1378–80). Teucer reciprocates by addressing Odysseus too as *aristos* (1381). *Esthlos* is likewise used both by Odysseus of Ajax and Teucer of Odysseus (1345, 1399). But quite different qualities are being commended in the two men. In praising Odysseus for his unexpected transformation from Ajax's greatest enemy into his protector against *hubris* (1381–5), Teucer is valuing not only his courage in resisting Agamemnon, but his tact, good sense, flexibility and respect for justice. When Odysseus calls Ajax *aristos*, we must assume that he is praising the other's excellence as a warrior (cf. 1340). Yet this tribute to his *arete* as such may also remind us that Ajax's might was employed, until the quarrel, on behalf of the Atreidae and the rest of the Greeks. He is a former *philos* of preeminent value.

Odysseus praises Ajax's prowess in terms that pointedly recall the contest for the arms, even alluding to Ajax's own claim. He admits that Ajax was his greatest enemy, 'ever since I won the arms of Achilles', but acknowledges that Ajax was '*aristos* of the Argives who came to Troy, except Achilles' (1336–41; cf. 418–26). Despite this praise, whose sincerity we have no reason to doubt, Odysseus neither asserts that Ajax was wronged, nor defends his own claim to the arms.[194] Yet by the end of the play he has proved *aristos* in a most practical way for Ajax's dependants, whom Ajax abandoned and Teucer could not save. The play itself demonstrates the excellence of Odysseus. But it does not thereby devalue the heroic *arete* of Ajax. The two are incommensurable, and each has its place.[195] Later defenders of Odysseus tried to make his virtues commensurable with those of Ajax by arguing that his intelligence was of greater military use than Ajax's physical courage: 'Battles may be won by brawn; but wars are ultimately won by brains' (Stanford xxi). But this introduces a different criterion for the contest, which we are told was for 'the most excellent hand' (934f.). Odysseus wins only if a different *kind* of *arete* is being assessed. Consequently the dispute over the arms is insoluble. And if this is insoluble, so is the quarrel between Ajax and his enemies. For the crucial question, 'Who started it?' can never

[194] These lines are often interpreted as an admission that the judgement was unjust, but cf. Kirkwood 72 and Hester, *Distemper* 245 (who rightly argues that the issue is left unclear). See also the exhaustive discussion of Machin 31–59.
[195] The contrast between them is often presented as a chronological one (e.g. by Segal 133), but both begin with Homer (Stanford, *UT* 108).

be answered as long as the disputants disagree on the proper criteria for assessing merit. It is therefore up to Teucer to acknowledge in the end the supreme *arete* of both Odysseus and Ajax (1381, 1415).

Odysseus' preamble, with Agamemnon's response and parting shot, make it clear that persuasion has here been accomplished by means of *philia* (1328–31, 1370–3). The friendship on which Odysseus relies is not just the basic bond of loyalty needed to unite any army, alliance or band of thieves. It involves honesty (1328f.), respect for a friend's opinion (1330f.), flexibility (1360f.) and a willingness both to accede to a friend's wishes (1353) and to grant honour (1351) and *charis* (1371) on the basis of *philia* alone – that is, without requiring a specific favour in return. These aspects of *philia* are what enable Odysseus to succeed in upholding his view of justice. And all these qualities were absent from Ajax's treatment of his *philoi*.[196] Far from proffering favours or honour without specific return, he expected unconditional support from his friends, ordering *them* to 'honour' *his* wishes (687f.), disregarding the suggestion that *philoi* might alter his resolve (483f.; cf. 330),[197] showing no respect for their opinions (e.g. 591), explicitly spurning flexibility (594f.), ignoring Tecmessa's appeal to reciprocal *charis* (520f.), treating her with distinct lack of honour (e.g. 369) and deceiving them all in his famous speech.

A distinctive feature of Odysseus' *philia* is that he both recognises the mutability of human relations (1359) and acts accordingly (1376f.). In sharp contrast are both Ajax, who takes his enmity to the grave (835–44, 1394f.) and Agamemnon, whose enmity follows him there (1372f.).[198] If enmity is immutable, then it is not only gratifying but logical to admit no compromise in the indulgence of hatred. But if enemies may later become friends, such hostility, as Odysseus sees (and Ajax claims to see in his deception speech), may no longer always be appropriate. As Odysseus warns Agamemnon, the pleasure and *kerdos* of gloating over an enemy are not always *kalos*

---

[196] He shares with Odysseus only the view that his own services deserve gratitude (cf. Easterling, *Homer* 8).

[197] Note especially that Agamemnon calls it 'senseless' (or 'insane') to reject a friend's advice (1330).

[198] Teucer too is unremitting in his hatred of the Atreidae on Ajax's behalf (1389–92), but he accepts for himself the new friendship of Odysseus who has given him cause to adapt.

(1347–9).[199] He requires from Agamemnon a self-discipline of the kind that Ajax failed to apply, implying that principle should constrain the passionate impulses of pleasure, hatred and personal *kerdos*, which fuel the most destructive applications of Harm Enemies. Odysseus himself, though moved by pity, is not a passionate character.[200] His hatreds and loves are directed by principle, leading to a position almost Socratic in its insistence that one should do no injustice even to an enemy. But Odysseus is no Socrates.[201] He considers it legitimate both to return abuse for abuse (1322f.) and to harm an enemy within certain limits (1347). He thus represents a modification but not an outright rejection of the talio.

Odysseus uses his preexisting friendship with Agamemnon to initiate new friendship with others who would normally be his enemies by association. Others in the play do not doubt that enmity extends to the *philoi* of an enemy, regardless of their role in a particular dispute. Ajax justifiably expects hostility from the whole Greek army, which owes loyalty to the Atreidae (408f., 458), and includes them all in his curse (844). The chorus, as his dependants, fear that they will be stoned to death with him (253–5) – a fate which Teucer, as his brother, only narrowly escapes (721–8). Odysseus, however, departs from another basic assumption of Help Friends/Harm Enemies when he breaks the chain of inherited hostility by offering friendship to the surviving *philoi* of his worst enemy.

In the prologue Odysseus' perception of Athena's operations gave him excellent reasons for cultivating a variety of virtues. In the final scene of the play he adheres consistently to the same virtues but develops them in interesting ways. Judgement of what is to be feared made him reluctant to encounter an insane enemy, but now provides the courage to stand up to Agamemnon for the sake of principle. *Sophrosune* was originally displayed as the prudent acquiescence to Athena's will, but now takes on a constructive value in relation to other mortals. When Odysseus sacrifices his desire to help with Ajax's funeral (1400f.), he is subordinating his own wishes, without

---

[199] 'Such a revenge is the gratification of a passion and so a *kerdos*' (Winnington-Ingram 67). For such *kerdos* cf. 107; *Ant.* 1056 (with Winnington-Ingram 126); Aesch. *Sept.* 684, 697 (with Winnington-Ingram, *Septem* 24–8); Lys. 1.4.

[200] This is one reason he is not a heroic figure (cf. Knox 29).

[201] Cf. Vlastos, *Justice* 320f., who finds him the closest thing to a precursor for Socrates' rejection of the talio.

the duress of 'timely fear', to those of an enemy, as a token of new friendship with his survivors. Reverence in face of the manifest power of a terrible goddess has become the more profound piety that upholds divine laws in the interests of another. The pursuit of an enemy to ascertain his guilt has become a defence of the same enemy in the name of an impartial divine justice. Pity based on the common fate of all living creatures has been put into action as positive help that transcends the boundaries of personal feuds. The separation of enmity from hatred has become a more far-reaching distinction between enmity and the objective evaluation of worth. Finally, Odyssean cleverness, displayed in the prologue as the crafty hunting and sifting of evidence, has become the adroit and tactful manipulation of a friend, praised by the chorus as wisdom (1374f.). Paradoxically it is this very flexibility which enables him to remain consistent, since the possibility of change is built into his moral framework. He thus provides a foil for the rigidity, shortcomings and inconsistencies of others, which persist even at the play's conclusion – Agamemnon's favour to Odysseus cannot be reconciled with his enmity for Ajax, while Teucer's new friendship with Odysseus clashes with Ajax's permanent enmity. In a further paradox, it takes Odysseus' variety of excellence to vindicate Ajax's heroic *arete*. His constructive, humane and supple view of the world offers an antidote to the effects of unbridled hatred.

The character who comes closest to Odysseus is Tecmessa (cf. especially 924). She does not call down destruction on Ajax's enemies (though cf. 961–5). She is pious (587f., 594), and offers herself as a paradigm for acquiescence to the blows of divine chance (485–9). She embodies in her own life the mutability of enmity to friendship (490f.), and begs Ajax to soften (594). She appeals to pity, gratitude and reciprocal favour (510, 520f.). Besides loyalty, she shows self-restraint and flexibility in friendship (294, 529, 490f.). These qualities are less striking in Tecmessa than Odysseus because they are expected of a woman in her position (cf. 527f., 580, 586). Moreover she is in no position to influence events. She does her best with the means at her disposal, but Odysseus, as the friend of Agamemnon, is uniquely placed to put his virtues into practice.

The play ends with Ajax's funeral, characterised as a co-operative endeavour by the repeated use of verbs compounded with *sun-* or *xun-*, which indicate joining or sharing in an activity. Tecmessa wishes for the arrival of Teucer to 'join in composing the limbs' of Ajax (922). Teucer, who addresses his brother as one 'joined in blood' (977; cf. 727), orders the chorus to 'join in the labour' (988). Menelaus commands Teucer not to 'join in lifting' the corpse (1048). The chorus welcome the arrival of Odysseus, if he is there 'to join not in intensifying, but in resolving [the crisis]' (1317). Odysseus convinces Agamemnon that he wishes to 'join in helping' him, as he always has before (1329). Then he proves his new friendship with Teucer by wishing 'to join in burying and working' with him (1378f.).[202]

Such cooperation is alien to Ajax. When Menelaus argues that he came to Troy as an ally or 'fellow fighter' (*summachos*), Teucer scornfully rejects the idea (1053, 1097–9). The only alliance he enters into, with his *summachos* Athena (90, 117), is grounded in delusion and leads to disaster.[203] *Sun-* and *xun-* words link him not with cooperative friendship but with evils (429), evil doom (123), sickness (338),[204] madness (611)[205] and death (854f.).[206] When 'joined with' his friends, he brings them not help but pain (273, 609f.).[207] When Odysseus asks to help with the burial, Teucer respectfully invites him to 'join in performing' other things (1396),[208] but is regretfully reluctant to let him touch the tomb (1393–6). Ajax abandoned *philia* when he thought it had been violated, but will not dismiss hostility

---

[202] συγκαθαρμόσαι (922); ξύναιμον (977; cf. 727); σύγκαμνε (988); συγκομίζειν (1048); μὴ ξυνάψων, ἀλλὰ συλλύσων (1317); ξυνηρετεῖν (1329) (literally 'rowing with'; this is Lobeck's commonly accepted emendation, but *xun-* is present in all mss.); συνθάπτειν ... καὶ ξυμπονεῖν (1378f.; cf. *Ant.* 41).

[203] On the use of *sun* for the cooperation of gods with mortals see above, n. 37.

[204] Cf. Stanford ad loc., and on the text Dawe, *Studies* ad loc., who attractively suggests παροῦσι ... ξυνών.

[205] Cf. Winnington-Ingram 33.

[206] Cf. also 361, where the Suda and Jebb take συνδάιξον to mean 'kill me along with the cattle' (Kamerbeek and Stanford take it as 'join in killing me'; Heath 178 n. 24 suggests it is intensive); and 577 where Ajax says his armour will be buried with him (κοίν' ἐμοί). Ajax's only 'cooperative' *sun-/xun-* word is at 861, where he addresses the Athenians as 'nurtured with me' (σύντροφον), thus emphasising his isolation at Troy and distance from his parents, especially the nurturing mother (cf. 849).

[207] Cf. also κοινός in 266f. with Stanford ad loc. and Winnington-Ingram 24 n. 42. The chorus use κοινός to describe Hades and Ares, in their condemnation of the 'cooperative' enterprise of war (1194, 1196).

[208] ξύμπρασσε (1396).

in response to a new, spontaneous favour. He thus sustains from the grave the anti-cooperative role he played in life.

Once again Teucer acts as his brother's surrogate, echoing the curse delivered by Ajax himself at the moment of suicide,[209] when he prays that Zeus, an Erinys and Justice may 'destroy those evil men evilly', just as they wished to cast out Ajax's body 'unworthily' (1389–92). This curse, and the rejection of Odysseus' help, underline the essential reciprocity of friendship. Not even an Odysseus can generate it single handed. It also reminds us of the fragility of the compromise reached with Agamemnon, who, like Ajax himself, refuses to abandon his hatred. But Ajax's friends can finally unite to give him burial, symbolising both the unity and the exclusiveness of Ajax's group of loyal supporters. Teucer pays tribute to his greatness: 'Come now, any man who says he is here as a *philos*, hurry, move, labouring for this man who was entirely excellent' (1413–15). But there is one last dissonant note. Odysseus is now a man who 'says he is a friend'. Yet he does not 'hurry' to help with the other *philoi*, but departs before the exodus (1400–1). Ajax casts his shadow over their new friendship even in death.

---

[209] Note especially the prayer to the Erinys (1390; cf. 837, 843), the formula 'just as ... so ...' (1391; cf. 840f.), the polyptoton with *kakos* (1391; cf. 839), and the reference to Zeus (1389; cf. 824, 831).

4

Antigone

Born to be arrested

OBEY ALL LAWS! BE A MODEL CITIZEN
Seattle graffiti (1985)

Antigone and *philia*

Antigone is the only character in Sophocles who explicitly purports to value *philia* above hatred. She does so in the course of a short dialogue, central to the play, which turns on the nature of *philia* and enmity. Creon has asked if she is not ashamed to differ from the compliant chorus:

> Antig.: No, for there is no disgrace in revering those born from the same womb.
>
> Creon: Was he who died on the other side not also of the same blood?
>
> Antig.: Of the same blood from both mother and father.
>
> Creon: Why then are you honouring the other with a favour irreverent in his eyes?[1]
>
> Antig.: The dead [Eteocles] will not attest to what you say.
>
> Creon: He will if you honour him on an equal footing with the irreverent one.
>
> Antig.: No, for it was no slave, but a brother who died.
>
> Creon: But he died ravaging this land, while the other died defending it.
>
> Antig.: Nonetheless, Hades desires these rites (*nomoi*).[2]
>
> Creon: But the worthwhile man (*chrestos*) does not desire equal honour with the bad (*kakos*).[3]

---

[1] I use 'reverence' for σέβας and cognates wherever possible, since the religious connotations of 'piety' are often inappropriate. On this theme cf. Kirkwood 236–8; Long 150f.

[2] In 519 I retain τούτους with most editors against Pearson and Müller.

[3] For the origin and meaning of *chrestos* see Redard 98–100.

Antig.: Who knows if in the underworld these things are
pure?
Creon: An enemy is never a *philos*, even after his death.
(511–22)

It is here that Antigone makes her famous rejoinder: 'My nature is to join not in enmity, but in *philia*' (523). The dialogue ends with Creon's biting command to go down to Hades to love her brothers, 'if you must love' (524f.). This stichomythic debate weaves together several threads of the play, such as the proper objects of honour and reverence and the nature of *nomos* ('law' or 'custom'). Above all, however, it brings into focus the clash between two opposing views of *philia*.[4] For fuller development of these views we must turn to the opening scenes, where they are presented in sequence.

Antigone's first words suggest a commitment to kinship. She opens the play with an intimate address to her sister, and builds up to the latest evil that afflicts them: 'Enemies are plotting harm against our friends' (10).[5] She explains that Eteocles is to receive the honour of burial which justice and *nomos* demand, whereas Polyneices will be left as a 'sweet treasure' for birds of prey to feed on (21–30). The penalty for disobedience is death, but Antigone is determined to defy the decree. Ismene cannot even move from amazement to refusal before Antigone starts to reproach her by emphasising their shared kinship with the dead man, declaring that she for one will not betray him (45f.). Creon, she argues, has no right to keep her from her 'own' (48; cf. 893).[6] Unperturbed by Ismene's reminder that their father died 'hated and in ill-repute' (50), she is confident that she will be reunited after death with Polyneices: 'I shall lie *philos* with him, my *philos*' (73). As we shall discover later, this expectation also embraces her parents, who are to welcome her precisely because

---

[4] The importance of *philia* and the central significance of this dialogue are seen by Winnington-Ingram 128–36. Cf. also Weinstock 134–41; Raphael, *Paradox* 106f.

[5] Or 'Friends are being harmed as only enemies should'. Although I prefer the former, both interpretations are appropriate and compatible with Help Friends/ Harm Enemies, provided that both articles are taken as generic, thus excluding any allusion to the enemy army (Antigone's feuds and friendships are purely personal). For various interpretations see the editors ad loc.; Winnington-Ingram 135 n. 55; Kells, *Antigone* 48–52.

[6] For the proprietorial phrasing of those who rely on family *philia* cf. *El.* 536, *OC* 830–2.

she has shown them the good offices of a *philos* even in death (897–902).[7]

Antigone's emphatic *phil-* language indicates a commitment to the obligations of kinship *philia*. Does it also show a warm personal love for her dead brother? One recent critic sees 'a special relationship of deep affection',[8] whereas others stress the fact that 'relationship is itself a source of obligation, regardless of the feelings involved',[9] and point to Antigone's lack of personal warmth, especially towards her sister. The truth lies somewhere in between. Nussbaum quite rightly contrasts Antigone's attitude with the deeply personal lamentations of a Hecuba. 'There is no sense of closeness, no personal memory, no particularity animating her speech' (Nussbaum 6).[10] It is true that *philos* and the superlative *philtatos* may be used substantively for one's close relatives regardless of sentiment. But when used attributively, as when Antigone calls Polyneices her *philtatos* brother (81), the epithet is redundant unless it adds an element of positive affection.[11] Antigone's later emphatic repetition of *phil-* words (898f.) implies more than the mere fact of kinship, which is not in question, while the unique verb 'join in *philia*' (523) has clearly been selected, if not coined, to express the special character of her devotion. It is quite natural, under the circumstances, that Polyneices should be singled out for affection. Antigone's picture of their reunion in death even suggests a lovers' embrace (73).[12] A further

[7] For other echoes of the prologue in Antigone's last speech see Else 65.

[8] Winnington-Ingram 130. Cf. also Else 33f.; Santirocco 187–90.

[9] Nussbaum 64. Similarly Perrotta 112f.; Weinstock 134–6; Linforth, *Antigone* 249f.; Lloyd-Jones 117. The two are not, of course, mutually exclusive.

[10] For Hecuba see Nussbaum 439f. n. 41. The best figure for comparison is Sophocles' own Electra. She expresses her love for her brother Orestes in a lengthy and personal speech of mourning, despite the fact that she has not seen Orestes since he was a small child. This love is matched, however, by caustic hostility towards a living sister, thus demonstrating the obvious fact that coldness towards one sibling does not exclude love for another.

[11] Cf. its frequent use by Electra (below, p. 155 n. 30). At *Ant.* 572 it is used by the affectionate Ismene for Haemon. The attribution of this line to Ismene, as in the mss., is now accepted by many (see Hester, *Unphilosophical* 30 n. 1 and most recently Winnington-Ingram 93 n. 7). But others still give it to Antigone (e.g. Müller and Kamerbeek ad loc.; Dawe, *Studies* 107; Scodel 138 n. 11).

[12] So also Musurillo 43; Winnington-Ingram 130. Her verb (κεῖμαι) may have an erotic connotation (cf. *Il.* 9.556 and the double entendre of Aesch. *Cho.* 894f., 906f.). At *Ant.* 1240f. it is used of Antigone and Haemon's union in death. But κεῖμαι is also a normal verb for lying dead, either before burial or in Hades (e.g. *Aj.* 899, *El.* 463, 1419; see Lattimore, *Themes* #70). For burial together of family members, including pairs of siblings, see Humphreys 105, 112–21.

dimension is added by the evocation of maternal tenderness in the guard's pathetic metaphor of the bereaved mother bird (423–5).[13] This image, together with Antigone's violent reaction to the un-covering of the corpse (426–8), provides a vivid vignette of passion-ate affection. Yet the impression of devotion remains a general one. A long and intimate speech of mourning like Electra's would shift attention away from the central fact of Antigone's dedication to all her dead family members, and the bond of *philia* that unites, or should unite, them all.

The prologue ends with Ismene's conclusion that her sister, though 'senseless', is rightly *philos* to her *philoi* (99). This judgement, embracing both 'beloved by' and 'dutiful/loving towards',[14] is a tribute to Antigone's unswerving loyalty. We shall soon see the de-gree of reciprocal devotion she inspires in her living *philoi*, Ismene and Haemon. But her steadfast pursuit of Help Friends beyond the grave is not prompted solely by love for the dead. It is also a matter of principle, reinforced by self-interest (albeit of a peculiar variety). The honour of Eteocles' funeral was a matter of justice and *nomos* (23f.). So too Polyneices' burial is an honour required by the justice of the gods and by their famous unwritten, immortal, infallible laws (450–60; cf. 76f., 519, 921).[15] Besides affection and family *philia*, Antigone's principal motivation is a prudent respect for the gods and their demands. Burial, especially of kin, was traditionally among those demands, and Antigone emphatically claims credit for a pious act of reverence (943).[16] She presents this pious deed to Ismene as a

---

[13] On this metaphor see Easterling, *Notes* 59–61. Cf. also Antigone's later com-parison of herself to Niobe (823–33), the grieving mother par excellence (Else 60f.).

[14] Knox 81, Else 35 n. 23, and Müller ad loc. prefer the active sense, Jebb and Mazon the passive. But given the essential reciprocity of *philia*, it is not possible to choose one to the exclusion of the other.

[15] On unwritten laws, see Hirzel, Ἄγραφος Νόμος; Ehrenberg ch. 2 and appendix A; Guthrie, *Sophists* 117–30; Bowra 97–101; Knox 95–8. Cf. also the works on *nomos* cited below, n. 87. On the parallel with *OT* 865–72 see especially Funke 40f.

[16] At the same time she acknowledges that her piety violates human law and may therefore incur a charge of 'villainy' (74) or even 'irreverence' (924, cf. 301); 924 is sometimes taken as an admission that violating Creon's law actually is impious (e.g. Schadewaldt 85; Webster 99). Such an admission from Antigone would be highly implausible (cf. Perrotta 79 n. 1; Pohlenz 195 and *Erläuterungen* 81), and the Greek does not require it (contrast *El.* 254, 616 where Electra unequivocally admits to shame at her behaviour). At the same time, Antigone's paradoxical phrase reminds us that hers is not the only perspective on her deed or on the nature of piety.

test of whether her nature is *eugenes* or *kakos* (38), and anticipates that
it will bring the greatest possible glory, since the citizens covertly
approve (502–5). Death in such a cause will be *kalos* (72, 97). It will
also, in a paradoxical sense, be prudent. Even though the burial violates the conventional prudence urged by Ismene, to Antigone it is
prudent in the long term. For she foresees some kind of post-
mortem existence, when she will be a 'resident' with the dead forever (76, 868; cf. 852).[17] It therefore makes perfect sense to sacrifice
short-term ties to the living in order to avoid alienating these permanent future companions (74f.; cf. 89)[18] – not to mention the immortal gods, who will punish her after death if she fails to obey their
laws (458–60; cf. 925f.). She therefore claims 'sense' in the eyes of the
dead (557) and the approval of 'those with sense' (904), despite
charges of folly from the more short-sighted. On the way to her
death her confidence wavers, but she still expects all to become clear
in the underworld (922–6).[19] She never anticipates extinction.
Finally, she considers her life so miserable that she has nothing to
lose. All mortals must die, and if death comes prematurely, that is a
positive gain (*kerdos*) for one in her circumstances, and would give
her no pain (460–6; cf. 2–6).[20] What would give her pain would be
omission of the action she believes is right (466–8). Ironically, Creon
is right when he attributes the burial to a desire for *kerdos* (222, 310,
312, 326).[21] Antigone's adherence to Help Friends is thus supported

17 On the 'concreteness' of Antigone's vision see Else 33. For popular beliefs on
the subject see Garland ch. 5 and cf. Dover 243–6.
18 Creon will die too (Wycherly 51), but Antigone does not care about pleasing
him in this life or the next. The argument of 74–6 is sometimes thought 'illogical', since greater length of time does not entail a higher authority (Linforth,
Antigone 186; cf. Wycherly loc. cit.; Gellie 32). But this misses the point of the
argument, which is a perfectly rational calculus. (At Eur. *Alc.* 692f. Pheres uses
a similar calculus to draw an opposite conclusion; cf. also Pl. *Rep.* 608c.) It is
perhaps a reluctance to attribute any prudential motive to Antigone which has
forced interpreters to see it as 'a supreme revelation of her elevated mood' (Linforth loc. cit.). The case is similar with the notorious calculus at 904–15
(Wycherly loc. cit. rightly observes that the similar tone of the two passages
supports the authenticity of the latter).
19 Line 926 is sometimes taken to imply that Creon's success in punishing her
shows she was wrong (it was so taken by Hegel; see Paolucci 280). But since she
has expected and even courted human punishment from the outset, it is more
likely to mean that she will discover after death if she is wrong.
20 For the emphasis on evils in her opening speech see Else 28–31.
21 On *kerdos* and the money theme see Goheen 14–19.

by a confluence of affection, principle and unconventional self-interest, involving piety, justice, renown, honour, *eugeneia* and her own long-term well-being.

Yet this character, whose principles and feelings require a heroic expression of family *philia* towards the dead, is harsh and scornful towards her affectionate and living sister. Ismene argues against Antigone's proposal by reminding her of their family history, their solitude, weakness and female *phusis* (49–64).[22] They must obey the more powerful 'in this and still more painful things' (64), rather than risk a 'most evil' death for flouting the decree and power of a *turannos* and defying the law (59f.). She will therefore ask pardon of the dead on the ground that she is 'forced' to behave this way (65f.; cf. 79). 'For', she concludes, 'there is no sense at all in performing excessive deeds' (67f.). The plea of duress implies that it is right to bury their brother, a suggestion confirmed at the end of the prologue when Ismene says Antigone is 'rightly' a *philos* to her *philoi* (99). At the same time, her expectation of forgiveness implies that omitting the burial is venial under the circumstances.[23] Moreover she suggests that Antigone is defying not only the law (59), but the will of the citizens (79).[24] Finally, her word 'excessive' (68) adds an element of positive disapproval by suggesting that Antigone's deed goes beyond the bounds of propriety.[25] This is picked up a few lines later when she warns that 'it is not fitting to pursue the impossible' (92).

Antigone makes no attempt to win Ismene over, and displays immediate disdain for the notion of forgiveness. She declares that even if Ismene changed her mind she would not want her help (69f.), thus foreshadowing her later rejection of her sister. She dismisses the argument from duress as a pretext (80), belittles Ismene's fears on her

---

[22] On Ismene as an embodiment of conventional Athenian womanhood see Weinstock 132f.

[23] Acceptance of a plea of duress goes back as far as the *Odyssey* (Mackenzie 102f.). This kind of plea might or might not be acceptable in court (cf. Lys. 12.28f. and see Dover 148). Cf. also Arist. *EN* 1110a4–b1.

[24] Cf. also the ambiguity of 44 between 'forbidden to the city' and 'forbidden by the city'. Note that Ismene characterises Antigone's defiance as 'violence' (59, 79) in a way that echoes the 'violence' to which she herself is subject (66) (Rohdich 31f.).

[25] σχετλία (47) also has pejorative connotations (see Jebb and Kamerbeek ad loc.). On περισσά (68) cf. Knox 24f. This is the first occurrence of the theme of limits and their transgression (cf. 449, 455, 618–20, 853, 874, 802f.).

behalf (82f.), and rejects her promise of discretion with an invitation
to denounce the plan to all (86f.). When Ismene declares that her sister is 'in love with the impossible', Antigone retorts that such words
will justly make her *echthros* to both herself and Polyneices (90–4).
Even the impossible, she implies, must be attempted.[26] Any failure
in unconditional support relegates a living *philos*, however well-
meaning, despite duress and despite the tie of blood, to the status of
enemy. Ismene has shown that she is not a legitimate member of
their noble family, not *eugenes* in her nature but *kakos* (38). Antigone
demands not affection but action, and that of the most extreme
variety. On behalf of the dead as well as herself she acts on a principle
she will later make explicit: she does not tolerate a *philos* who shows
philia only in words (543).

In this latter scene Ismene is doing her best to share the consequences of Antigone's deeds and die with her. This is scarcely to be
characterised as showing love 'only in words', but for Antigone the
unbridgeable gulf between friend and enemy has already opened.
No desire to share her sufferings can compensate for that initial
failure to act, and she bitterly rejects the love of one who 'cares for
Creon' (549). When Ismene asks the reason for this unfair and 'useless' taunt, Antigone answers that if she mocks (the response due to
an enemy) it is because of the pain her sister has caused her (550f.).[27]
Since Ismene did not share in the action, she is also 'justly' excluded
from its consequences (538f.), which Antigone chose for herself as a
kerdos. Ismene, who originally chose differently, must also abide by
the consequences of her decision (555, 559f.). She too now longs to
die (548, 554), but Antigone refuses to accept her sister's claim to
joint responsibility (536f., 558), or her conversion to the view that
life is no longer worth living. Antigone chose death in a noble cause
(72), whereas Ismene's death at this stage would accomplish nothing
(547). So Antigone both taunts her sister and at the same time obliges
her to abide by a choice that is, after all, preferable according to the

---

26 This ἀμήχανος theme (79, 90, 92) will be picked up in the first stasimon (363; cf.
    349, 365). Antigone is the 'awesome' being who performs the burial and goes
    'resourceless' to nothing but her own death (360–2).

27 Ismene asks the wrong question when she asks what *use* it is (550). There is no
    question of benefit. Mockery of enemies is a pleasure. My view is shared by the
    scholiast, who glosses 'I mock you because you were not willing to help me.'
    For other interpretations see Kells, *Antigone* 53–5; Winnington-Ingram, *Soph-
    oclea* 6f.

conventional values espoused by Ismene herself in the prologue. The only 'benefit' Ismene can now provide is to save herself, an 'escape' that her sister does not 'begrudge' her (552f.).[28] We need not doubt Antigone's sincerity when she leaves her sister with a final word of encouragement, which at the same time underlines the utter divergence of their outlooks (559).

In what sense, then, is it Antigone's nature to join not in hatred, but in *philia* (523)? The primary reference, in the context of the dialogue with Creon, is clearly to her dead brothers. She excludes herself from the hatred that divides them and abides by the claims of kinship-*philia* towards both.[29] But her verb, 'it is my nature', suggests a broader claim to *philia*.[30] Yet she speaks of enemies as does any other champion of Help Friends/Harm Enemies.[31] Like Ajax and Philoctetes, she prays before she dies that Creon may suffer the same evils that he is unjustly inflicting on her (927f.; cf. *Aj.* 839–41, *Phil.* 315f.). Like Achilles, she threatens hatred to a friend who sides with her enemy (93f.; cf. *Il.* 9. 612–15). Her dedication to *philia* and rejection of enmity, though useful rhetorical weapons at this moment of crisis, appear to be strictly limited in their application.

We might expect Antigone's commitment to kinship-*philia* to embrace at least Ismene. But despite her firm devotion to a brother who made war on his own brother and their native city, she rejects her sister for a perceived disloyalty of a much more venial kind. 'Justly' (94) indicates that this is not merely lack of self-control arising from her passionate temper, but a matter of principle. One critic has explained that for Antigone 'there is in fact only one case in which the tie of blood relationship can be cancelled – the betrayal of the sacred obligation that tie imposes' (Knox 82). What then of fratricide? Does this not constitute such a betrayal? Antigone is forced, like Creon, to take sides between her dead brothers, not just by patriotism but by her own values. Not only does the transitivity of friendship and enmity produce an insoluble conflict (as Creon

---

[28] As Rohdich 100 points out, the idea of 'escape' echoes the values of the guard (437f.). See also ib. 95–105 on the way Antigone isolates herself from Ismene in this scene.

[29] So e.g. Jebb ad loc. Her other *phil-* language (897–9) extends the claim to her dead parents.

[30] For the force of the verb see Lesky, *Zwei* 97–9.

[31] Cf. Winnington-Ingram 135.

realises), but kinship-*philia* itself demands rejection of a brother who attacked not only his own city but his family, and ended up destroying one of the closest of kin, his own brother. This is the dilemma that her fratricidal brothers have bequeathed to Antigone as her share of the family inheritance – a dilemma to which 'there is no solution' (597).

In an attempt to escape it Antigone denies the persistence of enmity beyond the grave. She makes no attempt to deny Creon's charge that Polyneices was *kakos*, but can evidently forgive in death his hostility in life towards both family and city. What is more, she expects Eteocles to do likewise. This is an extraordinary position for a conventional adherent of Help Friends/Harm Enemies. Electra convinces her sister that Clytemnestra's offerings at Agamemnon's tomb will not be welcomed in a friendly way (*El.* 442f.). In Homer, the hostility between Ajax and Odysseus persists in the underworld (*Od.* 11.543–64). In Sophocles' own *Ajax* Odysseus may draw the line at pursuing enmity beyond the grave, but Ajax's survivors expect his animosity to persist (*Aj.* 1347, 1394f.).[32] Moreover Odysseus' restraint is based on divine justice and Ajax's personal excellence, whereas Antigone relies solely on ties of blood to efface hostility amongst the dead. This extraordinary belief is questioned by Creon, but cannot be challenged by the dead themselves. Antigone is free to ascribe to them the values that support her own decision. The living may disagree, but by doing so they earn nothing but her contempt.

Yet Antigone's own first priority is to please the dead and thus secure their long-term approval (74f., 89). It is Ismene who relies on their forgiveness (65f.), and perhaps rightly so. If Antigone can forgive Polyneices, and he and Eteocles can forgive each other, will they not forgive their sisters for omitting burial under duress? The belief that her brothers are free from post-mortem resentment thus tends to undermine the practical urgency of Antigone's need to please the dead. This belief is not rationally grounded. 'Who knows', she says, 'if these things are pure below?' (521). Later she will express it as a strong hope or expectation (897),[33] without ruling out the possibility that she is wrong (925f.). But it is this conviction, be it

---

[32] The same assumption underlies the general belief that cult-heroes continue to help their friends and harm their enemies (see further below, p. 253f.).

[33] On the irrationality of 'hope' see below, p. 143.

wishful thinking or 'heroic fiat',[34] which enables her to avoid taking sides between her brothers. Despite the history of strife that has plagued her family, she can love them all in death. Not just their death, for the heroic expression of her devotion leads inevitably to Antigone's own destruction (cf. 559f.). This is a drastic solution to the underlying incoherence in her single-minded pursuit of family *philia*, an incoherence highlighted by the denial of Ismene's wish to share the death sentence. Driven, ironically, by her very devotion to the family, Antigone excludes her sister from the bounds of that 'joining in *philia*' which can be expressed only in death.

Creon

The gulf between Antigone and Creon is represented dramatically by their introduction in discrete scenes divided by the parodos. In this first choral song the chorus describes the defeat of Polyneices and his army in their assault on Thebes. The attack is defeated by Zeus himself (128–34, 141–3). But despite their rejoicing at the city's salvation, the chorus pass no judgement on the brothers' personal quarrel. They do not invite us to admire a patriotic Eteocles at Polyneices' expense, and refer even-handedly to 'quarrels with arguments on either side' (111). When the brothers' duel is described, the mutual character of their hatred and destruction is heavily emphasised (143–6).[35] We must await Creon for the portrayal of one brother as hero and the other as villain (only then, at 212, will the chorus echo his phrasing). Moreover the parodos leaves the chorus' political sympathies unclear, so that we cannot predict their response to either edict or burial.[36] As far as they are concerned, victory should bring 'forget-

[34] Winnington-Ingram 132, whose account is close to mine.

[35] They echo Ismene's description (13f., 55–7). Note especially κοινός (57, 146) and the use of the dual in 143–6 (also used by Antigone in 21).

[36] Gardiner 83f. After the parodos they maintain a character of unenthusiastic obedience and cautious advice towards Creon, coupled with an ambivalent disapproval of Antigone. They are introduced as Creon's supporters, which both distinguishes them from the *polis* as a whole (note ἐκ πάντων δίχα, 'apart from all', 164) and enhances Antigone's isolation. They also contribute to the dichotomies of male vs. female, old vs. young (appropriately, news of Antigone's support from the city comes from the youthful Haemon). At the same time, their lacklustre support (especially 211–20, 278f.), together with hints of intimidation (504f., 509, cf. 688f.), avoids conferring legitimacy on Creon. On their status and character see Burton 85–90; Gardiner 82–97; cf. also Alexanderson, *Antigone*. On their ambivalence see further Perrotta 66–71, 82–5; Kirkwood 205–9; Winnington-Ingram 137f.

fulness' (151).[37] The ode thus forms a fitting interlude between the entries of the two main characters with their antithetical viewpoints.

As Antigone's opening words stressed family ties, so Creon begins with 'the affairs of the city' (163).[38] In an attempt to sever the Gordian knot of conflicting loyalties, he has adopted the *polis* as his touchstone of worth: 'Whoever is well-disposed to this *polis* will be honoured by me in death as in life' (209f.).[39] Ismene's words in the prologue left no doubt as to the legitimacy of his authority, and even suggested some ambivalence about the decree (cf. 59, 79).[40] He is now introduced sympathetically as a new king who has called a council of elders (155–61),[41] and begins quite properly by attributing victory to the gods (163f.). Only the faintest of warning notes is struck when he speaks of 'reverence' for the power of the throne (165f.). This throne is his by inheritance (173f.), but it remains to be seen what kind of 'spirit, thought and judgement' the experience of 'rule and law' will reveal in him (175–7).[42]

After this moderate, untyrannical preamble, Creon sets forth the principles on which his rule is to be based, and which at the same time provide the justification for his decree. For a start, he condemns as *kakistos* any absolute ruler who allows fear to deter him from 'the best plans' (178–81).[43] Here is the first sign of a tendency of Creon's to utter worthy principles while seeming unable to apply them

---

[37] For the implications of this cf. Rohdich 50–2.

[38] Throughout the first half of the play his language is riddled with references to the *polis* (see especially Knox, *Polis* 13–16).

[39] He uses for the *polis* language appropriate to personal relations (209, 187). Cf. above, p. 44. On εὔνους ... τῇ πόλει see Connor 103f.

[40] On the language of 60 see Goheen 157 n. 31; Knox 63.

[41] For the sympathetic implications of 160f. see Knox 86. But 'new' (156) for a king can connote cruelty as well as inexperience (see Griffith on *PV* 35; Dodds, *Progress* 41).

[42] The programmatic significance of these lines has often been remarked. The scholiast and others compare the saying of Bias or Chilon, 'Rule reveals the man.' On the language of 176 see Long 53; Dodds 139. On φρόνημα ('thought') see also Long 38. Benardete (1) 172 notes that Creon combines two arguments for legitimacy: legality of accession and probable excellence of rule. These criteria are independent and could conflict, but Benardete goes too far in calling them 'contradictory'. As the scholiast on 164 observes, it is necessary for one entering power to appear well-disposed to his subjects.

[43] His words recall the Athenian bouleutic oath (cf. Lys. 31.2 τὰ βέλτιστα βουλεύ-σειν τῇ πόλει, 'to plan the best for the city'), and other patriotic sentiments (cf. Cleoboulus DK 10.3.a.9; Herod. 3.81.3, 7.10.δ.1f.; Thuc. 1.43.4, 4.74.3; Demos. 59.4; Diog. Laert. *Solon* 1.60).

appropriately to the case in hand.[44] The chorus will hint at this in his scene with Haemon, when they uneasily emphasise their approval of Creon's words – as opposed, perhaps, to his actions? (681f.; cf. 724f.). Haemon too, in an attempt to alter his father's behaviour, will refrain from questioning the correctness of his views, simply suggesting that others may deserve equal attention (685–7). Here in Creon's first speech, it is unclear what 'the ruler of the whole city' should have to fear which might deter him from 'the best plans'.[45] Unpopularity perhaps? Or insurrection? Under absolute rule, it is usually the subjects who have cause to keep their mouths shut out of fear, as Antigone will remind us later, in an unmistakeable echo of this passage (505; cf. 243, 690). And sure enough, this particular ruler's failure to adopt 'the best plans' will owe more to his locking his subjects' mouths through fear than locking his own. But a motive for the statement will soon emerge. It is an advance justification for a decree that Creon expects to be unpopular (219, 289f.). Evidently he does not trust the citizens to recognise and approve his 'best plans'. Hence the fear is a fear of dissent. But he shows no trace of understanding that the courage to risk unpopular measures must be balanced by a respect for legitimate grievances. On the contrary, the illegitimacy of any grievance is suggested by his most characteristic fear – the fear of insurrection.

Next we hear the criteria by which Creon judges which plans are 'best'. First, he has no regard for anyone who values a *philos*, a personal friend or relative (as Polyneices is to him), above his native land (182f.). This is no mere commonplace, for the clannish loyalties of *philoi* were a constant menace to the fabric of the Greek *polis*. Creon adds that he himself would never keep silent if he saw 'doom instead of *soteria*' approaching the citizens (184–6). This admirable avowal would seem trite were it not for the implication that one who values personal *philoi* too highly would keep silent in just this way. But again, Creon's own failing will be the opposite, for he will silence the voices of others when they warn him of approaching doom.

---

[44] This is related to his often remarked penchant for gnomic utterances (see Wolf 48–53, 126–31, and especially 49 n. 1 on their disjointed character). The respectability of his sentiments can be seen from parallels.

[45] This unclarity is brought out by the variety of suggested interpretations (see e.g. Ehrenberg 58; Podlecki, *Creon* 361; Winnington-Ingram 123).

Nor, Creon continues, would he ever befriend anyone hostile
to the land (187f.). This view that 'loyalty to the city is an essential
qualification for being a *philos*' has been called 'a radical idea for a
Greek' (Connor 52). But it is one that harmonises well with the
patriotic spirit of democratic Athens, and is echoed by later writers
such as Lycurgus, who claims that a just citizen should 'consider
those doing something illegal to their fatherland his private enemies'
(*Leocr.* 6; cf. also Plut. *Mor.* 809e). Creon justifies his attitude by
explaining that friendships can only be formed in the context of a
stable *polis* (188–90). Here is another commendable principle,[46] and
one that could form the basis of an effective argument for the punishment of traitors, including the Athenian practice of denying them
burial within Attica.[47] But further argument is needed to move
from this defensible premiss to the propriety of Creon's decree. For
he both suppresses other premisses – the rights of the dead man's
relatives, and the fact that he is Polyneices' uncle – and reaches a very
strong conclusion: denial of burial under any circumstances at all,
even outside the city by the victim's own relatives. The extremity of
his position is underlined by the fact that, as Polyneices' closest surviving male relative, he himself has the primary responsibility for
ensuring that the burial takes place.

Creon's view of *philia* and its conflict with the *polis* is arti-
ficially polarised. His choice of words is telling – for him *philoi* are
made, not born (188, 190).[48] He declares that his decree is 'brother'
to his principles (192), showing that for him 'brotherliness ... is a
harmony between political ideals and practice' (Seale 86).[49] He sees
burial rites as an honour due to a public benefactor, rather than a
right due to all from their families (cf. 196f., 284f.). For him there is
no middle ground. But loyalty to a natural *philos*, even one who is a

---

46 Cf. Democr. DK 68 в 252; Thuc. 2.60.2f.; Eur. fr. 798 (Nauck); Demos, 9.69,
    19.247 (where *Ant.* 175–90 are used against Aeschines). On the metaphor of the
    ship of state see Goheen 46f.; Musurillo 47f.; Nussbaum 58f.

47 But their relatives could bury them on foreign soil (MacDowell, *LCA* 176–8;
    see also Parker 43–8; Bremmer 90f.). The issue has been much discussed in rela-
    tion to *Ant.* See especially Hester, *Unphilosophical* 19–21 and appendix c; Lin-
    forth, *Antigone* 190–3; Pearson, *Ajax* 133f.; Perrotta 63–6; Kitto, *FMD* 147–9;
    Nussbaum 437 n. 14.

48 θείμην (188); ποιούμεθα (190) (also noted by Knox 87; Winnington-Ingram
    123; Nussbaum 57).

49 On this expression see also Knox 87; Nussbaum 57; and cf. Lys. 2.64; Pl. *Rep.*
    421c, 436ab.

public enemy, is itself an obligation and one that need not be subversive. Creon ignores the obligations that *philoi*, in particular relatives, bear towards each other independently of the *polis*. He needs
an argument, especially in view of the popular disapproval he fears,
to show what is dangerous to the state about burying this corpse.[50]

The justification he provides is, typically, not quite to the
point. Instead of spelling out the presumed deterrent effect of denying burial, and arguing that this overrides the obligations of kinship
(cf. 659f.),[51] he declares that Eteocles is a patriotic hero and Polyneices a traitor, and he will never honour the *kakoi* more highly than
the just (207f.). He will reaffirm this in his dialogue with Antigone:
the *kakos* should not receive equal honour with the *chrestos*, and an
enemy is never a friend, even in death (520–2). These passages exemplify Creon's tendency to ascribe a variety of ethical terms on the
basis of patriotism.[52] Eteocles, who is *aristos* in a patriotic military
sense (195–7), is also just (208) and *chrestos* (520). But the traitor is
irreverent (516) and *kakos* (208, 288, 520), just as the ruler who fails
to use the best plans was *kakistos* (181). In Creon's estimation such a
person is 'nowhere' and could never count as a *philos* (183, 187f.).
Accordingly, both living and dead are to be judged by their good
will towards the *polis* (209f.; cf. 211f.). As we have seen, this is a
legitimate line of argument as far as it goes. But it is limited in its
failure to take into account the rights and obligations of the family.
Creon does not adopt the standard plea that Polyneices, a former
philos, has made himself an enemy through unprovoked aggression.
He simply ignores not only his own blood relationship to a nephew
(his friends are 'made'), but also Antigone's to a brother. This scorn
for family ties is harshly expressed when he alludes to Antigone as his
'slave' (479).[53] When it comes to punishing her, he will not merely
disregard their relationship but openly repudiate it, coming omi-
nously close to blasphemy with his scorn for Zeus Herkeios (protec-

---

[50] Cf. Linforth, *Antigone* 189f.; Ronnet 87f.
[51] Mackenzie 115–20 discusses the rarity of such teleological justifications for
punishment in the classical period. But to her exceptions should be added Lys.
1.47; Demos. 25.17.
[52] Nussbaum 54–8 shows well how Creon redefines such words as 'just' in terms
of the *polis*, but she does not distinguish between loyalty to the *polis* as such and
to its leader (see further below, p. 123).
[53] She, by contrast, bases her faith in the reconciliation of the dead on the fact that
it was 'not a slave, but a brother' who died (517).

tor of the hearth) (486–9). Later he declares that he will kill Antigone rather than break his word to the *polis*; she may therefore call in vain on Zeus Xunaimos (protector of blood-kinship), for discipline must begin at home (655–60). Without the repeated defiance of Zeus as guardian of the family, this wish not to be false to the *polis* might seem a praiseworthy rejection of nepotism. But in context it hints at the danger of denying the claims of kinship.

Yet from his son Creon demands an unquestioning loyalty, just as Antigone did from her sister. He expects to be *philos* to Haemon whatever he himself does (634), for a son should be subordinate in everything to his father's judgement (639f.).[54] This is why men pray for obedient children: to reciprocate evil to their father's enemies and to honour his friends (641–4). Otherwise children are 'useless' — they bring nothing but trouble, and mockery from one's enemies (645–7). This demand for unconditional filial loyalty depends on just the kind of blood tie whose force Creon has belittled. But his language also suggests a one-sided and purely instrumental view of parenthood, where the son is not loved or valued for his own sake. The relationship is portrayed in simple, authoritarian terms without reciprocity or the spontaneous pleasure of natural affection.

The same insensitivity to the value of love in a reciprocal relationship is betrayed by Creon's view of Haemon's marriage. He sees it in one-sided, crudely reproductive terms: 'Others have fields for him to plough' (569).[55] This was, to be sure, a conventional view of marriage.[56] A different perspective, however, is provided by Ismene's response: 'But not as these two were fitted to each other' (570). She implies at the very least mutual compatability, if not special affection between them.[57] But Creon's only concession to marital love is a warning to his son not to lose his wits out of

---

[54] πανταχῇ δρῶντες (634) hints at the etymology of the pejorative *panourgia* (cf. 300f. and see below, p. 188f.).

[55] Cf. the agricultural image of 645. On Creon's denial of *eros* see Winnington-Ingram 96f.

[56] The metaphor is a common one and echoes the Athenian marriage contract (see Kamerbeek ad loc.; Roussel 65 n. 2; Vernant, *MP* 140f.). But for the idea that reproduction is only one element in the marital partnership see Xen. *Oec.* 7.11–13. On reciprocity in marriage see above, p. 46.

[57] Cf. Lloyd-Jones' review of von Fritz, *Gnomon* 34 (1962) 740. If ὡς in 570 means 'as' (so e.g. Jebb) it clearly suggests a personal bond. Roussel 65–7 takes it as 'since', which is necessary to justify his view that 570 refers merely to the contractual fact of betrothal (ἁρμόζω has this sense in Ionic; see the editors ad loc.).

'pleasure in a woman' (648f.). Erotic pleasure must be kept under the control of reason and subordinated to practical considerations. For a *kakos* woman in Haemon's bed will provide a 'cold embrace', and nothing is a greater wound than a bad friend, a *philos kakos* (650–2).[58] He should therefore 'spit away' Antigone as an enemy, and leave her to marry someone in Hades (653f.).[59]

What is it that makes Antigone a *philos kakos*? She is already a *philos* by virtue of blood-ties, but the pragmatic Creon is concerned with the formal tie of marriage. What makes her *kakos*, as a *philos* and a woman,[60] is her civic disobedience: 'For I caught her alone of the whole city disobeying' (655f.). If she is a *philos kakos*, it is because she has refused the compliance he demands of both citizens and *philoi*. Yet according to Ismene she is 'rightly a *philos* to her *philoi*' (99). She has shown herself capable of remarkable loyalty to one she loves, and moreover has done nothing *kakos* to Haemon. Creon, however, has already declared that he expects a son to share his father's friendships and enmities (641–4). He evaluates Antigone's future relationship to his son strictly in terms of his own authority, without concern for Haemon's feelings or judgement. Ismene is right when she exclaims that Creon is dishonouring his son (572), by 'riding roughshod over him' (Dawe, *Studies* ad loc.).[61] His last words in Haemon's hearing are a command to bring out Antigone (whom he calls an 'object of hate'), 'so that she can die in her bridegroom's presence, at his side, before his very eyes' (760f.).

This failure to grasp the reciprocal character of authentic *philia*, this myopic view of a child's obligations, help generate Creon's blindness to Haemon's efforts at persuasion. For if it is a son's duty to agree with his father in everything, then any attempt to alter the father's convictions or behaviour is an act of disloyalty. Yet Haemon is introduced as a devoted son, declaring in his opening words,

---

[58] The wound metaphor is part of Creon's penchant for military language (below, p. 124). At the same time it evokes the vulnerability engendered by *philia*.

[59] As Musurillo 52 well observes, 'Antigone will indeed become a "chilling embrace" for Haemon ... and Haemon will indeed "spit upon an enemy" – his own father, as the event proves – and find his betrothed wedded to the god of Death.'

[60] Creon twice condemns her not merely as 'bad', but as a 'bad woman' (or 'wife') (571, 651).

[61] Cf. the chorus' fears at 627–30. For the nature of the 'dishonour' see Linforth, *Antigone* 209 (other explanations in Jebb ad loc.; Roussel 68f.).

'Father, I am yours' (635). He is guided, he says, by his father's good judgement (635f.); no marriage is more important to him than his father's fine guidance (637f.).[62] He does not even deny the propriety of his father's present words (685f.). He is a model of tact, referring to his marriage only to dismiss it. Unlike Creon, he understands that *philia* means caring for another for that person's own sake. Though he also acknowledges a concern for his own interests, which he sees as identical with Creon's (749), he declares that nothing is more precious to him than his father's well-being (701f.; cf. 749). When he says he 'cares' about Creon (741), he uses a verb conveying the warm concern proper from child to parent.[63] He sees his natural role as watching out for Creon's interests amongst the people (688f.).[64] Unlike his father, moreover, he understands the reciprocal character of *philia*, though he puts it in terms of reputation rather than affection: 'What greater ornament is there for children than renown of a flourishing father, or for a father than that of his children?' (703f.). It is only when Creon has threatened to kill his bride before his very eyes that Haemon repudiates the filial tie, telling Creon to go and 'rave with those of your *philoi* who are willing [to endure you]' (765).[65]

Creon fails to comprehend the nature of *philia* (both familial and personal), fails to respect its claims, and at the same time makes rigid and counterproductive claims on his own presumptive *philoi*. His attitude towards his subjects is equally destructive. Just as he ignores the wishes and interests of his son, so his view of the state is relentlessly authoritarian. The two are related. As he tells Haemon, the man who is *chrestos* in his household will also be just in the *polis* (661f.).[66] This harmless sounding statement has ominous implications for Creon himself, whose behaviour in the *polis* rests precisely on the denial of family ties.[67] His next lines give it an

[62] For the 'studied ambiguity' of his phrasing see Linforth, *Antigone* 215f.

[63] προκήδομαι. Antigone uses a related adjective to taunt Ismene as 'caring' for Creon (κηδεμών 549). For the implications of these words see Knox 176 n. 7.

[64] Reading πέφυκα in 688 with most editors. πέφυκας (preferred by Pearson and Müller) would make a revealing comment about Creon's nature, but see contra Jebb and Kemerbeek.

[65] On this line see Else 52: 'The real point of Haimon's words is that Kreon will go on living alone: he will have no φίλοι left.'

[66] Cf. Aeschin. 3.78. I follow the mss. order of lines in this speech (with Jebb, Dain, Kamerbeek and others against Pearson, Dawe and Müller).

[67] For the ironies of 661f. see Rohdich 125.

authoritarian colouring: 'But he who transgresses by violating laws, or trying to give orders to those in power, this man cannot receive praise from me' (663–5). The well-being of the *polis* may be his own criterion for right action, but the criterion he proposes for the citizens themselves is unconditional obedience to their rulers (666f.), despite his own acknowledged inexperience in that role (175–7). Since he regards the *polis* as 'belonging to the one with power' (738), he can move easily, if illegitimately, from the criterion of serving the *polis* to that of obedience to himself. He ascribes moral terms even more often on the basis of disobedience (Antigone's fault) than lack of patriotism (that of Polyneices).

This shift away from the more persuasive criterion (*soteria* of the *polis*) to that of absolute obedience begins in the first scene with the guard, when Creon implies that it is just for a subject to 'keep the neck under the yoke' (291f.).[68] The spectre of disobedience then prompts a diatribe against money and bribery, which, he says, are responsible for the ruination of cities, for villainy, irreverence and disgraceful deeds (296–301; cf. 313f., 1045–7). Both here and to Haemon the demand for obedience is implicitly justified as a means of preserving the *polis*. The disciplined man is not only *chrestos* at home and just in the city, but good at both ruling and being ruled (669),[69] and a 'just and excellent' military comrade (671). Obedience saves cities whereas disobedience destroys them, and is thus the greatest of evils (672–6).[70] The insubordinate subject, as represented by Antigone, is shameful (510), hubristic (480) and above all *kakos*.[71] When Haemon defies his father he too is 'utterly *kakistos*' and also of 'foul character' (742, 746).

A consequence of these values is that the obligation to obey outweighs the subject's personal judgement of right and wrong: 'Whoever the city appoints must be obeyed in small matters, and in

---

[68] On this transition cf. Knox 108; Rohdich 130f. (though both associate it with the Haemon scene).

[69] For this ideal cf. Herod. 3.83; Pl. *Leg.* 643e, 762e; Arist. *EN* 1134b15, *Pol.* 1277a25–7, 1277b44–21; Plut. *Mor.* 806f.; Diog. Laert. 1.60.

[70] ἀναρχία (672) is literally 'absence of rule' (Long 54) but as opposed to πειθαρχία (676) it suggests absence of effective rule, resulting from disobedience. For parellels to the sentiment see Nestle 141; cf. also Thuc. 5.9.9.

[71] A favourite word of Creon's, used of Antigone or her deed at 495, 565 (twice), 571, 651, 652, 731f.; cf. also 489. In general, his abuse is remarkably unimaginative. Cf. the repetitious 678–80, and the anticlimactic flatness of 183 and 665.

just ones, and the opposite' (666f.). The Greeks were less inclined than ourselves to value individual moral judgement when it comes into conflict with the state,[72] and we have several parallels to Creon's statement. But their context tends to link them with slavery or the resigned obedience of the powerless, neither of which provides an attractive political paradigm.[73] The most plausible context for such a sentiment is warfare, where, as Creon rightly tells us, disobedience brings disaster (674f.). His own recent successes have been as a military leader (8, 1162),[74] and he frequently has recourse to military imagery.[75] But it is less easy to justify ruling a city at peace, or one's own family, on such terms,[76] when an act of disobedience does not automatically endanger the safety of the community.

As Nussbaum has suggested, Creon's authoritarianism and rejection of family in favour of *polis* bear a superficial resemblance to Plato's ideal state.[77] Plato's guardians are to love and care for the city, thinking its interests identical with their own, and to do whatever they think is in its interests; they must preserve at all costs the conviction that they should do what is 'best' for the city (*Rep.* 412c–e).[78] They will keep watch over both external enemies and internal friendships, 'so that the latter may be unwilling and the former unable to do any harm' (414b). The family is to be abolished in order to enhance civic unity (461d–65b). But Plato extends *philia* to the whole city not by dissolving natural ties, but by expanding them to embrace all fellow citizens: 'Will you not require them, not merely to use those family terms, but to behave as a real family?' (463cd, trans. Cornford). His aim is to put an end to precisely the kind of

---

[72] But see Daube for examples of civil disobedience.
[73] Cf. Paroem, Graec. 1.394.100; *Tr. Fr. Adesp.* 436 (Nauck²); Aesch. *Cho.* 78. The sentiment is more likely to be acceptable coming from Solon (30 (West) = 27 (Diehl)), though the context is unknown. (All these are quoted by Kamerbeek ad loc.)
[74] He is presented as the victorious general, which is hardly surprising in view of Eteocles' fate. Against the alleged difficulties with line 8 raised by Ehrenberg (105–12 and appendix B) see Lloyd-Jones' review, *JHS* 76 (1956) 113; Ronnet 86f.; Funke 38f.
[75] See Goheen 19–26. Cf. also Musurillo 39f.; Siewart 105–7.
[76] On Creon's treatment of the family as a miniature *polis* cf. Rohdich 124–6.
[77] Nussbaum 57 (but cf. 159 where she contrasts them). Plato like Creon uses the ship of state metaphor (*Rep.* 488).
[78] The word for 'caring' is κηδεμών (412c) (cf. above, n. 63); 'best' is βέλτιστα (cf. above, n. 43).

narrow family loyalties that Creon actually encourages by demanding his son's total support in pursuit of Help Friends/Harm Enemies
(641–4). The result of Plato's measure is to be a complete community of interest and mutual sharing in feelings of pleasure or pain
(464a). In other words, Plato wishes to broaden the traditional values
of mutual interest and affection in *philia*, whereas Creon curtails
them, reducing all interests to his own. Nor does Creon's authoritarianism fundamentally resemble Plato's, for he is politically inexperienced and certainly does not bring to his task the years of training in
virtue and wisdom enjoyed by the philosopher. Could those who
have gazed on the form of the just require their subjects to obey
them 'in just matters and the opposite'?[79] Plato stresses the harmony
between his rulers and their subjects, who will call each other
'saviours' and 'nurturers' respectively, in contrast to other rulers,
who call their subjects 'slaves' (463b) – as Creon does Antigone (479;
cf. 756).[80] Although Creon does not attain the grotesque stature of
the tyrant of Plato's lurid imagination (580a), he has more in
common with him than with a philosopher king.[81]

For Creon's failure in personal relationships is paralleled by a
failure in political *philia*, the *philia* extolled by Democritus under the
name of *homonoia*, 'unanimity'.[82] To be sure, *homonoia* is compatible
with several of Creon's values. For Democritus it enables the city to
make war (DK 68 B 250; cf. also 255); for Xenophon's Socrates, it
results in obedience to the law (*Mem.* 4.4.16). But in the myth of
Plato's Protagoras, this kind of *philia* comes in the train of *dike* and
aidos, justice and respect for others, which are the twin foundations
of democracy (*Prot.* 322c–3a). It is also closely linked with justice and
philia by Plato himself, for whom unity of feeling is the greatest

79 Plato's state incorporates such doubtful features as the 'medicinal lie' (389bc,
   414bc, 459cd), but revising the concept of justice is not the same as requiring
   obedience to unjust commands (on this feature of the *Republic* see Brickhouse
   and Smith). Creon too may be revising justice, by making it consist solely in
   obedience (cf. 291f., 662, 671), but 666f. shows this is not consistently carried
   through.
80 Cf. also *Aj.* 1235; Eur. *Ba.* 803, *Her.* 251. For further examples of this tyrannical
   trait see Funke 41 n. 55. Slavery is a one-sided instrumental relationship incompatible with true *philia* (cf. e.g. Xen. *Cyr.* 1.6.45). In Aristotle's view, there can
   be no friendship with a slave *qua* slave, though there may be *qua* human being
   (*EN* 1161b2–8).
81 Cf. Funke 36–8.
82 Cf. above, p. 44.

good that a city can have (*Rep.* 351d5, 462a–e; cf. also *Clit.* 409de). Aristotle even makes *homonoia* and *philia* prior to justice (*EN* 1155a22–8). 'People say that a city has *homonoia*,' he remarks, 'when the citizens agree about what is beneficial and choose the same things, and do the things that have been approved in common' (*EN* 1167a26–8). They agree, for example 'that offices shall be elective, or that an alliance shall be made with Sparta, or that Pittacus shall rule' (*EN* 1167a32). Thus even under a monarch (such as Pittacus),[83] the people must approve of the rulers and their practical decisions.[84] It is this same agreement, under the name of *sophrosune*, that sweetens Plato's absolute state (*Rep.* 431de).

Although Creon speaks of obeying 'whomever the city appoints', it is clear that his power has not been granted by the city but inherited, by the 'chance' of his nephews' death, through those very family ties for which he shows so little respect (155–7, 173f.; contrast *OT* 383f.). As he himself implies, a hereditary ruler must prove himself acceptable if he is to gain the approval of the *polis* (175–7). But throughout the play the evidence mounts that both his decree and his treatment of Antigone violate the sense of justice not only of Antigone herself (451f., 921, 928), but also of his own son (728, 743) and the rest of the citizens (cf. 693–5), including finally the noble chorus (1270).[85] According to Haemon, his father's decree is also impious (745) and disgraceful (747). Both he and the entire city deny that Antigone is *kakos* (731–3), while the city regards her deed as 'most glorious' (695) and worthy of 'golden honour' (699).

For Creon, however, even the citizens' expression of their opinions conflicts with their 'just' acquiescence to his rule (289–92). Their only outlet is rumour, whose 'dark and silent' character indicates the absence of communication between king and people (700). Creon shows no interest in his subjects' approval or contentment, and implicitly acknowledges their dissatisfaction through his constant fears of insurrection. He claims that loyalty to the *polis* is his cri-

---

[83] Pittacus, tyrant of Mytilene, was originally appointed with popular support. Aristotle calls this 'elective tyranny' (*Pol.* 1285a29–b1). In this chapter of the *Politics* the acceptance of the ruler by the subjects is a salient feature distinguishing other kinds of kingship from tyranny (cf. also Eur. *Hel.* 395f.).

[84] For Aristotle *homonoia* is essentially practical as well as political (*EN* 1167a28–32, *MM* 1212a14–16).

[85] On various views of justice in the play see Segal 168–70; id. *Praise* 47; Santirocco, *Justice*.

terion for *philia*, but sees all its citizens as potential enemies. He claims that the city's well-being is his criterion for action, but treats the *polis* as a personal possession (738) and ignores its opinions as outlined by Haemon. He is outraged at the notion of instruction from the *polis* that he purports to represent (734, 736) – an indignation that would certainly earn him a democrat's disapproval (cf. Eur. *Supp.* 406, 442). As Haemon retorts, he would make a good ruler of a desert, for if the *polis* belongs to one man then it is no *polis* (737, 739). The guard's nervousness, other hints that the citizens are afraid to voice their opinions (504–9, 690–2, 700), and the lukewarm choral support all suggest that despite his avowed concern for the *polis*, Creon is out of tune with its members. No wonder he needs Haemon as his spy amongst the people (688f.). This disharmony is confirmed both by Creon's own continual suspicions of rebellion, and by the tyrannical picture of his rule painted by others.[86] It seems that his policies have not brought *homonoia* in their train.

The most praiseworthy aspect of Creon's authoritarianism is his emphasis on *nomos*, 'law' or 'custom'.[87] He lays out at the start the *nomoi* by which he will rule (191), and accuses Antigone of *hubris* in violating the 'published laws' (481; cf. 449, 663). Both Ismene and the chorus are shocked at Antigone's violation of *nomos* (59, 381f.), and in the first stasimon the chorus link earthly *nomoi* with divine *dike* as factors that preserve a prosperous city (368f.).[88] Respect for *nomos* is prima facie laudable, for it is this which binds society together.[89] Such is the assumption that underlies Socrates' argument in Plato's *Crito*. But the broad semantic range of *nomos*, 'ranging from "law" as a political enactment to a custom or habit which may or may not have absolute validity, and from the rules of a game to that ordered society on which civilized existence rests' (Ostwald, *Pindar*

[86] Creon's tyrannical features have often been noted. See especially Funke; also Schmid 7–12; Bowra 72–8; Ehrenberg 57f.; Podlecki, *Creon*. He is defended by MacKay 169; Calder, *Antigone*.

[87] On *nomos* in general see Heinimann; Guthrie, *Sophists* ch. 4; Ostwald, *Nomos* 20–54, *Pindar* 120–31; Morrow 20–3. On *nomos* in the play see Kirkwood 239; Goheen 86–93; Segal 168–70.

[88] For interpretation of this passage see Ehrenberg 62f. His punctuation (also in most editors except Pearson) is clearly right. On ὑψίπολις (370) see Ehrenberg 64; Else 46; Knox 185 n. 47; Coleman 9 n. 1; and cf. Segal 168. For *nomos* and justice holding the city together cf. Anon, Iamb. DK 89.3.6.

[89] For pride in the rule of law cf. Demos. 25.15–17, 20–7 and see Guthrie, *Sophists* 74.

120), together with its notoriously relative character, meant that it could also be regarded with suspicion. If *nomos* is the 'master' who guarantees freedom (Herod. 7.135–6), it is also the 'king of all' whose rule may verge on tyranny (Pind. fr. 169 (Snell)). The demand for obedience loses much of its force when *nomoi* are promulgated at the whim of a ruler who will brook no criticism. As the chorus non-committally observe, Creon is free to use any *nomos* he pleases with regard to both the living and the dead (213f.).[90] His own view is that by *nomos* the city is his (738),[91] but this *nomos* is inherited monarchy, just the kind of established tradition that he is violating. If Antigone is 'a law unto herself' (821), so is he.[92] Accordingly, the other characters refer to the decree as his pronouncement, rather than the law of the land (8, 31f., 47, 59f., 382, 453f.).[93] If such a *nomos* conflicts with the sentiments of the *polis*, what claim does it have? The argument of Socrates' *nomoi* gains much of its force from the fact that any Athenian citizen could try to change the law democratically through persuasion, and if accused could defend himself before a jury.[94] Creon's *nomos* is not merely human as opposed to divine – it is one man's law. The 'laws of the gods' on which Antigone relies are not simply divine – they are the traditions sanctioned by the *polis*. They are, as Creon himself will eventually acknowledge, the established *nomoi* (1113).[95] There is no intrinsic conflict between divine and human law. An orator could eulogise *nomos* as 'an invention and gift of the gods, a decision of prudent mortals ... and an agreement of the *polis*' (Demos. 25.16). The clash in *Antigone* is not simply between divine and human law, but between *polis* and autocrat.

But it is also between autocrat and gods. Creon is convention-

---

[90] Note the emphatic placing of σοί, 'you' (211, 213).

[91] Vickers 529 notes his use of the first person singular for affairs of the *polis*. Cf. also the emphatic personal pronouns in his opening speech (Winnington-Ingram 123) and at 290, 292.

[92] On αὐτόνομος (821) see Else 60.

[93] The only contrary implication is in the phrase βίᾳ πολιτῶν (79, 907). (On the latter see further below, p. 147.) Others besides Creon call his decree *nomos* (59, 213, 382, 847), but both the laws of an autocrat (cf. Eur. *Supp.* 429–32) and an ad hoc decree (cf. Thuc. 3.37.3) may be referred to in this way.

[94] On persuasion in the *Crito* see Kraut 71–3.

[95] For the phrase cf. Ar. *Clouds* 1400, where the context brings out some of its implications.

ally pious (e.g. 162f.), and especially likes to invoke the name of
Zeus, king of gods as he is king of mortals (184, 304; cf. 756). Yet as
we have seen, he twice defies Zeus in a different capacity, as protector of the family.[96] He tries to rationalise this contradiction by portraying the gods in his own image. Just as Antigone adopts a novel
view of the dead which disguises the confusion in her values, so
Creon interprets the gods and their laws to suit his own narrow perspective. Perhaps, he sarcastically suggests, the gods wanted to
honour Polyneices exceedingly as a benefactor – him who came to
destroy their land and temples and scatter their *nomoi* (284–7; cf.
199–201). No, the burial is an irreverence, for the gods do not
honour the *kakoi* (288; cf. 301). He dismisses the pollution brought
by Polyneices' corpse, on the ground that mortals cannot pollute the
gods (1043f.).[97] But he undermines his own position when he
changes his mind about the method of Antigone's punishment. Instead of having her stoned to death, the published penalty (36), he
tries to avoid the pollution of killing by entombing her alive with a
little food (773–6, 889).[98] This cynical evasion is inconsistent with
his rationalised picture of the gods and undercuts his claim to divine
support.

Creon's gods, like Creon, treat burial as a reward for public
service. Like him they execute a retaliatory justice based on loyalty
to their city and laws. But in scorning those other divine *nomoi* to
which Antigone appeals, Creon is failing to perceive that the gods
resemble him more deeply. For like him they require unconditional
obedience to their laws, regardless of the rights or wrongs of the case
as he, their subject, sees it. When he invites Zeus' eagles to carry dead
human flesh up to the divine throne (1040f.), should we not recall
the words of the chorus in the parodos, 'Zeus utterly hates the boasts

---

[96] On conflicting notions of piety in the play, see Vernant, *Tensions* 34f.; Kirkwood 236–8; Segal, *Praise* 49–51; Bultmann 314–17.

[97] Cf. Eur. *Alc.* 22f., *Her.* 1232 (with Bond ad loc.) and see Parker 144–7.
Although it was popularly believed that mortals could pollute the gods, this
does not harm the gods, 'on the contrary, it is upon the offending mortal that
the pollution rebounds' (Parker 145f.). Criticism of this belief may have been
sophistic (see Nestle 138–40). On Creon and pollution cf. also Segal 174f.

[98] If Creon's reason is understood to be the fact of kinship, the conflict in his position is even stronger. As Kitto points out, there was no reason for Sophocles to
mention the form of punishment at 36 except to emphasise the change (*FMD*
166).

of a proud tongue' (128f.)?[99] The theme is reechoed both in the
story of Lycurgus (962) and in the final lines of the play (1349–53).
For it is Zeus, not Creon, who can use any *nomos* he wishes for both
the living and the dead – especially the dead. Creon's edict goes
beyond his jurisdiction, as Antigone implies in her famous speech
(450–5).[100] As Teiresias will confirm, he is interfering with the
divine order which declares that the dead belong to the underworld
and the living to the daylight (1068–73). Death is the limit to the
invention of 'resourceful man' (360–2). It is Zeus and the other gods
who remain untouched by time or death (606–10). And it is for
transgressing these limits, for violence against the gods and their laws
that Creon is crushed (1072f.; cf. 663). He must give up his son, 'a
corpse as payment in exchange for corpses' (1067; cf. 751), and suffer
'the same evils' as he inflicted (1076). As his punishment for reversing
the proper status of the dead and the living, by burying the living
and denying burial to the dead (1068–71), he will himself become a
'living corpse' (1167). Like him, the gods punish with the talio one
who violates their laws and so incurs their enmity. Teiresias warns of
divine avenging spirits, the 'Erinyes of the gods and Hades' (1075),
and Creon will himself acknowledge that a god has struck him
down (1272–5). But the gods do not intervene directly in the action.
Instead they allow Creon to fall victim to the rage and despair of
fellow mortals whose feelings and advice he has disregarded, and
who retaliate on the human level in the only way they can.[101]

Reason and passion

Creon's superficially rational principles and arguments in support of
the decree and his punishment of Antigone are undermined by a
passionate obsession with power.[102] His first speech, in which he
outlines his principles, sounds stiffly reasonable, but in the brief ensuing stichomythia he betrays a fear of revolt and suspicion of bribery

---

[99] With the surprising exception of Jebb, most critics agree that Creon's 'blas-
phemous defiance ... is unparalleled for its ferocity in all Greek tragedy' (Knox
109).

[100] See especially Bultmann; Rohdich 38f.

[101] On the element of revenge in Eurydice's suicide (cf. 1301–5), and perhaps also
Haemon's, see Delcourt 161–3; Seidensticker 121–3.

[102] Cf. Trousson 25f.; Ronnet 88f. It is sometimes said that he is moved by hatred
of Polyneices (e.g. by Funke 33; Linforth, *Antigone* 249; Ronnet 88), but there is
little evidence for this.

that turn out to be characteristic. When the chorus make a first attempt at advice, he reacts with passionate anger before going on to argue against their suggestion (279–81). He treats the guard brusquely, ignoring the reasonable objection that a messenger should not be blamed for the message (315–22).[103] When Antigone appeals to divine justice and law, he casts doubt on his own position by his failure to meet her arguments, warning instead (with heavy dramatic irony), that the most stubborn thoughts and spirits are most liable to be broken (473–8). He interprets her self-defence as mockery, declaring that if she wins this trial of wills she, not he, will turn out to be the man (482–5).[104]

The insubordination he abhors appears at its most extreme in a woman, whose status entails docile obedience. But he is not just a run of the mill misogynist. He reacts as though challenged in his status not only as a male, but as an adult, a father and a ruler. He shows not merely stubbornness but irrational wrath at every attempt to make him reconsider. With Haemon he responds angrily not just to the notion of learning, but to learning from a younger man (726f.).[105] When his son expresses concern for him, he answers by condemning him for arguing with his father (741f.). As for his subjects, he reacts equally defensively to the idea of learning from the humble guard (315–26), the noble chorus (278–81),[106] the *polis* as a whole (734f.) or the higher authority represented by Teiresias. In a revealing detail, he reacts to the prophet's advice by exclaiming '*all of you* are shooting at me like archers' (1033f.).

It is established at the outset that Teiresias, besides his religious credentials, is a reliable adviser who has previously helped Creon to govern successfully (992–5). He also has the authority of age, addressing the king as 'child' (1023).[107] As long as the chorus of

---

[103] Contrast Pentheus at Eur. *Ba.* 672f. (a character who has much in common with Creon). On Creon's exchange with the guard see Else 88f. and cf. Jens 298f.

[104] This is the first clear sign of a preoccupation with masculine status. Cf. 525, 578f., 678–80, 746, 756 and his reaction to Haemon's words at 741.

[105] Cf. *OC* 1116, 1181 and contrast Oedipus' reaction at 1204f.

[106] At 770f. he approves their words, but they were not offering advice. One consequence of delaying Ismene's reprieve until this point is that Creon need not be portrayed earlier as responding rationally to persuasion. Only at 1099 does he turn to the chorus for advice.

[107] Contrast the chorus, who defer to him as 'lord' (223, 278, 724, 1091, 1103), except at the pivotal moment of advice, when he is 'son of Menoeceus' (1098). Else 49 n. 38 notes that they never address him as 'king', but cf. 155.

elders are unwilling to speak out, Teiresias provides the only restraint on the king's untrammelled exercise of power. Creon's angry
reaction therefore reflects ironically on his claim that the disciplined
man will make both a good ruler and a good subject (668f.). He, the
authoritarian ruler, is himself undisciplined and heedless of authority, and would scarcely make a good subject by his own criteria. In
his rigidity and impatience he resembles Antigone, the embodiment
of disobedience. In his abuse of an old man he displays the lack of respect for age which he abhorred in Haemon (726f.; cf. 1087f.). After
warning the chorus not to be foolish at their age (281), his contempt
for the *polis* betrays a juvenile folly unworthy of his own years (735).
Only the most devastating suffering will teach him finally to learn
'good sense in old age' (1353).

Creon thus ultimately fails to honour his own principles, to put
the *polis* first and listen to the 'best plans'. All his decisions can be
rationally defended with general precepts, which may have value.
But his irrational anger and stubbornness (280, 718, 765, 1028, 1088),
and inability to tolerate rational criticism (757), prevent him from
adapting those principles to the particular circumstances and so lead
to disaster. That is why, despite the prima facie merit of his principles, he is fully responsible for the tragic outcome and accepts that
responsibility (1173, 1259f., 1268f., 1304f., 1312f., 1317–20). He
'killed' his wife and son 'against his will' (1340f.), but the blame is
his, for he rejected warning after warning. When he finally yields, it
is not to rational persuasion but to fear. The tyrant whose weapons
were threats and violence finally responds to the verbal violence of
the seer's angry 'arrows' (1085). To him these are even more terrible
than the humiliation of yielding (1096f.; cf. 1091). He is scared, not
persuaded, into compliance, while his passions still resist (997, 1097,
1105f., 1113).[108]

Antigone's decision to bury Polyneices may be seen as a
reasoned choice to keep faith with the gods and her *philoi*. Yet she
too is driven by passion.[109] Ismene attributes her decision to her 'hot
heart' (88),[110] and the chorus to her 'boldness' and 'self-willed pas-

---

[108] Cf. Agamemnon in *Aj.* who is truly persuaded but whose hatred persists
(above, p. 99).

[109] On reason and emotion in Antigone see especially Levy. Most critics see her as
acting from intense emotion or 'instinct', but see contra Waldock 138; Linforth, *Antigone* 250.

[110] Cf. also 20 (χαλχαίνουσα) with Jebb ad loc. and Goheen 139 n. 16.

sion' (853, 875; cf. 821).[111] After her first speech in self-defence the chorus comment that she has shown 'the savage spirit of her savage father' (471).[112] After her last speech they react similarly, in words that clearly recall their earlier description of the passionately violent Capaneus (929f.; cf. 136f.).[113]

This last choral response may offer a key to the notorious passage in the preceding speech, where Antigone argues that she would not have buried a husband or child in defiance of the citizens, but only a brother; for unlike a husband or child, a brother cannot be 'replaced' now that their parents are dead (904–15). Superficially, her argument here is drily logical – indeed, too logical for some tastes.[114] But on closer examination it appears quite illogical. In particular, it appears to conflict with the kind of reasons she has already given for her deed: the unwritten law; the *kerdos* of death for the wretched; fear of reprisals from the gods; desire to please the dead and share with them in *philia*. But Antigone has never expressed a commitment to the burial of all dead kin.[115] Nor does she specify that this is among the unwritten and immortal laws of the gods (451–7) – though in view of Greek feeling on the subject, the audience would no doubt assume this unless otherwise informed.[116] Her talk of pleasing the dead refers to those already dead, namely her parents and brothers. It is their loss that has made her life no longer worth living, so that death has become a *kerdos*. If these are all who are covered by the 'laws of the gods', there is no conflict with her final speech.[117] If so, her interpretation of divine law is highly idio-

[111] On 875 see Else 80.

[112] On ὠμός here see Linforth, *Antigone* 471 (though his conclusions are unconvincing).

[113] See Else 37 for the echo of Aesch. *Sept.*

[114] E.g. Gellie 47; Else 110. It is usually explained as an ill-fated attempt to rationalise a deed prompted by feeling (but see contra Reinhardt 83f.). Many now accept the passage as genuine, but there are still distinguished dissenters (e.g. Funke 41 n. 56; Müller 199f. and ad loc.; Else 64 and appendix B; Winnington-Ingram 145). For doxography see Hester, *Unphilosophical* appendix D. Blumenthal adds an interesting new argument for authenticity.

[115] Emphasised by Chamberlain 139f.

[116] Cf. Knox 97: νόμιμα are 'customary rites of burial'. But Antigone is less specific.

[117] Note especially how she moves from the laws of the gods to the burial of her own mother's son (466–8) (Chamberlain 140). We may recall that in a patrilineal society a woman's husband and child both belong to a different family from her parents and brothers (MacKay 171).

syncratic. Like Creon, she sees the gods in her own image. It is therefore not strictly contradictory, though it is most startling, if she now
restricts her other reasons for burial to brothers and (by implication)
parents, who are also irreplaceable. This criterion ingeniously
matches her previously expressed commitment to parents and
brothers, and accords with her apparent indifference to Haemon. As
Aristotle saw, such a set of priorities requires some justification to
carry credibility (*Rhet.* 1417a28–33). The precariousness of these
principles will be forcefully underlined after Antigone has died for
them, when Creon, despite his scorn for personal and familial ties, is
shattered precisely by the loss of those 'replaceable' relatives, a
spouse and child.

   Antigone's argument is most peculiar. Her distinction between
irreplaceable and other relatives for purposes of burial is highly
unorthodox, and the assumption that the gods condone her priorities
is even stranger. Moreover her apparent devotion to Polyneices is
undercut by the curiously generic character of a calculation which
implies, inter alia, that she would not bury him if their parents were
still alive.[118] But quite apart from all this, the argument is not properly applicable to the situation.[119] It makes some sense as a justification for saving a brother's life (as it is used in Herodotus),[120] but the
criterion of replaceability is undercut by the fact that Polyneices is
already dead. The argument becomes still more pointless in light of
the fact that Antigone is effectively committing suicide by burying
her brother. Once she is dead the replacement of a hypothetical husband or child will be equally impossible. Just as Creon's arguments
about loyalty, obedience and discipline are reasonable in themselves,
but collapse through his failure to consider all the relevant features of
the particular case, so Antigone's argument for the priority of
brothers is logically sound but not applicable to her circumstances.
Her counterfactual claim is safe, since she has ensured that she will
never have either husband or child of her own, but the spurious
rationality of the reasoning undermines her defence and reinforces
the impression of a deed prompted by passion.

   This passion is not just a violent love for a dead brother

---

[118] On this aspect of the argument see Rohdich 172–4.
[119] Cf. Kamerbeek 158; Schmid 28–31; Müller 198f.
[120] Herod. 3.119. For other parallels see Perrotta 120f.; Kakridis 152–64.

(though it is that). Nor is it merely the wrath of one whose will has been thwarted (though it is that too; cf. 32, 426–8). 'No one is so foolish as to be in love with death' declare the chorus (220), but they are evidently mistaken. Ismene accuses her sister of being in love with the impossible (90). Antigone does not deny it, answering, 'Then I shall stop when I run out of strength', and reacting with fierce hostility to the repeated suggestion that the impossible should not be pursued (91–4). She even sarcastically tells Ismene to announce her plan to all, otherwise she will be 'far more hateful' (to whom? Creon, or Antigone herself?) (86f.).[121] Yet she knows that the penalty is death (35f.), and makes no attempt to deny her deed or evade the penalty by pleading excuses (432–5, 443, 448). Instead she provokes Creon still further by a defiance that he interprets as mockery (482f.; cf. 495f.), then answers his tirade by asking why he does not kill her right away (497–9). Her present life, she declared in her opening speech, lacks nothing that is painful, dishonoured or disgraceful (4–6; cf. 857f.). She lives in such evils that death is a *kerdos* (463f.). Its pain means nothing to her, unlike the pain of leaving a brother unburied (465–8). She guards both responsibility and punishment for her deed almost jealously from her sister (538f., 542, 546f.). She has chosen death (555), and in spirit has already died, precisely in order to carry out the burial (559f.). Her deed was tantamount to suicide, and accordingly, once enclosed in the tomb, Antigone will kill herself rather than wait for starvation or possible rescue.[122]

Only on the way to her death does she bewail her fate. When the chorus suggest that she is 'paying' for her father's deeds (856), she responds by recalling the dreadful fate of her family, her 'most painful concern' (857). This was the theme of her opening words in the prologue (2–6), and it is this that has made her life no longer worth living (461–6). Yet it does not invalidate her grief that she must die prematurely, before knowing marriage or motherhood (867f., 876f., 917f.). A crucial function of Antigone's lament is to show an awareness of these ties she has sacrificed amongst the living, thus enhancing

[121] Note the mocking echo of Ismene's 'alas' (82, 86). In relation to the burial 86f. is utterly irrational since self-defeating. But Rohdich 41f. links it with Antigone's pursuit of glory.

[122] This does not mean the second burial is prompted by a suicidal desire for capture. For a sensible discussion of this issue see Bradshaw; for a more recent contribution see Scodel, *Doublets*.

her tragic stature.[123] But at the same time she reveals an insight into the disastrous consequences of marriage for the house of the Labdacids.[124] She laments both the fatal marriage of her parents, of which she is the doomed offspring (862–6), and that of her brother, which is the indirect cause of her own death (869–71). As heir to such a history Antigone can never know the joys of a normal marriage. But if she must die friendless (as far as she knows) and unwed, she will have friends in the underworld and be married to Hades. The 'bride of death' motif, which pervades the play, is a familiar means of arousing pathos for the fate of the virgin dead.[125] It is complicated here both by the eagerness with which Antigone approaches death in the earlier part of the play, and by her insight that this is the only 'wedding' available to a child of the Labdacids.

Antigone is exceptionally rich in the language of reason and intellect.[126] Antigone and Creon both impugn their opponents' wits (281, 469f., 561f., 754; cf. 927), claim good sense for themselves (179, 557, 904) and use rational arguments whose sincerity we have no reason to doubt.[127] But both are called foolish or mistaken by others (67f., 99, 383, 707–11, 753, 1015; cf. 49, 220, 683f., 743, 765); both violently reject rational warnings (324, 280f., 69f., 726f., 754, 1033f.); and both seem driven by passion to perform the deeds they rationally defend.[128] Antigone is aware of the unconventional nature of her claims to wisdom (95, 469f.), yet remains confident in it except for a brief moment of hesitation (927f.). But Creon will eventually acknowledge that he was wrong (1261–9).

With other characters, a gulf opens between the promptings of reason and passion. In the prologue, Ismene is a paradigm of conven-

---

[123] On the lament see especially Winnington-Ingram 138–44, also Else 58–64, 76–8. It is sometimes argued (e.g. by Perrotta 115–18) that it is inconsistent with the rest of her character. See contra e.g. Pohlenz 188, and for full doxography see Rohdich 11–17.

[124] Cf. Rohdich 158f.

[125] Cf. 654, 804f., 810–16, 832f., 891, 1205, 1240f. and see Kamerbeek on 801–5; Lattimore, *Themes* 193f.; Roussel 70–4. On marriage imagery see Goheen 37–41. For the close association between death and marriage see Lawson 545–60; Redfield, *Notes* 188–90; cf. also Keuls ch. 5.

[126] See especially Knapp; Goheen 75–100; Kirkwood 233–6; Nussbaum 436 n. 6.

[127] Pace those who call Creon a hypocrite (e.g. Trousson 26).

[128] For other similarities between them cf. Else 51; Santirocco 186.

tional prudence against which Antigone's folly and courage may be measured. She is shocked at her sister's boldness in defying Creon (44, 47) and afraid of the consequences (59f., 82). She urges prudence, recalling the dreadful fate which has dogged their family (49). Her repeated judgement of Antigone's proposal is to call it foolish and impossible (68, 79, 90, 99). The next we hear of her, she is 'raving, and not mistress of her wits' (492, trans. Jebb). For the passionate spirit (*thumos*), so Creon tells us, tends to betray those involved in some dark plot (493f.). Ismene the prudent has lost control of her wits as a result of *thumos*. And when she reappears, the chorus' description of her 'sister-loving tears' and distraught appearance will confirm his words (526–30). Prudence forgotten, she tries to share responsibility for the burial (536f.). She is not ashamed to join as a 'fellow sailor' in her sister's suffering (540f.). Death shared with Antigone now seems desirable, as she begs for the 'honour' of revering the dead by her own death (544f.). For life is no longer *philos* or even worth living without her sister (548, 566). Creon sourly comments that she now turns out to be 'senseless', just as Antigone has always been (561f.), to which Ismene replies that misfortune deprives people of their native wits (563f.). With this line, applicable to so many characters in the play (though not to Creon, who learns through suffering), she affirms that she still views her own and Antigone's actions as folly (cf. 558). Ismene the prudent has been moved to this folly by grief at the prospect of losing the sister she loves.

Haemon, when he first appears, is eminently tactful and reasonable. His opening words, with their emphasis on obedience and good judgement (635–8), seem to allay the fears of the chorus and Creon that he will arrive in a state of passionate grief (628–30, 633). In his long speech he seems to have heeded his father's warning not to lose his wits out of sexual passion (648f.). He begins and ends with praise for reason, tolerance and the wisdom of learning from others (683–7, 707–23). But when Creon rejects him, he warns that Antigone's death 'will destroy another' (751). Creon, characteristically, takes this as a rash threat against himself (752), perhaps with some justification (cf. 1232–4). But Haemon's final lines contain a transparent hint at suicide. The chorus comment on his exit 'swift with anger', adding uneasily that mental anguish is keenly felt at such an age (762–7). They will go on to attribute the quarrel to the power of erotic love, which has driven Haemon to this 'injustice' (791).[129]

The chorus' anxiety will be amply vindicated when we hear from the messenger of Haemon's passionate end. Silently glaring 'with savage eyes', he spits in his father's face and tries to kill him before turning the sword on himself, 'angry with himself',[130] and embracing Antigone with his last breath (1231–9). The dutiful son, who valued nothing more than his father's well-being (701), has become the violent agent of that father's downfall. Despite his claim to value Creon's good advice above any marriage (637f.), his loyalties to father and bride have proved as irreconcilable as the conflicting claims of family and *polis*.[131] His special tragedy is that unlike either Creon or Antigone he has a full understanding of the values of both. His concern for Creon and the *polis* are complemented by an appreciation of both personal and family love. As he tells Creon, he cares about him, Antigone, himself and the gods (948f.). Creon has placed him, like Antigone, in a dilemma to which the only solution is death. He has not, in Creon's crude image, had his spirit broken by the bit (477f.), but nor has he implemented his own sage advice to bend with the storm (710–17). In this he is as inconsistent as Creon, who fails to place the interests of the city above his personal impulses, or Antigone, whose claim to love extends only to the dead.

Haemon's arrival, attempt at persuasion and angry departure are paralleled by Teiresias.[132] He too starts out by winning Creon's approval (993f.). Like Haemon, he both begins and ends with warnings to take thought and learn from others (996, 1023–32). As with his son, Creon interprets the prophet's advice as a threat to his authority, and the ensuing stichomythia degenerates into abuse. This finally provokes Teiresias' dreadful prophecy. Even he can be provoked to passionate behaviour, calling his words 'arrows' shot in re-

---

[129] Von Fritz, *Liebe* argues that the chorus must be mistaken, if Haemon's arguments are not to be undermined. But it is an oversimplification to require one 'right' motive for Haemon's conduct (cf. Lloyd-Jones' review of von Fritz, *Gnomon* 34 (1962) 739f.; Winnington-Ingram 92–4).

[130] This phrase (1235) is usually taken to indicate remorse for attempted parricide (so e.g. Jebb; Gellie 51). But the motive could equally be anger at himself for failing to kill Creon (cf. Winnington-Ingram 94 n. 12; Seidensticker 122). Cf. also above, n. 101.

[131] On Haemon's dilemma see Rohdich 135f., 139.

[132] Cf. Reinhardt 85.

sponse to the pain and *thumos* stirred up by Creon (1084f.). The choral comment on his departure underlines the parallel with Haemon's stormy exit (1091; cf. 766).

Even Eurydice's brief appearance reflects this pattern. She reassures the messenger that she will listen as one 'not inexperienced in evils' (1191) – an implicit guarantee that she will not give way to excessive grief.[133] When she exits silently at the end of his tale, the messenger hopes she has departed to observe the proprieties by weeping indoors, 'for she is not inexperienced in judgement so as to err' (1250). The chorus observe that silence can itself be ominous (as Haemon's wordless frenzy has just illustrated), and the messenger leaves to see if her ominous silence conceals something suppressed in an 'impassioned heart' (1251–6). His expectation of sensible, rational behaviour was, of course, tragically misplaced.

Creon's reasoning gives way to reveal passionate underlying motives. Antigone's rational defence is called forth by challenges to the passionate undertaking she is set on from the start. Haemon, Ismene and Eurydice all turn from rational speech to passionate action that undermines that speech and is marked, in two cases, by silence (1232, 1245). As befits his authority, Teiresias' plea for reason is not undermined by his deeds but reinforced as he turns to angry prophecy, the blind seer's most effective form of action. Further commentary on all this may be found in the person of the guard, who represents the ordinary mortal with his everyday hopes and anxieties. In him we see neither a dichotomy between reason and emotion, nor the use of one to bolster the demands of the other. He reasons not under the influence of his pleasures and pains, but *about* them, performing the kind of hedonistic calculus analysed by Plato in the *Protagoras*. But he reasons rather more astutely than Plato's common man, who through an error in perspective allows small immediate pleasures to 'win' over larger more distant ones (*Prot.* 355d).

The guard performs two such calculations, and perhaps reports a third. When he first appears, he explains why he was so long on the road, because of 'pauses arising from reflection' (225).[134] For his soul kept addressing him: 'Wretch, why proceed to a place where you

---

133 Cf. Deianeira's more extended reassurance to Lichas at *Trach.* 436–69. She too will make a dramatic silent exit (813). On Eurydice's exit see Seale 105.
134 For the meaning of the Greek here see Long 85f.

will be punished?' (228). 'But if Creon finds out from someone else, you will certainly suffer pain' (230). Finally, the second consideration 'wins' (233). Only now, after he has done his best to determine which course will minimise the risk of punishment, does the comforting hope or conviction come into play that he can suffer nothing that is not his fate (253f.).[135] He eventually launches into his tale, which ends with an account of the guards' joint deliberations over what to do about the burial. The proposal to report it filled them with fear, but finally 'won' (274),[136] presumably after some such calculation of risks as that which prolonged the speaker's journey.

The guard performs another personal calculation after Antigone's arrest. He had sworn never to return (329, 390f., 394), but this prudent plan for the future has been overturned by the specially intense pleasure resulting from 'the joy that transcends hope' (392f.; cf. 330f.). Even his rationality is belied by the unforeseen eventuality that can make a mockery of prudent expectation and even oaths (330f., 388f., 394). The chance to deliver Antigone is a 'treasure trove' (397). Her confession was 'most sweet', because it brought him out of danger, though at the same time painful, since it meant involving a *philos* in such evils (436–9).[137] But, he candidly concludes, it is his nature to count everything else as less important than his own *soteria* (439f.).[138] We may infer that for this reason he has no hesitation in handing over Antigone, despite his pain on her behalf.

This guard, with his acknowledged hedonistic egoism outweighing the ties of *philia*, is a paradigm of amoral humanity.[139] As such he suggests that we are ultimately moved by whatever

[135] For this commonplace cf. *Il.* 6.487–9, 18.115–21; Theogn. 817; Callin. 1.8 (West); Bacchyl. 17.24–8; Eur. *Ba.* 515f. It does not justify apathy or rule out a vigorous choice of action. In the guard's case it is a consolation for a foreseeable risk estimated as the lesser of two evils. For a different account of the guard's deliberations see Nussbaum 53.

[136] This idiom is often used for political decisions. Cf. Rohdich 56–8, who sees the guards as a microcosm of human society.

[137] It is sometimes thought that he calls Antigone *philos* as a family slave, but there is no evidence of servile status (cf. Fitton Brown 19, though I find his conclusion unconvincing). Antigone may still, however, be called *philos* as a member of the royal house that he serves (cf. 1192). Is he perhaps one of the ordinary citizens (cf. 690) who, Haemon tells us, fear Creon and sympathise with Antigone?

[138] In this he contrasts strikingly with Antigone (see e.g. Seale 91). He has excited much opprobrium (colourfully expressed by Reinhardt 71).

[139] For parallels see Nestle 141–3.

brings us personal pleasure or pain, seeking our own pleasure or advantage like the birds of prey that feast on Polyneices' corpse (29f.).[140] This does not mean that the characters' rational arguments should be construed as insincere. But it is passion which sets the goals that reason defends. Antigone rejects both her sister and life itself for the pain they cause her (4–6, 465–8, 551, 857f.; cf. 64). Like the guard, she risks paying Creon's penalty from fear of a greater one, in her case to be inflicted by the gods.[141] She states her disagreement with Creon in terms of pleasure – she knows that they can never agree, since they take pleasure in different things (499–501).[142] But unlike the guard, and unlike Creon, Antigone's personal pleasure involves the well-being of others, her select group of *philoi*. Moreover she believes that her deed pleases the citizens as well as the dead (504f.). A similar involvement with the fate of others underlies the pleasures and pains of Ismene, who is willing to die for grief at the loss of a *philos*, and of Haemon and Eurydice, who do so. All three are moved by passionate despair at the fate of dearly loved *philoi*.

Creon too will finally experience this despair, but only as one consequence of his unwillingness to grant full personal value to close ties with others. He starts out with rational arguments directed towards the good of the state, but the emotions that drive him are ultimately self-serving and hostile to the common good. Despite his claim to revere Zeus, his 'reverence' is directed primarily towards his own prerogatives (304, 744; cf. 166). Like the guard he gives his own satisfaction priority over the interests of others, including those *philoi* who are entitled to his concern. Unlike the guard, however, Creon initially shows no overt interest in personal pleasure. He is moved to anger by pain when his authority is threatened (316, 573),[143] and apparently enjoys the conventional well-being of the tyrant who is free to do as he pleases (506f.; cf. 211–14).[144] But he belittles the pleasures of marriage and shows no appreciation of the joys of *philia*.

---

[140] Teiresias' birds will lose their lucidity when they feed on this flesh, symbolising the victory of disordered passions over the voice of reason, which has ceased to be comprehensible. On birds of prey as subversive of civilised values see Segal 157–9, 164f.

[141] Note the repeated idiom δίκην δοῦναι, 'pay the penalty' (228, 303, 459f.).

[142] On Antigone and pleasure see Goheen 76–82.

[143] Cf. also 292 which is ambiguous between 'endure my rule' and 'please me', depending on whether ἐμέ is subject or object (Funke 35 n. 32).

[144] Cf. e.g. Eur. *Hipp.* 1013–5; Pl. *Gorg.* 469c; and see Winnington-Ingram 126.

Only when his wife and son are dead does he realise that, as the messenger emphatically declares, life is not worth living for one who has 'betrayed' the pleasure of such personal ties (1165–7). 'Pile up great wealth in your house, if you wish; live in the style of a king; but if joy is absent, I would not give the shadow of smoke for these things compared with pleasure' (1168–71). Before this disaster Creon was 'flourishing in the noble procreation of children' (1164), a periphrasis embracing not only the child he has lost (his 'joy', 1275), but the wife he is about to lose (cf. 1300).[145] A reference to the loss of their other son, Megareus, is introduced to complete his desolation (1303). He too now longs passionately for death (1336), for he is reduced to 'no more than nothing' (1325), the 'living corpse' of the messenger's speech (1167). His utilitarian view of parenthood (641–7) has been answered by the death of a son, and his denial of pleasure in marriage (648f.) by that of a wife. He gives the lie both to Antigone's argument belittling such 'replaceable' relatives as a spouse and child, and to his own merely instrumental view of their value.

The chorus provide a deeper background against which to observe and interpret the interplay of human reason and passion.[146] In particular, they show how our passions may both lead us to wrongdoing or impiety and at the same time constitute the instrument of divine punishment. The parodos portrays the consequences of arrogance, hated by Zeus (128f.), and manic hostility (135–7), especially between those who should by nature be friends (144–6).[147] It becomes progressively clearer that Creon too has offended the gods, who, as the chorus tells us, send 'swift-footed harms' to cut down the 'bad-minded' (1103f.). They lead such people towards doom by confusing their sense of what is bad and good (*kakos* and *esthlos*) (622–5).[148] Creon thinks this is the effect of money, which 'alters

---

[145] On the significance of Creon's personal loss see Gellie 30, 43f.; Else 99; Seale 107; Nussbaum 62.

[146] Their lyrics have implications soaring well beyond their limited persona, and have been much discussed. For a general account see Burton ch. 3. Cf. also Goheen ch. 4; Müller ad loc.; Segal 197–206; Rohdich on the individual odes. Most valuable in the present context is Winnington-Ingram's ch. 5, which offers an outstanding interpretation of the last three odes, bringing out their emphasis on the irrational. Some further works on individual odes will be mentioned below.

[147] On the parodos see especially Else 35–40.

[148] Cf. Theogn. 405f. On this whole ode see Dawe, *Ate* 111–13; Lloyd-Jones 113–15; Else 11–18, 74–6; Easterling, *Antigone*; Winnington-Ingram 164–73.

worthwhile minds towards disgraceful deeds' (298f.) through the
hope of profit by which, he tells us, men are often destroyed (221f.).
But the chorus show a profounder understanding. Hope, they say,
benefits many of us, but it cheats many others with 'empty-minded
passions (*erotes*)' (615–17).[149] We do not understand our own ignorance until we unexpectedly burn a foot in the fire (618f.).[150] These
reflections on the delusive nature of hope echo both the guard's false
expectations (235, 330, 392) and the first stasimon's qualified optimism concerning human wisdom (366).[151] The theme will be picked
up again with the messenger's vain hope of Eurydice's prudence
(1246), and gives deeper implications to the hope in which Antigone
goes to her death (897).

The 'empty-minded passions' of the second stasimon (617) suggest that we are not so different after all from the 'empty-minded
birds' (342),[152] which are among the victims of rational human
ingenuity in the first stasimon. We humans may have our intellect,
but with its potential for both evil and good (*kakos* and *esthlos*) (367),
reason itself is a prey to powerful irrational forces. One such force is
the *eros* of passionate love, which drives us 'mad', as it does wild
beasts and even gods (781–90); it twists the wits of the just to injustice and stirs up family strife (791–4); it is unconquerable (781,
795–801), and like death, inescapable for mortals (787–9; cf. 361f.).
Thus passion as well as mortality sets limits to the power of human
reason. Unruly nature continues to resist 'ingenious man', in storms
of irrational human emotion (391, 528f.) as well as perturbations of
the natural world (417–21).[153] The chorus use the image of a violent
storm to describe the fate of a house doomed by the gods (584–92),
going on to attribute the fall of the Labdacids to 'the bloody dust of

---

[149] For the ambivalence of hope cf. Aesch. *PV* 250 with Griffith ad loc. For its
'emptiness' cf. *Aj.* 478, *El.* 1460. For its irrationality cf. especially Thuc. 3.45,
where it also goes hand in hand with *eros*.

[150] On the image see Musurillo, *Fire-walking* 172–5.

[151] On the ambivalence of the first stasimon, and the way its initial optimism is
qualified in the rest of the play, see Goheen 53–6; Linforth, *Antigone* 196–9;
Coleman 9f.; Müller ad loc. (with Knox's review, *WA* 169–71); Segal 152–70
and *Praise*.

[152] On the echo see Rohdich 64.

[153] Cf. also 163 and Creon's ship of state image (189–91) with its implications of
human control over nature. For a detailed discussion of storm and sailing
imagery see Goheen 44–50.

the nether gods, folly of reasoning and an Erinys of the mind' (601–3).[154]

In the mythological song after Antigone's last exit we hear yet again of the power of the gods (Danae), their punishment of impious human arrogance, passion and frenzy (Lycurgus), and the consequences of human savagery (Cleopatra and her children). The last ode is a hymn to Dionysus, who along with Aphrodite is the principal god of the irrational. He represents both the forces of untamed nature (1126–36, 1146f.) and a potentially benevolent version of the 'mad frenzy' that has been a recurrent theme of the play (1151; cf. 135, 765, 790, 961). He is also a child of Zeus (1116f., 1149) and the special protector of Thebes (1115–25), and as such the chorus pray to him for 'purification' of the city's 'sickness' (1140–5). We may recall that in the first stasimon one function of human ingenuity was to teach speech, thought and 'the mood and mind for law that rules the city' (355f., trans. Fagles). This suggestive phrase hints that passion should be not hostile but complementary to civic *nomos*.[155] But it is too late to channel the frenzy of irrational passion into the service of Thebes. The city's 'sickness' can only be healed through the most drastic form of 'purification', like the lightning that killed Dionysus' own mother, the Theban princess Semele (1139).

The desperate emotions of his son, his wife and Antigone all contribute to Creon's downfall. But ultimately, despite his alleged reliance on 'the best plans' (179), he is destroyed by his own failure in planning, that 'worst of all evils for a man' (1242). It is just because we are moved by passion that we need rational advice. But to profit from such counsel it is necessary to respect those *philoi* who are concerned for our well-being and with whom our interests are linked. Creon makes an error of judgement, but what prevents him from correcting it is his failure in *philia*. Antigone's judgement of the religious issue is, by contrast, clearly right, yet she too rejects the prudent advice of a loving friend to have 'sense' (49). But she remains true to her own conception of *philia* and is willing to take the con-

---

[154] 'Reasoning' is λόγος (603), which also means 'speech'. On this line see Else 74f.; Winnington-Ingram, *Sophoclea* 7f. Contra Pearson I retain κόνις in 602 (defended by Goheen 142f.; Booth, *Antigone*; Linforth, *Antigone* 212f.; Easterling, *Antigone* 147f.).

[155] The Greek ἀστυνόμους ὀργάς cannot be literally translated, but includes *nomos* alongside words for 'city' and 'passion'. Cf. also Rohdich 65f.

sequences, whereas Creon learns that his rationalisation of *philia* is false to the emotional ties whose force he acknowledges only once they have been destroyed forever. And although Antigone's *philia*, like Creon's, is limited – she seems able to love only the dead – the *kerdos* that she seeks rises above conventional self-interest to embrace personal loyalty even at great personal cost. But Creon's loftier principles are progressively belied.

With her last words Antigone denounces the injustice of her sufferings, and emphatically repeats the claim that her deed was one of reverence (942f.). She thus responds to disaster by reaffirming her original decision despite the consequences, which she foresaw clearly from the outset. Creon, however, loses his earlier preoccupation with *polis* and *nomos* after his confrontation with Haemon. He reacts to disaster by quite accurately condemning his own error (1261–9), and really does learn the inadequacy of his blinkered viewpoint. He acknowledges the power of Antigone's *nomos* (1113), and when the chorus finally speak out, remarking that he has seen justice at last, he cries, 'Alas, wretch that I am, I have learned' (1271f.). The final lines of the play, sung by the chorus, are immediately applicable to him: 'sense' is the most important part of true well-being and is taught by the terrible consequences of arrogant words (1347–53). The play ends with the word 'teach' (1353).

As we have seen, Creon and Antigone are alike in several ways, especially the inconsistency of their values and the way they are driven by passion below a surface of rational argument. Both are also one-sided in their commitments. The poet could have given the champion of the *polis* a much stronger case.[156] But he could also have let Antigone meet and conquer Creon on his own ground (for example by arguing that her two brothers were equally responsible for the war). The narrowness of both is revealed by their failure really to engage in argument. Creon's two main statements of principle actually occur in Antigone's absence. When they do confront each other, in the brief passage of stichomythia with which we

---

[156] This is the chief weakness of the Hegelian view that Antigone and Creon are both right and yet both wrong (for Hegel see Paolucci, especially 73f., 325, and Steiner 19–42; for the history of Hegelian influence see Funke 29–33). Significant interpretations in this tradition include Schadewaldt; Knox ch. 3 and 4; Rohdich; Nussbaum ch. 3. See contra Pohlenz 190f.; Perrotta 86–8; Vickers 526–46; Müller 10f.; and cf. the judicious remarks of Bowra 65f.

began, they argue at cross purposes, repeatedly missing each other's point.[157]

This does not mean, however, that they are equally limited in the values to which they adhere. Antigone is sometimes accused of being as narrowly one-sided as Creon in her allegiance to the family and disregard for the interests and *nomoi* of the *polis*: 'If one listened only to Antigone, one would not know that a war had taken place or that anything called "city" was ever in danger' (Nussbaum 63f.). Nor can it be denied that she ignores competing concepts of *nomos* and justice which have their claims,[158] no matter how shoddily Creon may represent them.[159] Creon's misapplication of his principles does not undermine their claim to consideration, and the rightness of Antigone's cause does not of itself justify the passionate narrowness with which she pursues it.[160] But although she does not acknowledge the authority of the *polis*, she never explicitly rejects it, as Creon does the family. Moreover she acts ultimately to the city's advantage. As Creon himself so ironically puts it, 'the man who is worthwhile in family matters will also turn out to be just in the *polis*' (661f.). It is Creon's own scorn not just for the family but for public opinion (734) which finally brings the *polis* 'doom instead of *soteria*' (185f.).[161] He who began by saving Thebes from its enemies (1162) ends by stirring up other cities with enmity (1080). He tells Antigone she is alone in her views, but she retorts that, on the contrary, all those present (namely the chorus of the city's elders) are on her side (504f., 508f.).[162] Moreover she foresees great glory from her deed

---

[157] For the 'different languages' that they speak see Reinhardt 77–9; Goheen 17; Knox 181 n. 57; and cf. Pohlenz 187.
[158] Cf. especially 368f., 853–5. On the ambiguities in 368f. see Else 44f. For interpretation of 853–5 see Perrotta 78 n. 2; Lloyd-Jones 115; Else 62, 77f.; Winnington-Ingram 141 n. 68. Lesky, *Zwei* 92–5 argues for 'fall suppliant' in 855. But the context suggests that what Antigone does at this crux is something bad, a deed of 'rashness' (θράσους, 853) to be explained as payment for some past deed of her father (ἐκτίνεις, 856). θράσος is not always reprehensible, but it seems inappropriate to an act of supplication (cf. 371).
[159] Cf. Schadewaldt 91–5; Gellie 34; Else 48. Although Antigone defeats Creon (at bitter cost to herself), 'the family' does not thereby defeat 'the city'.
[160] On this distinction see Nussbaum 436 n. 7.
[161] Cf. Perrotta 88; Pohlenz 193f.; Knox 112.
[162] Knox 88 plays down this passage, noting the lack of choral support. But Antigone suggests that they are silent out of fear (505). In any case, it is not safe to identify this chorus with the city as a whole (cf. above, n. 36). The important point is that Antigone at this stage *claims* general support from the Thebans.

(502–4), which the context suggests is to derive from none other than her fellow citizens.[163] Creon can make no such claims for himself. Indeed Haemon will hint that his father's behaviour may be destroying a glorious reputation (703f.).[164] With the loss of his son's loyalty, Creon also loses the last shreds of his claim to represent the *polis*.[165] But Antigone's words are vindicated when Haemon reports the admiration of the ordinary citizens (cf. 690), echoing her own evaluation of her deed (694–9; cf. 502–4).[166] Even the chorus, while withholding direct approval of Antigone's actions, promise her praise and glory for the manner of her death (817f.).

Antigone does once suggest that she is violating the will of the *polis* as represented by its citizens (907). But she does so only in the extremity of her isolation, lamenting that she is 'friendless' (876; cf. 881f., 919) and even questioning her divine support (922f.). She has cut herself off from her sister and quarrelled with the chorus, and has not, of course, heard Haemon's report of public sympathy for her fate. Under the circumstances it is not unreasonable that she should now believe she is defying the will of the citizens. But she claims that she would do so under the most extreme provocation, implying respect for the *polis* if not its present king.[167] She restricts her defiance to the drastic circumstances of the present crisis, acknowledging the potential conflict between her own priorities and the demands of civic life.

As Antigone goes to her death, she emphatically calls the city itself (843, 844–6, 937), its gods (938; cf. 839f.) and its most prominent citizens, the chorus (806, 843f., 940), to bear witness to her fate. Does this tell us that she has learned the limitations of her own narrow principles?[168] Or is it a reproach to the apathetic chorus?[169] Surely the latter. She shows no sign of regret or new-found insight into the civic value of obedience. But she addresses the chorus in ways suggesting their special responsibility not just as citizens, but as Theban aristocrats who might be expected to play a role in public

[163] For the connection of glory with recognition by the *polis* cf. Rohdich 36.
[164] Cf. Rohdich 128.
[165] Cf. Rohdich 135.
[166] For the echo cf. Else 55.
[167] Cf. Rohdich 171f. For a different view of 907 see Knox, *Polis* 16.
[168] Cf. Schadewaldt 99; Jens 307f.; Nussbaum 66.
[169] So Jebb on 940; Rohdich 185; Winnington-Ingram 141; Gardiner 91.

life.[170] She calls them 'citizens of the fatherland' (806), 'wealthy men of the *polis*' (843f.), 'leading men of Thebes' (940). When she refers to herself as 'the last remaining daughter of the royal house' (941),[171] she is reasserting her status as a member of the ruling family, to which the chorus are supposedly loyal (165–9), and to which Creon is tied only by marriage. This royal status is linked with her reverence for the gods (937–43), especially her ancestral gods (938; cf. 839f.). Her obligations to the *polis* and her dead family are not mutually exclusive. She has not failed the citizens, for the burial was both in their best interest and called for by their 'established laws' (cf. 1113). But they, intimidated by Creon, have abandoned her.[172] She therefore accuses the chorus of mockery and *hubris* (839–42),[173] the same hostile laughter that she inflicted on her sister (551) and (in his view) on Creon (482f.).

One-sided and 'autonomous' though she may be, Antigone's obsession is less sterile and destructive than Creon's. He, as he so much likes to remind us, is the sole ruler of the *polis*. In order to achieve a just and stable social order, such a ruler must acknowledge and balance competing claims and values. If these are ultimately incommensurable,[174] he must attempt a compromise, however uneasy. As Haemon eloquently insists, he must know how to bend with the storm (712–17).[175] He must respect the ties of natural *philia*, and at the same time promote political *philia* by adopting policies that meet the citizens' approval. Antigone abides heroically by the first variety of *philia* as she interprets it, and can make some claim to the second, but Creon is a failure at both.

---

[170] Teiresias emphasises the status of the chorus by addressing them along with Creon as 'lords of Thebes' (988). Creon calls them simply 'men' (162). On their new-found authority at the end of the play see Gardiner 94–7.

[171] On the text of 940f. see Else 67f. Antigone ignores Ismene, who has proved herself not to be *eugenes* (38).

[172] Note her plurals at 927f., 942 (cf. Gardiner 92). Does she interpret the chorus' meekness as complicity? Creon seems to (cf. 577).

[173] I take her complaint to be that the glory they foresee for her is based merely on the unusual *manner* of her death, whereas she aspires to recognition that her deed was *right* (cf. 502–5; so also von Fritz, *Liebe* 239; Burton 119).

[174] As argued by Nussbaum ch. 3.

[175] On the importance of this metaphor for the meaning of the play see Musurillo 59; Nussbaum 79f.

5

Electra

A mother and a daughter – what a terrible combination of feelings and confusion and destruction! ... The mother's injuries are to be handed down to the daughter, the mother's disappointments are to be paid for by the daughter, the mother's unhappiness is to be the daughter's unhappiness. It's as if the umbilical cord had never been cut. The daughter's misfortune is the mother's triumph, the daughter's grief is the mother's secret pleasure.

Ingmar Bergman, *Autumn Sonata*

Helping friends and harming enemies

Electra presents us with a world in which Help Friends/Harm Enemies remains unquestioned. In the prologue Orestes announces his intention 'to shine out like a star against my enemies' (66), and when he reappears, declares that he will stop his laughing enemies in their tracks (1295). Electra expresses similar sentiments (453–6, 979f.), and makes loyalty to friends a cardinal principle (345f., 367f., 395). Like Orestes, she assumes that their enemies are indulging in hostile mockery (277, 807, 1153).[1] Clytemnestra prays that if her dream is hostile it may recoil on her enemies, and that she may enjoy prosperity with her present friends (647, 652f.).[2] The chorus console Electra with the assurance that Orestes is 'noble (*esthlos*), so as to help his friends' (322), and their general approval of Electra's values is clear from their praise and sympathy. When they advise her to moderate her hatred, they are thinking of her welfare, and add that she should not forget it entirely (177f.). Neither they nor Chrysothemis, in their efforts to restrain her, maintain that she is wrong in principle. Clytemnestra does suggest that Electra should not treat her *philoi* as she does (518), but she casts no doubt on Help Friends/Harm Enemies – in fact her criticism of Electra depends on it.

---

[1] Cf. also 1299f. where Orestes foresees himself and Electra 'laughing freely' in their turn.

[2] The commonplace general terms of Help Friends/Harm Enemies make Clytemnestra's prayer seem less outrageous than if she mentioned either her friends or her enemies by name (cf. Eur. *El.* 805–8).

The justice of the talio is likewise accepted by all. No character modifies or softens in any way the harsh ethic of revenge. It receives its initial sanction from Apollo, who commanded Orestes to exact his just revenge by stealthy deception (*dolos* 37). *Dolos* will be paid for *dolos*, blood for blood.[3] Clytemnestra claims in turn that the killing of Agamemnon was just (528), since he had no right to kill Iphigeneia. Electra throws this principle of reciprocal murder back in her face as a threat (577–83), yet relies on it herself. At the very moment of revenge she denies her mother pity because she herself displayed none (1411f.). The chorus pray that the present roles of Electra and her enemies may be reversed, and present the killing of Clytemnestra as an enactment of the talio (1090–2, 1420f.). On the verbal level, Clytemnestra argues that rebuking Electra does not count as *hubris*, since it is a response to provocation, while Electra takes care to deny her this justification (523f., 552f.).

Reciprocation of benefits is less prominent. Electra's address to the chorus suggests a reciprocal basis for their friendship (134), and she reproaches Orestes for not showing the courage that she did in rescuing him (321): she saved him then (cf. 12f., 1133), and now he in turn is her only hope of *soteria* (cf. 924f.). If he is dead, her nurture will go unrequited (1143–5). Orestes does eventually 'repay' her, but positive reciprocation is not emphasised. The theme occurs most clearly not amongst humans, but in the choral ode in praise of the birds, which unlike human beings provide nurture for their parents and reciprocate other benefits (1058–62).[4] Although the chorus go on to apply their words to Electra, the principal effect is to throw into relief the dislocated human world in contrast to the natural, harmonious life of the birds.

Electra thus presents us with a deed of vengeance performed in a world where the legitimacy of such revenge passes unchallenged.

---

[3] *Dolos* and cognates: 124, 197, 279, 1392, 1396; φόνος ('murder', 'blood') and cognates: 14, 34, 96, 99, 116, 248, 263, 272, 447, 953, 955, 1422. 1476f. recalls the death of Agamemnon in Aesch. *Ag*; 1422f. echoes 96. On the similarity of the two murders cf. Minadeo 134–9. On the talio in this play cf. Segal, *Electra* 534–9.

[4] Winnington-Ingram 244 n. 89 attractively takes 1060–2 to refer to reciprocal obligations between parents and offspring (not just the duty of offspring to parents, as it is usually interpreted). The second clause ('from whom they find benefit') suggests an even broader reference, extending beyond the family to the general principle of reciprocation.

There is, however, a major complication, for the natural relationships of family *philia*, as represented by the birds, have been seriously
disrupted.[5] The murders of Iphigeneia and Agamemnon have
created two warring groups of *philoi*, cutting across the normal lines
of family solidarity. Clytemnestra evinces maternal feelings, generated by the sheer physical fact of motherhood, for both Iphigeneia
and Orestes (530–8, 766–71). Hatred for a child militates against this
natural sentiment, but because of the division of loyalties within the
family she is led first to desire her son's death and then to rejoice at it
in an unnatural way (783–7; cf. 804–7).[6] Through her own dis-
ruptive act she has thrust herself into a situation where family ties are
distorted, so that what benefits her in practical terms (*kerdos* and
soteria) is also 'terrible' and 'evil' (767f.). She is despondent about
Orestes' death as she is not about Agamemnon's (769; cf. 549f.).[7]
Though she regards both as enemies, the tie of blood prevails over
the tie of marriage as it did with her feelings for Iphigeneia. The conflict is painful (767), but she overcomes her maternal impulse, declaring that although Orestes received life from her he has abandoned
her maternal care, and performed no filial duty but threatened her
with revenge (775–9). By remaining loyal to his father, he has lost
his role as her son. Electra protests that Clytemnestra's words are
hubris and it is not 'well' (*kalôs*) for a mother to speak so of her dead
son (790). Clytemnestra replies, in her most callous line of the play,
'Not well for *you*. But he is well off as he is' (791). She uses *kalôs*, as
she used *esthlos* earlier (646), for whatever benefits herself. When
Electra prays to Nemesis for vengeance on Clytemnestra's un-
motherly behaviour, Clytemnestra replies that Nemesis has already
done her work (792f.) – no doubt by punishing Orestes for his un-
filial behaviour. After a further exchange of abuse, she departs with a
laugh (807), the antithesis of the emotion a mother should feel at
such a moment. This final reversal of her natural relation to her son
is highlighted by Electra's ensuing lament to 'dearest Orestes' (808).

[5] On the inversions of nature and *philia* in the play see Segal, *Electra* 485–505; cf.
also Vernant, *MP* 134–8.
[6] Clytemnestra wanted and even planned Orestes' death (see Gardiner 168). But
this does not mean her maternal feelings for him are to be construed as insincere
(see Reinhardt 261 n. 19; Whitman 273 n. 46). On the tragic impact of this
scene see Kells 7–9 (though he exaggerates the positive effect of Clytemnestra's
love for Orestes).
[7] ἀθυμεῖς (769); οὐκ εἰμὶ ... δύσθυμος (549f.). Contrast Eur. *El.* 1105f.

From Clytemnestra's perspective it was Agamemnon who first violated her own and her family's rights, by killing Iphigeneia and thus failing in his obligations as a father (546). But her own revenge has perpetuated this drastic violation of the family structure. By betraying her husband and treating him as an enemy she has forced her children to choose between their parents (126, 407, 433, 444). So while she occasionally speaks on the assumption that all family members are *philoi* (518), she usually shows an awareness that most of these presumptive *philoi* are now her *echthroi* (638, 647; cf. 803),[8] above all Electra, who claims that her mother calls her a 'godless thing of hatred' (289). This will lead to the total alienation of 'a house empty of *philoi* and full of murderers' (1404f.).

The problem of allegiances generated by the murder of Agamemnon is conveyed by a confusion of social and familial roles. As we saw, Clytemnestra finally denies Orestes the status of a son. Electra in return emphatically rejects Clytemnestra as a mother to both herself and Orestes: she has rejected her own offspring (589f.) and become 'a non-mother mother' (1154), deserving the name not of 'mother' (273f.) but of 'slave mistress' (597f.).[9] Electra's impassioned speech to the chorus is based on this perversion of family relationships and her resulting misery. Her first grievance is, 'my relationship with the mother who bore me has become *echthistos*' (261f.; cf. 814f.).[10] By emphasising Clytemnestra's biological motherhood Electra's form of expression underlines the unnatural state of affairs between mother and child, a reversal that encapsulates the total disruption of family *philia*.

This violation of the natural order leads to a whole series of role reversals. The breakdown of kinship-*philia* is expressed through the metaphorical use of family terms for *philoi* outside the family. Clytemnestra may have lost the role of mother, but the chorus have adopted it.[11] In the parodos they liken themselves not just to a mother, but to a 'faithful' one (234). Electra greets them warmly (134), and continues to address them with affection as *philoi* (226, 307, 1398). She also calls them 'offspring of noble (*gennaios*) family'

---

[8] This gulf between presumptive and actual *philia* is exploited for ironic effect (cf. 667, 671f., 1451).

[9] Cf. Bowra 231–5; Gardiner 167–70.

[10] On the primacy of Electra's hatred for her mother see Kirkwood, *Electra* 91.

[11] On the relationship between Electra and the chorus see Gardiner 142–5, 160f.

(128), in contrast to Clytemnestra whom she bitterly calls 'gennaios in word' (287).[12] Electra herself took on the role of mother and nurse, provider of nurture and *philia*, to the young Orestes (1143–7).

The role of husband and father has been usurped by Aegisthus. Electra dwells on this substitution at length and in painful detail: Aegisthus sits on her father's throne, wears his clothes, pours libations on the very hearth where he killed him, and, worst of all, sleeps with his wife (266–74).[13] Appropriately enough, in Clytemnestra's fateful dream Agamemnon appears bearing his sceptre which Aegisthus has usurped (420f.)[14] Electra emphatically rejects this usurpation, and identifies herself with her father when she declares that she has been betrayed and murdered with him (205–8). She identifies even more strongly with her 'dead' brother (808, 1162–9), whom in turn she links closely with Agamemnon (1316f.).[15] Most explicitly, however, she addresses her brother's mentor, the paedagogus, ecstatically as 'father' (1361). We see him fulfilling this function of father-substitute in the prologue: he was the purveyor of *soteria* and nurture to the young Orestes, whom he has raised for vengeance, and now he prompts discussion of a plan (13–16). Orestes addresses him as *philtatos* and *esthlos* (23f.), defers to his judgement (29–31), and praises him through the slightly odd metaphor of the noble or well-bred (*eugenes*) horse: he has never lost heart, but always urged them on (25–8). We shall soon see him in this advisory role (82–5; cf. 1364–71).[16] Electra thus identifies all her male *philoi* with her father, and herself with both father and brother. Despite her friendship with the chorus, she has in general nothing but scorn for the female *phusis* (1240–2; cf. 302, 997).[17] But her attitude towards her sister is

[12] Most editors take 287 as a sarcastic reference to Clytemnestra's own words, though it might also mean 'called noble because of her birth' (cf. *Aj.* 1095 and Kaibel ad loc.).

[13] On Electra's preoccupation with the adultery, and the theme of sexuality, see Jones 149–53; Segal 261.

[14] Letters 249 reminds us of the special significance of Agamemnon's sceptre at *Il.* 2.100–8.

[15] This effect is enhanced by Orestes' 'death' (e.g. 1417–21, 1477f.). On the confusion of living and dead see Scodel 80–3.

[16] Lines 82–5 are perfectly appropriate to the Paedagogus, but Sandbach's proposal to give him 78–81 and 82–5 to Orestes is still tempting. If he is right, the scene would foreshadow Orestes' rather than the servant's subsequent coldness towards Electra, and confirm his practical, rational concern with 'victory' (below, p. 174).

[17] See Woodard (1) 168; Winnington-Ingram, *Women* 242–4.

ambivalent. For the most part Chrysothemis falls in Clytemnestra's camp (341f., 365–7, 1033). When Electra is trying to enlist her sister's help, however, she addresses her as *philos* (431, 986).[18]

The dislocation of the household is also expressed through the inversion of social roles. Orestes, exiled from his mother's affections, is also a literal exile (775–7).[19] When Electra believes he is dead, she laments at length his death and burial amongst strangers (865–70, 1131–42). Chrysothemis lives in material comfort, but she too is deprived of the rights belonging to her position (359–64, 959–62). Electra herself lives as an alien or a slave, in subjection to her father's murderers (189, 264f., 597, 814–16, 1192).[20] Her material circumstances, poor food and meagre clothing, are inappropriate to a king's daughter (189–92; cf. 959f.). She is also, as she frequently complains, prevented from fulfilling the female social and biological roles of wife and mother (164f., 187f.; cf. 961f., 1183).[21] Her total alienation from her mother and the whole household finds physical expression when she is left outside to cry (802f.), and declares her intention to take no further part in the household, but to remain outside the gate until she dies there, friendless (817–19; cf. 948f.).[22]

The language of rule and subjection suggests a political sphere extending beyond the household.[23] Political disruption is implicit in Aegisthus' adoption of Agamemnon's regalia (267f., 420f.; cf. 651), and the paedagogus ironically refers to both him and Clytemnestra with the ambivalent word *turannos* (661, 664).[24] Aegisthus himself, in his speech over the corpse, betrays the tyrannical character of his

---

[18] Cf. Segal, *Electra* 502f.

[19] For the political language of 776 see Segal, *Electra* 498.

[20] On the imagery of enslavement see Musurillo 95–7. The theme is complemented by that of freedom. Electra is physically constrained, but her tongue is free (312f., 517f., 911f.). Chrysothemis, by contrast, buys physical freedom at the expense of freedom of speech (339f.). Electra scorns this freedom (cf. 387), maintaining that real freedom can be achieved only by killing Aegisthus (970f.). Orestes' arrival brings a new freedom of speech (1256, 1300), and the chorus declare at the end that at last the house of Atreus is free (1509).

[21] In antiquity her name was taken to mean 'unbedded' (see Segal 464 n. 41; Kamerbeek 2).

[22] This physical symbol of her alienation gives added point to the repeated references to Electra's defiant presence outside the house (312f., 328–31, 516–8, 1052) Cf. Steidle 92f. She will re-enter, but only after the removal of the conditions that required her exclusion (1383).

[23] Cf. Whitman 157.

[24] Cf. Sheppard (1) 86.

rule, especially in the harsh phrase that any dissident should now accept his 'bit' (1458–63).[25] He is emphasised not only as the adulterous lover but as the usurping ruler. This political dimension is enhanced by the use of free citizens for the chorus, rather than the slave women of Aeschylus' *Choephori*.[26]

It is only Electra who, by denying Clytemnestra the name of mother and rejecting Aegisthus as substitute father and ruler, deprives the new social, political and familial order of the appearance of legitimacy. But this alienation from her mother is counterbalanced by loyalty to her father. She alone fulfils the natural duty of lamenting his death (100f.), and so maintains, in this relationship at least, the proper unity of kinship and *philia*. She alone resembles the birds of the choral song (1058–62), though the situation precludes the fully bird-like behaviour of honouring both parents alike.[27] The chorus liken her to that tragic bird, the nightingale (1077), an image she has already used twice of herself (107, 147–9; cf. 241–3).[28] Their language also suggests a natural order with which she is in harmony (1081, 1095f.).[29] This devotion to her father extends also to her living *philoi*. She and her supporters are united by a bond of *philia* brought out by the repeated use of *phil*-words, frequently in the superlative and used mostly by Electra.[30]

Her devotion to Agamemnon is implicitly justified on independent grounds. Besides being 'the dearest of all mortals' (462f.), she calls him 'most excellent of all fathers' (365f.). The chorus support her by applying various terms of approval to her and her *philoi*. Orestes is *esthlos* (322); the death of Aegisthus is 'a confrontation with justice' (1441); Chrysothemis will show *sophrosune* if she does as Electra asks (465). Above all they sing Electra's own praises for risking her life in the cause of vengeance: she is the 'noble child of a

---

[25] Cf. *Ant.* 477 and further parallels in Whitman 272 n. 31 and 32.

[26] See Jebb, *Introduction* §15 and cf. Gardiner 162f.

[27] It also obliges her to express her devotion to her father in a perverted form (Segal, *Electra* 488; cf. also Seaford).

[28] On the ambivalence of τεκνολέτειρα (107) see Jebb ad loc.; Segal, *Electra* 495. For the sinister connotations of bird imagery see Beare; Sheppard (1) 82f.; Segal, *Electra* 492f.

[29] βλάστοι (1081), ἔβλαστε (1095f.); cf. ἔφυ (236), ἔβλαστε (238). 1095f. recalls *Ant.* 454f. *OT* 865–71.

[30] She uses *philtat*- 15 times, as against five other occurrences in the play which are all used by her *philoi* of each other (15, 23, 871, 903, 1224).

noble father' (1081);[31] she has proved her excellence by refusing to
live 'badly' and disgrace renown (1082–6); she has chosen what is
kalos,[32] and is a 'wise and most excellent child' (1087–9),[33] she has
supported the 'greatest laws' by her 'reverence' (1095–7).

These are very much the terms of approval that Electra claims
for herself: a *eugenes* woman cannot fail to act as she does (257f.); it
cannot be *kalos* to neglect the dead (237); she is following the path of
'sense' (403; cf. 145f., 1023, 1047, 1350).[34] Her values emerge most
clearly from her attempt to persuade Chrysothemis to join her in
killing Aegisthus. She laments both the deprivation of their ancestral
wealth, and their unmarried condition (959–62; cf. 522), and argues
that if they succeed they will receive reverence from the dead,[35]
regain the freedom that is their birthright and attain a worthy marriage (967–72). Moreover they will win praise, *philia*, reverence,
honour and renown from the general public, both citizens and
strangers, for courageously risking their lives in pursuit of vengeance
on their enemies and salvation for their house (973–85).[36] Expecting
everyone to judge, as she does, by the standard of what is *chrestos*
(972), she foresees a burgeoning of *philia* (981). Conversely, she desires no honour from those she considers despicable (239; cf. 364,
605–7). There is no explicit mention of justice here (the rewards of
virtue are well to the fore, as befits the persuasive function of the
speech), but the propriety of both the talio and Help Friends/Harm
Enemies is implicit (978–80), and underlies the whole speech. The

---

[31] εὔπατρις (see Jebb and Kamerbeek ad loc.).

[32] On the text of 1087f. see Jebb's appendix; Burton 213; Kamerbeek ad loc.;
Lloyd-Jones, *Sophoclea* 95. Whatever solution is adopted, τὸ μὴ καλόν seems too
important thematically to be abandoned.

[33] The chorus previously questioned Electra's wisdom (1015f.), but it was primarily her prudence that was in doubt. They have now become convinced that she
is φρονιμώτατος (1058), and applaud her lack of prudential 'forethought' as
courage (1078f.). On their increasing solidarity with Electra see Gardiner 161.

[34] At the same time Electra acknowledges a failure in conventional prudence
(345f., 1027). The nature of prudence is an important theme of the play,
especially prominent in the second scene between the sisters.

[35] No doubts are expressed this time as to whether the dead appreciate favours
(contrast 355f.).

[36] While Electra spurns material honours at the price Chrysothemis pays for them
(239, 364), she is still highly sensitive to dishonour (240–3, 356, 444, 1035,
1214). She also insists that her situation is an 'outrage' (102, 191), a strong word
echoed by the chorus (216, 486, 511, 515; cf. also above, p. 65 n. 25). On the
importance of honour and glory for Electra cf. Segal, *Electra* 510.

complex motivation of duty to the dead, honour, principle and self-interest is summarised in her conclusion: join me in labouring for your father and brother, and save both of us from misfortune, knowing that it is disgraceful for the well born to live disgracefully (986–9).

Electra and Chrysothemis

The chorus introduce Electra's sister in a way that reminds us of their shared *phusis*, their 'nature' or biological inheritance: 'your sister, of the same father by nature, Chrysothemis, and the same mother' (325f.). Their elaborate word order pinpoints the issue of the divided family, raising the question of which parent will retain this daughter's loyalty.

Chrysothemis' opening speech involves a certain amount of ethical confusion. First she offers an argument for failing to put her avowed pain (333) into action by 'doing something' (336), even when that action is merely the public expression of disapproval.[37] Such words remain words, she argues, and will accomplish nothing. There is therefore no point in inconveniencing oneself by airing them publicly. This argument would be effective against, for example, a solitary Philoctetes, who achieves nothing beyond self-satisfaction by abusing the enemies who abandoned him. But Chrysothemis' claim that she lacks the 'strength' (333) for action overlooks the fact that Electra's abuse *is* an effective form of action. She has already suggested that her vocal protests are a source of intense displeasure to her mother and Aegisthus (282–302), and will shortly claim to be avenging and honouring her father by bringing pain to her enemies (349, 355f.). This claim is vindicated when Clytemnestra complains of the distress Electra has caused her (784–7; cf. 556f., 654, 379–82). She is doing all she can to fulfil her own prayer for vengeance (209–12), and to thwart Clytemnestra's for a happy relationship with her remaining *philoi* (652–4). Accordingly she isolates the flaw in Chrysothemis' argument: it is useless to claim that if she had the strength she would prove her hatred in action, when she will not even give Electra any encouragement, let alone help her, in doing what she can to avenge their father (347–50). Chrysothemis hates merely in word, while cooperating with the

---

[37] For an extensive discussion of word and deed in the play see Woodard (1) 174–99.

murderers in deed (357f.). Electra brands her sister's fault as cowardice (351) – the lack not of physical, but of moral strength.

Chrysothemis undercuts her own confused argument by conceding that justice is on Electra's side (338f.). She explains that she
'must' obey those in power 'in all things' in order to remain free
(339f.; cf. 219f., 396).[38] Her 'freedom' is thus no better than the servitude of Creon's subjects in *Antigone* (cf. *Ant.* 666f.). Electra affirms
the justice of her own cause (245–50) and acts accordingly. But
Chrysothemis fails not only to act on her alleged distress but to do
what she admits is just. She produces no argument to explain this
lapse beyond the 'necessity' of physical convenience (339f.).[39] That
this is her only motive is confirmed later, when Electra asks scornfully if she must follow '*your* justice' (1037). Chrysothemis implies
an affirmative answer (1038), but Electra's use of 'just' has forced on
her a moral weight to which she does not herself lay claim. She soon
backs down, admitting once more that *dike* is on Electra's side, but
rejecting it because it 'sometimes brings harm' (1041f.). Her apolo-
getic tone in the earlier passage suggests a recognition that justice
should outweigh personal comfort.[40] This will shortly be confirmed. When Electra convinces her to thwart Clytemnestra's
funeral offerings to her husband, Chrysothemis responds, 'I shall do
it; for justice allows no argument, but demands immediate action'
(466f.). With these words she acknowledges that she has been failing
to live up to her own moral standards. It is here that her lack of
strength really lies.

Electra presents their disagreement in terms of the irreconcilable claims of their two parents: siding with the mother is a betrayal
of the nature Chrysothemis has inherited from her father (341f.). She
presses her sister to make a choice, 'either to lack good sense or to
keep your sense and forget your *philoi*' (345f.). Only Agamemnon
counts as a *philos*. No compromise is possible. Chrysothemis' pru-

---

[38] Cf. Ismene's arguments (*Ant.* 63–7, 78f.). But Ismene is much more sympathetic than Chrysothemis. She does not call her own behaviour unjust, or give
personal comfort as a motive. She shows a warm affection for her sister (82,
84f., 99), acknowledges immediately the need for forgiveness from the dead
(65f.; cf. *El.* 400), and finally judges life not worth living without her sister
(548).

[39] For the use of impersonal expressions of necessity to support a dubious moral
standpoint cf. below, p. 188, n. 16.

[40] Note καίτοι, 'and yet' (338), on which see Denniston 556.

dence contradicts Electra's own paradoxical claims to 'sense'. She is also endowed with *sophrosune* in the conventional sense of restraint and decorum – a sense in which her sister manifestly lacks it. Electra earlier acknowledged her own deficiency in this virtue, but now paradoxically redefines it and reclaims it for herself (307, 365).[41] Their conceptions of advantage are equally opposed. Electra provocatively asks what *kerdos* she could gain by following Chrysothemis' advice (352f.). The conventional answer is obvious, but Electra uses the term in order to reject its conventional associations in favour of her own form of self-gratification.[42] She needs no *kerdos* beyond mere existence, provided she can continue to torment her enemies and thereby give honour and gratification, if possible, to her dead father (352–6). She is not blind to conventional comforts, as her appeal to Ismene shows (959–89), but she ranks them below the fulfilment of Help Friends/Harm Enemies, declaring that she would never sacrifice her values for the sake of Chrysothemis' luxury (359–64). She prefers physical to moral pain: 'Let my only food be not to pain myself' (363f.; cf. *Ant.* 466–8). For this her sister's variety of honour is contemptuously sacrificed (364).[43] She sums up by invoking once more the unbridgeable gulf that divides their family, adding an explicit appeal to reputation: Chrysothemis must be called 'mother's child', rather than 'child of the best of fathers', 'for thus you will appear manifestly *kakos* to most people, for betraying your dead father and your *philoi*' (365–8).[44] Electra ends as she began, with loyalty to their father, the only legitimate *philos*.

Chrysothemis' warning of the 'greatest evil' which is approaching (374) constitutes a direct challenge to Electra's claim that mere existence suffices for her (354). She answers that if there is anything worse than her present state, she will give up her protests (376f.), but her notion of 'worse' evidently rules out any kind of physical privation. On hearing of Clytemnestra's dream, however, she addresses Chrysothemis for the first time as *philos* (431), urging

[41] For the flexibility of *sophrosune* as a term of approval see North and cf. MacIntyre 127f. On Electra's 'private interpretation' of the virtue see North 65.

[42] The chorus will vainly attempt a compromise (369–71, 1015f.). On *kerdos* in 1486 see Segal, *Electra* 522. Cf. also Antigone's *kerdos* (above, p. 110).

[43] For the scornful use of the possessive cf. 359f., 1037, *Phil.* 1251. For the sentiment cf. *Il.* 9.607f.

[44] According to Jebb ad loc. 'mother's child' implies cowardice, at least when used of a boy. Electra judges her sister by masculine standards.

her not to fulfil their mother's instructions. She claims that it is
neither 'permitted' nor 'holy' to take gifts to their father from a wife
who has become his enemy (432f., 440, 444), and reinforces her
argument with further unpleasant details of Agamemnon's murder
(444–6). The chorus echo her form of address (465), and Chrysothemis reciprocates by calling them too 'friends' (469).[45] The chorus
also agree that Electra's suggestion shows piety and *sophrosune*
(464f.). They have apparently become convinced of the value of her
brand of *sophrosune*. But in this instance it is perhaps not incompatible with the conventional *sophrosune* of decorum. Here is a deed that
needs no physical strength, that can be performed with discretion
and without great personal risk (though the possibility of painful reprisals is not ruled out; cf. 470f.). Chrysothemis can act in relative
safety as justice demands. The weakness of her moral position has
laid her open to persuasion, which will sharpen our interest when she
reappears.

After Electra succeeds in convincing her that Orestes is dead,
Chrysothemis is initially willing to cooperate: she will do anything
that brings benefit, and 'join in enduring' as far as she has strength
(944, 946). But when she hears Electra's scheme, she castigates her for
her foolishness and failure to acknowledge her female *phusis* and lack
of physical strength (997f., 1014). The latter argument has rather
more force than in their first dispute, if Electra's proposal is as suicidal as her sister claims (100f.). Previously Chrysothemis was refusing
to participate in a form of vengeance well within her power. But
must justice be pursued however slight the chance of success?
Chrysothemis' objection is strengthened by the fact that Electra suggests killing Aegisthus, with no mention of Clytemnestra. This gives
Chrysothemis her argument from female weakness. At the same
time it deprives her of a potentially powerful appeal to the impiety
of matricide. The emphasis on Aegisthus thus creates a starker contrast between Electra's foolhardy pursuit of justice and Chrysothemis' sensible though cowardly rejection of the impossible.[46] But

---

[45] Gardiner 147 suggests that this produces the effect of a 'united conspiracy of
women'.

[46] Cf. Alexanderson, *Electra* 88f.; Gellie 119. The omission of Clytemnestra from
Electra's plan has been much discussed, often fancifully (see e.g. Kirkwood,
Electra 88–90; Linforth, *Electra* 103f.; Woodard (1) 204 n. 74). If an argument
from character is needed, we need only consider the likelihood of convincing a
Chrysothemis to commit matricide (cf. Waldock 185). It will later become

pragmatic objections are irrelevant to Electra's aims, for she is not motivated solely by the prospect of successfully enforcing justice. Although she paints a picture of glorious success, she also regards it as honourable to die in the attempt (989, 1320f.).

When Chrysothemis refuses to help, Electra again tries to force the issue into a strict division of loyalties, sneering 'go and tell your mother' (1033). But Chrysothemis, who in a more cheerful moment called her sister *philos* (916), still refuses to adopt the role of enemy which Electra thrusts upon her, answering 'I do not hate you with such great hatred' (1034; cf. *Ant.* 84–7). Like the chorus, with their prudent concern for Electra's well-being (cf. 990, 370f., 1015f.), Chrysothemis acts not to dishonour her sister but out of 'forethought' for her (1036). Yet this very concern underscores their total disagreement. They may share both friends and enemies and a single conception of justice, but they differ radically on a wide range of other values.[47] They diverge not just over intellectual and prudential terms, but over the proper treatment of friends (395f., 400f.), over honour and dishonour (364, 983, 1035f.), renown (973, 985, 1005f.), and what counts as *kakos* (395, 430) and *kalos* (384, 393f., 398f.). In every case Chrysothemis' first priority is prudence (1036, 394, 1005f.), which even leads her to violate her own conception of justice. Each sister rejects the other's whole outlook – her *nomoi* or her 'ways' (1043, 1051). Electra uses the language of physical separation to emphasise the unbridgeable gulf between them, declaring with an emphatic future denial, 'Go inside. I will never follow you' (1052). Chrysothemis belongs in the household of Clytemnestra, which Electra has declared she will never rejoin (817–19).

Electra and Clytemnestra

The fact that Clytemnestra claims to have right on her side makes her a far more formidable opponent than Chrysothemis. She uses the

clear that Electra herself has no such scruples (cf. Sheppard (3) 164; Bowra 218; Kirkwood, *Electra* 91; contra Letters 259f.). The significance of Clytemnestra's death is downplayed e.g. by Owen 51. Such critics seem excessively influenced by the fact that Aegisthus is more prominent than in Aesch. *Cho.* But in Sophocles' play he is still insignificant compared to Clytemnestra. Electra's fundamental hatred is for her mother, while Aegisthus is hated as her mother's lover and her father's replacement. The confrontation with her mother is central to the play, and the fact that Aegisthus dies last does not alter this (see below, n. 121).

[47] Cf. Kirkwood 137f., 240f.

talio to deny Electra's charges of both *hubris* and injustice (521f.). On the level of words, she denies that her insults are *hubris* since she is simply responding to similar abuse which she herself receives (521–4).[48] On the level of deeds, she claims that she killed Agamemnon as a just penalty for his killing of Iphigeneia (528, 538).[49] It is Electra who lacks 'just judgement' (551), and who should 'pay a just penalty' for saving the hostile Orestes (298).

But while Clytemnestra claims that her actions are justified, they are condemned by Electra and the chorus as unjust (113, 521, 561), 'unlawful' (494), *hubris* (271), a 'most disgraceful outrage' (487; cf. 559), 'evil villainy' (1387; cf. 126) and an affront to both *aidos* and reverence (249f.; cf. 124, 1383). If they are right, then Clytemnestra's particular application of Help Friends/Harm Enemies, based on her own quite reasonable evaluation of who her friends and enemies are, must inevitably violate a whole series of moral norms. But if she is right, then their pursuit of the code is equally reprehensible. Both sides cannot simultaneously pursue Help Friends/Harm Enemies and at the same time adhere to other independent moral standards approved by all. This irreconcilable conflict brings into focus the risk of relativism inherent in the code, in so far as it involves evaluating others by their relationship to oneself (loyalty or hostility) rather than some independent assessment of their actions or character.

One way to dignify personal applications of Help Friends/Harm Enemies with the appearance of impartiality is to claim, as Clytemnestra does, the support of an impersonal justice: '*Dike* overcame him, not I alone' (528). The personification suggests for her deed an absolute validity transcending her partial perspective.[50] But this *dike* is itself based on personal friendship and enmity. It is just because one of Clytemnestra's *philoi* (Iphigeneia) has been harmed that she claims the justice of the talio in harming her enemy in return. This is brought out clearly by the cynical suggestion that one of Menelaus' children should have died instead of hers. The question

---

[48] *Hubris* and cognates are used in this play only of verbal taunts, except at 271 (of the adultery) and perhaps 522 (though context suggests verbal abuse here too).

[49] On these two levels of the talio in the play see Winnington-Ingram 222f.

[50] For the personification of *Dike* cf. especially Aesch. *Ag.* 1432f., 1500–4; cf. also *Ant.* 854, *OC* 1381f.; Hes. *Theog.* 902, *WD* 256–62; Solon 4.14–16 (West); and see Hirzel, *Themis* 138–56; Havelock, *Justice* index s.v. *Dike*. For a similar technique in court cf. Lys. 1.26; *Rhet. ad Alex.* 144467f. Burton 212 notes the legal overtones of the verb ἑλεῖν (528, 1080), which can mean 'convict'.

is not one of independently just punishment for unwarranted killing, but of revenge based on personal interest in the victim. The justice of simple retaliation may be presented as a universal law, but it is used to justify human behaviour prompted by the fiercely personal standards of Help Friends/Harm Enemies.

The combination of personal criteria for censure and approval with claims of impersonal validity is a sure recipe for vendetta and ceaseless argument. Intensely personal estimates of what constitutes legitimate provocation set the stage for the kind of relentless application of the talio that we see in *Electra*, which soon acquires an impersonal momentum of its own. Each side's belief in the absolute justice of her cause blinds both to the interminable nature of their dispute. Although the action of the play represents just one climactic moment, the feud has clearly been under way far longer, without any hope of resolution. Electra's opening lament and many subsequent lines emphasise the incessant character of her complaints. In her first speech she recounts a particular argument with her mother. The present tenses in this report, indicating customary or repeated action, show that this is merely one typical instance in a whole series of such disputes.[51] These repeated verbs of abuse are the keynote of the exchange, which is far more vitriolic, at least on Clytemnestra's part, than anything we actually observe. Ironically, Electra shows no awareness that such terms may be equally applicable to her own abuse of her mother.

This speech gives us a background of constant daily quarrels against which to interpret the debate we witness. The repetitive air is maintained by Clytemnestra's language when she first enters.[52] Like her daughter, she at once starts to report her adversary's stock accusations: Electra claims that she rules 'boldly and beyond justice', committing *hubris* against herself and her property (521f.). Since we have plenty of evidence that Electra makes precisely such charges (cf. especially 271, 293), these lines contribute to the cumulative effect of interminable argument. Each is well aware of the other's complaints, but this brings them no closer to a resolution. This effect is reinforced by Clytemnestra's contention that she is merely responding

[51] ἐξονειδίζει (288); ἐξυβρίζει (293); βοᾷ (295); ὑλακτεῖ, ἐποτρύνει (299). Cf. Woodard (2) 198–200.
[52] αὖ (516; cf. 328); ἀεί (517, 525, 530; all at line end); πολλὰ πρὸς πολλούς (520); θαμά (524).

to Electra's taunts (523f.). From what we have seen of Electra this claim is plausible enough, but according to her it is (at least sometimes) Clytemnestra herself who starts it (285–8, 552f.). Evidently these are disputes of such a kind that it is impossible to say 'who started it', for each incident is just one in a series of retaliations going back to an original act of provocation. Since neither party can agree on what counts as legitimate provocation, the continuing feud can never be resolved.[53] The altercation that follows exemplifies the process. It shows us the talio in action on the level of words, but its subject is the far more serious matter of retaliation through deeds. It is ostensibly about the justice of Clytemnestra's murderous act, but because of the nature of the talio Agamemnon is also on trial, and there are serious implications for Electra's actions as well.

Clytemnestra does not deny that she killed her husband, but claims to have done so justly (528). In terms of the talio this is true. It was Agamemnon who first disrupted the natural ties of family *philia* by initiating the sequence of killings. But although she relies on the talio, whereby a death is 'paid' for a death, Clytemnestra does not seem perturbed by the thought that her own death is now owed in turn. Nor is it, necessarily. If the murder of Iphigeneia was a crime, then the murder of Agamemnon has, according to the harsh logic of the talio, restored the status quo by 'paying' for it. But such simple compensation only works when all parties agree as to who was initially at fault. In Electra's eyes the sacrifice of Iphigeneia was excusable, making the murder of Agamemnon the act of aggression that now demands punishment. As with their verbal exchanges, it is impossible for the two women to agree who started it.

Clytemnestra goes on to anticipate her opponent's objections – a rhetorical move which gains added point from the impression that these arguments have been rehearsed many times before. Did Agamemnon sacrifice Iphigeneia for the Argives (535)? That would be no excuse, since they had no right to kill her 'own' (536). Clytemnestra's possessive language indicates a proprietorial sense of family *philia* (536, 538),[54] but by avenging one child she herself has alien-

---

[53] Cf. the dispute in *Aj.*, where Ajax's grievance dates from the allocation of the arms, while for the Atreidae the first offence is Ajax's attempt on their lives. In *El.* the competing causes are more finely balanced, both being kin-murders.

[54] Cf. *Ant.* 48. Like Clytemnestra, Antigone places an absolute value on kinship, and uses a male relative's violation of blood ties to justify defying his authority.

ated at least two others. Or did Agamemnon do it for his brother Menelaus (537)? But why kill Iphigeneia instead of one of Menelaus' own children, since the whole voyage was caused by his wife Helen (539–41)?[55] This is a strangely artificial argument, for there was never any suggestion that one of Menelaus' children would have been an acceptable sacrifice. The idea that Menelaus should have kept the murder in the family shows once more Clytemnestra's apolitical family-centred outlook. From this perspective her complaint is legitimate. But any sympathy aroused by her maternal feelings is dispelled by the narrowness of her interests and the suggestion that it would have been 'more reasonable' to kill some other child than hers (540).

In the same vein she asks sarcastically whether Hades had a greater desire to 'feed' on her child than Helen's (542f.). This comes ironically close to the truth, since from the divine point of view Iphigeneia's death was required precisely on account of her parentage. The idea of killing one of Menelaus' children is a misleading rhetorical flourish. She likewise belittles the problem by her sarcasm when she asks if Agamemnon's behaviour was not that of 'a foolish father with bad judgement' (546). It is true that if a father's first obligation is a prudent concern for his family's well-being, Agamemnon's action was foolish, to say the least. But Clytemnestra's position is weakened by her refusal to judge the issue from any perspective beyond that of the family, as well as her willingness to rupture other family bonds in pursuit of revenge. She adds defiantly that she feels no remorse (549f.), and ends by condemning Electra's 'judgement' as she did Agamemnon's, reemphasising the justice of her case (550f.).[56]

Clytemnestra dwells on Agamemnon's relationship to Iphigeneia, while ignoring her own to him. Electra, however, opens with the claim that nothing could be 'more disgraceful' than the simple admission of murder, regardless of the justice of the deed (558–60).[57] This must mean that in virtue of their relationship a wife

Cf. also OC 830–2 where Creon uses similar language for a different purpose. Note also 'your sister' (531), which reminds us that Electra too has sacrificed some loyalties (cf. Ant. 45).

[55] On the text of 541 see Kaibel and Kamerbeek ad loc.

[56] On the repeated γνώμην cf. Easterling, Repetition 26f. For the meaning of the word see Dihle, Will 28–30.

[57] On the theme of shame and disgrace in their debate cf. Kirkwood 140f.

is never justified in killing her husband, even if the killing is just according to the talio. These lines have ominous implications for Electra's own position.[58] If the conjugal tie overrules strict retaliatory justice, then so should the most powerful kinship bond of all, the blood-tie uniting parent and child.[59] Electra relies passionately on the justice of her cause, but does not consider whether any other claim, in particular her relationship to her mother, may override strict justice or qualify her own right to implement it. She may argue that Clytemnestra has forfeited the rights of kinship. But Clytemnestra could say the same of Agamemnon (cf. 546). If kinship per se is to have overriding force, then it cannot be invalidated at the speaker's convenience.

Adkins uses 558–60 to support his view that 'to say that an action is *aischron* is to play the ace of trumps: to justify performing it, one cannot press the claim that it is *dikaion*, for this is of less importance, but must maintain that it is in fact not *aischron* after all' (Adkins 156). He compares Euripides' *Electra* 1051, and concludes, 'Sophocles and Euripides maintain that in fact justice should not be exacted. There is a higher standard which may be set against the claims of strict justice' (Adkins 186). But apart from the fact that 'Sophocles and Euripides' say no such thing,[60] there is a weakness here internal to Adkins' own system. He asserts that *aischros* was the 'only conceivable word' that could be used to override the claims of *dike*, because it is drawn from 'the more powerful, competitive system of values'; to call actions *aischros* is 'to say that they are unworthy of the *agathos*; and as the conduct of the *agathos* embraces not merely successes and failures but a whole way of social – though not, traditionally, quiet moral – life, these actions are stigmatized as "not done"' (Adkins 186). But Adkins himself concedes that, 'as a result of the nature of women's *arete*' (45), *aischros* may be used *of women* to condemn breaches of the 'quiet' virtues which are the province of *dike*. Moreover Clytemnestra's murder of her husband was the breach par excellence of women's *arete*, stigmatised in Homer as bringing disgrace on all women, even the virtuous (*Od.* 11.433, quoted by

[58] As realised by e.g. Kitto, *GT*[1] 132; Johansen, *Elektra* 18f.; Winnington-Ingram 220f.

[59] Bowra 219f.; Jones 150 n. 1.

[60] Cf. Dover, *Evaluation* 42f. See ib. 41 for a different criticism of Adkins' handling of this passage.

Adkins himself, loc. cit.). It follows that even in Adkins' own terms we do not have here a 'competitive' term being used to override a 'cooperative' one. *Aischros* may be used to 'trump' *dikaios*, but Electra is also careful to argue that her mother's claim to justice is unwarranted. The suggestion that a deed which is just according to the talio can also be *aischros* is not Sophocles' 'solution' (Adkins 185), but part of the problem – the problem of relating this *dike* to other moral values.

Electra, wisely, does not spell out the implication that family ties overrule justice, or rely on it in her subsequent argument. Instead she proceeds to deny the justice of Clytemnestra's case on the ground that her real motive was not justice but 'the persuasion of an evil man' (561f.).[61] This 'unmasking' of motives underlines one difficulty with allowing the injured party to act as executioner: does the motive for retaliation affect its justice? The phrase in which Electra denies the justice of her mother's case is ambiguous between 'not in justice' and 'not from justice' (561). It can mean both that Clytemnestra acted unjustly (suggested by 'justly', in the previous line), and that justice was not her real motive (suggested by the contrast with persuasion).

In its strictest form the talio requires no consideration of motive.[62] But Electra's case depends on her father's innocence, so that his motive for killing Iphigeneia becomes crucial to her argument. Neither she nor her mother disputes the facts. But whereas Clytemnestra argued that hers was a deed of justice, Electra defends Agamemnon as having acted under duress (the excuse she denied her sister). She implies that the collective needs of the Argives outweighed narrow family allegiances. Agamemnon performed the sacrifice to release the fleet, 'under much compulsion and with great reluctance', and not merely as a favour to his brother (573–6). Like her mother she manipulates the events of Aulis so as to support the rhetoric of her own case, thereby belittling their tragic potential.[63] Agamemnon becomes a pawn in the debate between his wife and

---

[61] On this kind of 'unmasking' cf. MacIntyre 69. For the erotic connotations of 'persuasion' cf. 197 and see Buxton 31–52. For a discussion of Clytemnestra's motives see Jones 151–3.

[62] See above, p. 29. Aeschylus' Furies are unmoved by the fact that Orestes acted under duress (cf. Winnington–Ingram 208).

[63] On the way Agamemnon's dilemma is 'trivialised' see Winnington–Ingram 220 n. 15. Cf. also Kitto, GT^3 137; Segal 271.

daughter, each of whom interprets his motives at Aulis in the light of her own emotions and loyalties.

Electra now makes a rhetorical concession: supposing Agamemnon *did* kill Iphigeneia as a favour to his brother, he still should not have been killed in turn (577–9). The only principle that could justify such a killing would be the talio: 'Take care, in setting up this law for mortals, that you do not set up for yourself grief and regret. For if we kill one for another, you would be the first to die, at least if you should meet justice' (580–3). The dramatic irony is obvious, and is alone enough to cast doubt on any straightforwardly optimistic interpretation of the play.[64] It undermines Electra's position so that her rhetorical concession actually weakens her argument. There have already been hints of this difficulty. In her lyric dialogue with the chorus Electra sang that unless the murderers paid 'the justice of blood in exchange', '*aidos* and reverence' would depart from all mortals (245–50; cf. 1382f.).[65] She uses a reciprocal form of expression which carries the same ironic implication as her words to Clytemnestra.[66]

For her clinching argument Electra returns to the question of motive. She inquires sarcastically whether Clytemnestra's adultery, 'the most disgraceful of all deeds' (586), is also 'a penalty in exchange' for Iphigeneia's death (591f.). If so, she says, it is still disgraceful, for it is not *kalos* to marry an enemy in revenge for a daughter (593f.).[67] The suggestion is not merely that she has violated the talio by failing to reciprocate in kind, but (as in 558–60) that some deeds are disgraceful regardless of provocation. As the son of Thyestes, Aegisthus is a family enemy, but he is Electra's enemy primarily for his part in Agamemnon's murder. To Clytemnestra, however, this makes him a *philos*. The argument from enmity is thus a weak one. As for the notion that it is inappropriate to repay mur-

---

[64] Cf. Kitto, *GT*[1] 133; Winnington-Ingram 221; Segal 251f.; id. *Electra* 537 (where he notes the similarity to 1505–7). Scodel 85 observes that 'first' (583) suggests further deaths to follow. A minority view, that we 'do not notice' the import of Electra's words, is held by Waldock 181; cf. also Alexanderson, *Electra* 87; Perrotta 310; Heath 136f.

[65] 'An awkward principle for a person intent on murder' (Gellie 110). Segal, *Electra* 536 notes that language associated with *dike* in this play tends to be violent and destructive (e.g. 37, 248, 476).

[66] ἀντιφόνους (248); cf. 582, 592 and above, p. 29 n. 17.

[67] Cf. Hyllus' horror at the idea of marrying Iole (*Trach.* 1236f.).

der with adultery, what of repaying adultery with murder?[68] Simple retaliation is not nearly as workable in practice as it may at first appear.

At this point in her speech Electra turns from argument to invective, telling her mother, 'It is not even possible to advise you' (595). Once more the irony is unmistakable, and it extends into the next lines, where Electra says that Clytemnestra complains of her abuse (596f.). Such complaints are completely justified, for Electra does abuse her, and will go on to do so in her very next words. She derives the right to do so from the fact that she regards Clytemnestra as a 'mistress' more than a mother (597f.). But is she entitled to disown their natural relationship in this way? Not if her earlier arguments are to bear any weight.

Electra goes on to raise the sore issue of Orestes (601–5; cf. 293–7), who, so she hopes and her mother fears, will arrive as a *miastor* – an ambivalent word, indicating primarily a 'crime-stained wretch who pollutes others', and only secondarily the 'avenger of such guilt' (LSJ s.v.).[69] She concludes still more provocatively, inviting Clytemnestra to denounce her publicly as *kakos*, loud-mouthed and shameless, for such traits are worthy of the *phusis* she inherits from her mother (605–9). This need not mean that she accepts Clytemnestra's evaluation of her behaviour, only that she is indifferent to having it so described by her mother. Despite her desire for a glorious reputation, Electra, unlike Clytemnestra, is not embarrassed at public abuse (cf. 518, 638–42). Yet her final words also hint that her behaviour is indeed reprehensible. With their sarcastic colouring, these four lines have an elusive ambivalence. The ironic claim that she is living up to her mother's *phusis*, besides being an ingenious insult, manages to distance her from Clytemnestra while highlighting their similarity.[70]

The chorus rightly perceive that Electra's rational opening has degenerated into wrathful invective: 'I see her breathing passion; but I no longer see any thought for whether justice is on her side'

---

[68] Electra makes the Furies avengers of adultery as well as murder (112–14), a function adumbrated at Aesch. *Ag.* 1191–3 (see Winnington-Ingram 231f. and cf. Gardiner 148f.).

[69] It is also used of Aegisthus (275); cf. Winnington-Ingram 245 n. 93.

[70] On this passage and *phusis* in the play see Segal, *Electra* 498–501; Winnington-Ingram 245f.

(610f.).[71] Electra's passion has overwhelmed her moral sense — righteous indignation has degenerated into mere indignation.[72] This need not vitiate her arguments, but it does cast doubt on the rational basis of her lust for revenge. Clytemnestra picks up and echoes the word 'thought', answering in essence, 'If *she* no longer has any thought for the justice of her case, then why should I?'[73] Clytemnestra can exploit Electra's passion so as to avoid responding to the rational portion of her speech. She brings out the similarity between them by reciprocating her daughter's charge of verbal *hubris* (613; cf. 293). Electra tried to disown their relationship, but Clytemnestra reemphasises it, basing her demand for acquiescence on the inviolable tie of blood. As at Aulis, she relies solely on her rights as a mother. Electra's conduct is disgraceful (615; cf. 518, 622), for it violates the norms of family *philia*. But Clytemnestra herself, through her treatment of her husband, has devastated such norms.

Electra denies her mother's charge: 'I *am* ashamed of these things, even if you do not think so. I understand that my behaviour is unseemly and not appropriate to me' (616–18). This picks up on a number of earlier admissions. Her opening lyrics give the first hint of awareness that her behaviour has its reprehensible aspects: 'In terrible circumstances I have been forced to [do] terrible things; I know it, I am aware of my passion' (221f.). The theme is developed in her subsequent speech, where she admits to a sense of disgrace at her friends' disapproval, repeats that her conduct is forced upon her, and begs indulgence (254–7). She concludes as she began: 'So in such circumstances it is not possible, friends, to show *sophrosune* or reverence. Rather in evil circumstances there is great necessity to practice evil things' (307–9). 'Necessity' appears in all these passages, and will recur (221, 256, 309, 620). It denotes the force of principle, which for

---

[71] With Jebb I take both lines to refer to Electra. Others (including Kaibel and Kamerbeek) think they refer to Clytemnestra. But we expect the chorus to comment on the preceding speech (Burton 187; Gardiner 149f.). Jebb's view has been well supported by Booth.

[72] It is sometimes argued (e.g. by Kamerbeek ad loc.; Gardiner 150) that the chorus would not question Electra's concern for justice. This not only prejudges the issue, but confuses Electra's concern for justice with the justice of her cause. The chorus have already rebuked her for excessive passion (213–20), and there is no reason why they should not do so again here.

[73] There is no need for 'thought' in 611 as well as 612 to refer to Clytemnestra. It is perhaps more pointed if it does not.

Electra is irresistible.[74] Twice the point is strengthened by the word *bia*, 'force' or 'violence' (256, 620). This normally suggests physical compulsion (cf. the use of 'necessity' and 'force' at 1192f.), but Electra is obliged to *resist* physical duress in order to lament as she thinks fit.

The sentiment of 308f. (evil things give rise to evil things) and 221 (terrible things give rise to terrible things) is echoed once more: 'Disgraceful things are taught by disgraceful things' (621).[75] Clytemnestra replies, 'My words and deeds make you talk much too much', and Electra agrees, 'You said it, not I' (622–4). As the doer of shameful deeds, Clytemnestra is responsible for the shameful words that result (624f.). But this does not remove Electra's own sense of shame. Her tragic stature is enhanced by an awareness that she is violating accepted norms, and by the fact that she does not reject such norms out of hand.[76] Her own characterisation of her misfortunes may be applied to her moral dilemma: 'These things will be called insoluble' (230; cf. 142).

Electra never suggests, however, that the course of action she has rejected has an equal moral claim. Conventional virtues are acknowledged as such, but there is a definite ranking. She is doomed by moral 'necessity' to shameful and excessive behaviour, but she has no doubt whatsoever that this is the lesser of two evils. A *eugenes* woman could not act otherwise (257f.). *Dike*, reverence and *aidos* towards a murdered father take unquestioned precedence over *sophrosune*, reverence and *aidos* towards a murderous mother. Electra feels a certain shame, but no guilt at her choice.[77] Yet some of her own arguments against Clytemnestra tend to undermine the legitimacy of her self-righteousness. Moreover her talk of self-perpetuating evils opens the door to broader implications. For it underlines one of the major flaws in the justice of the talio: if wrong may always be returned for wrong, then a further wrong may always be returned for the second, and so on ad infinitum, as long as the second wrong

---

[74] Cf. *Phil.* 1366, *OC* 1178f. For the semantic range of ἀνάγκη, ('necessity') see Dover, *Aspects* 65.

[75] Cf. Winnington-Ingram 223f.

[76] On the significance of this conflict for Electra's tragic situation see especially Sheppard (1) 84f.; Bowra 240f.; Johansen, *Elektra* 13; Winnington-Ingram 225.

[77] On the 'remainder' when one moral imperative overrides another see especially Foot 381–9.

(the first act of revenge) is considered a wrong (rather than a rightful punishment).

Electra has the last word, for her opponent is unable to answer her final thrust and turns instead to threats (626f.). But it is perhaps too simple to say with Jebb and many others that 'the better cause has the advantage which it deserves' (Jebb, *Introduction* §15).[78] It is Electra who first descends to invective in her speech, thus paving the way for the exchange of abuse that follows. And like her mother, Electra uses a veneer of dubiously rational argument to justify behaviour prompted by passionate feeling. There are other persistent hints that they are more similar than their violent opposition might suggest.[79] Electra accuses her mother of excessive passion and an inability to listen (628f.; cf. 595), both prominent characteristics of her own (222, 1011; cf. 369). Each claims justice for her own deeds while accusing the other of injustice (113, 245–50, 298, 521f., 528, 538, 551, 561, 1041). Each additionally charges the other with *hubris* (293, 613), 'boldness' (521, 626; cf. 995, 1446) and disgraceful behaviour (559, 593, 615). Each enlists 'sense' on her own side (403, 529, 550f.; cf. 145f., 546). Each has her male champion: Clytemnestra relies on threats of Aegisthus' return to chastise Electra (517–20, 626f.), while Electra's trump card is to threaten the arrival of Orestes (293–5, 601–4).[80] Finally, just as Clytemnestra took on the masculine task of killing her husband, so Electra intends to defy her female *phusis* and kill another man, Aegisthus (956f.).

Orestes and vengeance

Orestes' motives, as expressed in the prologue, are very similar to Electra's: desire for revenge, justice, renown, 'profit' and 'salvation', honour and restoration of the family wealth (33–7, 59–72; cf. 14, 1181, 1426f.).[81] He also plays his own part in perpetuating the evils

---

[78] For more ambivalent views see Woodard (1) 185f.; Segal, *Electra* 536f.

[79] For their shared basic assumptions see above, p. 149f. On their similarities cf. also Kitto, *GT*[1] 133–5; Johansen, *Elektra* 17; Segal 261f.; id. *Electra* 501, 525f.

[80] This parallel is noted by the scholiast on 607.

[81] The most prominent additional factor is his obedience to the gods (32–5, 67–70; cf. 1264, 1374f., 1425). Electra places little emphasis on the help of heaven (though cf. 1265–70, 1376–83). Note in particular her response to the chorus' optimism about divine justice (173–5): long-term justice is of little use to her. She has already lived out the best part of her life unmarried and childless, with the status of an alien (185–92).

of retaliation. In particular, it is insisted throughout the play that he is retaliating for Clytemnestra's use of deception in the murder of Agamemnon.[82] He himself places a curious emphasis on his own duplicity (59–66). Deception against an enemy is defensible, and no character in the play condemns it. Moreover Apollo has explicitly sanctioned this particular means of attack (35–7). But Orestes shows just how far he is willing to go when he instructs the paedagogus to add an oath that his fictitious tale is true (47). This is both uncalled for and arguably reprehensible.[83] The servant discreetly ignores the suggestion, so that the passage has no dramatic function other than to illuminate Orestes' unscrupulous use of deceit in the pursuit of 'profit' (kerdos 61).[84] Apollo's command does not alter the fact that dolos is another of those self-perpetuating evils that are only made 'right' in some sense by the talio. So too the 'profit' Orestes will reap from killing his mother (61) is akin to the 'terrible profit' she thinks she is gaining from his death (767).

Orestes is not a heroic figure in the Iliadic mould. The wording of the oracle contrasts his use of deception to 'steal' his revenge with the use of open warfare (36f.), a method appropriate to his father Agamemnon, who is named in the opening lines of the play as the commander at Troy (1f.).[85] The 'messenger' speech presents us with Orestes as he might have been – the heroic and glorious son of the

[82] Cf. above, n. 3. So also in Aesch. Cho. especially 555–8 (cf. Winnington-Ingram 335). Note other language emphasising the underhand nature of Orestes' approach (37, 56, 1228f., 1397, 1440; cf. 159, 1494).

[83] Some have found it ill-omened (e.g. Sheppard (2) 5; Segal, Electra 483). The scholiast feels the need to justify it by the command of Apollo, but does the oracle condone even perjury?

[84] See Kells 6 for parallels, to which add Herod. 3.72.4 with Dihle 98f. For the pejorative associations of kerdos cf. Ant. 221f.; OT 380–9 (where it is associated with dolos); fr. 28, 807, 833 (Radt); and above, p. 33 n. 38. Orestes has much in common with Odysseus in Phil., one of Sophocles' least sympathetic characters, but one in whom deception could easily have been condoned as part of his traditional personality. Both are willing to lie in pursuit of kerdos (cf. Phil. 111), and are underhand (Reinhardt 259 n. 3 compares El. 37 with Phil. 55; cf. also Phil. 133 with El. 1395–7), cool, rational, prudent and ruthless in pursuit of their goals. Cf. also Shucard 136f.; Strohm 112f. Woodard (1) 202 n. 37 notes that both instruct a false messenger, and finds similarities between Orestes and the Homeric Odysseus (171f.). But many of these are merely the result of story type, and in others the analogy is weak.

[85] Seale 80 n. 1 suggests that this reference to Agamemnon serves 'to illuminate the unheroic task which faces his son'. This helps to counter the aesthetic objection raised by Haslam 166–8 in support of a tenuous case for deleting the line.

great Agamemnon (694f.) – in contrast to the cool and devious Odyssean figure of the prologue. 'Shining' (685) echoes Orestes' wish to 'shine forth' (66), and the athletic victory (687) recalls the 'victory' that prevents Orestes from approaching Electra (85).[86] The Orestes of the speech is the hero whom Electra awaits,[87] and who our Orestes aspires to be, but the victory he wins is not the glorious triumph of the speech.[88] The account of the chariot disaster is also unsettling in itself, echoing the ominous precedent of Myrtilus (504–15).[89] The paedagogus even affects to draw the moral that when a god causes harm, none can escape (696f.). This is, to be sure, a commonplace (cf. e.g. *OC* 252–4; Soph. fr. 680 (Radt)). But it is applicable to more than one character in the play, as is the paedagogus' aphoristic summary: 'What evils he meets, after doing what deeds!' (751).[90]

Just before revealing himself to Electra, Orestes declares that he has long felt pity for her (1199). This emotion has so far been little in evidence,[91] but seems here to introduce a new warmth. For according to Electra, Orestes is the first to pity her lot (1200). In *Ajax*, Odysseus' pity went beyond the narrow code of Help Friends/Harm Enemies to create a new bond of friendship. Electra and Orestes are already *philoi* by birth and loyalty, so Orestes' pity functions instead to provide emotional confirmation of their alliance. But the most striking aspect of this pity is that it is so short-lived.[92] After recognising his sister Orestes shows her little affection,[93] and any warmth from his moment of pity is soon dispelled, when Clytemnestra begs for pity on the basis of kinship and Electra denies it with the talio (1411f.). Pitilessness breeds pitilessness, just as shameful, terrible and evil deeds perpetuate themselves.

[86] If Sandbach is right, 85 should be assigned to Orestes. 'Victory' is a key word for Odysseus in *Phil.* (below, p. 187f.).

[87] See Gellie 117 and cf. Wilamowitz, *Elektren* 238f.

[88] For the contrast between the heroic language of the speech and its unheroic purpose see Segal 289 with n. 94. Cf. also Seale 64–6.

[89] Winnington-Ingram 236f.; Segal 267–9; Sheppard (2) 6f. On the Myrtilus ode see Burton 201–3. Segal 256 observes that 'virtually every ode in the play deals with the destruction of a house'.

[90] For the speech as 'a fable of common Greek morality' see Scodel 82f.

[91] Agamemnon died pitifully (102, 145, 193f.); Electra pities Chrysothemis' 'ignorance' (920); the strife of the sisters is pitiful (1067f.).

[92] Cf. Winnington-Ingram 229.

[93] Apart from a perfunctory *philtatos* (1224) – not directly addressed to her – Orestes does not reciprocate Electra's abundant *phil*- language.

Orestes appears at his least heroic in the scene leading up to the murder. As he takes Pylades inside, he addresses him by name for the first and last time (1372f.).[94] In Aeschylus, Orestes also addresses Pylades just before the matricide, in a final moment of hesitation (*Cho*. 899).[95] But in Sophocles' treatment he shows no trace of reluctance beforehand or regret afterwards. So why is attention drawn to Pylades as they enter the house? Perhaps to emphasise that two men will be attacking a single women, for the paedagogus has just laid great stress on the fact that Clytemnestra is alone and undefended (1368–71). Here is a different twist to the theme of strength and *phusis* debated by the two sisters. Orestes has a healthy respect for the female *phusis* (1243f.),[96] and takes every precaution when attacking his mother. There could be no clearer contrast with Electra, whom Clytemnestra could not control (519f.), and who was ready to defy her own *phusis* to attack Aegisthus.

Before the murder Electra prays to Apollo to display the gods' reward for 'irreverence' (1376–83).[97] Her prayer recalls her mother's earlier one (cf. especially 655 with 1378, 1379; 649 with 1381), and is usually interpreted as 'the accents of authentic prayer as contrasted with Clytemnestra's humbug' (Waldock 188). But the word 'irreverence' (1383) reminds us of Electra's own previous admission of failure in a different kind of 'reverence' (308). It is by no means obvious that the daughter's prayer for the death of her mother is preferable to the mother's for the death of her son.[98] At the actual moment of death Clytemnestra calls for Aegisthus (1409). But her daughter's male champion and source of (physical) strength has now arrived. Electra does her best to make the deed her own by calling out 'if you have the strength, strike twice' (1415).[99] Here is the chilling outcome of using one's 'strength' to the full. The chorus cannot

---

[94] The only other such address is that by the paedagogus in the prologue (16), which serves to identify Orestes' silent companion.

[95] He is more strongly reluctant in Euripides (*El*. 964–87).

[96] A remarkable attitude for a Greek male (cf. Dover 98–102). Opstelten 39f. aptly contrasts Aesch. *Supp*. 748f.

[97] On εὐσέβεια ('reverence') and cognates in *Electra* see Long 151f. and cf. Torrance 313.

[98] Cf. Segal, *Electra* 525.

[99] For the way Electra 'stage-manages' this scene, taking Orestes' place in the dialogue, see Seale 74f.; cf. also Johansen, *Elektra* 26; Steidle 93f. On the double stroke as repayment for the two blows that killed Agamemnon (Aesch. *Ag*. 1297) see Hirzel 441f.

blame the killers for their deed (1423),[100] but their language
prompts thoughts of a continuing cycle of bloodshed: 'The curses
are at work; the buried live; blood flows for blood, drained from
the slayers by those who died of yore' (1417–21, trans. Jebb).[101]
When Orestes makes his famous announcement, 'All is well in the
house, if Apollo gave his oracle well' (1424f.), his 'well' (*kalôs*)
echoes the triple *kalôs* in Clytemnestra's reaction to his own 'death'
(790–3).[102]

Unlike Clytemnestra, Aegisthus has a brief confrontation with
his killers. When he realises the truth, he is denied the opportunity to
defend himself, on the grounds that 'spinning out words' is profitless
for one about to die (1482–6). Electra's words recall Creon's harsh
curtailment of Antigone's lament (*Ant.* 883f.). Like Creon she demands that the offender be killed 'as quickly as possible' (1487; cf.
Ant. 885–8), adding that he should be cast out without burial
(1487f.).[103] Aegisthus does his best to fight back, asking 'Why, if the
deed is *kalos*, does it need darkness?' (1493f.). Orestes answers in
terms of the talio – Aegisthus must die on the spot where he killed
Agamemnon.[104] But Aegisthus' words suffice to remind us that the
deed of revenge is not in every respect *kalos*. The uneasiness that this
generates is reinforced by his mention of 'the present and future evils
of the house of Pelops' (1498). This must refer to future punishment

---

100 Accepting Erfurdt's ψέγειν in 1423, on which see Dawe's review of Kamerbeek,
    Gnomon 48 (1976) 233f.
101 This and the brief song during Electra's absence (1384–97) are distinctly
    Aeschylean in tone. But as Kitto observes, the concept of 'the dead reaching
    out to kill the living' is also characteristic of Sophocles, appearing in five of the
    extant plays (*FMD* 193).
102 *Kalôs* is also emphatically repeated at 1320f. (meaning 'nobly') of Electra's de-
    cision to kill Aegisthus or die in the attempt, and at 1345f., where the sense is
    unclear. Does τὰ μὴ καλῶς ('what is not well') refer, as Jebb takes it, to Clytem-
    nestra's improper rejoicing at her son's death? Even if this is the surface mean-
    ing (which is not clear to me), the words also suggest that the impending
    matricide itself is not *kalôs*. Cf. Sheppard (2) 8; Kirkwood 241 n. 22;
    Winnington-Ingram 234 n. 60.
103 Her language in 1490 echoes Clytemnestra's attempted purifications (635, 447;
    cf. Segal 276). The sense of 1487f. is controversial. I follow the scholiast and the
    majority of critics in taking it to refer to dogs and birds (i.e. to no burial at all).
    For the alternative view (that it refers to a humble burial) see Bowra 254f.;
    Letters 260; Johansen, *Elektra* 28 n. 34. Cf. also Gardiner 167.
104 For other examples of the talio according to place see Hirzel 442–56.

for the matricide.[105] The fact that Orestes himself seems blind to this possibility, and sneeringly dismisses it (1499), does not alter the implications of the remark. And Aegisthus caps the sneer by pointing out that 'this prophetic skill you boast of was not your father's' (1500).[106] The mention of Agamemnon, whose name opened the play, ties up past, present and future, suggesting in a single line the cycle of deaths that plagues the house.

The encounter ends pettily, as Orestes forces Aegisthus to enter the house ahead of him (1502). His reasoning is that Aegisthus' execution should not be at his own pleasure, but must be made 'bitter' (1503f.). The harsh tone is not relieved by Orestes' final lines, whose merciless authoritarianism again recalls Creon or the Atreidae in *Ajax*: 'There should be this *dike* right away for all who want to go beyond the *nomoi* – to kill them. Then there would not be much villainy' (1505–7). The position of the delayed verb 'kill' is particularly emphatic. Should death really be the penalty for breaking every *nomos*? What of the *nomos* demanding reverence for one's mother?

The chorus announce that by this deed the house of Atreus has attained freedom (1508–10).[107] But there is no celebration of its beneficial consequences.[108] As if to avoid a conclusion of rejoicing and reconciliation, Electra's joy has been transferred to the moment of recognition, and even there a shadow is cast by Orestes' repeated attempts to subdue her (1236, 1238, 1251f., 1257, 1259, 1271f., 1288–92). Before the murder they envisage a future where they will talk and laugh together, but which must for the present be postponed (1251f., 1299f.; cf. 1364–6). We are not permitted, however, to witness any such joy.

---

[105] Cf. Sheppard (3) 164f.; Johansen, *Elektra* 29; Alexanderson, *Electra* 95–7; Winnington-Ingram 226f. Owen 50f. gives parallels, but underestimates the line's significance. Others take it to refer merely to Aegisthus' own impending death (e.g. Bowra 257f.; Ronnet 214f.), but see contra Alexanderson, *Electra* 96; Knox, *WA* 185 (both of whom rightly point to the limiting force of γοῦν in 1499).

[106] On the prophecy motif see Winnington-Ingram 237f.

[107] As Linforth 122 and Kirkwood, *Electra* 94f. observe, this statement corresponds in both sentiment and position to the ode at Aesch. *Cho.* 935–71, immediately after the death of Clytemnestra and Aegisthus. Since Sophocles ends the story here, this parallel may be more germane than the contrast with the end of *Cho.* which is more often remarked.

[108] Cf. Winnington-Ingram 227. Contrast the end of *Oresteia* (*Eum.* 903–1047) and the relatively cheerful close of *Phil.* (1445–71).

The last, tantalising, word of the play is 'ended'.[109] We know that the myth does not end here, and the play has suggested that such cycles of revenge are endless. Yet in human terms, the cycle of revenge *is* over – no other mortal avenger will arise. This leaves a delicate problem for a dramatist more interested in human dilemmas than supernatural solutions. The play accordingly ends with assurances from the participants that the conflict is at an end. But it is typical of Sophocles' characters, especially at moments of success, to have only a limited understanding of events that the audience may appreciate more fully. His choruses in particular are notoriously prone to premature rejoicing (cf. e.g. *Aj.* 693–718; *Ant.* 1115–54; *OT* 1086–1109). Even the apparently sunny ending of *Philoctetes* is clouded by a veiled reference to the impious sacking of Troy (1440f.; cf. also *OC* 1769–72). Aegisthus' reference to 'future evils' has a similar effect, enhanced by the familiarity of the myth.[110] Thus, without the introduction of supernatural avengers, *Electra* ends on a characteristically ironic note with intimations of humankind's limited understanding of its own predicament.[111]

Matricide, revenge and justice

Because the play contains no overt criticism of the matricide, and because there is no reference to the hounding of Orestes by the Furies, many critics have thought that Sophocles is condoning the matricide or at best ignoring its moral difficulties. Others think that he is raising such issues by subtler means.[112] The difficulty is exacer-

---

[109] It is the last in a series of words from the same root (1344; 1399; 1417; 1435; 1464; it is traced back further by Woodard (2) 229 n. 32; Segal, *Electra* 531). Cf. also the language of finality at 1397, 1451, 1490. Such language also appears at the end of *Trach.* (1255–7, 1263), which suffers from a similar controversy about the continuation of the story outside the play (cf. *Trach.* 1270 with *El.* 1498).

[110] As Knox points out, this does not just depend on knowledge of the Aeschylean version, for 'Orestes' flight to Athens was firmly based in local Athenian cult' (*WA* 185).

[111] Interpretations of the ending vary widely, corresponding in general to each critic's view of the play as a whole (see next note). But many who think Sophocles approved of the matricide still find the ending harsh (e.g. Bowra 256f.; Letters 244).

[112] Jebb speaks of 'the calm condonation of matricide' (*Introduction* §19), and many more or less agree with him. For 'ironic' readings see especially Johansen, *Elektra*, Woodard, (1) and (2); Winnington-Ingram; Segal. For doxography see Kells 1–5.

bated by the fact that plays on this theme by all three tragedians have survived, providing dangerous fuel for over-interpretation. In particular we must beware of assuming that Sophocles is somehow 'answering' either Aeschylus or Euripides.[113] Yet it is hard to deny that *Electra* has many Aeschylean overtones.[114] These succeed in conveying a morally ambivalent and oppressive atmosphere without incorporating the entire Aeschylean ethical and religious framework. Thus a reference to the Erinys punishing Clytemnestra may remind us of the similarity between particular acts of vengeance and suggest the futility of the continuing cycle, without the need to portray Orestes himself under pursuit, which Sophocles had his own reasons for wishing to avoid.

What kind of reasons were these? First, the play is self-contained, not part of a trilogy. A conclusion with Orestes exiting pursued by Furies would leave the audience dangling and vitiate the tight dramatic construction. Second, it is Electra's play, and Orestes must not upstage her. But such formal explanations must be complemented by considerations of meaning. If Sophocles remains silent about the Furies' pursuit of Orestes, we may infer that it is not important for the play. This does not mean, however, that problems of revenge and justice are ignored. On the contrary, the play explores the nature of revenge by presenting us with characters who believe in their own justice, with their arguments, motives and passions, and demonstrating the rationally insoluble character of their disputes. We see how the talio can be used as an objective mask for the passions that give rise to deeds of irrational brutality — passions of lust, hatred, grief and wrath.[115]

There are repeated references to Electra's passionate spirit (218, 222, 331, 369, 610, 1011).[116] The violence of her emotion is underlined by the reaction not only of Chrysothemis (330f., 1009–11), but also of the loyal and sympathetic chorus, who consider it self-destructive and futile in its excess (137–44, 153–5, 213–19; cf. 369, 610f., 830, 1015f.). They will come to approve of Electra's behaviour, but their admiration is in part inspired by what would conventionally be considered her imprudence (cf. 1078f.). And indeed

---

[113] Cf. the cautions of Waldock 191–3; Dale, *Electra* 227; Stevens, *Electra* 112.
[114] See especially Winnington-Ingram 217f.; Johansen, *Elektra* 25f.
[115] Cf. Winnington-Ingram 221f.
[116] Cf. also 1283, though the text here is difficult (see the editors ad loc.).

her plan to kill Aegisthus is arguably suicidal folly of a kind that exceeds the demands of justice. Still more revealing is her reaction to Chrysothemis' warning of impending exile. She welcomes the new punishment, for it will take her out of the company of her enemies (387, 391). This new threat is proof of her efficacy as an interim avenger, for its aim is to deprive her of that function. But she does not allude to this thwarting of her main purpose. Instead, her anxiety to be gone betrays the passionate hatred which motivates her beyond the ethical requirement of maintaining her integrity. The most striking testimony to this hatred is in her own words: 'my hatred has sunk into me from long ago' (1311).

With Orestes Electra is overcome by different emotions – first grief, then passionate joy, which is cast into relief by his contrasting coolness and the brusqueness of the paedagogus (1364).[117] She who was ruled by wrath and hatred, who lived gratifying her *thumos* (331), is now 'conquered by pleasure' (1272), an overpowering emotion which actually inhibits the vengeance she has awaited so long. She attributes similar wrath and violent pleasure to her mother (628, 1153), and agrees with the chorus that *eros* was Clytemnestra's 'real' motive for killing her husband (197; cf. 561f., 584–9). At the end of the play Electra is willing to sacrifice her own pleasure, profit and *thumos* to those of Orestes – a sign of the sincerity of her *philia* (1301– 5, 1319). Yet their joint harshness towards their enemies differs only in degree from Clytemnestra's treatment of her husband. The visitation of external Furies, whether in person or in the more naturalistic form of madness,[118] would detract from this spectacle of human beings acting as their own Furies from the combination of destructive, self-deceptive passions with a self-defeating conception of justice.[119]

---

[117] Woodard (1) 193f. and 204 n. 78 points out that 'Orestes has no lyric anywhere in the play; and Electra has a greater proportion than any other protagonist in Sophocles.' The only exceptions are brief interjections (1276, 1280) which seem insufficient to justify Segal's claim that Orestes 'joins sympathetically in her cries despite himself' (*Electra* 514).

[118] I cannot agree with Kells 10f. that Electra herself goes mad (see the rebuttal by Stevens, *Electra* 116). But he is right to observe that the traditional Furies were 'too outward a phenomenon for [Sophocles'] conception' (Kells 9).

[119] The resemblance of Electra to a Fury is most striking at 784–6 (cf. Aesch. *Cho.* 577f., Soph. fr. 743 (Radt); see Winnington-Ingram 233 and cf. Kamerbeek ad loc.). Cf. also 1386–8 with Bowra 258f. Clytemnestra and Aegisthus in turn are

In a play so full of passion there is an ironic emphasis on teaching and learning. Electra accuses her mother of being inaccessible to reason (595), while remaining impervious to teaching herself (330, 370f., 1032; cf. 889). Yet each invites the other to 'teach' her (534, 585). Electra issues the same invitation to Chrysothemis (352), after rebuffing her advice on the ground that it has been 'taught' by Clytemnestra (344), and before rejecting her 'teaching' again as disloyalty (395). Yet there is also a sense in which Electra has herself been 'taught' by her mother. As she herself puts it, 'Disgraceful things are taught by disgraceful things' (621). When the opportunity for honest 'teaching' to a sympathetic listener finally arises, Orestes brusquely forestalls it (1289f.). The cumulative effect is a sense of the futility of reasoned human teaching in a world governed by passion. This impression is reinforced by one of the most ironic scenes in a play full of ironies, when Electra manages to convince her sister that what we know to be true is false, and vice versa. Coming as it does so soon after the 'messenger' speech, with its powerful assault on our rational beliefs, the scene demonstrates the fallibility of human means of acquiring knowledge. When Chrysothemis correctly accounts for the grave-offerings, Electra's alternative explanation (932f.) suggests, like her debate with Clytemnestra, that we interpret events in accordance with our own presuppositions.[120]

The play focusses primarily on the murder of Clytemnestra qua revenge, not matricide. This is one reason why Aegisthus dies last. We are left with the grim brutality of summary vengeance, without the complicating emotion of horror at matricide.[121] This is also why, in Jebb's words, 'Sophocles has been careful to remind us again and again how completely Clytemnestra has forfeited all *moral* claim to a son's loyalty' (*Introduction* §13). Jebb objects that 'the question here

a 'double Erinys' to Electra (1080). On these and other references to the Erinyes in the play see Winnington-Ingram ch. 10 passim and cf. Burton 211f.

120 'Teaching' is successful first when Electra releases the urn that symbolises her delusion and sees her father's ring (1222f.), and again when Aegisthus receives the answer to his requests for knowledge (1450, 1454) – the irrefutable evidence of Clytemnestra's corpse (145; cf. 1458). The direct evidence of the eyes, undistorted by erroneous human interpretation, is finally vindicated (1454f., 1475; cf. 1461f.).

121 On the order of the killings see especially Kirkwood, *Electra* 90–4. Cf. also Bowra 218; Johansen, *Elektra* 24f.; Winnington-Ingram 234f. All dispute the view that the order shows the matricide is not of central importance.

is, however, not moral but religious; a matter, not of conduct, but of kinship'. But it is precisely the religious aspect of the matter which the play avoids. An emphasis on impiety would weaken the impact of the conflict between justice and expediency in Electra's confrontations with Chrysothemis. It would also weaken the play's portrayal of the psychology of revenge. Clytemnestra must put forward a claim to justice, rather than simply relying on a mother's claim to 'reverence'. At the same time her character is blackened, not to provide a naive justification for matricide, but to show that however guilty a victim of the talio may be, and however much we may sympathise with the avenger, it remains a harsh, destructive and fatally subjective form of justice. Further, the fact that Electra and her mother have so much in common means that her mother's character generates a special ambivalence about her own. The inextricable bonds of kinship – the shared *phusis* of mother and daughter – are more significant than the strictly religious implications of matricide. It is not necessarily weak or evasive, as Jebb thought, to ignore these implications. On the contrary, the play dares to suggest that *if* revenge is just (and this is the *premiss* of the play, or at least of all the characters), then it should logically be applied impartially to family and stranger alike.[122]

Those who think Sophocles positively approved of the matricide may point to Apollo. Although the god does not place Orestes under duress as he does in Aeschylus,[123] nevertheless the mission clearly has his approval.[124] It is arguable that the young man who pursues this mission, unclouded by passion, represents an objective, rational, divine confirmation of the rightness of Electra's position.[125] But we cannot assume that the playwright's approval is coextensive with that of Apollo. The interests of different divinities

[122] For an awareness of the potential tension between religious obligations towards parents and the demands of justice cf. Pl. *Euth.* 4b (though admittedly Euthyphro is something of an eccentric).

[123] Only in Sophocles does Orestes explicitly take the initiative in consulting Apollo. His question to the oracle implies that he is already determined on revenge (33f.), and no divine sanctions are threatened for failure to obey (contrast Aesch. *Cho.* 269–97).

[124] Attempts such as Sheppard's ((2)4) to exonerate Apollo are misguided (cf. Linforth, *Electra* 122f.; Winnington-Ingram 236; Segal 280). Note that Ares (1384f., 1422f.) and Hermes god of *dolos* (1395–7) also preside over the matricide (cf. Segal 272).

[125] Whitman 168–72 goes so far as to call him a *deus ex machina*.

may themselves conflict. It was Artemis, Apollo's twin sister, who initiated the whole cycle of killings, in return for an apparently trivial offence (563–9). We are reminded of this when she is invoked twice more in the play, once each by Electra and Clytemnestra (626, 1239).[126] If she can enforce a disproportionately cruel application of the talio (blood of a child for blood of an animal), then how much confidence can we have in the instructions of Apollo? At a climactic moment we are invited to ask this very question, when Orestes tells us that all is well, *if* Apollo gave his oracle well (1425). Whether or not these words indicate doubt in Orestes himself,[127] they may still raise a question in the minds of the audience. For as we saw in *Ajax* and *Antigone*, the gods use the same standard of retaliatory justice as humans, with all the complications which may ensue. The chorus even speculate as to a divine role in the murder of Agamemnon (199f.), and with characteristic caution qualify their curse on his killers by adding 'if it is permitted for me to say such things' (127). This despite their assurance that Electra should have confidence in the power of Zeus (173–5). Nor are the gods immune to the talio's weaknesses of self-interested application and insufficient attention to motive. Artemis disregards the careless or accidental nature of Aga-memnon's offence, just as Clytemnestra ignores the circumstances of Iphigeneia's death. Divine approval may vindicate the avengers on one level – vengeance is the justice of the gods, and avenging a father is clearly 'reverence' from one perspective – but this does not resolve the problems of vengeance on the human level. The murders are in-deed just, according to the talio, but the talio is a grim and prob-lematic form of justice.

---

[126] According to Wilamowitz only young women swear by Artemis in tragedy, unless there is special reason for someone else to do so (*Elektren* 220 n.). Jebb and Kamerbeek think Clytemnestra invokes the virgin goddess at 626 because of Electra's 'unmaidenly conduct', but this is not incompatible with an oblique reference by the poet to the events of Aulis (cf. Kaibel ad loc.).

[127] Critics diverge widely on the significance of the conditional. For various views see Kells and Kamerbeek ad loc.

6

Philoctetes

> There are times ... when reality bears features of such an
> impellingly moral complexion that it is impossible to follow
> the hewn path of expediency. There are times when life's ends
> are so raveled that reason and sense cry out that we stop and
> gather them together again before we can proceed.
>
> Richard Wright, *Native Son*

Odysseus and Neoptolemus

Philoctetes is the most ethically complex of all Sophocles' plays.
Philoctetes, Odysseus and the background figure of Achilles present
various paradigms for the young Neoptolemus, who must decide in
the course of the play which, if any, to adopt as his model.[1] Philoctetes and Odysseus are both endowed with established convictions,
but Neoptolemus' moral character is still in the process of formation.
Moral argument and choice take on a peculiarly dynamic role in the
plot as we see him exposed to the influence of each of the two older
men in turn.

Odysseus has come to Lemnos to steal Philoctetes' invincible
bow, which, according to the oracle of Helenus, is necessary for
Greek success at Troy.[2] But he knows that Philoctetes hates him bitterly (75f.), so his plan requires the cooperation of Neoptolemus.
Odysseus characterises the scheme as a joint one (25), but also makes
his own controlling role quite clear. Neoptolemus is to serve (15),
and to listen while Odysseus explains his plan (24f.). The young

---

[1] On Achilles and Odysseus as contrasting paradigms of heroism see Knox 121f.
with notes; Nagy 42–58; King 69–71. On Neoptolemus' moral education see
Rose 85–9 and my *Phusis*.

[2] The question of the precise terms of the oracle has been much discussed, largely
because of a number of apparent inconsistencies or illogicalities. For a 'naturalistic' defence of Sophocles, see Linforth, *Philoctetes* 101–4. Most critics, however, following the lead of T. von Wilamowitz, now accept that information
about the oracle is 'dispensed by Sophocles according to his dramatic convenience' (Winnington-Ingram 292). See especially Kitto, *FMD* 95–9; Knox
187–90 n. 21; Hinds 168–80; Steidle 169–73; Robinson 46–51; Gill, *Bow* 139–42;
and most recently Machin 61–74.

man's task is to exploit deceitfully the trust and friendship that may be expected to develop between him and Philoctetes when the latter discovers that he is Achilles' son (cf. 57, 70f., 242). Deception is appropriate to Odysseus' own traditional persona, but he rightly anticipates that the son of Achilles will object to such methods.[3] He therefore tries to forestall any scruples by the persuasive use of moral language. Neoptolemus must be 'noble' (gennaios), not just in body, but in performing whatever unusual task is now required of him, 'to serve the purpose for which you are here as a helper' (53). He reinforces his plea with the word gennaios (51), an aristocratic term of approval which appeals to Neoptolemus' pride in his birth and desire to be true to his parentage.[4] By suggesting that Neoptolemus owes him obedience, Odysseus exerts pressure on the young man to agree to his plan.[5] At the same time he provides him with an ethical escape-hatch by enabling him to disown any deed performed under orders.[6] He will shortly ask Neoptolemus to abjure personal moral responsibility, with the notorious exhortation to 'give me yourself' (84).[7] He will also exert additional moral pressure by pointing out that if the young man fails to obey he will give pain to all the Argives (67), thus, it is implied, failing in the obligation to help his friends.

Odysseus' scheme will bring the Greeks (including himself and Neoptolemus) salvation (109), the pleasure of victory (81), the removal of pain (67), and kerdos (111) (perhaps a hint at plunder, an obvious benefit not explicitly mentioned). He apparently aims to benefit himself and his friends or allies in these conventional ways.

3 Since ancient times critics have adduced Il. 9.312f., where Achilles declares to none other than Odysseus his hatred of deception (see the scholiast ad loc. and cf. Pl. Hipp. Min. 364e–5b).

4 See Knox 125 and my Phusis. On gennaios in Sophocles see Freis 51–61. For its general implications cf. also Thuc. 3.38 with Creed 229f. and Nussbaum 404f. On this kind of persuasive use of moral terms see Long, Morals 134; Dover 51.

5 Both ὑπηρέτης and ὑπουργεῖν (53) suggest subordination; cf. ὑπηρετεῖν (15). Note that Neoptolemus does not portray his own role in this way, but calls himself a 'fellow worker' (ξυνεργάτης 93). On Odysseus' wording cf. also King 68, 71f.

6 On Greek attitudes towards such a plea see Dover 147f, 155.

7 The expression itself is not unique and may be colloquial. See Stevens, Aesch. and Soph. 104, who compares Trach. 1117, Ter. Ad. 838. Cf. also Ar. Knights 739f. (where the context is sexual). For a parallel with similar implications of moral and intellectual influence see Diog. Laert. 2.34 (Aeschines says to Socrates, 'I give you myself').

According to Help Friends, this is a perfectly respectable, indeed an admirable goal. But if Odysseus is motivated by Help Friends, then his treatment of Philoctetes is reprehensible even by his own standards. According to Help Friends, he and the Atreidae had an obligation of loyalty to their loyal ally Philoctetes, an obligation which they violated by abandoning him. The legitimacy of Philoctetes' grievance is indicated not only by his assertion that the Atreidae and Odysseus each blame the other for the abandonment (1026–8), but also by Odysseus' defensive claim to have been acting under orders (6), and his evasive refusal to discuss the matter further (11f.). He does claim that Philoctetes' cries interfered with sacrifice (8–11). But Philoctetes will dismiss this as a pretext, pointing out that such considerations have not prevented his enemies from seeking him out now that they need him (1031–5). We may also note that religious scruples play no part in Neoptolemus' dilemma over whether to rescue Philoctetes. The emphasis is strictly on the discomfort caused by the sick man's foul odour and terrible cries (e.g. 519–21, 890f.).

Odysseus and the Atreidae are therefore guilty of treating a friend as an enemy and causing his justified hostility towards them. For this reason, even though he is well aware of Philoctetes' hatred (46f., 75f.), Odysseus cannot use Harm Enemies to justify plotting against him, for this would mean acknowledging his own culpability. He therefore skates over this embarrassing issue, failing to give a coherent reason for not approaching Philoctetes himself (72–4).[8] He cannot defend his conduct by appealing to Help Friends/Harm Enemies, or ask Neoptolemus to share in his enmity, without admitting that he has personally violated the code in the past.

Help Friends can with some plausibility be attributed to Odysseus as a fundamental principle that the audience would take for granted. The chorus allude to Help Friends/Harm Enemies within the deception (507–18) and even use Help Friends to justify Odysseus (1143–5).[9] The code is likewise presupposed by other characters, though (as we shall see) they disagree on how to interpret and implement it. Odysseus himself seems to presuppose it when trying to persuade the conscientious Neoptolemus that *his* behaviour must be determined by loyalty to the Greek army (66f.). But he never claims to be moved himself by Help Friends, and his language is conspicu-

---

[8] Cf. Linforth, *Philoctetes* 99f.
[9] On this passage see further below, p. 209f.

ously lacking in *phil-* words.[10] He does identify himself as a representative of the Greek army, but invokes it not as his *philoi* but as a threat to Neoptolemus: 'Aren't you afraid of the Achaean army, doing this?' (1250); 'I shall go and tell this to the whole army, which will take vengeance on you' (1257f.; cf. 1243, 1294). In his clearest statement of motivation there is no mention of *philia* or the common good (1049–52).[11] On the other hand, he places no emphasis on his own pleasure or advantage. We may safely assume that success in his mission will bring him personal power, prestige and material rewards, but the 'pleasure' of victory (81) with which he tempts Neoptolemus is impersonally expressed, and we know that his self-interest coincides with the public good. In the absence of any explicit statement, it remains unclear whether he should be construed as acting from Help Friends, self-interest, or some union of the two.

There are hints in Odysseus' language, however, that his overriding aim is the fulfilment of his own goals, which just happen to coincide with the public good.[12] He sets up an alternative criterion of behaviour, irrespective of morality. This criterion is explicitly identified as 'salvation' (109) or *kerdos* (111). The former is in itself irreproachable, but the latter is an unsavoury term suggesting prosperity gained at the expense of others, often by treacherous means.[13] 'Victory', however, is the key word for Odysseus. In normal usage, *nike* can be used for 'winning' any kind of goal, but is generally positive, connoting enviable achievement and success on a personal or public level. At its first appearance in *Philoctetes* it apparently refers to the pleasant consequences of victory over Troy (81), which will follow from 'victory' over Philoctetes. Odysseus admits that his scheme is 'shameless' (83) and (by implication) *kakos* (80), unjust (82) and irreverent (84f.). But, he argues, 'victory' should outweigh any moral squeamishness, for it is 'sweet' (81f.). If they succeed, they will

---

[10] See Nussbaum, *Consequences* 36; Rose 89f.

[11] Nussbaum, *Consequences* 31 and others interpret the 'hedonistic calculus' of 66f. as the commendable subordination of self-interest to the needs of the majority. But see contra my *Odysseus*, where I argue more fully for the view of Odysseus presented in this chapter.

[12] It is possible to represent society without having the well-being of its members at heart, as Plato's Thrasymachus knows well (*Rep.* 343).

[13] For its pejorative associations see above, p. 173 n. 84. For its connection with Odysseus see King 74.

subsequently be revealed as just (82), and Neoptolemus will be called 'most reverent' (84f.).[14]

In two other places *nike* is closely associated with Odysseus. As he leaves the stage after winning over Neoptolemus he invokes his patron goddess as Athena Nike (134).[15] When he reappears he tells us that *nike* is his first priority: he acts in whatever way is 'necessary' in any given situation;[16] when men are being judged for justice or *arete*, none will be found more reverent than himself; but it is in his nature to crave victory 'in everything' (1049–52). As in the prologue, he admits by implication that his present behaviour is deficient in justice, *arete* and reverence, but declares that for him *nike* overrides such considerations. In this case only will he make an exception, conceding 'victory' by allowing Philoctetes to have his way and stay on Lemnos.[17]

A 'victor' in this sense, then, is one who gets what he or she desires, regardless of the contrary wishes of friends or foes.[18] An Odysseus, who craves victory 'in everything' (literally 'everywhere', 1052), is one determined to get his own way regardless of the needs or desires of others. His own aims may be more or less creditable, but if he is *never* willing to respect the desires of others, then he threatens to make nonsense of the whole basis of morality.[19] That this accords with Greek ways of thinking is shown by the pejorative adjective *panourgos*, which literally means 'one who does all'. It acquires its common meaning 'villainous' through its use for one who disregards moral constraints to do anything at all in pursuit of his or her own goals.[20] Philoctetes uses the noun *panourgia* of Odysseus in a

[14] ἐκφαίνομαι is always used for revealing something clearly to be the case, not for a deceptive appearance (see Jebb ad loc. and LSJ s.v.). But as 85 makes clear, Odysseus' emphasis is on how the deed will appear to others, not on the deed itself which he admits to be shameful. Cf. Nussbaum, *Consequences* 51 n. 29.

[15] On the goddess Nike and her identification with Athena see Jebb ad loc. and cf. Segal 138f.

[16] Odysseus repeatedly uses such impersonal expressions of necessity, which enable him to express the demands of expediency while evading responsibility for any dubious implications (cf. 50, 54, 57, 77, 111, 982, 988, 993, 994, 1060). See further my *Odysseus* and cf. Benardete 297; Nussbaum, *Consequences* 29f.

[17] On the question of whether he is bluffing see below, n. 89.

[18] Cf. especially *OC* 849–55; also *OC* 1204, *El.* 253; *Aj.* 330, 1353; Aesch. *Ag.* 941f.

[19] Cf. above, p. 3 n. 8.

[20] In Soph. fr. 683 (Radt) it is associated with trampling on justice and *sophrosune*. Cf. also Pl. *Ap.* 38d–39a (quoted below, p. 211, and discussed in my *Odysseus*).

way that brings out its etymology (407f.), and of Neoptolemus when he is under Odysseus' influence (927).[21] So when Odysseus exhorts Neoptolemus to be 'bold' and cast aside his scruples (82),[22] he is not offering a new moral system so much as ditching morality altogether.

Neoptolemus responds to Odysseus' first attempt at persuasion with an unequivocal rejection: he 'loathes' to do something that is 'painful' for him to hear about (86f.). Such scheming, as Odysseus feared, is alien to his *phusis* (88f.; cf. 79f.). As we shall soon discover, he shares the conventional assumptions that profit is desirable and gratuitous suffering undesirable, but disagrees over what means are admissible to attain these ends. He therefore makes a counter-suggestion – why not take Philoctetes by force? (90f.). After all, he says, Philoctetes will not have a chance with his wounded foot since we outnumber him (91f.). It is remarkable to a modern sensibility that he should regard deception as shameful and yet propose the use of force against a defenceless cripple.[23] The crucial point, however, is that force would be open and honest. For Neoptolemus (at this stage) this makes it an acceptable alternative.[24] But even now he is swayed towards deception by the obligation of loyalty (93f.). His final word, however, is an explicit rejection of the Odyssean view that 'winning' justifies anything – he would rather 'fail honourably (*kalôs*) than win basely' (94f.).

At this point the two opposing standpoints are clear: for Odysseus, the desirable fruits of victory overrule anything that may interfere with the reaping of such fruits. Neoptolemus is torn between two claims, his loyalty to Odysseus and the army (which apparently coincides with self-interest), and his desire not to do what he con-

[21] Cf. also 448. For the etymological point cf. 633f.; *Ant.* 300f.; *OC* 761f.; fr. 189, 567 (Radt); and see Long 154f. Similar language is used of Odysseus at *Aj.* 379f., 445; fr. 567 (Radt). Philoctetes himself is willing to 'suffer anything' rather than be taken to Troy (999). Here is the converse of Odysseus' *panourgia*: the one will do anything to achieve his goal, the other suffer anything to thwart it.

[22] 'Boldness' or 'daring' (τόλμα) is morally neutral. It may be a commendable courage or a reprehensible daring (cf. 110, 363, 369, 481, 634, 984 and see Dihle, *Will* 22f.). In its negative sense the idiom 'daring all' may be used much like *panourgos* (cf. *OC* 760f., fr. 189 (Radt)).

[23] Cf. Rose 88.

[24] Cf. Knox 122. This attitude vanishes as soon as he comes into contact with Philoctetes. Although he persists for a while in using force, he no longer tries to justify it as acceptable per se.

siders *kakos*. The resulting dilemma gives Odysseus an opening. He starts with some worldly wisdom, taking advantage of Neoptolemus' youth and respect for authority:[25] 'I too when I was young had a slow tongue and an active arm; but now with experience I see that it is the tongue, not action, that rules in everything among mortals' (96–9).[26] He rephrases the conflict between deception and force as one of word and deed, allying force with youthful rashness and deception with wise maturity, and thus translating the moral issue into terms favourable to himself.[27]

Neoptolemus, however, is not fooled. He tries another suggestion: persuasion, the honest counterpart of deception (since both employ words rather than deeds). Odysseus replies that neither persuasion nor force would work. The three possible methods of achieving their goal – persuasion, force and deception – are here clearly distinguished, and Odysseus has ruled out the first two.[28] So they are back with the original question: is it disgraceful to speak falsehoods? (108). But Neoptolemus is now asking Odysseus' opinion, rather than categorically stating his own. Odysseus' reply is crucial: it is not disgraceful if it brings salvation (109). This shocks Neoptolemus, who asks, 'How shall one have the face to speak those words?' (110, trans, Jebb).[29] Odysseus justifies himself with his explicit appeal to *kerdos*, transforming outrage at a morally reprehensible 'daring' (110) into an exhortation to courage: 'when you do something for profit, it is not proper to hang back' (111).

With the morally tinged reference to 'profit' Neoptolemus begins to weaken. He wants to know what 'profit' is in it for him

---

[25] Neoptolemus is frequently referred to as 'child', even by the chorus, his social subordinates (1072). For the relative frequency of such forms of address and a discussion of the paternity theme see Avery 285–90; cf. also Reinhardt 164–6; Knox 122; Vidal-Naquet 172f., 177. Respect for Odysseus' superior status is shown by the way Neoptolemus addresses him as 'lord' (e.g. 26), even when disagreeing with him (94).

[26] On 'tongue' as a label for intellectuals see Denniston, *Aristophanes* 120. It is used pejoratively by Philoctetes (408, 440). Cf. also *OC* 806f.; fr. 201a (Radt); Eur. *Ba.* 268f.

[27] For the commonplace that wisdom is proper to age cf. *Ant.* 281; *OC* 804f.; fr. 260, 664, 694 (Radt); *Il.* 3.108–10, 4.322f.; Eur. *Ba.* 251f., *Phoen.* 528–30.

[28] On these three options as a structural principle for the play, see especially Garvie; Buxton 118–32. Cf. also Knox 119f.; Easterling, *Philoctetes* 31.

[29] The English idiom approximates the Greek, on which see above, p. 70 n. 52. For the force of λακεῖν see Jebb and Kamerbeek ad loc. Cf. also King 73.

(112), for he has been told that he is the one who will sack Troy (114). As we shall discover later, he regards this military enterprise as glorious and *kalos* (352, 1344–7).[30] When Odysseus spells out the need for Philoctetes' bow (115), Neoptolemus' heroic ambitions finally defeat his instinctive scruples. When he does give way, it is with an Odyssean impersonal – the bow 'must be hunted' (116) – which evades full responsibility for the decision.[31] Odysseus fortifies this reluctant acquiescence with a further appeal to self-interest: 'If you do this, you will get two gifts' (117). Neoptolemus is interested in the gifts: 'Tell me what they are, and I would not refuse to act' (118). His decision is confirmed when Odysseus specifies two 'gifts' perfectly designed to appeal to the son of Achilles – not material gifts, but two virtues, or at least the reputation for them: 'You would be called at once wise and good (*sophos* and *agathos*)' (119). Odysseus, here as elsewhere, sees virtue only in terms of reputation, as potentially useful in a pragmatic sense, and couches his moral appeals to Neoptolemus accordingly (82, 85, 119).[32] Neoptolemus himself wants to *be* virtuous (86–8), but also shows concern for his moral reputation (93f.). He is vulnerable on both counts to Odysseus' promised 'gifts'.

But these are flexible terms. *Sophos* may refer to the prudence and good judgement that guide proper action, but also to sophistic cleverness of a morally suspect kind.[33] This ambivalence makes it especially appropriate to the ambiguous cunning of Odysseus' traditional persona. Neoptolemus apparently wants to be thought *sophos*, but will come to realise that it is not Odysseus' cleverness that he desires. This is first hinted at during his deception of Philoctetes (431f.). It becomes explicit when Neoptolemus declares that although Odysseus is by nature *sophos* (clever), his words are not *sophos* (wise) (1244). He admits that his present behaviour is not *sophos* (clever), but asserts that it is more important for it to be just (1246). He thus

---

30 At 352 *kalos* is associated with Odysseus, but only as reported in a deception speech, and moreover in a persuasive context where it is not explicitly attributed to Odysseus himself. On Neoptolemu˟ ˟nbition' cf. King 74.

31 For Odysseus' usage see above, n. 16. For N˟ ptolemus cf. also below, p. 207.

32 Contrast 51 (which refers to the task at hand, not the future). For this and other sophistic traits in Odysseus see my *Odysseus*.

33 For the former cf. 421–3, where Philoctetes uses both *sophos* and *agathos* of his old friend Nestor. Cf. also *Aj.* 1374. For the latter cf. 14, 77. For the contrast cf. Eur. *Ba.* 395 with Dodds ad loc. and see O'Brien 33–8; Dover 118–23.

leaves open for himself the possibility of being *sophos* (wise), if Odyssean *sophia* fails to qualify as true wisdom.

Agathos is never pejorative, but it too is fluid in content. In Homer it often describes the powerful king or warrior like Achilles, whom his son Neoptolemus aspires to emulate. But by the end of the fifth century, when *Philoctetes* was produced, *agathos* and *arete* could commend not only other kinds of success (cf. Pl. *Meno* 71e–72a, 73c, 76b), but also such virtues as justice and *sophrosune*.[34] *Agathos*, like *sophos*, is flexible enough to attract Neoptolemus, who desires both military glory and moral rectitude, without being utterly inappropriate to Odysseus, the advocate of success at all costs.[35] Neoptolemus has already rejected the notion that the end justifies the means (94f.), but he does want to be, and to be thought, *agathos* in other ways, so he is susceptible to Odysseus' suggestion. He does not pause to consider whether it is really Odysseus' *arete* that he wants to have, or to be known for.

He will be made aware of an alternative *arete* when Philoctetes says that he may hold the sacred bow, because he has promised to take him home and restore him to his family and *philoi*, and taken his part against his enemies (662–6). Philoctetes concludes that Neoptolemus may touch the bow on account of his *arete*, which is equated with the service Philoctetes himself performed for his friend Heracles (667–70). Like Odysseus, Philoctetes promises Neoptolemus a name for *arete*. But he offers this recognition for a very different kind of behaviour. His *arete* involves service to a friend in need and hostility to his enemies.[36] As with *sophos*, two versions of the same term come into direct conflict. Neoptolemus will eventually be forced to choose between them. In the prologue, however, enticed by Odysseus' arguments without regard for their implications, he completely capitulates (120). His resolve to 'dismiss all sense of shame' (120) shows that deception is still disgraceful in his eyes. But

---

[34] Such usage is conspicuously Socratic (see Vlastos, *Happiness* 3), but Socrates was not the first to use *arete* in such a way (cf. Theognis 147f. with Dover, *Evaluation* 48).

[35] In Dio's paraphrase of the prologue to Euripides' *Philoctetes*, Odysseus calls himself '*aristos* and most *sophos* of the Greeks' (Dio 59.1).

[36] Even those who think *arete* in Sophocles means 'supreme valour or the reputation for it, nothing less and nothing more' (Winnington-Ingram 301; cf. Adkins 193) must admit this as an exception (so Torrance 323 n. 8; Winnington-Ingram 309 n. 16; Adkins does not discuss the passage).

the prospect of a reputation as *agathos* and *sophos*, combined with loyalty, obedience and personal profit, is enough to outweigh the shame which was his natural response.

Neoptolemus and Philoctetes: deception

The chorus are eager to help (142f.) and alert to opportunities for success (150f.). They are Neoptolemus' subordinate *philoi*, standing in the same relationship to him as he does to Odysseus.[37] Their eagerness to grasp opportunities for their master is exactly what Odysseus wants from his subordinate (151; cf. 131, 1069). Their actions are determined solely by loyalty, and they defer to Neoptolemus' judgement in almost everything.[38] They appear to act on the principle suggested to Neoptolemus by Odysseus, that loyal obedience to orders removes responsibility from the subordinate. This will be confirmed later by their claim to have had no part in the deception (1117f.), and their defence of Odysseus (1143–5). Unlike their master, however, they are troubled by no moral scruples. They provide a foil to Neoptolemus' developing awareness that obedient loyalty to superior *philoi* may be challenged by other principles.

After affirming their solidarity with Neoptolemus, the chorus go on to express the pity, already hinted at (151), which is their most characteristic response to Philoctetes. They have not yet seen him, but imaginatively conjure up his hardships, apparently sharing in that general human sympathy which Philoctetes himself will urge as a ground for pity and help (177–9; cf. 501–7). Their ode begins to fill out the bare and unsympathetic account of his predicament given by Odysseus in his opening speech (16–21). But Neoptolemus replies strangely to their compassionate words. Philoctetes' sufferings, he says, were divinely caused, and he has been kept from Troy until now so that it should not fall before its due time (191–200).[39] But

---

[37] They use the same verb for their role as Odysseus does of Neoptolemus (ὑπουργεῖν 53, 143). ὑπηρετεῖν (above, n. 5), is not used of them but indicates etymologically precisely their role, meaning literally 'to row for'. On their status see Gardiner 16f.

[38] Besides this first song see 963f., 1072f., and cf. 886–8. The only exception is 843–64, where they think they are advising him in his best interests. Gardiner ch. 2 argues that they become progressively more deferential as Neoptolemus learns to assert himself.

[39] On this passage see Linforth, *Philoctetes* 107f.; Winnington-Ingram 284f.; cf. also Kitto, *FMD* 111–13.

this detachment, like his earlier advocacy of violence (90), will be altered when he encounters the man himself. Neoptolemus' emotional response to Philoctetes will be an important factor in his moral education, helping to counteract the insidiously rational arguments of the cool Odysseus.

When Philoctetes finally appears he at once appeals strongly for pity, on the same grounds as those just given by the chorus (227–9). This appeal is backed up by a long speech detailing his miseries. Odysseus' skeletal account is now fully fleshed out from the point of view of the victim.[40] He accuses his enemies of acting in an impious and disgraceful way, and of gloating in his misfortunes (257f., 265; cf. 271, 1023, 1125). His grievance, as he later makes clear, is their ingratitude towards a loyal friend (1026–8, 1216f.). He lives according to the 'expediency of the stomach' and other such basic physical needs, which must be satisfied with extreme pain by a severely handicapped ingenuity (285–99; cf. 35f.). This provides a poignant contrast to, and commentary on, Odysseus' belief in the use of 'skill' to acquire what is 'necessary' for 'profit', 'victory' and 'salvation'.[41] The contrast is most pointed when Philoctetes expresses his dependence on fire with the same phrase, at the same position in the line, that Odysseus used of his relationship to Athena Nike: it 'always keeps me safe' (297; cf. 134).[42] He ends by blaming the Atreidae and Odysseus for all the sufferings he has so vividly recounted, and praying that they may suffer likewise in return (314–16; cf. 275, 791–5). He even sees his relationship to the creatures of the island in terms of the talio (954–60). But in this case it was he who began hostilities by preying on them, in return for which he invites them to feast upon his flesh (1155–7).

In the final portion of his speech Philoctetes tells of the visiting sailors who would pity him verbally and even leave him food or clothing, but refused to take him home (307–11). Expressions of pity are mere words, which must be put into action if they are to deserve praise.[43] This imparts a heavy irony to the chorus' claim to pity

[40] On the contrast between Odysseus' description and the realities of Philoctetes' situation, see Rose 63; Inoue; Segal 324.

[41] See Rose 58–64, 82–5 and cf. Segal 296.

[42] On the implications of *soteria* for the different characters see Rose 64–7, 84f.; Avery 296.

[43] Conversely 'pity' may refer to deeds alone, regardless of words or sentiment (Dover 195f.).

Philoctetes 'as much as' the other strangers who visited the island (317f.).[44] For they apparently pity him just that much and no more – or even less, since they will subsequently try to abandon him in a worse condition than that in which they found him (835–8). The pity they express is fundamentally flawed by the fact that they have no intention of acting on it.[45] These ineffectual expressions form a dramatic contrast both with Neoptolemus' initial coldness and with his subsequently developing pity, which will eventually be confirmed in action and lay the foundation for friendship.[46] When the chorus deceitfully urge him to pity Philoctetes (507) and take the sick man home (516–18), their pretence brings out all the more poignantly the gulf between the words and deeds of pity.

Neoptolemus launches the deception by recounting his quarrel with Odysseus and the Atreidae. It is hard to draw a line between fact and fiction in this puzzling narrative.[47] But however we interpret the tale, its effect relies on the assumption that depriving Neoptolemus of his father's arms would have been a justified cause of anger. Odysseus, who fabricates the story, expects it to be plausible, and Philoctetes accepts it without question as an outrage typical of his enemies (403–6). He considers Neoptolemus fully justified in leaving Troy, since the others committed the *hubris* of taking away his 'prize' (1364f.), just as Agamemnon took Achilles' in the *Iliad*.[48] There is thus a set of values, reminiscent of Achilles, subscribed to by Philoctetes and implicitly acknowledged by both Odysseus and Neoptolemus, whereby Neoptolemus would have a legitimate grievance against Odysseus if the latter kept the arms (cf. 62f.).

Philoctetes' propensity for affection and loyalty have already been displayed. The very sight of the new arrival, then the sound of

---

[44] Cf. Gardiner 22.

[45] There is no reason, however, to doubt their sincerity. The first ode, sung before Philoctetes appears, makes this clear. Thus we have no reason to question later expressions of sympathy, such as at 676–17, on which see now Tarrant, *Philoctetes*; Gardiner 31–6.

[46] This contrast is weakened if we do not take the chorus' pity as sincere (see previous note). Alt 154 points out that the chorus express pity only while Neoptolemus is playing a part. Once he starts to show it himself (759 etc.) they speak of it no more.

[47] For a discussion of various views (though his own is unacceptable) see Calder, *Philoctetes* 389–407.

[48] For this analogy see Knox 123; Segal 345; Scodel 94f. Hamilton 131–7 emphasises the correspondence of Neoptolemus' story to Philoctetes' own situation.

his voice, prompt an effusion of *phil-* words which reach a climax
with the disclosure of Neoptolemus' identity (224, 228, 229, 234,
237, 242). When Neoptolemus goes on to express rage towards the
Atreidae, shared hatred creates an instant bond. Prejudiced by his
own hostility, Philoctetes applauds Neoptolemus' anger before dis-
covering the cause (327f.). When he hears the full story he responds,
'You have sailed here to me, it seems, with a clear counterpart to my
pain' (403f.). As the scholiast on 59 remarks, 'those injured by the
same person have *philia* for each other'. Neoptolemus himself will
later claim that Philoctetes' hatred for the Atreidae makes him his
'greatest friend' (585f.).

The strength of Philoctetes' loyalties is brought out by his repeated wishes that his enemies had died instead of his friends (416–
18, 426–30).[49] Here and elsewhere he aligns his friends with various
terms of approval. Achilles, who is *philtatos* (242), is also *eugenes*
(336) and *aristos* (1284). Nestor, who is '*agathos* and my *philos*', prevents evils and is *sophos* in counsel (421–3), thus enjoying two of the
epithets that Odysseus earlier promised Neoptolemus (119). The cata-
logue of friends/approved persons consists of those who Philoctetes
believes would have supported Neoptolemus' claim to his father's
arms, all of whom are dead or incapacitated like Philoctetes himself.
Conversely he charges his enemies, who are still alive, with impious
and disgraceful behaviour (257, 265), 'bad words', 'villainy' and injustice (407–9). Besides Philoctetes' personal enemies,[50] this group of
the wicked/living/enemies is represented by Thersites, a paradigm of
the despicable, who is introduced in a way that makes Neoptolemus
(and the audience) think immediately of Odysseus (439–41).[51] By
aligning his enemies with baseness in this way, Philoctetes implicitly
provides an ethical defence for his vigorous pursuit of Harm

[49] This whole scene has excited much critical comment. My view is close to that
of Whitman 182. Cf. also Winnington-Ingram's appendix F.

[50] Diomedes (416) is not explicitly represented as a personal enemy, but he is associated with Odysseus in many tales, and accompanied him to Lemnos in
Euripides' play (see Jebb, *Introduction* §8), a version to which Sophocles seems to
allude in the false merchant's tale (570f.).

[51] In order to introduce Thersites Sophocles has altered the legend of his death (see
the scholiast on 445 and Jebb on 442). Huxley 33f. (followed by Calder, *Philoctetes* 159f.) argues that we are meant to assume he is in fact dead and Neoptolemus is lying. But we cannot tell whether this part of the tale is supposed to be
fictitious (pace Huxley, 445 proves nothing). For the significance of Thersites
here see further my *Odysseus*.

Enemies. The revenge he craves is also, in his eyes, a just punishment of the wicked (1035f.). This alignment is extended to a general statement about the gods: they leave what is *kakos* and villainous alive, and destroy the just and worthwhile (446–50). Philoctetes thus confirms Neoptolemus' aphorism that war spares the bad man and takes only the 'worthwhile' (436f.). We might expect this apparent commonplace to refer to the respective fates of the coward and the hero in battle.[52] But the inclusion amongst the living of Diomedes (416), one of the greatest warriors of the *Iliad*, makes it clear that mere courage is not the relevant criterion.[53]

Neoptolemus responds equivocally to Philoctetes' characterisation of his enemies. He professes to share Philoctetes' attitudes – he prefers the *agathos* and 'worthwhile' to the 'worse' and the coward (456–8) – but the content of these evaluative terms remains unclear. The aristocratic language may remind the audience of Neoptolemus' originally stated desire to live up to his father's heroic standards, in contrast to his present Odyssean deceit. But on the surface it is an innocuous statement of preference which could offend no one. Neoptolemus is hedging his bets. This is the kind of vacuous moral statement about which he will have to make up his mind by the end of the play.

Philoctetes' observations on the nature of warfare bring him face to face with the problem of evil. He shows proper reverence for the gods, often calling for aid in their name (736–8, 747, 770, 933, 967, 1181–5). He also believes that they sanction his hatreds and friendships, for these are based on values that he thinks the gods share and enforce. In the strongest statement of this belief he declares that his desire for revenge is just, and the gods will fulfil it if they care about justice; but they *do* care about justice, as Odysseus' very arrival proves (1035–9). The logical conclusion to this impassioned syllogism is that the gods will indeed punish his enemies, but at this point confident assertion is replaced by prayer (1040–2). Conversely, Philoctetes refuses to let Odysseus use the gods to justify his actions. Odysseus is 'most hateful to the gods' (1031) and his reference to Zeus a mere pretext, for unlike Odysseus, the gods are not 'liars'

---

[52] Cf. fr. 724 (Radt) and further parallels in Jebb on 436f.; Bowra 277. King 45 and n. 137 observes that the same four figures mentioned here as dead appear elsewhere as the cream of the Greeks who died at Troy.

[53] Cf. also the reminder of Odysseus' bravery in rescuing Achilles' corpse (373).

(992). The religious excuse for abandoning Philoctetes was likewise a pretext (1034).[54] For in Philoctetes' view the gods sanction his own values and condemn those of Odysseus. This is summarised as 'praising things divine' (452).

At the same time, however, Philoctetes has good reason to feel 'hated by the gods' (254), considering the injustice, suffering and ignominy to which he has been exposed.[55] So in his own case he finds the gods 'bad' (452).[56] Yet they will turn out to be just in the long run, 'in time' (1041), if they answer his prayers and eventually give him the compensation of revenge. This is the only way he can reconcile faith in the ultimate justice of the gods with the conviction that his own sufferings are unjust. But can this attempted reconciliation work? Only if there is an equivocation on 'justice'. Philoctetes' gods, it seems, dispense rectificatory justice – they will compensate the victim by penalising the injurer.[57] But they do not display distributive justice – they do not hand out good fortune according to worth. Moreover while Philoctetes treats Odysseus' arrival as evidence of divine concern for justice, he ignores the possible implications of this belief. If Odysseus' mission was commanded by the gods as a just recompense for his sufferings, perhaps that recompense consists precisely in the opportunity to sail for Troy.[58] Philoctetes speaks as though the gods have caused the Greeks to need his aid purely so that he may be in a position to withhold it, thus obtaining his revenge. He craves a vengeance which is wholly negative, and destructive to the point of self-destruction. Even when explicitly promised the divinely sanctioned recompense of cure and glory (1324–42), he would rather sacrifice such compensation for the sake of revenge

---

[54] This presumably means that the argument from sacrificing was insincere, and therefore an abuse of piety and hateful to the gods. Alternatively, it could mean that the gods care more about justice than about the interruption of sacrifices by involuntary ill-omened cries.

[55] On πικρός as 'hated' (254) see above, p. 98 n. 189. For the injustice of the 'divine chance' that caused Philoctetes' wound (1326; cf. 192–4) see Segal, *Piety* 150–2.

[56] εὕρω (452) means 'I find from my own experience', as opposed to his more general conclusions about the gods.

[57] For 'rectificatory' and 'distributive' justice, see Arist. *EN* 1130b30–32b20.

[58] Philoctetes does not yet know of the cure in store for him (919 is vague; the cure is not revealed until 1329–34; cf. Wilamowitz 309). But he does know that he is to be rescued and is needed to take part in the sack of Troy (919–22; cf. 610–13).

than forgo revenge and obtain compensation. But compensation is all that divine justice has on offer.

After the first deception scene Philoctetes 'persuades' Neoptolemus to take him home. First he makes a formal supplication (468–72). Then, like Odysseus in the prologue, he begs him to endure for one brief day (475, 480, 481). [59] The two appeals have a superficial similarity, but Philoctetes is exhorting the young man to have the courage of his convictions, whereas Odysseus urged him to abandon them. The courage demanded by Philoctetes means enduring the physical 'discomfort' of his presence (473; cf. 481–3). Avoiding such discomfort was one of the original reasons for abandoning him (1031f.), and Odysseus urged the pleasure of victory as a reason for 'enduring' the deception (81f.). Philoctetes' appeal is therefore directly opposed to the values of an Odysseus. When Neoptolemus starts to abandon these values, it will be at the prompting of a different kind of 'discomfort' (902f.).[60]

The parallelism of the two attempts to influence Neoptolemus is made particularly clear when Philoctetes supports his appeal with the word *gennaios* (475; cf. 799, 801, 1402). He gives it quite a different content from Odysseus, who suggested that it was *gennaios* to obey orders, no matter what (50–3). It is the 'no matter what' that creates the problem, for loyalty and obedience are not in themselves objectionable principles. According to Philoctetes, however, one who is *gennaios* hates disgrace and pursues the 'worthwhile' as a source of renown (476f.). His language accords with his own implicitly moral criteria for friendship and enmity (disgrace is *echthros* to him). He goes on to apply this 'nobility' to Neoptolemus' case in such a way that the conflict with Odysseus' view becomes inescapable: if Neoptolemus abandons Philoctetes he will acquire an ignoble (non-*kalos*) reproach, while if he rescues him he will achieve great renown (477f.). Philoctetes thus appeals to the desire of Achilles' son to do what is *kalos*, to avoid disgrace and to achieve a reputation for noble deeds.

This appeal is couched in the language of heroic morality, but

---

[59] For the echoes of 79–85 see Kirkwood 243 n. 23. Note especially the parallel phrasing of ἔξοιδα ... ἀλλά ... τόλμα (79–82) and ἔξοιδα ... ὅμως δὲ τλῆθι (474f.).

[60] On δυσχέρεια (473, 900, 902) and εὐχερής (519, 875) see Segal 312f. and 473 n. 91. Cf. also Kitto, *FMD* 120.

the behaviour that Philoctetes urges is rather different from a deed of Achillean heroism.[61] Philoctetes, himself an Achillean figure, is in a predicament where the value of justice and compassion are all too apparent. He uses heroic, aristocratic language to urge a course of action that conforms to intrinsic moral standards rather than the approval of the community at large, and to justice rather than heroic accomplishment. His appeal competes with Neoptolemus' desire for military glory, and with Odysseus' earlier promise of a reputation as *agathos* and *sophos* (119). That promise convinced Neoptolemus to dismiss all sense of shame (120), but now his sense of shame is coming home to roost. He cannot have both these promised reputations.

Philoctetes ends with a final appeal for both pity and salvation (501). He requires pity translated into action, as opposed to the mere 'words' of the other strangers who came to Lemnos (307–9). He implies that active pity is a proper response to one's fellow human in misfortune, since disaster can befall anyone, however prosperous (501–6; cf. *Aj.* 121–6, *OC* 565–8). This view of pity is endorsed later in the play, both by Philoctetes himself and by Neoptolemus. Philoctetes begs the gods, if they pity him, to punish his enemies, suggesting that they too should be moved by pity to justice (1040–2).[62] Thus pity is elevated into an instrument of justice and given a place in a moral scheme. Active pity, at least for the victims of injustice, is not merely legitimate but right. Similarly Neoptolemus implies that when someone is forced by circumstances to suffer misfortune, pity is a just response (1320). He does not restrict this to the victims of human injustice, but extends it to all those who cannot improve their own lot.[63] One corollary is that those who reject a chance to escape their misery forfeit the right to pity from others (1316–20). Another is that both failure to act on one's pity and hard-heartedness or lack of pity become reprehensible. In *Philoctetes* both the chorus and Odysseus fall short according to this standard, the chorus by failing to live up to their feelings of pity, and Odysseus by failing to have any (cf. 1074f.). Neoptolemus, by contrast, though he devotes fewer words to it than the chorus, both develops feelings of pity and is eventually willing to act on them (965f., 1074f.). His compassion

---

[61] See Rose 68 and my *Phusis*.

[62] Cf. *Il.* 24.23, 44f. On divine compassion see Dover 78f. and on pity and justice ib. 196.

[63] Rose 77 n. 63 cites Pl. *Prot.* 323c–24c. Cf. also Arist. *EN* 1109b31f.

for Philoctetes is an essential catalyst both in the formation of his friendship with Philoctetes and in the development of his moral character.[64] But if the gods pity Philoctetes, it is only so far as to compensate him for his sufferings. They never give him the revenge for which he prays. Neoptolemus too, though inspired by pity to befriend Philoctetes, forestalls his revenge on Odysseus (1300–4). It is perhaps appropriate that this humane emotion should prompt justice in the form of compensation for the victim rather than punishment for the offender.

At the end of Philoctetes' great speech the chorus pretend to back him up out of pity (507). They speak in terms of friendship and enmity: rescuing Philoctetes will transform his enemies' harm into a *kerdos* (510–18).[65] They do not seem troubled by the possibility (which they themselves introduce) of *nemesis* from the gods.[66] Their willingness to exploit piety in the cause of deceit is closer to Odysseus than to their master Neoptolemus, who never goes so far.[67] Their inconsistency forms an effective counterpoint to Neoptolemus' growing awareness of the importance of ethical consistency.[68] But at this stage he and they are equally involved in a charade of

[64] It has rightly been observed (e.g. by Alt 157f.) that it is the direct experience of Philoctetes' disease which marks the emotional turning point for Neoptolemus (759f.). His cry of mental pain (895) clearly echoes Philoctetes' scream of physical anguish (745f.) (cf. Knox 132, Winnington-Ingram 288). On these inarticulate cries, see Podlecki, *Word* 234f.; Rose 72; Segal 333–6.

[65] The harm and *kerdos* in question are to Philoctetes, but within the fiction his rescue will also produce harm for the Atreidae and *kerdos* for Neoptolemus. The latter would thus supposedly be helping his friends and himself and harming his enemies.

[66] In context this *nemesis* (518) doubtless refers to the consequences of spurning a suppliant. But it has broader implications for the deception of which it forms a part.

[67] Though he too will refer with ominous irony to the *nemesis* of the gods (601f.). Cf. also the discordance of 656f. (below, p. 203). On the chorus' 'misuse of religious matters' (especially at 391–402) see Reinhardt 171 and 267 n. 9; Gardiner 23–6. For Odysseus cf. 84f., 989f., 1050–2. On the general similarity of the chorus to Odysseus see Gardiner ch. 2 passim and cf. my *Odysseus*.

[68] Reinhardt 182 argues that the chorus has two distinct functions and therefore cannot be blamed for inconsistency, a 'Tychoism' followed e.g. by Alt 152; Burton 249. But since as Burton himself puts it, they 'perform the part assigned to them as fellow-conspirators with their captain in an enterprise involving trickery', it is reasonable to attribute some of their inconsistencies to deceit as well as to Sophocles' desire 'to move his audience' (Burton loc. cit.). Cf. also Rose 71 n. 51.

concern for principle which only serves to highlight their treachery. When Neoptolemus admonishes them to be sure their actions live up to their words, they answer that they will never fail to do so, for this would be a 'reproach' which may 'justly be brought as a reproach' (523).[69] Yet they are all planning to fail in their promises far more radically than Neoptolemus suggests. This ironic exchange strikes a warning note. It portrays the chorus and Neoptolemus as well aware that their behaviour is liable to blame, thus laying them open to criticism for precisely the fault they are condemning.[70]

Neoptolemus pretends to give way to the chorus, on the ground that it would be disgraceful to fall short of them in helping a stranger (524f.).[71] Like his exhortation to the chorus, this is both ironic and ominous. He claims to be moved by honour while in the very act of disregarding it, recalling both his own assumption that one should avoid disgraceful deeds (108; cf. 94f.) and his attempt to abandon this sensitivity at Odysseus' instigation (120f.). In the event this attempt will fail, as his own principle of moral consistency catches up with him and he more and more decisively rejects disgrace (842, 906, 909, 1228, 1234, 1249). For the moment, however, this shunning of disgrace remains a lie. Philoctetes responds with a joyful affirmation of friendship: 'Oh dearest day, sweetest man, dear sailors, how can I prove to you in deed how friendly you have made me!' (530–2). In a further twist of irony he too endorses the view that deeds should match up to words, while affirming the reciprocity of favours and *philia*.

Their departure is forestalled by the arrival of the false merchant, sent by Odysseus to relate a fictitious tale of the need for Philoctetes at Troy. Neoptolemus receives him with language that

---

[69] They echo Philoctetes' warning of an 'ignoble reproach' (477; cf. 968) and foreshadow Neoptolemus' decision not to incur a 'disgraceful reproach' (842). Winnington-Ingram 285 n. 18 makes the attractive suggestion that τοῦτο (522) is emphatic – *this* reproach, hinting at other kinds.

[70] Strictly speaking there need be no inconsistency in the chorus' position, since the whole scene is a deception and they could be merely fabricating their disapproval of inconsistency. But if so, they have some unconventional views not articulated or justified elsewhere. We know from 86f. that Neoptolemus himself believes in matching deeds to words, so for him the inconsistency is clear.

[71] He invokes the principle of noblesse oblige by suggesting that his status places the onus of such generosity on him. Cf. 385–8 (though like the present passage, the lines form part of a deception); *Aj.* 1093–6; Eur. *Hipp.* 409–12. This attitude accords with Neoptolemus' aristocratic faith in his *phusis*.

ironically echoes both his own preoccupation with his *phusis* and Philoctetes' affirmation of friendship: 'The *charis* shown by your concern, stranger (*xenos*), will remain a source of friendship, if I am not *kakos* by nature' (557f.).[72] This apparently casual utterance underlines the extent of Neoptolemus' betrayal both of his *phusis* and of the ideal of friendship initiated through *charis*.

Philoctetes' reaction to the false merchant's story proves Odysseus right in his original belief that persuasion would not work (though this does not necessarily justify his refusal to try it).[73] Philoctetes would sooner be persuaded to return from the dead than to go to Troy (624f.) – in other words, it is beyond the logical realm of persuasion (cf. Arist. *EN* 1113b26–30). Still more vividly, he declares that he would rather listen to the snake that bit him, which he calls *echthistos* (631f.). Odysseus, he implies, is like that snake – slippery, venomous and gratuitously hostile – but even more repellent. He wants to leave at once (635–8), but Neoptolemus now shows his first sign of hesitation by trying to delay departure because the wind is against them (639f.).[74] Then he finally gets his chance to inquire about the invincible bow. The two men discuss it with an elaborate piety (657, 661f.), which produces a jarring effect, appearing as it does in the course of a scheme that even Odysseus implicitly acknowledges as impious (85, 1051).[75] Their friendship is apparently

---

[72] Note especially the echo of προσφιλής (532, 558; cf. 587), which may explain the slight awkwardness of expression. The word occurs five times in this play (also at 224, 469) but only three times in the other extant plays of Sophocles (plus the adverb once; see Ellendt s.v.). For the idea that Neoptolemus' *phusis* is not *kakos* cf. 79f., 88f., 1013–15, 1371f.; cf. also 94f., 971f.

[73] An important function of the 'merchant' scene is to show Philoctetes' reaction to the very idea of persuasion by his enemies (cf. Alt 155f.; Steidle 170). For a useful discussion of the scene see Garvie 215–19; see also Masaracchia 92–5.

[74] That this is a sign of hesitation has been disputed, but provides the most natural and pointed explanation for the delay. For the wind motif cf. 464–7, 779–81. This is a metaphorical as well as a literal wind. The adverse wind, which provides Neoptolemus with an excuse not to depart, is a symbol that the apparent opportunity (καιρός 151, 466, 525, 637, 837) is not what it seems. Only when Neoptolemus has abandoned all attempts to grasp the καιρός through words (1279), and a full reconciliation has taken place, can the wind be perceived as favourable (καιρὸς καὶ πλοῦς ... 1450). This symbolic significance of the wind comes out most clearly in the words of Philoctetes himself, who sees the voyage in superbly illogical terms reflecting his own moral convictions (641–4; cf. also 237).

[75] On Neoptolemus' response to the bow see Segal, *Piety* 144.

sealed, and Neoptolemus in turn affirms the principle of reciprocal
philia, yet again enunciating a moral principle in the very moment of
violating it: 'I am not sorry to have met you and taken you as a
friend; for someone who knows how to do a good turn after receiving one would become a friend better than any possession' (671–3).
Philoctetes welcomes his support in the most literal sense, asking
Neoptolemus to accompany him into the cave as a 'fellow helper' in
his sickness (674f.). At this point, then, about half way through the
play, Neoptolemus has achieved his goal as Odysseus' 'fellow
worker' of deceptively winning Philoctetes' trust and friendship.[76]
It remains only to exploit them.

     After reemerging from the cave, Philoctetes is overcome by an
attack of his sickness. He begs for pity (756) and Neoptolemus asks,
'What shall I do?' (757).[77] Philoctetes answers 'Do not betray me'
(757). His exhortation recalls Neoptolemus' earlier reluctance to be
called a 'traitor' to the Greek army (94). Yet another value term is
being used to exert two conflicting claims. These two loyalties will
be brought face to face when Philoctetes cries, 'I have been
betrayed', and Neoptolemus replies with his allegiance to 'those in
power' (923–6). But for now Philoctetes trustingly hands over the
bow, after begging Neoptolemus not to give it up to his enemies
(771–3). Neoptolemus assures him impersonally that the bow 'will
not be given' to anyone else (774f.) – a safe promise, since the scheme
does not oblige him to give it up (he is hedging his moral bets again).
Philoctetes adds a wish that the bow may not bring down divine
envy on Neoptolemus as it has brought trouble to its previous
owners, himself and Heracles (776–8).[78] This should be a worrying
moment for Neoptolemus. He knows that he may only touch this
sacred weapon because of his supposed friendship for Philoctetes,
and now he finds that it is liable to bring divine envy on its possessor.
After acquiring it treacherously, it can scarcely do him much good.
The bow thus symbolises his relationship to Philoctetes: each needs

[76] Strohm 117 n. 28 notes the parallel between ξυμπαραστάτην (675) and
ξυνεργάτης (93).

[77] This is the first occurrence of the question that will pinpoint his moral dilemma
with increasing urgency (757, 908, 969; cf. 895, 963, 974). Philoctetes will eventually face it too (1350; contrast 949). Cf. also above, p. 81.

[78] For the bow's malignant history see Kott 176. For its significance in the play see
Harsh 411–14; Musurillo 121f.; Vidal-Naquet 170–2; Taplin, *GTA* 89–93; Gill,
Bow 138f.; Seale 36f.

the other, but their friendship cannot bear fruit unless it is based on authentic mutual trust and loyalty. Neoptolemus' prayer for a prosperous voyage (779–81), ambiguous though it is, is unlikely to be fulfilled under these conditions.[79]

In the extremity of his pain Philoctetes once more identifies with Heracles, the innocent sufferer, and asks Neoptolemus to set fire to him as he himself once did to Heracles. He twice calls Neoptolemus *gennaios* (799, 801), and in a gesture of trust declines to put him under oath, implying that the true *gennaios* will remain loyal to a friend without any such religious sanction (811).[80] Similarly when he wakes and thinks his trust has been vindicated, he attributes this to the inherited nobility of Neoptolemus' nature, in contrast to the so-called *agathoi* Atreidae (873f.).[81] Philoctetes thinks Neoptolemus is living up to his father's standard of excellence (cf. 904f.). But Neoptolemus was quite safe in promising not to leave Philoctetes behind (810), for he knows it is no use taking the bow to Troy without its owner (812, 839–41).[82] A single line neatly summarises his double motivation for staying: 'It is a disgraceful reproach to boast of a treacherous deed without even succeeding' (842). If he quits now, he will lose both ways.

Neoptolemus, Philoctetes, Odysseus

When it comes actually to taking Philoctetes away on false pretences, Neoptolemus starts to crack (895). The preceding scene has provided repeated reminders of his moral inconsistency. The virtues that Philoctetes has praised in him – *arete* (669), nobility (874), piety (662) – are incompatible with those that Odysseus used to tempt him

---

[79] Cf. his false farewell to Philoctetes (461–5). Both passages use the wind motif (above, n. 74). On 463 see Rose 67.

[80] For the implication that an oath of loyalty is a sign of distrust cf. *OC* 650; Eur. *Med.* 731–3; Isoc. 1.22; Diog. Laert. 1.54, 1.60.

[81] This description of the Atreidae may be merely sarcastic (cf. 447), or it may exploit the ambiguity of *agathos* ('They may be good fighters, but they are not good men'). On this and other ironic uses of *agathos* in Sophocles see Freis 92–9, who rebuts Adkins 193 n. 23.

[82] I agree with Bowra 281 and others that the hexameters at 839–41 are oracular in tone, suggesting Neoptolemus' insight into the prophecy (though there need be no close connection with the words of the 'merchant'). At the same time, the use of the epic metre may suggest that Neoptolemus is learning to live up to his father (Gardiner 38; cf. also Winnington-Ingram, *Tragica* 48–50, but I am not convinced by his suggestion that στέφανος in 841 refers to Philoctetes himself).

(82, 85, 119). The two older men also represent incompatible perspectives on treachery and loyalty (93f., 757, 910f.), courageous endurance (82, 111, 475, 481, 869–73) and renown or reputation (81–5, 119, 476). Moreover Philoctetes' values harmonise with Neoptolemus' own initial conviction that noble failure is preferable to base victory (94f.). Accordingly he fails to put aside his sense of shame as he intended.

The net result is bewilderment (897).[83] Neoptolemus admits that he has departed from his *phusis* (902f.) and that he is both *aischros* (906) and doubly *kakos*, once for using deception to obtain the bow and a second time for failing to reveal their true destination (908f.). He now suffers from a moral discomfort (902), instead of the physical discomfort caused by the sick Philoctetes' company. He admits that he has 'for some time' been feeling distress, both at his own behaviour (906) and at causing Philoctetes mental pain (912f.; cf. 1011f.),[84] despite the fact that his actions will lead to the healing of the physical wound (cf. 919). This concern for the other man's feelings is Neoptolemus' first sign of honest friendship. It accompanies the realisation that he can no longer adhere to Odysseus' view that it is permissible to be *kakos* for a sufficiently valuable end. He therefore determines to avoid at least his second fault, by informing Philoctetes that they are on their way to Troy. This does not palliate his original deceit, but he seems to think that Philoctetes will acquiesce when he hears what is in store for him (917). If this first perfunctory attempt at persuasion is successful,[85] it will relieve him of the shame of deceit. He still wants to have his cake and eat it. But this solution is spoiled by Philoctetes' utter refusal to cooperate.

Now that Neoptolemus has encountered Philoctetes and been moved to pity it is less easy to regard 'honest' force as an acceptable

---

[83] His language recalls the *aporia* or bewilderment to which the Platonic Socrates reduces his victims by demonstrating that they hold incompatible moral beliefs or principles (cf. *Meno* 80a). In Neoptolemus' case, his general moral desires (94f., 108) conflict with the obligations of loyalty and obedience as well as with self-interest. From the chorus' pragmatic perspective he gets into a different kind of *aporia* by deciding to stay with Philoctetes (854).

[84] He uses the same phrase in both cases (906, 913). On πάλαι, 'for some time' (806, 906, 913, 966) see Winnington-Ingram 283f.; Kirkwood 159f. Steidle 174–81 detects early hints of Neoptolemus' distress. For a contrary view see Erbse 189–93.

[85] On its inadequacy see Kitto, *FMD* 121f.; Alt 161f.

alternative.[86] He therefore adopts an Odyssean strategy, employing impersonal expressions like 'great necessity' to justify forcing the unwilling Philoctetes to accompany him to Troy (921f.; cf. 915, 925). But his original moral sensitivity, though misdirected by Odysseus, is still functioning. He continues to support his pursuit of self-interest with the only plausible principle available: 'Both justice and expediency make me obey those in power' (925f.). But Philoctetes now addresses him as *xenos* (923), a title that ranges from 'friend' to 'stranger' (cf. 557, 791) and thus accentuates the breakdown of their burgeoning *philia*. He is not fooled by the Odyssean impersonals, but persists in using the active second person singular for Neoptolemus' actions, thus ascribing full responsibility to him (921, 924, 928f., 931, 940; he does not yet know of Odysseus' role). He calls Neoptolemus *echthistos* (928), and appeals as a suppliant to the young man's most sensitive point: the sense of shame that prompted his original confession (929f.). Philoctetes' words underline the inadequacy of merely revealing the deception. If Neoptolemus' sense of shame is really his prime motivation he should not just placate it with words, but act on it. Philoctetes presses him to do so with a series of reproaches and pathetic appeals (927–51). He still believes the young man's values are fundamentally the same as his own (950; cf. 971f., 1009). It is not too late for him to change his mind (961f.).

This impassioned appeal brings Neoptolemus to the point of surrender, as he admits to a 'terrible pity' for Philoctetes (965f.). Philoctetes begs him to act on this pity and avoid reproach (967f.), telling him he is not *kakos*, but has learned disgraceful things from those who are (971f.). Odysseus, however, has a different notion of what is *kakos*. Neoptolemus is about to return the bow when he intervenes, rebuking Achilles' son as '*kakistos* of men' (974). Again two incompatible ethical positions come into direct conflict by laying claim to the same value term. This intervention by Odysseus extenuates Neoptolemus' behaviour by placing him under duress. He is not yet ready to defy Odysseus openly,[87] and fades into the background

---

[86] Knox 132 suggests that 'the only snag' with this return to honesty is that 'he won the bow not by Achillean violence but by Odyssean lies'. But from Philoctetes' perspective both are equally bad. Nor is the dichotomy so simple, since (as we shall soon see) 'violence' is also characteristic of Odysseus.

[87] Compare 982 with Odysseus' similar but totally ineffectual threat at 1298.

for the rest of the scene, while Philoctetes finally confronts his most hated enemy.

Now that the plot has been uncovered, Odysseus no longer relies on persuasive words but resorts to threats of 'force' (983, 985), and even to its use (1003).[88] Yet after Philoctetes' tirade he unexpectedly gives way, allowing him to remain upon the island without his bow (1054f.).[89] This second abandonment is tantamount to murder, since Philoctetes is utterly helpless without his bow.[90] It reenacts in still more brutal form the original abandonment of Philoctetes on Lemnos, thus underlining the callousness and culpability of Philoctetes' enemies, above all Odysseus himself.[91] This time he cannot claim to be following orders (cf. 6).

But Neoptolemus instructs his sailors to remain, out of pity and the hope that Philoctetes may acquire 'better sense' (1075–9). Accordingly they try to persuade him to change his mind. They argue that he is now responsible for his miserable lot: 'It was *you* who decided; there was no external compulsion; you chose the

---

[88] He also threatens violence at 1241–3, 1297. The Homeric periphrasis Ὀδυσσέως βία ('force of Odysseus') is used three times of him, always conspicuously at a line end (314, 321, 592). For the implications cf. Schein 135f. Long 102 and n. 138 notes only one other such use of βία in extant Sophocles.

[89] Many think Odysseus should be construed as bluffing here. But since there is no indication to the contrary, I take it that he is sincere (see especially Knox 134; Robinson 45–51; and for a contrary view, Hinds 177f.). It is true that Odysseus has prevented Philoctetes from committing suicide (1003), but this precedes Philoctetes' outpouring of hatred, which might plausibly provoke such a response (for a closely analogous situation cf. *OC* 848–55; no one suspects Creon of bluffing). Moreover suicide would not only conclusively rule out a successful outcome by any means, but bring down a dangerous curse, whose content can be seen by Philoctetes' reaction (cf. 1019 and see Delcourt 165f.; cf. also above, p. 71 n. 55). It is not the case, as some have argued, that the bluff interpretation ruins the effect of Philoctetes' lament (though it does alter it; cf. Electra's lament over her 'dead' brother in *El.*). But it does weaken the contrast between Odysseus' irreverent lack of insight into the bow's function (1055–60) and Neoptolemus' reverence (656f., 839–42), and destroys the effect of reenactment of guilt (see text).

[90] Cf. 931–3, where Philoctetes puns on the similar words for 'bow' and 'life'.

[91] For the technique of reenacting guilt incurred outside the action with a different but analogous deed within it cf. the 'carpet' scene in Aesch. *Ag.* and Pandarus' violation of the truce in the *Iliad* (which recapitulates Paris' guilt). The parodos of *Aj.* works rather differently, since it shows the continuation of the original guilty deed. The debate at the end of *Aj.* reenacts but also revises the judgement over the arms of Achilles. Oedipus' curse in *OC* reenacts his previous curses in climactic fashion (cf. below, p. 258 n. 116).

worse when you could have thought better' (1095–1100). In Aristotelian terms, they claim that the 'beginning' was in Philoctetes and he made a choice, without duress or external force (cf. *EN* 1109b30–10b17). He must therefore take full responsibility for his decision. Had he agreed to go to Troy, he could have disclaimed responsibility on grounds of duress.[92] But the decision to remain despite duress was entirely his own, even though it has left him in such appalling straits. He has chosen what he considers the right course (because it harms his enemies, who are wicked, and is therefore just). But the chorus call this the 'worse' choice (1099f.), certainly pragmatically, and perhaps also morally, since it is harmful to the rest of the Greeks. They are quite right that this persistent refusal is Philoctetes' assertion of his own autonomy. But the way they ignore their own and their masters' responsibility for reducing him to such a choice makes their reproachful tone hard to stomach.[93] His choice is 'free from external compulsion' only in the narrowest sense.

When Philoctetes totally ignores them and persists in his lament, the chorus try another approach. They suggest that it is fate from the gods which has overtaken him, 'and not any deception on my part' (1116–22). The second part of this claim is manifestly false, since the chorus were a party to the deception and could theoretically have foiled it.[94] They seem to operate on the assumption that obeying orders removes responsibility, and will shortly defend Odysseus in such terms, arguing that he acted under orders as a representative of the whole army, and was serving the common good of his *philoi* (1143–5). This favourable interpretation is appropriate to the chorus and suits their persuasive purpose (they are not, after all, disinterested). It is also sometimes cited out of context as evidence for Odysseus' public-spirited motivation. But even if the chorus are correct, Odysseus is not exonerated in his handling of the affair. It was open to him (as it was not to Neoptolemus) to try and fulfil his orders by other than treacherous means.[95] Moreover the passage

[92] What Dio Chrys. 52.2 calls 'forced persuasion' (πειθὼ ἀναγκαία, on which cf. Schlesinger 122–4). Cf. Odysseus' use of πειστέον (994), which hovers between 'you must obey' and 'you must be persuaded'.

[93] Cf. Kitto, *FMD* 124–6; Gardiner 42–4.

[94] Their role in the scheme is well emphasised by Gardiner ch. 2.

[95] Philoctetes calls Odysseus a servant of the Atreidae (1024), and assumes that they are implicated in his actions. But Odysseus himself never uses their authority to justify his methods (contrast 6 and 1028 on the abandonment of Philo-

occurs just after his cruel treatment of Philoctetes has undermined
any possible claim on our approval, and just before the spectacle of
his final discomfiture. Its dramatic purpose is to illustrate Philoctetes'
stubborn resistance to every kind of appeal. It is too late to rehabili-
tate Odysseus.

However shameless it may seem for the chorus to deny their
own involvement in the deception, it does have the advantage of
enabling them to appeal to Philoctetes as friends (1122). But he continues, understandably enough, to ignore them. He addresses only
the stolen bow as *philos*, endowing it with the human emotion of
pity while he bitterly imagines a gloating Odysseus, his 'loathed
enemy' wielding it (1123–39). At this the chorus rebuke him again: it
is proper for a man to assert what is just, but not to add angry invective (1140–2).[96] Here is an implicit acknowledgement of the justice of
Philoctetes' cause (cf. 680–5). But at the same time, they seem to
propose a separation of justice from hostile abuse that is never con-
templated by Philoctetes. As far as he is concerned, impersonal
justice thoroughly sanctions his outpouring of personal hatred, and
he is scarcely in the mood to draw a logical distinction between
them.

The chorus try one more appeal, asking Philoctetes 'by the
gods' to respond to their friendly good will and acquire some sense,
and reemphasising that it is up to him to escape his painful lot (1163–
6). He himself appealed repeatedly to Neoptolemus 'by the gods'
(747, 770, 933, 967, 1185), tried to make him change his mind
(961f.), and declared that he would respond to friendship (530–2).
But he continues to ignore the chorus. This failure to respond to the
kind of appeals he himself makes to others is only superficially
inconsistent. His own appeals were utterly sincere, but he has every

ctetes). In the false merchant's story (for what it is worth) Odysseus is the
instigator of the expedition (614–18).
96 This is the general sense of this vexed passage according to Jebb, who follows
Arndt's emendation of 1140. For other suggestions see the editors ad loc.
(including Dawe's apparatus), and Kells, *Philoctetes* 7–9. Although the text is
problematic, it seems fairly clear that a contrast is being established between
merely stating (that something is just or good?) and adding further gratuitous
abuse. On most interpretations, the speaker referred to is Philoctetes, but
Mazon and Kamerbeek take the chorus to refer to themselves. An alternative
interpretation, 'it is a man's part to call the expedient just', is ruled out by the
μέν ... δέ construction (see Jebb ad loc.).

reason to mistrust the chorus' overtures, even couched in language to which he might otherwise respond. He does in fact make some response, calling them 'best' of those who have visited him (1171). But when they suggest that it would be best for him to go on to Troy (1176), he refuses to listen. Even if he trusted them, he would have no reason to accede to their persuasion unless he also trusted Neoptolemus or Odysseus, and at this point he has excellent reasons to distrust them all. His final words encapsulate his grievance: 'I came to support the enemy Greeks' (1216f.). He came to Troy to help those he thought were friends, but they treated him as an enemy and thus have earned his enmity. Now he has been betrayed a second time by his new 'friend', Neoptolemus. It is hardly surprising that the chorus' declaration of 'good will' (1164) leaves him unshaken in his resolve.

When Neoptolemus reappears, his earlier hesitation has been replaced by decisive action. His treatment of Odysseus is no longer deferential, but peremptory. He has unequivocally chosen Philoctetes' values, which chimed with his own instincts, over those of Odysseus: disgrace must be shunned unconditionally, regardless of obedience, 'victory' or duress. He openly acknowledges that he is at fault (1224f., 1248f.),[97] emphatically reaffirming his previous sense that deception is disgraceful (1228, 1234, 1249; cf. 108). He is no longer willing to subordinate his sense of shame to expediency, loyalty or authority.[98] He is finally putting into practice his original unconditional faith in acting 'nobly' (kalôs) despite the consequences (94f.). In the prologue we saw him abandon this principle and succumb to the temptations of Odyssean panourgia. We now see him confronting panourgia once more and rejecting it in the face of Odysseus' threats.

This rejection is reminiscent of Socrates, who granted that there are many ways to escape death, 'if one is bold enough to do and say everything,' but declared that in his own case, 'I have been convicted through a deficiency, not of words, but of boldness and shamelessness' (Pl. Ap. 38d–39a). Neoptolemus shares the Socratic

---

[97] He now uses 'error' (1224, 1248) not for failure to achieve nike (95) but in Philoctetes' sense of a moral lapse (1012). Cf. Segal 342.

[98] For his rejection of authority cf. 1226. Mazon translates βουλεύειν τι νέον (1229) as 'devenir un rebelle'. This attractive interpretation also makes the next line more pointed.

view that justice outweighs all considerations of personal advantage (cf. 1246, 1251).[99] In his own way Philoctetes shares it too, for he prizes the justice of revenge above the conventional benefits of physical rescue. Such views lead Socrates to accept death, Philoctetes to face probable death on Lemnos, and Neoptolemus to renounce a glorious future. The only way to counter them is to argue that some other principle of justice or morality carries greater weight. Crito, Odysseus, and Neoptolemus all try to do this by pointing to the claims of others.[100] Crito suggests, amongst other things, that Socrates should not 'betray' his sons (Pl. *Crito* 45cd); Odysseus invokes the needs of the Argives (*Phil.* 66f.); Neoptolemus will exert his own claim on Philoctetes as a *philos*. Neoptolemus was originally swayed by Odysseus' arguments, but now, like Socrates and Philoctetes, rejects them as subordinate to the claims of justice as he sees it.

Odysseus, however, cannot understand why the deception is 'inappropriate' to Neoptolemus (1227; cf. 111), despite an implicit admission that his own behaviour is not *gennaios* (1068; cf. 51). Nor does he see why Neoptolemus thinks it 'just' to frustrate his scheme, despite his own previous acknowledgement that the scheme is unjust (1246f.; cf. 82).[101] He tries to restrain Neoptolemus in the name of the whole army (1243), and when this fails resorts to explicit threats of violence and open accusations of disloyalty (1250–5). But Neoptolemus has abandoned his respect for Odysseus' authority and his loyalty to the army in favour of his own principles, which are now strong enough to resist duress. He effectively accepts the charge of disloyalty, burning his boats with Odysseus by declaring, 'So be it' (1254). He now has two loyalties, to Philoctetes as well as to the Greeks. Since he is forced to choose, he chooses the friend with justice on his side.

Neoptolemus' dilemma illustrates the inadequacy of Help Friends as a general moral principle. It provides no built-in criterion for deciding a conflict of loyalties, though it could easily be modified to include one (e.g. simple majority of *philoi* – a utilitarian position available to Odysseus). Yet such conflicts are highly likely to arise. The rigid adherent of Help Friends/Harm Enemies with two friends

---

[99] For Socrates see e.g. Pl. *Crito* 48cd with Vlastos, *Happiness* 6–8.

[100] Pearson, *Ethics* 200 notes the parallel between Socrates and Philoctetes. The prototype for this pattern of persuasion is *Il.* 9 (cf. Schlesinger 103–5).

[101] On these and other inconsistencies in his language see my *Odysseus*.

who are or become mutual enemies confronts an insoluble dilemma. By choosing to help one friend, he or she will make an enemy of the other. Such cases reveal the need for an independent, non-vengeful means of deciding such divisive disputes. Neoptolemus adopts one. Rather than taking sides with either Odysseus or Philoctetes merely on the basis of *philia*, and thus violating his friendship with the other, he chooses according to neutral moral criteria, which support Philoctetes' case against Odysseus. These criteria happen to coincide with an important distinction in his relationships to these two *philoi*. Odysseus is Neoptolemus' military ally and partner in a mutually profitable enterprise, and a certain intimacy is suggested by Odysseus' paternal tone, but there is no sign of affection between them. The friendship with Philoctetes, on the other hand, is a bond of personal sympathy. The fact that moral criteria support the claims of personal friendship is not merely fortuitous, for the friendship is based on a foundation of shared values.

But this unanimity is not absolute. Neoptolemus is prepared to defend, with force if necessary (1255), Philoctetes' just rights, and accepts that enmity with Odysseus and the Greeks may be a consequence (1253f.). But he does not automatically adopt Philoctetes' unqualified hostility towards his enemies. He tries to undo Odysseus' misdeeds, yet defends him from Philoctetes' vengeance (1300–4). Philoctetes cannot understand why he should not kill this enemy without further ado (1302f.). At last he is in a position to implement personally the destruction of his enemies, which he has craved so long. But Neoptolemus tells him that this is not *kalos* for either of them (1304).[102] Yet Neoptolemus does regard the sack of the enemy city of Troy as *kalos* (1344; cf. 352). The implication is that Trojans are legitimate enemies, but that not every enmity should be pursued with the hostility of warfare.[103] Neoptolemus does not see friendship and enmity in exclusive terms, but realises that it is in none of their interests to fight merely out of hatred. Nor does he choose his allies exclusively for their moral worth, for he refuses to allow his

---

[102] Webster 42 thinks the line 'implies that the just man ought not to harm anyone', but although Neoptolemus' words are consistent with this Socratic position, they do not entail it.

[103] On the relative simplicity of Help Friends/Harm Enemies in warfare see above, p. 52f. The Trojan war may also be justified by the guilt of Paris (cf. 1426), but no human character alludes to this.

disapproval of Odysseus' values to provide a foundation for personal hostility.

When Odysseus declines to stand up to Neoptolemus, the contrast between his failure to act on his threats and Neoptolemus' apparent readiness to do so gives the encounter the force of a moral confrontation (1254–7). Philoctetes will accuse Odysseus of cowardice (1306f.), but Neoptolemus does not endorse this judgement, and even characterises Odysseus' caution as *sophrosune* (1259).[104] After Odysseus backs down his defeat is total, and we shall see no more of him, except for a brief reappearance and undignified exit which only serve to underline the futility of his threats.[105]

Neoptolemus and Philoctetes: persuasion

Neoptolemus is left with the task of overcoming Philoctetes' extreme and amply justified mistrust. He turns to words once more, this time honestly, but has by now exhausted his persuasive capital (1267–72, 1275f., 1280).[106] He announces that he has changed his mind (1270), which is precisely what Philoctetes had begged of him earlier (962), but Philoctetes is no longer willing either to believe in a change of heart or to undergo one himself. So Neoptolemus turns to the only form of persuasion that remains: 'manifest action' (1291). Philoctetes has declared that he will never become well-disposed to Neoptolemus, and condemned him in the strongest terms (1281–4). But all this is changed by the simple but momentous act of returning the bow.

Neoptolemus has now wiped his slate clean and made good the friendship originally flawed by deception. Philoctetes once more calls him *philtatos* (1301; cf. 1290), agrees that he no longer has any cause for blame or anger (1308–10), and praises him as his father's true son (1310–13). But now, as Neoptolemus tactfully points out, it is Philoctetes' turn to match deeds to words (1314–16) and respond to friendship and good will (cf. 1322, 1375, 1385) by coming volun-

---

[104] The tone here may be scornful, but there is no reason why the words should be taken as insincere. North 66 interprets them as a taunt of cowardice, but this is surely incompatible with the restraint Neoptolemus urges on Philoctetes at 1304. I would take them in a simple prudential sense, which as North 3 shows, is one of the oldest meanings of *sophrosune*.

[105] See Taplin, *Philoctetes* 37.

[106] On the repetition of λόγοι ('words') see Easterling, *Repetition* 29.

tarily to Troy. But he does not present this just as a personal favour, for he tries to convince Philoctetes that it will be the best course for both of them. The reformed Neoptolemus combines the best of Achillean forthrightness and Odyssean persuasiveness, while avoiding the concomitant vices of violence and treachery. With his restoration of the bow and speech of persuasion we have for the first time a morally irreproachable attempt to get Philoctetes to Troy.

First Neoptolemus repeats the chorus' argument that Philoctetes' suffering is now self-inflicted, so that he has forfeited his right to pity (1316–20). Though he persists in lamenting his solitude and friendlessness, he refuses to make himself accessible to the good will of others, rejecting potential friends as hostile enemies (1321–3). Such arguments carry more conviction coming from Neoptolemus, who has now proved both his pity and his friendship in action and is therefore entitled to friendship and trust in return. He goes on to give a full and unequivocal account of the prophecy, backing it up with the strongest assurances of veracity that mere mortal words can provide (1324f., 1341f.). Although he speaks again in terms of necessity (1339, 1340), this is no longer an excuse for conveying Philoctetes to Troy by fair means or foul, but a way of convincing him that it is in his best interests to rejoin the expedition. In the light of the prophecy, he concludes, Philoctetes should come willingly to Troy to achieve both cure and glory (1343–7). The fact that Neoptolemus is willing to sacrifice martial to moral reputation does not mean that he has lost interest in the former. We should also expect Philoctetes, with his aristocratic values, to be influenced by such considerations (cf. 254–6).[107]

Philoctetes in turn now faces a moral dilemma with the question, 'Alas, what shall I do?' (1350). Earlier, under the illusion that Neoptolemus was a sincere friend, he affirmed a commitment to reciprocal friendship (531f.) and promised Neoptolemus any benefit in his power (658f.). Now he acknowledges Neoptolemus' sincere good will and the claim that it has on him (1350f.). 'Are you forcing this upon me?' he asks (1366), when the only force that has been applied is moral pressure and persuasion. But he will not yield. He could not endure even to associate with his old enemies, let alone benefit them in any way (1352–7). His eyes could not bear to see him

[107] See Alt 149f.; Avery 296 n. 1; Podlecki, *Word* 238 n. 13.

in their company (1354).[108] He is now urgently needed by the
Greeks, and could presumably demand abundant human compensation in addition to the divinely promised cure and glory. But the
vengeance he craves is beyond price or arbitration.[109]

Philoctetes also suspects future harm from his enemies, claiming that this worries him more than their past offences (1358–60).
Given his feelings about the past, this claim may seem implausible.
On the other hand, the past is past, and may provide valuable lessons
for the future. Philoctetes' fear is not merely of hostility but of
further treachery, to which he would be exposed by entrusting himself once more to formerly treacherous allies (cf. 1390). Honest open
enmity is more easily dealt with, as he suggests by his confidence that
he can repulse the hostile Greeks with his bow (1405–7). Neoptolemus asks him to have trust, both in the gods and in his words, the
words of a friend who will accompany him (1374f.). But Philoctetes'
suspicion extends both to the new friend who has earned his moral
approval, and apparently to the gods themselves, or at least to Neoptolemus' report of their plans. This distrust rules out reconciliation
with old enemies, and even outweighs new friendship. But such suspicion is becoming harder to justify. By resisting every attempt at
persuasion Philoctetes, in his anxiety to avoid the snares of persuasive
'words', also precludes reaping their benefits.

Philoctetes is also surprised that Neoptolemus no longer seems
to share his values, but refuses to harm his 'enemies' at the cost of his
own glory. Even though the real purpose of Neoptolemus' mission
has been revealed, Philoctetes is incredulous at his lack of rancour
against those who allegedly deprived him of his father's arms. He
thinks Neoptolemus should not go to Troy himself, and should even
prevent Philoctetes from going, in order to thwart those who committed this *hubris* against him (1363–5). However we interpret this
controversial passage,[110] its implications for Philoctetes' values are

---

108 His language suggests shame at such a prospect. Cf. 110, 929 and above, p. 70
     n. 52.
109 His situation is now analogous to that of Achilles in *Iliad* 9, who declares that no
     amount of gifts can win him over (378–87).
110 The most recent and exhaustive discussion is that of Machin 74–81. Most com-
     mentators explain the failure to clear up the question of the arms by Neoptole-
     mus' embarrassment at the extent of his lies. Certainly the quarrel between him
     and Odysseus must be taken as fictitious (this is shown not only by 57–64, but
     by the way Neoptolemus tries to exculpate Odysseus at 377f., 385). It is there-

clear. He cannot conceive of Achilles' son failing to agree that a single injury means unremitting hatred at whatever cost to oneself. The injury that he himself sustained was extraordinarily severe, involving betrayal, dishonour and severe physical hardship. The resulting thirst for vengeance is so fierce that he is prepared to forgo the rectification of both dishonour and hardship in order to deny satisfaction to his enemies. This priority is powerfully expressed when he declares that if they were destroyed, he would feel his disease was cured (1043f.). He would rather remain an outcast from society than reenter it on terms that compromise his hatred. But Neoptolemus has already shown that he does not share Philoctetes' rigid criteria for enmity, and here again he refuses to condone the other's relentless hatred. Whoever now possesses Achilles' arms, to act as Philoctetes urges would benefit no one and destroy Neoptolemus' chance to live up to his father by winning renown at Troy.

In rejecting Neoptolemus' attempt at persuasion, Philoctetes is pursuing Harm Enemies to the exclusion of the complementary principle Help Friends, as well as the exclusion of significant personal benefit (the pleasure of health is outweighed by that of destroying his enemies, 1043f.; cf. 1019f.). Moreover he is failing to abide by his own principles of reciprocal friendship and active gratitude (531f., 658f.). It is true that he has not yet received the assurance of rescue for which he originally promised this gratitude. Yet Neoptolemus has saved him from a desperate predicament at considerable cost to himself, and the false condition of friendship on which Philoctetes' promises were based is now a reality. Neoptolemus, as a friend, is entitled to his loyalty and support. It is thus misleading to say that Philoctetes has 'no moral grounds' for agreeing to go to Troy (Whitman 184). Yet it is equally an oversimplification to say that 'he may rightly be condemned' for his refusal (Bowra 293).[111] The problem is created precisely by the fact that his own values give him obligations in both directions. But a choice must be made, and he allows his concern for a friend to be outweighed by the conviction that Neoptolemus is wrong to persist in his desire to fight at Troy.[112] Philoctetes has already shown that he expects others to re-

fore most economical to infer from 62f. that Odysseus did hand over the arms to Neoptolemus as in the epic tradition (see Knox 191 n. 30).

[111] For a view closer to my own see Steidle 191; cf. also Beye 73–5.
[112] Cf. Linforth, *Philoctetes* 145; Alt 170.

spect his wishes and moral judgements, at the cost not only of their own desires, but of their view of his best interests. (The return of the bow was a deed of this kind.) Yet he not only refuses to honour Neoptolemus' wishes and judgement, but continues to press him for further assistance, which will involve just the kind of subordination of one's own desires that he himself is unwilling to accept. In asking Neoptolemus to keep his promise and take him home, he is exerting pressure on him to redeem those treacherous words by putting them into action. Yet he himself will not act on the principles that he pronounced in all honesty.

He continues, however, to promise gratitude – 'double *charis*' from both himself and his father (1370f.) – for both helping him and thwarting his enemies.[113] He also adds another incentive: by staying away from Troy Neoptolemus will avoid appearing to be *kakos* by helping *kakoi* (1370–2). His wording echoes and contrasts with his earlier commendation of Neoptolemus as 'helping an *esthlos* man' (905). It follows from the inflexible alignment of loyalty and hostility with his conceptions of who is *esthlos* and *kakos*, that it is *kakos* to help in any enterprise whatsoever those he considers *kakoi*. Despite the benefit to himself and Neoptolemus, going to Troy would be disgraceful (1381f.). He cannot understand how Neoptolemus can take him to Troy and still be his friend, for this would be handing him over to his enemies (1386). No course of action that benefits his enemies (even incidentally) can be truly beneficial to himself: the two are mutually exclusive (1384).

Both Philoctetes and Neoptolemus regard some means as inadmissible in the pursuit of even the most desirable end. In this they are both the converse of Odysseus. But they differ in the values to which they give this ultimate authority. Both wish to avoid what is *aischros* and *kakos*, but Neoptolemus does not place the Trojan war in this category. He admits that Philoctetes' position has some plausibility (1373),[114] but still maintains that going to Troy is the best course for both of them (1381). He sees no disgrace in benefiting oneself and

---

[113] The significance of 'double' in these lines is disputed. For various interpretations see Kamerbeek ad loc.

[114] His vague expression (λέγεις μὲν εἰκότα) may mean that Philoctetes has some justification for his lack of trust, or that his enemies are indeed *kakoi*. It may also indicate embarrassment at Philoctetes' continuing belief in his quarrel with Odysseus.

one's friends in an honourable enterprise (1381–3), regardless of any incidental benefit to one's enemies.[115] For him, unlike Philoctetes, Help Friends outweighs Harm Enemies. Indeed he has never endorsed the harming of enemies (except the Trojans), so he can quite consistently affirm that an action which benefits personal enemies is not in itself disgraceful. Philoctetes, on the other hand, takes Harm Enemies to its logical conclusion, so that it clashes with Help Friends, and in doing so shows how rigid adherence to the traditional code can become mired in insoluble conflict.[116] His implicit moral defence of his friendships and enmities gives him an underlying justification for Harm Enemies and hence for refusing to go to Troy. But the conflict between this refusal and Help Friends becomes all the clearer, if all and only friends are to count as virtuous.

After failing to convince Philoctetes to take his own more constructive view of their friendship, Neoptolemus agrees with only a moment's hesitation to take him home (1395f., 1402). He thus faces, and passes, a still more stringent test to his Socratic concern for principle. For keeping this promise will be extremely troublesome to him. Philoctetes originally promised him 'the greatest prize of renown' for his compassionate help (478). But the decision to provide such help will not only deprive him of the renown he hoped to win at Troy, but put him at odds with the army and its leaders and expose him to charges of disobedience and treachery (cf. 1404f.; also 67, 1241–3, 1250, 1257f.). However much glory Philoctetes may personally bestow upon him for his honourable action, it will cost him his honour and reputation amongst the rest of the Greeks. It will

---

[115] If the ms. reading at 1383 is retained with Pearson and Dain, the line cannot be taken at face value without conflicting radically with Neoptolemus' previously stated principles, since it suggests that personal benefit removes disgrace from an action. Furthermore 1345 strongly suggests a sense of *active* benefit in 1383 (so Jebb, contra Segal 476 n. 27). Buttmann's conjecture ὠφελῶν φίλους (adopted by Jebb and Dawe; cf. also Kamerbeek ad loc.) is therefore attractive. For a defence of ὠφελούμενος (accepted by Webster) see Linforth 146 n. 27. But Linforth's argument, that it is acceptable to seek benefits promised by the gods, does not solve the problem. Odysseus too is seeking such benefits, but this does not exculpate him, and Neoptolemus' sense of shame is not limited to thoughts of divine disapproval. If the ms. reading is retained, Neoptolemus must be understood to mean that *ceteris paribus* profit is no disgrace. He is still subordinating enmity to other values.

[116] Cf. Winnington-Ingram 295–7.

benefit him in neither heroic nor pragmatic terms.[117] As he says himself, the easiest course would be to abandon Philoctetes as he found him (1395f.). Yet he agrees to take him home, evidently in the belief that one should keep a promise, even one made under false pretences.[118] This is apparently an altruistic decision, prompted by pity, friendship and a concern for moral consistency, and arising from self-respect rather than thoughts of reputation.[119] It is this that once more earns Philoctetes' seal of ethical approval as *gennaios* (1402).[120] He expects Neoptolemus to accede to a friend's wishes in a way that he himself is unwilling to do, or unable to do consistently.

It is only after agreeing to keep his promise that Neoptolemus expresses anxiety about reprisals from the Greeks, for a deed that he expects them to blame and punish (1404f.). In response, Philoctetes promises to defend him with the invincible bow (1405–7). At last he is offering Neoptolemus some benefit from their friendship. But the help he proposes is still not fully reciprocal, for he is promising protection from hostility incurred only through the act of doing him a favour. Neoptolemus has thus proved beyond the shadow of a doubt the unselfish nature of his friendship, and they are on the point of departure, when Heracles appears.

Heracles

The ending of *Philoctetes* has been the subject of interminable controversy.[121] On one side stand the proponents of the 'nod to the myth', who hold that the human ending is the 'real' one, and Heracles is

---

[117] There is no mention of the usefulness of a virtuous reputation (which in any case would have to compete with a reputation for treachery). Another self-interested motive might be divine reward or punishment, but such considerations are not aired.

[118] He treats his promise as a performative utterance (the expression is Austin's).

[119] On his altruism see O'Brien 33–5, and on altruism in general Dover 220–6. 'He is also asked to respond to a claim of a kind hardly recognized in the Greek theories of friendship, the claim that he respect his friend's wishes rather than act for what seems to him his friend's good' (Gill, *Bow* 142; cf. Nussbaum, *Consequences* 47 and above, p. 35f).

[120] There is a metrical anomaly in this line, but attempts to emend it have not been successful. It is best accounted for by the moment's emotional intensity and dramatic significance. See Jebb and Kamerbeek ad loc. and Tarrant, *Philoctetes* 134 n. 45.

[121] For doxography see Linforth, *Philoctetes* 150–2; Hamilton 135 n. 17; Easterling, *Philoctetes* 35f.

merely introduced to get Philoctetes to Troy and thus satisfy the requirements of the legend.[122] The intervention of Heracles is a mere device, which has no effect on our understanding or evaluation of the events that precede it. Thus Robinson (53f.) rightly argues that Heracles' words do not change any dramatic or moral judgements already made by the audience. This does not mean, however, that he or his words are irrelevant to the rest of the play, and other critics have tried to show in various ways that his arrival forms a fitting climax.[123] Certainly, had he so wished, the dramatist could have used some more arbitrary and external device to engineer Philoctetes' presence at Troy. For Heracles has a close personal relationship with Philoctetes, which has been alluded to several times during the play (262, 726–9, 1131).[124] The essence of that relationship is reciprocal favour. It was in return for helping Heracles by lighting his pyre that Philoctetes received the famous bow (670, 801–3).

The intervention of Heracles clearly counts on one level as the final triumph of persuasion which brings Philoctetes willingly to Troy.[125] Neoptolemus, the original advocate of 'force' (90f.), eventually turned to honest persuasion and thus built a foundation for constructive cooperation. But it is only now, with the divine pronouncements of Heracles,[126] that we can see an ironic truth in Odysseus' claim for the primacy of the tongue (96–9). Although Heracles makes a factual prediction, rather than an appeal or a command, Philoctetes happily accedes to the 'longed-for voice' (1445) of a personal friend. But he is also obeying a *philos* with superior status (like Neoptolemus at the beginning of the play), thus combining the theme of authority with that of persuasion.[127] This double motivation is captured by Philoctetes' response, 'I will not disobey' (1447), which in Greek suggests not just obedience but acquiescence to persuasion.

---

[122] See e.g. Wilamowitz 311f.; Linforth, *Philoctetes* 150–2; Kitto, *FMD* 136f., *GT*[3] 308–10; Robinson 51–6.

[123] E.g. Bowra 301–6; Whitman 187; Letters 275–7; Seale, *Surprise*; Taplin, *GTA* 93; Gill, *Bow* 142–4.

[124] See Bowra 301–3; Garvie 226 n. 40.

[125] So also Easterling, *Philoctetes* 31, 33f.; Rose 101; Buxton 128f.; contra e.g. Podlecki, *Word* 245.

[126] His words are μῦθοι (1410, 1417, 1447), in contrast to the mere λόγοι of ordinary mortals (Podlecki, *Word* 244f.).

[127] Cf. Easterling, *Philoctetes* 35; Gill, *Bow* 143f.

Heracles' persuasion differs from that of Neoptolemus in another important respect, namely the special authority conferred by his immortality.[128] Although he was once mortal,[129] and can appeal to Philoctetes on the ground of shared experience (1418–22), his assurance of the rewards that lie ahead is absolutely reliable. His *philia* is different too. It antedates the present crisis and has never been marred by deception. Nor has Heracles any personal interest in getting Philoctetes to Troy. On the contrary, he is doing his friend a favour (*charis* 1413). Philoctetes' distrust therefore cannot come into play. He has no conceivable reason to doubt this manifestation of the 'judgement of friends', which, as he now sees, coincides with 'great destiny' and the 'all conquering divinity' (1466–8). In this harmonious finale, 'friends' may embrace both Heracles and Neoptolemus. Philoctetes ends up persuaded by one friend and thereby helping another. Yet he is never moved by the disinterested desire to serve a friend's wishes or interests. He accedes to Heracles' absolute assurance that, besides being the plan of Zeus, going to Troy will be in his own best interests and provide some compensation for his sufferings. Heracles, like Neoptolemus before him, is helping a friend. Sophocles thus manages to get Philoctetes willingly to Troy without having him do anyone but himself a favour.

Heracles says nothing about justice. But he does provide a kind of justification for Philoctetes' apparently gratuitous misery, by offering himself as a role model. He too has endured hardships and has now achieved 'deathless *arete*' (1418–22).[130] For Philoctetes, the equivalent will be the *arete* and glory of sacking Troy, which Heracles acknowledges is 'owed' to him (1421f., 1425). If this is a theodicy, it is a minimal one, confirming that the gods are just only with respect to rectificatory justice, and indeed only one aspect of that. The only hint that they may also be concerned with punishing the guilty comes when Heracles predicts that Philoctetes will kill Paris, the 'cause of evils' (1426). But Paris can scarcely be held responsible for the evils of this play. Philoctetes' faith in divine justice is therefore confirmed only to a very limited degree, and certainly not in

---

[128] Cf. Segal 351f.

[129] Emphasised by Winnington-Ingram 318.

[130] Cf. Erbse 200; Hamilton 135–7; Segal 322. The two men are verbally linked by
πόνος ('labour') (1419, 1422) and *arete* (1420, 1425). On ἐκ (1422) see Garvie
255; on πόνος Knox 140f.; Segal 346.

the way he most desires.[131] Heracles has come to announce 'the plans of Zeus' (1415), which like Zeus' famous 'plan' in the *Iliad* (1.5) may include all manner of evil.[132] He does not exhort, but simply predicts (note the future tenses in 1423–30). The gods, it seems, are more concerned with what will be than with what ought to be. The question of precisely how far the two may be expected to coincide remains unanswered.[133]

The fact of Heracles' arrival is in some ways more significant than what he says. Sophocles could easily have allowed Neoptolemus to win over Philoctetes. What did he gain by avoiding that tidy ending and introducing Heracles instead? First, the portrayal of Philoctetes as so intransigent in his hatred that he prefers to sacrifice the best interests of himself and his friend to that hatred, despite the claims of reciprocal friendship.[134] So while some of his values (notably honesty) are vindicated, flaws are also revealed, especially that inability to live up to all his principles which results from the potential incoherence of Help Friends/Harm Enemies. Second, if Neoptolemus had succeeded in persuading Philoctetes, we could never be quite sure that returning the bow was not just another device to gain Philoctetes' trust and make him amenable to persuasion. After all, one of the first things Neoptolemus says after restoring the bow is, 'Listen to what I want to get from you' (1315f.). If he achieved his goal at this juncture he would remain open to the suspicion of Odyssean self-interest. His agreement to take Philoctetes home, followed by the intervention of Heracles, is necessary to guarantee the purity of his motives.[135]

---

[131] Rose 102 sees in 1440–4 an allusion to the eventual divine punishment of Philoctetes' enemies. But the Greek leaders (including Neoptolemus) were punished for their impiety at the sack of Troy (here alluded to), not for their treatment of Philoctetes. If Sophocles wanted to indicate that Philoctetes would finally get his revenge, he would have had to say so more explicitly. For this Heracles would have been the perfect vehicle. What better way to induce Philoctetes to come to Troy?

[132] Cf. also *Phil.* 555, 990; but the play demonstrates that the plan of Zeus is not to be fulfilled by Odyssean scheming.

[133] On the absence of a theodicy in the play see Kitto, *FMD* 105; Robinson 54; Garvie 225; Alt 174; contra Kirkwood 273; Letters 279.

[134] Cf. Kitto, *FMD* 130, *GT*³ 307.

[135] Cf. Robinson 51f. Philoctetes could have changed his mind after Neoptolemus agreed to take him home. But then Neoptolemus' offer could still be interpreted as a ruse to win Philoctetes' trust. Divine intervention is uniquely effect-

It is essential that we believe in the sincerity of Neoptolemus' altruism, for only this can provide the basis for the completely trusting friendship with which he and Philoctetes together will conquer Troy. Heracles puts in what Odysseus in the prologue left out: it is crucial for success at Troy that Neoptolemus and Philoctetes work together as friends and allies.[136] He 'turns the two men back from the road they had started on ... but, in a deeper sense, he confirms the personal "road" they have taken (the establishment of true friendship), and associates the continuation along that road with the fulfilment of the oracle' (Gill, *Bow* 143). The significance of this partnership is underlined by the Homeric lion simile with its use of the dual (1436f.).[137] Friendship is to be rooted in the reciprocity of mutual protection (1434–7), the foundation for which was established in the preceding scene. Heracles himself, returning favour for favour with Philoctetes, will be the model for this friendship. Philoctetes' willingness to let revenge overrule friendship must be abandoned, and Neoptolemus' conception of a friendship based on trust (1374) and mutual advantage (1381) has been vindicated.

On a more general level, the need for divine intervention demonstrates the impasse to which the characters have been brought by their various incompatible claims and convictions. The arrival of Heracles pinpoints the insoluble nature of the conflicting demands on Neoptolemus and Philoctetes.[138] In particular, it confirms the danger of incoherence in Help Friends/Harm Enemies in two different ways. Philoctetes is unable to live up to both principles, and is forced to sacrifice one to the other. Neoptolemus is unable to help all his friends, and must choose between them at severe cost to himself. But at the same time Heracles' intervention points towards a solu-

---

ive here, since it is entirely unpredictable on the human level and thus could not enter into Neoptolemus' plans. But despite the dramatist's best efforts, some still see Neoptolemus' repentance as a ruse (so the scholiast on 1402 followed by a few perverse modern critics).

[136] As Tony Long has pointed out to me, Heracles at 1434f. echoes and revises the words of Odysseus at 115, altering 'without the bow' to 'without him'. Neoptolemus shows a progressive understanding corresponding to his transition from self-interest to altruism: 'I shall sack Troy' (114; cf. 347, 353); 'I shall sack Troy with you' (920); 'you will sack Troy with me' (1335); 'you will sack Troy' (1347). Cf. also Hamilton 132 n. 6.

[137] Cf. also Segal 349–51 on the use of 'me and you' to convey *philia*, and Steidle 187 n. 72 on the pronouns in 1437.

[138] Cf. MacIntyre 124.

tion. By confirming the importance of *philia* between the two men he indirectly ratifies Neoptolemus' decision to do as his friend asked. The play thus approves his choice of honest friendship based on shared values, and shows that such *philia* must involve a willingness to sacrifice self-interest to the demands of one's friend. This sacrifice is required of Neoptolemus, not Philoctetes, for it was he who sabotaged *philia* by stooping to deception. Moreover his act of friendship in returning the bow, however admirable and self-sacrificing, in practical terms merely restored the status quo. Despite the destructive consequences of Philoctetes' position, the onus is on Neoptolemus to prove beyond any doubt his commitment to their *philia*. Only this can create the trust in which a true friendship of mutual support may flourish, a friendship that can finally afford to disregard the threats of enemies.

7

Oedipus at Colonus

Make my misery serve thy turn: so use it
That my revengeful services may prove
As benefits to thee, for I will fight
Against my canker'd country with the spleen
Of all the under fiends.

Shakespeare, *Coriolanus*

Oedipus, friendship and enmity

The twin principles Help Friends and Harm Enemies are fundamental to the structure of *Oedipus at Colonus*.[1] At the outset Oedipus reveals Apollo's prophecy which he wishes to fulfil, and whose fulfilment will constitute the action of the play. He is to find rest at Athens, 'bringing profit by dwelling here to those who welcomed me, but doom to those who sent me away, driving me out' (92f.). The dual theme is restated more explicitly when he tells the chorus that if they help him they will gain 'a great saviour for this city, and troubles for my enemies' (459f.). For the first 700 lines of the play, until Creon arrives, Oedipus' two-edged hopes and emerging power to implement them are constantly stressed. He shows his benign aspect to the Athenians, to whom he promises *soteria* and benefits if they help him (72, 287f., 576–8, 642; cf. 462f., 487).[2] The arrival of Ismene shows his love for his daughters (324–33), and through her message his power over Thebes is revealed (389f., 402). It gradually emerges how he intends to use that power, and the scene culminates in a curse on his sons and a prayer that he may indeed have the control over their fate which the oracle has promised him (421–4). Later, in his long speech to Theseus, it is made clear that the same event will simultaneously bring help to his friends and harm to his foes (621–8), and Theseus' response shows a full understanding of this (635 and especially 646f.).

---

[1] See especially Hester, *Friends*; also Bowra 311f.; Kirkwood 60–2.

[2] For retention of the ms. reading in 487 see Burian, *Suppliant* 414 n. 12. On the *soteria* theme see also Wigodsky 155–7.

After the Colonus ode (668–719), which marks Oedipus' full acceptance as an Athenian, the dramatic action polarises the two aspects of the double theme. First Oedipus encounters those natural *philoi* who have become his enemies, and denounces them with a series of curses of increasing ferocity (787–93, 864–73, 1370–96). This hatred is set in relief by the love between him and his daughters, displayed most intensely after their rescue (1099–1114). When they are restored to him, Oedipus prays gratefully that the gods reward Theseus and Athens as he wishes (1124f.). But it is only after the most terrible curse of all, and Polyneices' tragic exit, that the emphasis switches abruptly to the benign aspect of Oedipus' power. From this moment on he displays both complete confidence that he is following divine guidance, and an urgent desire to reward his friends as he has promised (1489f., 1508f., 1518–55; cf. 1496–8). The prophesied defeat of Thebes is now presented only as a blessing to Athens, not as the destruction of Oedipus' enemies (contrast 621–3). Both here and in the final scene the emphasis is firmly on the beneficial aspect of Oedipus' power.

The whole play is thus structured around Oedipus' overwhelming desire and special power to help his friends and harm his enemies. This desire is rooted in the reciprocity of the talio, which he also uses to justify killing his father: 'How am I *kakos* in my nature? I acted in retaliation for what was done to me, so that even had I done it in full knowledge, not even so would I be *kakos*. But as it is I reached the point I did knowing nothing, whereas those who acted against me tried to destroy me knowingly' (270–4).[3] He extends the right of retaliation within the family not only to fathers against sons – which is uncontroversial – but also to sons against their fathers, which is quite a different matter. He takes the doctrine of retaliation within the family to its logical conclusion: if striking back is right, why should parents be exempt?[4] Later on, however, he justifies his

3 On the importance of the talio in Oedipus' self-defence see Winnington-Ingram 261–4. But I cannot accept the view (which he shares with many) that 274 refers to Oedipus' parents' attempt to expose him as a baby. The context is Oedipus' ignorance in killing his father and marrying his mother. I would therefore (despite *OT* 1454) refer the line to the attack by Laius and his men, which Oedipus later represents as murderous aggression (991–6). (Mekler's emendation of 547, adopted by Jebb, expresses the same sentiment. But see contra Kamerbeek ad loc.).

4 For a comic parallel showing the untraditional character of the idea cf. Ar. *Clouds* 1400–24. Cf. also Howe 140f.

deed as self-defence against a murderous attack (991–6). Self-defence
is retaliation at its most justifiable,[5] and indeed need not be attributed to the talio at all, but Oedipus makes it quite clear that he does
consider retaliation just (cf. especially 1381f.; also 868–70).

Creon and Oedipus' sons have forfeited their presumptive
philia. As Oedipus bitterly tells Creon, 'This "kinship" was in no
way *philos* to you *then*' (770f.). His sons not only failed to prevent his
exile, but did not recall him until their own interests were at stake
(427–30, 418f., 448f., 599f., 1354–7).[6] Accordingly Polyneices is
'loathed', his voice is *echthistos* and brings great pain (1173f., 1177).
He is disowned as a son, and a fortiori as a *philos* (1369, 1383).[7]
Oedipus reinforces these personal judgements with a thorough
moral condemnation. His sons are *kakistoi* (418, 1354, 1384), while
Creon is *kakos* (783), *kakistos* (866f.), unjust (806f.), irreverent (823),
and shameless (863). His daughters, on the other hand, have fulfilled
the obligations of kinship-*philia* by subordinating their own immediate pleasure and advantage to his interests. The role of Ismene is ingeniously introduced and developed so as to produce a pair of
concerned daughters to balance the pair of callous sons (see especially
337–56). They remind us that the sons' behaviour was not inevitable,
for even if Oedipus' exile was unavoidable there were ways in which
they could have eased his lot.[8] The touching reunion of Ismene with
her sister and father, and the mutual affection emphasised after the
rescue and at Oedipus' death, make it clear that he is not deficient in

---

5   But Oedipus explicitly distinguishes retaliation in self-defence from 'justice',
    which might have been investigated had circumstances permitted (995f.), thus
    distinguishing evaluation of the deed from evaluation of the doer (in Aristo-
    telian terms it is an ἄδικον but not an ἀδίκημα, *EN* 1135a15–23).
6   The apparent inconsistencies in these passages have prompted much discussion.
    See e.g. Méautis, *L'Œdipe* 45f.; Kitto, *GT*[3] 390f.; Gellie 165–7; and most
    recently Machin 104–49. There are also difficulties in trying to pin down the
    precise terms of the oracle (see Linforth, *OC* 82–92). But Oedipus should cer-
    tainly not be regarded as distorting the 'facts'. This misses the point of his griev-
    ance: both sons, whether actively or otherwise, are equally responsible for both
    his exile and his neglect. Not even Polyneices tries to excuse their past be-
    haviour, so neither should we.
7   At 1323f. Polyneices himself suggests that he is the son not of Oedipus, but of
    an 'evil fate'. This adds pathos to his predicament, but at the same time recalls
    the rift in family relations which is Oedipus' strongest card. His reference to
    their common fate (δαίμονα 1337) backfires similarly.
8   Note especially γάρ ('for') in 1379. On the contrast between the daughters and
    sons see Easterling, *Oedipus*.

philia for those children who behave as children ought.[9] He is bound to them by the natural affection of kinship, for as Antigone puts it, 'Everything is *philos* to its parent' (1108). This line is highly ironic in view of the forthcoming confrontation between Oedipus and his son, but it also serves to underline the natural state of family relations which has been perverted by the sons' behaviour. The company of such *philoi* should bring pleasure (cf. 324f.) and delight (cf. 1121f., 1140).[10] After her father's death Antigone realises there is such a thing as 'longing for evils' (1697), and that the non-*philos* can be *philos* (1698), for the pain caused by caring for her father was outweighed by the pleasure of his presence. The messenger reports Oedipus' claim that 'the single word "love"' is sufficient recompense for all his daughter's hardships (1615–18).

Oedipus also initiates *philia* of a different kind by supplicating at the shrine of the Eumenides, where the chorus of local citizens promise him protection (176f.).[11] But as soon as they learn his identity they react with a horrified revulsion, which leads them to break their assurance of sanctuary (226). They persist in this rejection, despite pity for the old man, out of fear of divine reprisals (254–7). This is not a very promising start. But as soon as they act on their pity – swayed also by promises of benefit to their land – and advise Oedipus in his best interests (461–4), he addresses the chorus leader as *philtatos* (465). The seed of a future relationship of mutual benefit has been sown.

The chorus take Help Friends/Harm Enemies for granted in advising Oedipus to adapt to local custom. In accordance with the transitivity of *philia*, the outsider must adopt the city's entire system of friendships and enmities: 'Endure as a stranger in a strange land to loathe what the city holds as non-*philos* and revere what is *philos* to it' (184–7). They also try to use the talio to justify breaking their promise of protection: 'No destined vengeance comes for paying back what one has suffered first; a second deception laid beside a first gives in exchange trouble, not *charis*' (229–33). The first clause is a very strong general statement of approval for the talio.[12] The second

---

[9] Cf. Easterling, *Oedipus* 12f.; also Torrance 285.

[10] Cf. also 615 where 'delightful' is used as a synonym for *philos*, and 'bitter' for *echthros* (for the latter cf. 606, 615, 951, 990 and above, p. 98 n. 189).

[11] On the chorus' role as guardians of the land see Gardiner 116.

[12] Cf. Winnington-Ingram 268f. n. 56.

is particularly interesting because of the ambiguity of its tortuous language. The chorus must mean that the proper return for deceit is further deceit, which brings trouble in its train.[13] But their words could also be interpreted, 'If deceit is returned for deceit, then it brings nothing but trouble in its train.' In other words, their language can be construed as condemning the retaliation of which they approve. This is a form of irony characteristic of Sophocles, who likes to put words in the mouths of his characters that implicitly undermine the sentiment they explicitly convey (e.g. *OC* 743f., 738f.; *El.* 580–3; *Phil.* 519–23).

The chorus' use of the talio here is specious. Oedipus avoids telling them who he is (143–5), but can scarcely be said to deceive them. It is they who insist that he move away from the shrine before answering further questions (166–9). They do not directly ask who he is until he has left sanctuary with their promise of protection (203–6, 176f.). But even if he had deliberately concealed his identity, it is not clear that this would justify them in breaking their promise. Their horror at his identity is powerfully expressed by the fact that it leads them to do so. They are acting out of a kind of piety (cf. 256), as Antigone acknowledges when she calls them 'respectful' (237). This is the piety on which Creon will rely in his attempt to abduct his brother-in-law (cf. 944–6). But piety also demands respect for suppliants. Moreover Oedipus is 'sacred' and 'reverent' (287) not only as a suppliant, but in an as yet mysterious sense related to Apollo's oracle (cf. 105) and the 'benefit' that he brings (287f.).[14]

Theseus' reaction to Oedipus is in pointed contrast to that of the chorus.[15] He comes straight to meet the stranger and immediately offers to help him, not only out of pity (556), but on the basis of personal sympathy with his sufferings and an understanding of the transience of human life (560–8). Although we shall later discover that he has a proper respect for supplication, the initial offer of assistance is made without reference to religious constraints. Nor does he mention here the alliance between Thebes and Athens to which he later alludes (632f.). The absence of such factors from this first encounter establishes the human foundation of their friendship.

---

[13] So it is explained by the scholiast and subsequent editors.
[14] On Oedipus' sacred status see Torrance 290–2. For the significance of ἱερός, 'sacred' (287, 1545, 1763) see Burkert 269.
[15] Cf. Lesky, *Zwei* 101–3.

Theseus' pity, sympathy and understanding provide the initial impulse for *philia* between two people with no prior personal relationship. This human sympathy recalls Odysseus in *Ajax*, who pitied his enemy and initiated friendship with his survivors on similar grounds.[16] Here it enables Oedipus to retain his dignity as he goes on to offer real reciprocal benefit instead of the usual helpless gratitude of the suppliant (576–8).[17]

Besides his sympathy, Theseus' offer of protection is based on a preexisting military alliance with Thebes (632f.),[18] Oedipus' status as 'a suppliant coming from the gods' (634), and the offer of substantial though mysterious recompense to himself and Athens (635). The practical benefit that goes hand in hand with principle is not to be scorned, for as Oedipus says, 'What good man (*esthlos*) is not friend to himself?' (309). But such benefit is not Theseus' overriding motive. Even after it has been offered (576–8), he must be persuaded that it would not be more *kalos* for Oedipus to return to Thebes (590). Conversely he seems unperturbed by Oedipus' warning that accepting him will involve Athens in 'no small struggle' (587).

Theseus is thus moved by sympathy, piety, loyalty, self-interest and the interests of his city. For all these reasons he promises to protect Oedipus and establish him as an Athenian citizen (637; cf. 1156).[19] This reverses Oedipus' status as 'citiless' (1357; cf. 207), providing him with a new city and new *philoi* with whose help he can reject the advances of the old. In return for this *charis* (586) he will bequeath to them a unique *charis* of his own (636, 1489, 1498), the paradoxical 'gift' of his ravaged body (576f.; cf. 647).[20] This will en-

---

[16] But Odysseus' sympathy was grounded more generally, whereas Theseus' friendship is rooted in the specific shared experiences of hardship and exile, as well as common humanity.

[17] In virtue of their situation suppliants cannot normally offer an immediate concrete return to their rescuer. On their self-abasement see Gould, *Hiketeia* 94f.

[18] On these lines see Reinhardt 271 n. 14. Ironically, Theseus' respect for the alliance will lead to the destruction of Thebes.

[19] This is the usual understanding of Musgrave's attractive ἔμπολιν in 637. Burian defends the conjecture and notes that in making Oedipus a citizen Theseus both goes beyond the normal treatment of a suppliant and beyond Oedipus' own request (*Suppliant* 416f.). If the manuscripts' ἔμπαλιν is retained (with Dain and Kamerbeek) the sense is basically the same (though without the possible reference to citizenship), but the verbal echoes are reduced.

[20] For the *charis* theme cf. also 1183, 1753, 1776 and see Kirkwood 151, 244f.; id. *Melos* 110f.; Segal 380–2; Gellie 182. It is used especially for the mutual relationship between Theseus and Oedipus in contrast to the false *charis* offered by Creon.

sure that their land, now his, remains 'free from pain forever' (1765).
He can now afford, in addressing Creon, to call Thebes 'your city'
(785),[21] and refer to Polyneices' quest for power as 'your throne'
(1380). His new status also gives added point to the introduction of
Polyneices as 'not your fellow citizen but your kin' (1156f.). The
claims of city, family and friendship are now absolutely distinct.
Creon will argue in vain that Oedipus' original home has a prior
claim over his new one (759f.). Although Theseus too assumes that
ceteris paribus exile from one's native city is not *kalos*, he adds the important proviso that Oedipus should only return if he wants to (590).
Unlike Creon, he behaves like a true *philos* in respecting Oedipus'
desires. Before leaving, he gives his new friend the choice of whatever course of action is 'sweet' to him (638–41).[22]

As we shall discover, what does eventually give Oedipus such
pleasure is the orderly preparation for the death he desires (1604f.; cf.
1704–6, 1713).[23] Before dying, he entrusts his daughters to Theseus'
care (1631–7), and they accordingly inherit the newly initiated
friendship. Abundant *phil*-language in the final scene of lamentation
expresses not only their love for their father (1698, 1700) and each
other (1718, 1724), but a bond of affection between them and the
chorus (1677, 1721, 1737). Theseus' continued friendship is shown in
his final lines, where he agrees to send Antigone back to Thebes and
promises to do all he can to benefit the sisters or bring *charis* to the
dead Oedipus (1773–6). Ironically, this very deference to Antigone's
wishes will lead to her destruction.[24]

Creon

When Creon appears, his veracity has already been undermined by
Ismene (399f.).[25] The hypocrisy of his opening speech is underlined
by the ironic claim that he above all wishes to recall Oedipus, 'in so
far as I above all feel pain at your misfortunes, unless I am by my

[21] I owe this telling detail to Knox 156.
[22] Note the repetition of ἡδύ, 'sweet' (638, 640) (see Easterling, *Repetition* 30f. and
cf. 18f.).
[23] Meineke's ἔρωτος in 1604 is tempting (printed by Dawe and defended by Jebb;
contra Pearson and Kamerbeek).
[24] The irony is compounded by Theseus' promise not 'willingly' to betray his
friend's daughters (1634).
[25] Oedipus needs no 'special insight' (Bowra 337) or 'prophetic knowledge'
(Kitto, *GT*[3] 383) to know that he is lying.

nature the most *kakos* of all mortals' (743f.). Oedipus' estimate of his enemy is fully confirmed by Creon's dishonesty, disregard for suppliancy and use of violence against the defenceless. Once his deception has been exposed he makes no attempt to justify it, and accepts the charge of *hubris* for his threats of violence (883).

Creon has much in common with the Odysseus of *Philoctetes*. He claims to be acting under orders as a representative of the community (850f.; cf. especially *Phil.* 6); he is a man of the tongue (806f.; cf. 774, 782, *Phil.* 96–9), who tries deceptive persuasion (756) but then resorts to violence; he is ruthless and unrepentant towards his own victim; he treats a prophecy as something to be manipulated by fair means or foul,[26] without any thought as to how the divine plan is likely to work itself out.[27] His departure with the kidnapped girls, Oedipus' 'crutches' (848), recalls Odysseus' abandonment of Philoctetes after stealing his bow (cf. especially 849–52 and *Phil.* 1052f.). But Odysseus is cool and rational (he threatens violence but prudently steps down), whereas Creon is impulsive: he carries out his threat of violence, even against his better judgement (732–4, 874f.), and ignores the limitations of his age (958f.). Moreover unlike Odysseus he claims categorically to have justice on his side. Despite his admission of *hubris* (883), when the chorus reprove his present conduct as unjust (831; cf. 824f.),[28] he replies that on the contrary it is just (832; cf. 742, 760, 880, 957), defending this assertion with the claim, 'I am taking my own' (832; cf. 830). This is an implausible justification. How can an uncle have a stronger claim than a father? Jebb on 830 explains, 'He considers himself as now the guardian of his nieces – their father having forfeited all rights at Thebes.' This is arguable for Ismene, who has been living at Thebes under Creon's care, but it is hard to extend it to Antigone, who has shared her father's exile.[29] Yet even if a father could be deprived against his will of his parental

---

[26] Cf. Diller, *Wissen* 26.

[27] It would surely be naive to imagine that the tomb of a deceived and resentful Oedipus, in any location, could benefit Thebes (cf. 402f.), while the tomb of a hostile Oedipus on the borders of Thebes would only bring the fated disaster closer to home.

[28] At 825 they condemn his previous actions too, but it is not clear whether this refers to his expulsion of Oedipus or his treachery.

[29] There may be an allusion to *OT* 1503–9, where Oedipus entrusts his daughters to Creon's care. But the situation in *OC* is quite different. Antigone has suffered precisely the fate from which Oedipus the king wanted Creon to protect her.

rights, and Creon had a prior claim on his nieces, this could scarcely justify their forcible removal from sanctuary.

Creon also exploits the presumption of kinship-*philia* with Oedipus for his own ends. In maltreating his brother-in-law he behaves as if such *philia* can be forfeited, reserving the right to retaliate when Oedipus infringes their alleged *philia* (813f.). He freely admits that he has been roused to wrath by Oedipus' 'bitter' curses (951f.) and wants to cause him pain (816). Yet he does not allow Oedipus himself to retaliate for the wrongs he has received. Disregarding his own past behaviour, or refusing to admit that it was offensive, he trades heavily on the presumptive *philia* of kinship, calling himself a *philos* sent by *philoi* (813, 850). He even seems to treat this as the only legitimate claim, when he answers Theseus' charge of poor judgement by saying that he expected no one else to take an interest in his kinsman (939–43).[30] But if, as he professes, he is Oedipus' *philos*, he should promote his interests and help to satisfy his wishes. Yet he has not only thwarted Oedipus' desires in the past, but is now trying to trick him, through an ostensible favour, into another action that will cause him pain (764).[31] Either Creon's claim to be Oedipus' *philos* is false , or he is treacherously thwarting the wishes of a friend. Either way, his avowed *philia* is suspect.

Creon could have harmonised his conduct with Help Friends by arguing that Oedipus' best interests are in conflict with his desires, and that he, Creon, is acting for Oedipus' own good. This paternalistic approach may be useful to anyone enforcing an unpopular course (it is perhaps implied at *Phil.* 917–20), and Creon does hint at it. He cannot comprehend Oedipus' insistence that all he wants is to stay in Athens as he is, enjoying his own form of 'delight' (798f.) – the 'greatest pleasure' that will result from being left alone by Creon (802f.). Since Oedipus' present life is Creon's idea of 'misfortune' (800f.), he suggests that Oedipus is only damaging himself (800f.), and rebukes him for his folly (804f.) – folly that he thinks Oedipus himself will recognise in time (852). But unless people can be convinced that their interests do diverge from their present desires, they will never be amenable to paternalistic 'favours' that give no

---

[30] This point is distinct from the next one based on pollution (944–6).

[31] Oedipus has good reason to distrust apparently desirable offerings, after accepting the 'gift' (540) of his mother Jocasta as a wife. Cf. Whitman 278 n. 41.

pleasure or even bring them pain. Oedipus argues eloquently that Help Friends should be based on the friend's actual wishes, however misguided these may be. After blinding himself he longed for death: this would have been 'sweetest' (434), while exile would have been a 'gift' (432) and a 'delight' (766).[32] But no one would 'help' him by satisfying his passion (*eros*) for death (436), nor would Creon grant him the *charis* of exile when he wanted it (767). Later he regretted letting his passionate temper (*thumos*) go so far (438; cf. 434, 768), and it became 'sweet' to stay in the palace (769), yet Creon gave him the 'gift' (779) of throwing him out (770). But what 'delight' is there in alleged manifestations of *philia* that violate one's own will (775)? Such a *charis* can bring no *charis* (779); such a 'pleasure' is futile (780). What is 'sweetest' for a friend may thus not match that friend's long-term interests or future desires. But, Oedipus implies, a true friend should perform such a favour regardless.

The paternalistic claim of Creon and his ilk to know what is best for another is based on the assumption that conventionally accepted 'goods' (wealth, health, status etc.) are not only intrinsically desirable, but must be desired by all. This leaves no room for an Oedipus, a Philoctetes, an Antigone or a Socrates – for all those who see their own well-being as consisting in the satisfaction of unconventional desires, of which the most extreme is the desire for death.[33] Moreover, in the absence of a desire for conventional goods, how can the alleged *philos* prove that they do promote well-being? Oedipus' life has been one of such unparalleled suffering that he has nothing left to desire but a painless and glorious death, along with the discomfiture of his enemies. This is also what his true friends want for him (e.g. 1560–4). And he gets exactly what he wants: revenge on his enemies, blessing for his friends, and an end to his own sufferings by means of a miraculous death that confirms his heroic powers. As in the case of Ajax, it would be hard to find an outcome which would be 'better' for Oedipus than the one he

[32] On the repetition of τέρψις ('delight') and wishing words in 763–82 see Easterling, *Repetition* 31.

[33] Plato of course respects Socrates' unconventional desire to die rather than escape from prison. But rather than admit that people's conventional desires may actually coincide with their best interests, he argues that such desires are not 'real'. 'Real' desires will coincide with what he, Plato, regards as their 'real' interests (see e.g. *Rep.* 583b), in the cause of which he admits an unlimited paternalism (see Mackenzie ch. 9 and 10). On paternalism cf. also above, p. 36f.

chooses for himself. The play's ending shows that Creon's judgement of what is 'best' for Oedipus is as suspect as his *philia*.

Creon's strongest card (though he does not make very good use of it) is his appeal to the wishes and interests of the Theban people. He says the entire people is summoning Oedipus back 'justly' (742), and that his native city has a 'just' claim on him (760). Later he suggests that Oedipus is failing to help his friends, arguing that it is not *kalos* for him to resist the wishes of *philoi* and give *charis* to his own passionate temper, 'which always ravages you' (852-5).[34] The last clause apparently alludes to Oedipus' physical sufferings, thus giving a prudential colouring to the rebuke. But as we have seen, it is misguided of Creon to assimilate Oedipus' present wrath to his previous destructive fury, for this time the outcome will certainly be *kalos* for Oedipus himself. And although Oedipus himself has argued vehemently that a friend's wishes should be respected, the dubious character of Creon's *philia* undermines his own claim to this kind of respect. As for the rest of the city, Oedipus' alienation extends to Thebes as a whole, for he is an involuntary exile. As he puts it, 'the *polis* drove me out of the land by force' (440f.). It is therefore debatable how far he retains the obligations of a *philos* towards Thebes. Moreover Polyneices will attack regardless, so by helping the incumbent rulers Oedipus would not be saving the city from civil war. Disastrous though his wrath will be for its victims, it will not harm his true friends or even increase the suffering of the Theban people. Finally, even if Oedipus were failing in the obligation to help his friends, Creon would not be justified in the means he uses to carry out the wishes of those 'friends'. He uses this argument only before Theseus arrives and confirms that Creon's actions are not approved by the Thebans. Thebes, he says, does not produce unjust men, nor would it approve of Creon's impiety and violence (919–923; cf. 937f.). He speaks in general terms, but for dramatic purposes this

---

[34] His words may imply that it is non-*kalos* to give way to anger at all. But if this is true (which is at least debatable) the irascible Creon is on even weaker ground. His intemperate indulgence of his anger (874, 954f.) and Theseus' rebuke (930f.) undermine his taunts to Oedipus (804f.; 852–5). The two old men are equally a prey to *thumos*. This is a morally neutral force (cf. Pl. *Rep.* 440a–d), but on balance the evidence of this play is that it does more harm than good (cf. 434–9, 592, 768, 778, 874, 951–5, 1192–8, 1420). See further Winnington-Ingram 257–60.

clearly constitutes a rejection of any appeal by Creon to the wishes of the Thebans.[35]

Creon claims that he would not have acted as he did had he not been provoked by Oedipus' curses on himself and his family (951f.). His invocation of the talio suggests self-justification (953),[36] but his admission that the retaliation was provoked by *thumos* looks more like mere extenuation (954f.). Indeed it could simply express regret for a moment of poor judgement. But even if he is appealing to the talio in self-justification, it is doubtful whether it is applicable here. The essence of retaliation is the return of like for like. A return with interest may be acceptable, but kidnapping is a response of a different order from mere verbal abuse, for it raises the stakes from words to deeds.[37] More important, however, is the fact that Oedipus did not formally curse Creon and his family (868–70) until *after* his daughters had been kidnapped (818–47) and *after* Creon had threatened Oedipus himself with violence (860f.). Therefore Creon's defence, if it is one, could only justify his later repeated threat to abduct Oedipus (874f.).

Moreover Creon's argument that he was provoked is severely weakened, if not utterly invalidated, by the fact that Oedipus' formal curse was itself an instance of retaliation provoked by Creon's own violence and threats. Since the kidnapping took place before the· curse,[38] which was Oedipus' response to it, Creon's attempt on Oedipus himself is a further injury and not justified by a strict principle of retaliation, whereby the response should 'repay' the original injury and restore the status quo. As we saw with *Electra*, this scheme fails whenever the aggressor will not admit to being in the wrong, which is, naturally, most of the time. The enemy's response then becomes a fresh provocation which must in turn be

---

[35] Cf. Burian, *Suppliant* 420.

[36] Note especially ἠξίουν, 'I thought fit'.

[37] It will gradually become clear that 'mere' is not quite the epithet for Oedipus' words, which have a peculiarly effective power. But his curse on Creon resembles those of other Sophoclean characters against their enemies (cf. *Aj.* 835–44; *Phil.* 1040–2).

[38] Would an audience remember this? I think so, considering the solemnity of the curse and the fact that it is explicitly a response to the kidnapping. Oedipus' earlier imprecation (421–7) was directed against his sons, was not a formal curse, and came well before Creon's entrance. In his first tirade against Creon he merely referred to his avenging spirit (ἀλάστωρ 788).

avenged. Accordingly Creon, despite his earlier admission of *hubris* (883), now treats Oedipus' curse as a serious injury to which he was entitled by the talio to respond (953).[39] He even threatens violent retaliation to Theseus, and gives way to him only under duress (956–9). In claiming to be justified by the talio, he is either ignoring the kidnapping (because he considers it just?), or adopting a vendetta-like justice. The vendetta will be unending as long as it is open to a Creon to argue, 'He provoked me', whether the alleged provocation was itself just or unjust, aggressive or provoked.

Polyneices

After Creon's lies and violence, Polyneices represents a challenge of a different kind.[40] Oedipus' first reaction to the anonymous suppliant betrays a fundamental respect for his status: 'This suppliant posture merits no small consideration' (1163). When he finds out who it is, he begs Theseus not to force him 'by necessity' to receive him (1178), for the sight and sound of his son are hateful and will give him pain (1173–78).[41] Antigone and Theseus overcome this revulsion by calling on principles that overrule the indulgence of personal desire. Theseus appeals to piety, a crucial virtue for Oedipus, who not only emphasises his own sacred status (287), and believes that divine justice sanctions his personal revenge (623, 1381f.), but declares that the gods enforce human piety in general: 'Believe that they look towards the reverent mortal and the irreverent, and that there has never yet been an escape for any impious mortal' (278–81; cf. 1536f.). Since piety demands respect for supplication, Theseus answers Oedipus' fear of 'necessity' with the 'necessity' of religious compulsion: 'But see if his suppliant posture does not force you, lest you fail to preserve respect for the god' (1179f.). Such principles have a binding force, and if Oedipus is to retain his moral stature as he wields his demonic power to bless and curse, he too must respect these laws.

Antigone, in her longest speech of the play, adds to Theseus' brief reproof an eloquent appeal to Oedipus that he consent to see his

---

[39] Cf. 871 where he calls the chorus to witness, suggesting that the curse is an act of aggression.

[40] On the contrasting ways they are introduced see Linforth, *OC* 161f.; Burian, *Suppliant* 422–4.

[41] Another motive – fear of renewed violence – is also implied (1185, 1207).

son.[42] She has already exerted a moderating influence in the prologue, advising Oedipus to conform to local custom (170–2) and acting as a tactful intermediary between him and the chorus, whom she begged for pity (241), respect (*aidos* 247) and *charis* (249). Later she will also mediate between Oedipus and Polyneices (1280–3), and will try to prevent her brother's fatal enterprise (1414–41). Now she supplements Theseus' religious argument with an appeal to reciprocal *charis*, begging Oedipus to grant Theseus' request as a favour to him as well as to the god (1182.; cf. 1202f.). She will end similarly by insisting that it is not *kalos* for a person with a just request to be obliged to persist, nor is it just for one who has received good treatment to refuse to repay it (1201–3.).

Antigone not only approves of helping friends and reciprocating benefits, but denies that it is ever right to return one's son harm for harm:

> Yes, and you're his father –
> so even if he'd inflict on you the worst wrong,
> the worst outrage, father, it isn't right
> for you to strike back in kind.
>
> (1189–91, trans. Fagles)

This sentiment is all the more remarkable in that it seeks to curb the father's right to revenge on the son, rather than vice versa.[43] But rejection of the talio for this kind of case does not entail modification of Help Friends/Harm Enemies per se. Antigone retains her own friendship with her brother (cf. 1415, 1442f.). This suggests she is not arguing that some enemies (sons) should remain unharmed, but rejecting the notion that a son may forfeit his father's *philia*. If a son remains *philos* no matter what, then it can never be right to harm him, even in retaliation.[44] The blanket rule Help Friends/Harm Enemies remains intact (though the talio does not). But the criteria for enmity must be modified, since not everyone who injures me will count as my enemy. Nor is Antigone's *philia* confined to the virtuous, for she admits that her brother is *kakos*, as is her father's temper (1187–92, 1197f.). Like her other self in *Antigone*, she places an inalienable value on kinship.

---

[42] On her speech see Winnington-Ingram 259f.

[43] Dover 274 (though his reference is wrong) remarks that the passage 'sounds a note unusual for the fifth century'.

[44] Cf. Winnington-Ingram 263.

Although Oedipus ultimately rejects the notion that one should not retaliate against a son, Antigone's speech, together with Theseus' words, achieves its immediate purpose. He capitulates without a murmur, making his point with an oxymoron, 'you two win a grievous pleasure from me with your words' (1204). He thus acknowledges that there are times when helping or giving pleasure to a *philos* should overrule one's personal desires. This has been a litmus test of true friendship throughout the play, in contrast to the duplicity of Creon, who claims to be Oedipus' *philos* (813) but thwarts his desires at every turn (763–80). Ismene declares, 'Even if it is troublesome to aid one's parents, one should not be mindful of the trouble' (508f.), and places great emphasis on the pain and difficulty she has undergone to come to her father's aid (325f., 328, 361–4; cf. 1697f.).[45] The chorus, in their passionate desire to hear about Oedipus' past (512), ask him a favour that they know will cause him pain (510f.), on the grounds that they have done what he asked (520). Theseus is willing to sacrifice his own pleasure in a case that is trivial, but symptomatic of his character (890). He goes on to risk his life in rescuing his friend's daughters (1040f.). The favour that Oedipus now grants to Antigone and Theseus may seem small in comparison, but it is represented as extremely painful to him (1169–78). Polyneices is so loathsome to Oedipus that his very voice is *echthistos* and will therefore bring his father the greatest pain (1173f., 1176f.). The converse of Oedipus' pleasure and delight in the company of his daughters is his intense revulsion from the presence of his son.

But Oedipus must do more than allow his son to appear. Polyneices originally supplicated for 'some brief word' from his father (1162), and can thus claim to be 'dishonoured' by Oedipus' initial silence (1271–4, 1278f.).[46] Antigone encourages her brother to speak on, suggesting that his words may arouse a response by giving

---

[45] On 'trouble' (πόνος, 509) and its connection with nurture in the play see Easterling, *Oedipus* 3.

[46] Polyneices supplicates a second time in the course of his plea for help (1327) and is rejected (1380f.). But this is a merely 'figurative' supplication (cf. 1414, 1754), in contrast to the complete and binding ritual at the altar. (For this distinction see Gould, *Hiketeia* 77). Both Antigone and Theseus say Oedipus may listen to Polyneices (thus, it is implied, respecting his suppliancy) without consenting to do as he asks (1175f., 1185–8; cf. also the chorus at 1346f.) The respect due to his supplication is thus distinguished from acceding to his request.

'delight', or by expressing anger or pity (1280–3).[47] Polyneices has expressed pity for his father, and will go on to declare anger at his brother, but we have already been warned of the unlikelihood that the sound of his son's voice will bring Oedipus 'delight'. When he does finally speak it is for Theseus' sake (1346–53).[48] Friendship once more promotes respect for supplication. The irony is that only by speaking, and thus 'honouring' the suppliant, does Oedipus finally seal his son's fate.

Oedipus' subjugation of personal desire to the wishes of others removes him from the ranks of those Sophoclean protagonists who pursue their own gratification at the expense of both moral consistency and the wishes and/or interests of their friends. Creon brings this kind of charge against his brother-in-law (849–55), but he is wrong. Unlike Philoctetes or Ajax, Oedipus gives Help Friends equal weight with Harm Enemies, and remains open to the persuasion of his friends. This both enhances his moral stature,[49] and enables him to avoid inconsistency with two fundamental principles, the piety of respecting suppliants and the justice of reciprocal *charis*. This concern for moral consistency, and willingness to subordinate his desires to those of others, put his final intransigence into a different light from that of an Ajax or a Philoctetes. We cannot assume that he is motivated solely by lust for revenge, since he has shown a concern to stand by other potentially conflicting principles.

Polyneices' suppliancy places him in the same position as Oedipus himself.[50] Like Oedipus and Antigone he piously appeals for the honour and respect (*aidos*) that are the suppliant's due (1273f., 1278f., 1267f.; cf. 49, 247, 285f.). Unlike the hypocritical Creon he admits that he has been *kakistos* towards his father (1265f.; contrast 743f.). But he begs forgiveness, promising to do his best to make up

---

[47] We might expect the participles in 1282 to be causal, but see contra Jebb and Kamerbeek ad loc.

[48] At the same time his language (δικαιῶν 1350; cf. ἀξιωθείς 1352) recalls the moral arguments of Theseus and Antigone, and he does not present his action solely as a favour to a *philos* (contrast *Aj.* 1370–3). Cf. also Easterling, *Repetition* 32.

[49] Cf. Buxton 144f. Openness to persuasion is 'an essential characteristic of any concept of a moral agent' (Long, *Morals* 133).

[50] See Burian, *Suppliant* 422f.

for the past and reinstall Oedipus in Thebes (1269f., 1342f.).[51] Yet
Oedipus disowns him and condemns him, like Creon, as *kakistos* of
kakoi (1383f.). He announces that he will always think of his son as a
murderer (1361), and curses him with death in return (1387f.). Oedipus, like Odysseus in *Ajax*, recognises the mutability of human
friendship and enmity (607–15).[52] But he does not apply this insight
to his own hostility, resisting both Antigone's suggestion that it
could revert to friendship and Polyneices' own attempt at reconciliation.

When Polyneices reminds his father of their shared experience
of exile (1334–7) he echoes the sympathetic words of Theseus (562–
6), whose friendship Oedipus gladly accepted. But the parallel is a
specious one. Shared experience does not compel sympathetic
friendship under all circumstances. Polyneices' exile is less a reason
for sympathy than a just return for reducing his father to such
straits.[53] He sympathises with Oedipus' condition now that he is
forced to share it (1337), but the kinship bond gave him, unlike
Theseus, a prior obligation. Oedipus may therefore consistently
accept Theseus' offer of sympathy and friendship while rejecting
Polyneices'. The mutability of friendship does not oblige us to
accept every opportunity for change that may present itself.

Polyneices also begs for *aidos* (1268), echoing Antigone's plea
to the chorus on Oedipus' behalf (247). Oedipus himself accused
Creon of 'shamelessness' or lack of *aidos* (863, 960). But this does not
make him inconsistent in rejecting his son's appeal. *Aidos* does not
exactly mean mercy or forgiveness (as it is often translated) so much
as a sense of respect or obligation towards another. It is associated
with reconciliation, with *philia*, and often, as here, with supplication.[54] But if Oedipus is justified in rejecting his son's proffered
friendship, then a fortiori he may refuse the plea for *aidos*. It does not

[51] To some critics Polyneices is 'unquestionably sincere' (Whitman 196), to others
'transparently insincere' (Vickers 473). But we are given no reason to doubt his
sincerity. According to Ismene, Oedipus' pollution prevents his return (407; cf.
600f.), but this is only the reported view of those now at Thebes. Not even
Oedipus accuses his son of duplicity (cf. Burian, *Suppliant* 424).

[52] On this speech and the theme of time see Torrance 286f.

[53] See Saïd 211 for the way the same language is used to describe their fates.

[54] See Glotz 94–103; Benveniste 340f. (for the association with *philia*); Gould,
Hiketeia 85–90 (for supplication).

add a further consideration but enshrines Polyneices' claim to forgiveness, for better or worse.

Forgiveness per se is not a characteristically Greek virtue.[55] Yet Polyneices, like Neoptolemus in *Philoctetes*, promises to try to make up for his fault (1269f., 1342), and such an offer should not be rejected out of hand (cf. *Phil.* 1308–10).[56] When Neoptolemus returns the bow Philoctetes accepts his repentance and friendship, persisting in hostility only towards his unrepentant enemies. But the compensation offered by Polyneices is both inadequate and inextricable from his own self-interest. Still more important, the time for it has passed. Oedipus has already found new *philoi* and his fated resting place. There is nothing left that his son can do for him. Polyneices speaks truly when he laments, 'Wretch that I am, I learn this far too late' (1264).

Oedipus confirms this in his tirade: 'You drove me, your own father, into exile, and made me citiless, and made me wear this garb which you now weep to see when you have come to the same stress of misery as I. The time for tears is past. No; *I* must bear this burden while I live' (1356–61, trans. Jebb). This denunciation is also his answer to the claim of kinship, so movingly presented by Antigone. In rejecting it, Oedipus has popular sentiment on his side. Any relative who initiated hostilities might forfeit the rights of *philia*, and the greatest possible opprobrium was reserved for children who mistreated their parents. But Antigone's speech is enough to suggest that conventional morality is open to criticism on this point. We therefore cannot dismiss kinship out of hand as a reason for forgiveness.

In the house of Oedipus, however, any appeal to kinship is a two-edged sword. Not only is it precisely against the obligations of kinship that Polyneices has offended, but if Oedipus were to give way and forgive this one son, he would still be condemning Thebes

---

[55] Cf. Hester, *Friends* 29; Earp 35–40; contra Dover 190–205. But Dover has difficulty finding convincing cases of forgiveness. Most of his examples are from the orators, and leniency from a jury out of pity for starving dependents is a far cry from forgiveness of a personal enemy. Moreover Polyneices is asking even more than this – he wants a positive favour from Oedipus. As Dover 192 admits, 'Returning positive good for ill, an important stage beyond mere refraining from requiting ill, does not seem to be exemplified in the available literature.' Antigone's plea to Oedipus at 1189–91 comes closer than any of Dover's examples to an appeal for forgiveness for a serious personal injury.

[56] Cf. also *Il.* 9.496–523 with Lloyd-Jones 17; Arist. *Rhet.* 1380a6–b1.

to civil war and his other son to death. There is no indication that
Eteocles deserves this any more or less than his brother. The only dis-
paraging reference to him comes from Polyneices himself: 'The
turannos in the house ... luxuriates laughing at both of us alike'
(1338f.). This is a stereotyped description of an enemy (cf. 902f.,
1422f.), designed to assimilate the hardships of father and son by pitting them against a common foe. By itself it is slim evidence that
Eteocles is any more to blame than Polyneices himself. Ismene tells
the story of the quarrel without taking sides (365–81). She makes
clear that it was culpable, or at best irresponsible, for either brother
to take power: their original desire to leave the throne to Creon is
attributed to rational reflection on their family history (367–70),
whereas the subsequent 'evil strife' for power 'entered the pair of
wretches from some god and a sinful mind' (371–3). Nor can Ismene
deny the painful fact that both sons knew of the oracle and gave the
throne priority over desire for their father (416–20).[57] The similar
behaviour and equal responsibility of the two brothers is emphasised
by the repeated use of the dual number, both by Ismene (365, 372,
417) and especially by Oedipus himself, in the great speeches where
he contrasts them with his loyal pair of daughters (337f., 344f., 423,
430, 445, 448).

In other versions of the legend Eteocles is clearly in the wrong.
After the brothers agreed to rule alternately, he refused to give up
the throne at the end of his first year.[58] In Sophocles' version he is
also at fault, for usurping the throne from Polyneices. But it is not
clear that this is any more reprehensible than Polyneices' original
assumption of power, which was based solely on his rights as the
elder son (374f., 1293–5, 1422f.).[59] Since primogeniture was not a

---

[57] The sense of 418f. is unclear. Jebb and most editors take it to mean that since the
new oracles have rescinded Oedipus' exile, his sons should have restored him to
the throne, but they failed to do so because they desired power for themselves.
But if this were his complaint, we might expect Polyneices' overtures to meet
with his approval. The lines are more equally applicable to both sons alike if the
complaint is that only on hearing the new oracle did they become concerned
about their father (since their rule now depends on him). They thus showed
that they valued power more than their father, since they had never sought him
out for his own sake.

[58] For the various accounts see Roscher s.v. *Polyneikes*.

[59] Euripides makes Eteocles the elder (*Phoen.* 71f.) and the scholiast on *OC* 375
finds Sophocles' variation worthy of comment. Aeschylus does not specify (cf.
Sept. 576, 890, 932, 940).

Greek institution,[60] this makes his grievance less clearly justified than under the power-sharing arrangement. The fact that the quarrel now turns on an issue of family status instead of contractual obligation (note the language of 1293–6) makes it all the more fitting that Polyneices' appeal to his father should backfire. To claim one's inheritance as Oedipus' son is to court disaster.

Moreover Eteocles took over not by force but 'by persuading the city', a procedure with at least prima facie democratic respectability (1298).[61] Polyneices explicitly contrasts persuasion with other means of gaining power, namely argument or single combat (1296–8). The latter is particularly suggestive since he himself has chosen to overcome his brother by 'force' (1343), the antithesis of persuasion and a prominent characteristic of the villainous Creon's (867, 874, 903, 916, 922).[62] This scorn for political persuasion, while it may not exonerate Eteocles, helps to establish Polyneices' character as a man of violence and so to undermine the legitimacy of his claim.

Sophocles has thus left the moral status of the quarrel ambivalent. He has also given each brother a turn as king, unlike other versions in which Polyneices never rules at all. This assimilates the brothers still more closely to each other, and provides a further reproach for Oedipus to cast at Polyneices. As the first to rule, he was the first who might have recalled his father (1354–7). There is thus no reason at all why Oedipus should take his side against Eteocles. This ambivalence is sustained by the poet's use of Creon as the messenger from Thebes. Creon identifies himself as the ruler (*turannos* 851), and does not suggest that he was sent by Eteocles or even mention him. The way his character is dissociated from the city prevents his villainy from reflecting on Eteocles, so that we are not tempted to compare the two brothers. If Eteocles appeared instead of Creon he would either have to be more virtuous or villainous than his brother, thus forcing us to choose between them, or closely similar, which

---

60 For Athens cf. MacDowell, *LCA* 92. But the practice was doubtless familiar (cf. Xen. *Cyr.* 8.7.9, and for the prerogative of age cf. e.g. *Il.* 9.160f.).

61 On persuasion in Athenian political contexts see Buxton 53–6.

62 On the antithesis see Buxton 58–63. 'Argument' (λόγῳ 1296) is less easy to understand, since one might expect it to coincide with persuasion. It is usually taken to mean that Eteocles did not prove by argument his right to the throne. But cf. 369, where the same expression is used for the rational consideration that initially prevents the brothers from taking power.

would be monotonous. As it is Polyneices represents both, and both are equally damned.

The case for relenting is therefore far from obvious. If the war is inevitable, why should Oedipus take one side rather than the other? His resistance to persuasion is superficially similar to Philoctetes', but its consequences are very different. If Philoctetes had given way to Neoptolemus the results would have been beneficial for all the Greeks – Philoctetes himself, Neoptolemus and the army collectively, including, incidentally, both Philoctetes' friends and enemies. But Oedipus' resistance is ultimately constructive. If he gave way it would save neither his city nor his sons from war, but would merely help one undeserving son at the other's expense, while depriving his new friends, who have proved their moral worth, of friendship and assistance. In *Philoctetes* the gods' plan required Philoctetes to give Help Friends priority over Harm Enemies. In *Oedipus at Colonus* they seem to endorse a relentless application of Help Friends/Harm Enemies, which can in this case be pursued without contradiction. They make Oedipus the instrument of his family curse, but at the same time give him a unique power to help his friends. The two are intimately linked, for it is only by rejecting Polyneices that he can leave his tomb to protect Athens. Help Friends and Harm Enemies are fully complementary, so that the potential conflict between them does not arise.[63]

The choral couplet after Polyneices' speech is non-committal, directing Oedipus, for Theseus' sake, to 'say what is expedient' before sending his son away (1346f.). After Oedipus curses him, their rebuff to Polyneices is firm, but mild compared with their reaction to Creon (1397f.; cf. 834f., 937f.). Nor do the other characters explicitly endorse Oedipus' treatment of his son as they do his response to Creon.[64] Yet they do not attempt to excuse Polyneices' original behaviour. Theseus and Antigone argue only that he should be given a hearing, and Antigone that his relationship to Oedipus should bring him forgiveness. Nor does Polyneices himself offer any excuses, but

---

[63] The curse will indirectly harm Antigone, but Oedipus does his best to protect her (1631–7) and it is her own choice to return to Thebes (1769–72). The reminder of her fate (1405–13) may show a limitation in Oedipus' prophetic powers (so Winnington-Ingram 275). It certainly shows the same limitation in merely human powers of understanding and foreknowledge that we see at the end of *Phil.* and *El.*

[64] Cf. Bowra 330.

condemns himself as *kakistos* for neglecting his father's nurture: 'Hear what I am from myself and no other' (1265f.). He is guilty. Oedipus' revenge is harsh, but just.[65]

Polyneices tries to make Oedipus abandon his wrath, but when he fails, is unwilling to abandon his own.[66] The epilogue to his encounter with his father, where Antigone tries to dissuade him in turn from his chosen course, is the final vindication of Oedipus' decision. Polyneices is bent on destruction, either of his brother, or of himself and his allies (cf. 380f.). Like Oedipus himself he has found new friends who will back his interests against former family *philoi*. The detailed listing of these allies (1313–22) gives them a reality which makes not only Oedipus' curse but also Polyneices' final decision the more terrible. He rejects Antigone's appeal, as Oedipus did his, arguing that if he turned back now he would never be able to lead the army again (1418f.). Antigone makes the natural response: Why should he ever want to? What *kerdos* will he gain from destroying his fatherland? (1420f.). He answers that it is 'disgraceful' to be an exile and mocked by his younger brother (1422f.), making no mention of the practical benefits of regaining the throne (as we might expect after 1335–7). This emphasis on honour brings out the tragic futility of Polyneices' decision. He even declares that the 'worthwhile' commander should not tell his troops the bad news of Oedipus' curse, and thus rules out the possibility that his allies might dissuade him from the war (1429f.).[67] His heroic language disguises Odyssean deception, and like Odysseus in *Philoctetes*, he evades responsibility with impersonal expressions of necessity (1418, 1426, 1441, 1442).[68] Although he is a pathetic, even a tragic figure, he is as intransigent as Oedipus himself, rejecting any solution other than the violent one on which he has determined.

Oedipus implicitly reproaches his son with the use of violence against kin, using language that recalls his own offence against kindred blood (1385; cf. 407). But Oedipus' deeds, as he frequently

---

65 For bibliography on this issue see Hester, *Friends* appendix C.

66 On the likeness between Oedipus and Polyneices see Winnington-Ingram 277. Antigone too, though she tries to restrain both father and brother, shows a passionate impetuosity in the final scene.

67 Cf. above, p. 36. But Polyneices is deceiving not his troops, but his fellow chieftains, at a stage when war can still be avoided.

68 For Odysseus see above, p. 188 n. 16. The scholiast justifies 1429f. in Odyssean style, by remarking that lies are necessary for schemes if truth is not 'useful'.

reminds us, were involuntary, unlike Polyneices' wilful neglect of his father (985–7). Polyneices must likewise bear full responsibility for the violence against his brother and his native Thebes. For Oedipus' curse is contingent on Polyneices' attempt, and as Antigone tells her brother, he is bringing the curse upon himself (1371f., 1424f.). One function of this touching farewell scene is to arouse our sympathy for Polyneices, especially by the affection he displays for his sisters (1415, 1444–6).[69] But it also demonstrates unequivocally that he, as well as Oedipus, is responsible for his fate. He justifies his attempt as retributive justice (1306, 1329), but at the same time he is treacherously leading his friends into a foreseen military disaster.[70] He is willing to sacrifice not only his own life but the lives of allies to enmity and personal honour. Once more Sophocles reveals the potential for conflict between Help Friends and Harm Enemies, and the destructive futility of giving revenge priority over friendship.

Theseus

Theseus is a model of ethical propriety.[71] He instantiates all the cardinal virtues:[72] piety, especially in his respect for supplication (634–7, 922f., 1179f.; cf. also 664f., 887–9); justice in his treatment of both Oedipus and Creon; courage in his rescue of the women; *sophrosune* in his restraint towards Creon and refusal to boast about his exploits (904–8, 1148, 1209; cf. 1143f.);[73] wisdom, or at least rational prudence, throughout. He is a loyal friend who need not be put under oath (650f.).[74] He matches his virtuous words with deeds, risking his life for his principles (1040f.) and showing a benevolent use for force, not to make right, but to enforce it.[75] Finally, he shares with the Odysseus of *Ajax* a sympathetic desire to help the unfortunate on the basis of common human experience. Not surprisingly Oedipus re-

[69] Cf. Kirkwood 152f.; Easterling, *Oedipus* 11.

[70] How clearly it is foreseen appears to fluctuate: cf. 1407f., 1424–6, 1432–4, 1441, 1435–8, 1770–2, and see Linforth, *OC* 165.

[71] As he regularly is in tragedy (e.g. Eur. *Supp.*, *HF*). No one in the play criticises him (except for Creon's insinuations at 939–49). For a full discussion of his character see Bowra 331–5, 338–40.

[72] On which see Ferguson ch. 3.

[73] Contrast Polyneices (1344f.) and see North 55.

[74] See above, p. 205 n. 80 and contrast the chorus' breach of their promise.

[75] Cf. Solon's claim to have united force (*bia*) and *dike* (36.16 (West)). But Theseus' force is never characterised as *bia* (which tends to be pejorative) except in Creon's invidious phrase (943).

gards him as *gennaios* (569, 1042; cf. 1636),[76] and as *aristos* in every way (1458).

If Theseus is a paradigm, it is of very much the same values as Oedipus himself. He stands by loyal friends and is eager to make and defend new ones. He does not protest at Oedipus' vengeance on his enemies, or object to the prospect of harming his own in the future, and he punishes Creon according to the talio (907f.; cf. 1025f.). Both men believe in (and put into practice) respect for suppliants, reverence for the gods, moral consistency (suiting actions to words), punishing injustice and reciprocating favours. But in Theseus these values are tempered by reason. He remains consistently rational and restrained, appearing immune to the kind of emotional response that we see in other characters. His initial reaction to Oedipus is in marked contrast to the chorus' near-hysteria at the prospect of religious pollution.[77] He tells him to name his request, 'for you would have to say something *deinos* for me to back away' (560f.). Oedipus' deeds clearly were *deinos* in any normal sense − both 'terrible' and 'awesome' (cf. 141, 510). But as he insists in his extensive self-defence, they were not intentional (266–74, 521–48, 960–99).[78] This factor, crucial for the ascription of blame, means his deeds were not 'terrible' in Theseus' eyes.[79] By accepting Oedipus' supplication and friendship he implicitly accepts his self-justification, which he does not even need to hear. By welcoming him not only to Athens, but even under his own roof, he implicitly denies the danger of pollution.[80] He requires no persuasion in order to evaluate the situation

[76] Also used of Oedipus himself (8, 76). See Torrance 287f.

[77] On pollution and its complex relation to intention and law see Parker, especially ch. 4 on bloodshed and 318–21 on *OC*. See also Dodds 35–7; Adkins ch. 5; Vickers 138–55, 226–30; MacDowell, *AHL* 141–50, *LCA* 109–22.

[78] This defence has been much discussed, especially in relation to *OT*. See e.g. Whitman 202–4; Gellie 162f., 173; Adkins 105; Winnington-Ingram 261f.

[79] Contrast Odysseus in *Aj.* who uses human sympathy as an argument for burying Ajax despite a crime committed only in intention. Oedipus did the deeds, but without the intention, so Theseus ignores the deeds altogether. On intention and blame in Attic law see MacDowell, *AHL* 45–7 and ch. 6; cf. also Arist. *EN* 1109b30–11b3, 1135a28–30.

[80] Cf. Whitman 207; Adams 170. He is evidently right, for Oedipus' presence will not endanger but benefit Athens. There are hints that Oedipus has undergone ritual cleansing. He claims to be 'pure by law' (νόμῳ καθαρός 548) which can denote ritual purification as well as innocence (cf. Aesch. *Eum* 474; for the ambiguity see Parker 367). The same could be implied by his claim to 'holiness' at 287 (so the scholiast ad loc. and Adkins 136).

rationally.[81] He remains equally unmoved by fear of human reprisals, having nothing but scorn for the threats born of *thumos*,
which are soon dispelled by reason, and remaining calmly confident
that his own superior arms will prevail over Creon's rash attack
(658–63). But while he disapproves in general of *thumos*, and rebukes
Oedipus for indulging it (592), he is also willing to listen to Oedipus'
justification of his passionate feelings, and asks him to 'teach' him the
facts, 'for I must not speak without judgement' (594).

Theseus diverges furthest from Oedipus in his refusal to harm
enemies except as necessary for self-defence or the defence of friends.
He makes it clear that Creon deserves the full vengeance that anger
might prompt (904–6), but moderates his righteous indignation and
confines his exercise of justice to a speedy restoration of the status
quo. Creon will be punished with the same 'laws' that he brought
with him: he will be physically detained until the kidnapped women
are returned (907–10). The suggestion of exact reciprocity is spelled
out by the scholiast on 908: 'Just as he seized others from a foreign
(*xenos*) land, so he himself will be seized in a foreign land.' Theseus
thus adheres quite literally to the talio, but goes not a step further,
showing how strict reciprocity may act as a restraint rather than an
incitement to savage revenge. He employs the talio to rectify injustice, not to gratify personal enmity. In doing so he displays the virtue
of 'fairness' or 'equity', which deprecates an excessively rigid pursuit
of retribution, however just, and which is said to be characteristic of
Athens (1127).[82]

This rational control over the passions enables Theseus to function as the moral conscience of the other characters when they
become carried away by emotion. He reinforces and complements
Oedipus' passionate outburst against Creon with a thorough, calmly
reasoned condemnation, calling him (explicitly or by implication)
kakos (919), unjust (920, 1026f.), impious (921–3), disgraceful (929),

---

[81] Oedipus himself appears to acknowledge an ineradicable pollution (1130–6),
but rejects the notion that this might legitimise his exile (407f.). He retains an
emotional revulsion, but denies it any moral or religious significance (cf.
Dodds, *Misunderstanding* 43f.; Adams 172; Howe 134f.). On Theseus' reaction
see Parker 310f.

[82] On this virtue (ἐπιείκεια) see Dihle 46f.; Dover 191; and cf. Herod. 3.53.4;
Gorg. DK 82 B 6.15f.; Arist. *EN* 1137a31–38a3. In Soph. fr. 770 (Radt) it is
linked with *charis* and both are contrasted with 'absolute justice' (τὴν ἁπλῶς
δίκην). For its connection with Athens see Kirkwood, *Melos* 100–4.

senseless (931) and guilty of *hubris* (1029).[83] He concludes, 'Do you understand any of this, or do such words seem to you now as futile as when you were planning your scheme?' (1034). The question suggests that if Creon understands the force of Theseus' arguments he will be moved to shame or repentance. While such an intellectual manner of speaking is common in Greek,[84] it is specially appropriate to Theseus. He also steps in with the voice of principle when Oedipus' strong feelings tempt him to violate the rights of a suppliant. At the end of the play he plays a similar role, when Antigone is overwhelmed by grief and longs passionately to see the secret place of her father's death (1725–7). Ismene objects, but Antigone cannot understand why, and begs to be killed on her father's tomb (1729–33). (The exchange echoes – or prefigures – their relationship in *Antigone*.) But when Theseus corrects her with the voice of reason and piety (1758–67), she accepts his explanation of Oedipus' 'mind' and acquiesces (1768f.). In this play reason is not a morally neutral force (as it is, for example, in *Philoctetes*), but sides with both principle and the divine plan.

Theseus shares his rejection of personal vengeance with both Odysseus in *Ajax* and Neoptolemus in *Philoctetes*, neither of whom is willing to harm an enemy except in the course of helping friends. Odysseus and Neoptolemus provide a critical perspective on the destructive protagonists of their plays, as Antigone does for Oedipus. But Theseus does not condemn Oedipus' treatment of his son, and implicitly endorses his revenge by accepting its consequences. This need not be construed as approval of vengeance per se. Theseus' emotional response to provocation is less than the occasion warrants, and his reason dictates the justice of the talio in its strictest and most rational form. But he is also the ideal just ruler, and as such can provide Oedipus' revenge with the validation of an impartial justice. As both judge and executor, his judgements have a validity independent of the demands of private vengeance.

Theseus' authority receives wider sanction from his status as king of the great city of Athens and the surrounding land of

---

83 This rebuke is directed towards Creon's behaviour within the play, not his previous behaviour or his ultimate objective (as opposed to his present means; cf. 925). But the latter are implicitly condemned by Theseus' tacit acceptance of Oedipus' case.

84 See O'Brien chs. 1 and 2; Dover 116–29; Dihle, *Will* ch. 2.

Attica.[85] His prestige is closely tied to the idealised city and its ability to resist intruders like Creon (666f., 917f.; cf. 842, 879, 939f.). Oedipus appeals to the city's reputation for piety and benevolence towards unfortunate strangers, demanding that the chorus live up to it (258–62; cf. Thuc. 2.61.4; Pl. *Ap.* 29de). The chorus' ode in praise of Colonus and Attica is suffused with piety, and elicits from Antigone a similar exhortation to live up to their words (720f.). Even Creon has a good word for Athens (758f.; but cf. 1002f.), and exploits its reputation, saying he did not expect the city of the Areopagus to accept someone tainted with parricide and incest (944–9). Oedipus answered in the same terms: how could Creon expect to get away with kidnapping a suppliant from a city with such a pious reputation? (1005–9).

The Athenian stranger and the chorus, after their initial revulsion, display an openness to persuasion and deference to authority which show that the Athenian concern for reason and order is not confined to Theseus alone (47f., 77–80, 294f.)[86] But it is Theseus who really redeems the city's reputation. Oedipus emphasises that he is indebted to the king personally for rescuing his daughters (1121–3, 1129). He therefore calls down blessings on both Theseus and the land (1124f.), 'since I have found reverence amongst you alone of all people, and fairness and absence of duplicity' (1125–7). In the confrontation with Creon, Theseus is the mouthpiece of Athens: in contrast to Creon's lawless violence, this is 'a city that practises justice, and does nothing without *nomos*' (913f.).[87] As the voice of law between states he declares, 'If I entered your land, not even with the most just cause in the world would I seize or kidnap anyone without the permission of the ruler, whoever he was; I would know how a stranger should conduct himself amongst citizens' (924–8). He thus represents an impartial standard of rational human justice between both persons and cities. His tacit approval of Oedipus shows that by

---

[85] On the strong sense of locale in the play see Kirkwood, *Melos* 104–9. For the idealisation of Athens in tragedy cf. Eur. *Med.* 824–65 and see Heath 64f.

[86] These citizens might meet with approval in Plato's ideal state. They are pious but amenable to reason, courageous and proud of their city but aware of their humble status and inability to make important moral or political decisions.

[87] Note that Oedipus too uses *nomos* in his self-defence (142, 548). Contrast the appeal to *nomos* by unsympathetic characters elsewhere in Sophocles (e.g. *Aj.* 1073–6, *Ant.* 191).

this standard Oedipus is indeed just, even though the passionate and vengeful spirit which moves him is not that of a Theseus.

Oedipus, the gods and justice

The gods have caused Oedipus immeasurable undeserved suffering. 'So it was dear to them,' he says, 'perhaps from anger with my family long ago' (964f.). But like Philoctetes he believes that heaven is on his side and will see to it that justice is eventually done (1380–2, 1536f., 278–81). For Philoctetes this turned out to be true only in a limited sense. Oedipus, by contrast, is in a privileged position which places him in close contact with the gods and their plans. It is clear from the outset that he has received prophecies that are now in the process of fulfilment (cf. 45f., 84–95, 101–3, 452–4, 623). As the play develops, we see his increasing faith in the certainty of his predictions and the power of his blessings and curses.[88] Even before explicitly cursing, he claims to know the course of future events on the authority of Apollo (450–4, 616–23, 644–6, 787–93). His predictions manifest his confidence that his desires coincide with the will of the gods. Although he speaks of his sons' quarrel as 'fated' (421), he willingly accepts his role as instrument of that fate.

As has often been observed, this play presents us with the 'heroisation' of Oedipus.[89] It is as an incipient cult-hero that his desires not only coincide with the divine plan, but have the power to implement it. As such a hero he will have a uniquely effective ability to help his friends and harm his enemies. In contrast to Philoctetes' vain wish (*Phil.* 1035f.), or Ajax's unanswered prayer (*Aj.* 835–42), Oedipus' curses have validity, and his predictions can be made with assurance. But this special power does not place him 'beyond the boundaries of ordinary moral judgment' (Burian, *Suppliant* 427).[90] His emotions and actions are entirely explicable in human terms and are not exempt from human judgement. What distinguishes him

---

[88] Cf. Kitto, *GT*[3] 387–93.

[89] See e.g. Bowra 307–22; Knox 147–62. On hero–cult generally see Rohde 115–55; Farnell; Méautis, *L'Œdipe* 9–24; Burkert 203–8. On the cult of Oedipus see Farnell 332–4; Méautis, *L'Œdipe* 42–56; Edmunds, *Oedipus*; Henrichs.

[90] Similarly Rosenmeyer, *Wrath* 104; Bowra 330; Torrance 293; and cf. Reinhardt 219. Oedipus' humanity is stressed by Linforth, *OC* 120–8; Hester, *Friends* 30; Easterling, *Oedipus* 1f. On the heroic vs. the human in Oedipus, see the sensible remarks of Burian, *Suppliant* 425 n. 39.

from other mortals is his heroic power. That power is not something divorced from human standards. Not only were cult-heroes human beings,[91] albeit in a special class, but their power was simply an extension of the natural human desire, elevated by the Greeks into a moral code, to help one's friends and harm one's enemies.[92]

Oedipus assumes that his misfortunes were somehow caused by the gods (964f., 998). Yet the justice he demands and foresees is not divine compensation, but the power of vengeance on the human beings who failed to support him in the midst of his divinely inflicted sufferings. Only the chorus suggest that his strange death is a just compensation from the gods. They pray that he may have a painless death, for his sufferings were futile, but now 'a just god may be raising him up' (1560–7).[93] This recalls their earlier meditation on the action of time, which 'sees everything always, casting some things down, but raising others up from day to day' (1453–5).[94] The theme is a familiar one, especially in Sophocles.[95] Oedipus himself develops it when he explains to Theseus that everything human changes with time (607–15). This process may be perceived as a divine justice that rewards the good and lays low the wicked in the end, as the chorus here suggest. But it appears more often as an impersonal universal cycle, dispensing alternately good and bad fortune to mortals with little regard for merit.[96] Oedipus' end scarcely seems

---

[91] See Burkert 205. The deified Heracles is the prime exception, who proves the rule (Burkert 208; Méautis, *L'Œdipe* 17).

[92] For the dual power of the hero see Rohde 132–7; Burkert 206–8; Merkelbach; Bowra 320f.; Burian, *Suppliant* 411 n. 9 (who aptly cites Eur. *Heracl.* 1043f.); Henrichs, *Sobriety* 94 n. 30.

[93] This shows that their fear of divine punishment for harbouring a polluted man, which continues until his departure (1483–5), is self-interested and independent of any moral judgement.

[94] The text here is corrupt (see the editors ad loc.) but this must be the general sense.

[95] Cf. *Ant.* 162f., 1158f.; *Aj.* 646–83, 1087f.; *Trach.* 112–35; fr. 871 (Radt); Eur. *HF* 215f. For some non-tragic parallels see Bowra 335.

[96] This is the amoral *dike* that Kitto sees as the ruler of the Sophoclean universe (see especially *SDP* 47–54). Linforth, *OC* 187–91 understands 1565–7 essentially as I do, but even he can say that 'the alternation of fortune is demanded by justice' (*OC* 190). This shows the danger, warned against by Kitto, of translating this *dike* as 'justice'. Thus Bowra 349f. equates the 'rhythmical law of change' with a benevolent divine justice, and Jebb asserts that the gods' honour to Oedipus comes 'only as the final justice (1567) prescribed by a divine sense of measure' (*Introduction* §5).

an adequate compensation for what he has suffered, nor does he himself so interpret it. Ismene remarks that the gods who destroyed him are now raising him up (394). But he remains unimpressed, answering, 'It is a poor thing to raise up in old age one who falls in youth' (395). His only 'compensation' is a painless death.

It is true that it is a miraculous death, and that he will have the powers of a cult-hero beyond the grave. But the emphasis of the play is on death as the end. The chorus see death as a 'deliverer', who puts an end to the increasing pain and absence of delight experienced by the very old (1215–23). For as Creon says in a different context, no pain touches the dead (955).[97] Oedipus looks forward to his own death not as a glorious future, but as a terminus and respite from his sufferings (cf. 88–91, 101–3, 583–5, 1473, 1551).[98] Others pray that it may be painless, and then rejoice that it took place according to his wishes (1560–4, 1585, 1604f., 1663f., 1704–6). This is no reward for suffering or compensation from a just divinity. His death is 'amazing' (1665; cf. 1586) and fulfils his desires, but it is not the gateway to a blissful hereafter. The chorus declare that he has 'blessedly closed the end of life' (1720f.).[99] The 'blessing' for Oedipus is that he has died, and died without pain. In Theseus' words, he is one of those for whom death is a *charis* (1751–3).[100] This is directed as a gentle rebuke to Antigone, who, despite her father's miraculous end, still laments that he is 'clothed forever in underground darkness' (1701; cf. 1706f.).

Nevertheless, while Oedipus' fate may be no Christian heaven, the gods who cast him down have in some sense raised him up, by enabling him to help his friends and harm his enemies even from the grave.[101] Although the emphasis of the play is on death as the end of

---

[97] He may be wrong, however, to suggest that *thumos* ends with death (954f.). It is precisely the wrath of the dead Oedipus that he is trying to forestall.

[98] Note also the emphasis on dying in his final scene (1509, 1521, 1555) and cf. 1220, 1583f., 1612f., 1705f. On 103 see Long 88f.; on 91 Campbell ad loc.; on 1220 Burton 285. See also Linforth, *OC* 99f.; Hester, *Friends* 23; Gellie 181.

[99] On this phrase see Jebb and Kamerbeek ad loc. (the translation is from Jebb's note).

[100] In 1752 Martin's νύξ (printed by Pearson) is not an improvement on the received text. Most editors print Reisig's elegant ξύν' ἀπόκειται, which underlines the reciprocity of the *charis* between Theseus and Oedipus (cf. Kirkwood 244 n. 24).

[101] The need to avoid religious anachronism has been emphasised especially by Jebb, *Introduction* §4; Linforth, *OC* 102–4, 114–19; Hester, *Friends*;

Oedipus' troubles, the audience would think of him, like other cult-heroes, as somehow present in his tomb, and highly sensitive to the behaviour of friends and enemies, just as the dead Agamemnon in *Electra*, for example, is responsive to the prayers and offerings of both friends (453–60, 1066–9) and foes (442–6; cf. also *Trach.* 1201f., *Aj.* 1393–5). In Oedipus' final speech he emphasises the permanence of his legacy to Athens, ending with the propitious words 'in your prosperity remember me, a dead man, when you are fortunate always' (1554f.; cf. 1525, 1765).[102] In contrast to his own last years, the benefits he bequeaths will remain 'untroubled by the pain of old age' (1519). For the gods have given him a demonic power that in some ways resembles their own. His wrath, like theirs, is harsh, unforgiving and effective.[103]

Oedipus calls to witness his curse the divinities of strife, revenge and hatred, including Ares, who he says cast the terrible hatred into his sons, and 'the hateful paternal darkness of Tartarus' (1389–92). Why the epithet 'paternal'? Perhaps because of Oedipus' affinity, as the father of his sons, to the chthonian deities of whom he will soon be one. He also calls to witness the goddesses of the grove, to whom he is now consecrated. He avoids addressing them by name, calling them simply 'these divinities' (1391), as he does when cursing Creon (864; cf. 1010).[104] Their cult-name at Colonus was apparently Eumenides ('kindly ones') (cf. 42, 486), and an identification is suggested with the Semnai Theai ('august goddesses') worshipped in Athens (cf. 41, 89f., 458). Moreover since their primary role in the play is as Oedipus' saviours, their beneficial aspect is emphasised.[105] These factors may explain Oedipus' elliptical form

Winnington-Ingram 255. But Linforth's view that the hero was completely extinct and cut off from the world of the living is exaggerated. For popular views on the afterlife, which are often vague or inconsistent, see Vermeule; Garland ch. 5.

[102] Contra Pearson I retain the imperative in 1555 (see Jebb and Kamerbeek ad loc.). On the theme of permanence cf. Kirkwood, *Melos* 116.

[103] It is called μῆνις (1328), a word commonly used for the wrath of gods and cult-heroes (cf. 965, 1274; *Aj.* 656, 757; LSJ s.v. μῆνις; see further King 248 n. 109). It is described as 'heavy' (1328; cf. 402) like the wrath of Athena at *Aj.* 656 and the hostility of the Furies at Aesch. *Eum.* 711, 720. For Oedipus' anger cf. also 411, 855, and Rosenmeyer, *Wrath* 110.

[104] These and related goddesses enjoy a multiplicity of names which is a matter of some confusion. Cf. 42f. with the scholiast ad loc., and see most recently Brown, *Eumenides* 260–5.

[105] Cf. Kirkwood, *Melos* 108f.; Brown, *Eumenides* 278.

of address when invoking them in their destructive aspect, in which they resemble the Erinyes ('Furies').[106] But this darker side is not forgotten.[107] They are introduced by the Athenian stranger as 'the fearful goddesses, daughters of earth and darkness', whose precinct is not to be touched or inhabited (39f.). He adds that in other places they are known by other names (42f.) – a discreet allusion to the name Erinyes?[108] The chorus likewise emphasise their destructive potential, mentioning local apotropaic behaviour in the vicinity of the shrine (125–33). They fear that Oedipus' transgression will bring down curses on them all (153f.),[109] and dread dire consequences for him if he omits the proper rites (490–2).

Oedipus himself, however, recognises at once that this fearful place is where he is to find sanctuary (44f.).[110] To him the goddesses are paradoxically 'sweet' (106). For Oedipus, the pariah, has a good deal in common with these divinities.[111] The chorus' reaction to him as 'awesome to see, awesome to hear', echoes their response to the goddesses, who are passed by without looking or speaking, and are 'of awesome visage' (84, 128–33, 141).[112] Despite his blindness, he will speak 'seeing everything', the same phrase just used by the stranger for the Eumenides (42, 74).[113] He comes 'sober to the wine-less ones' (100),[114] and envisages his corpse drinking his enemies' blood like the Aeschylean Furies (621f.; cf. Aesch. *Cho.* 577f.). He also shares their double nature, their ability to bless and curse. Their benign aspect is represented not only by their salvation of Oedipus, and the benevolent welcome accorded to him by Theseus, but also by the blessing he himself bequeaths to Athens. Theseus calls this his

[106] I do not find Brown's attempt to dissociate them from the curses persuasive (*Eumenides* 278f.).

[107] On their ambivalence see Winnington-Ingram 265–8; Brown, *Eumenides* 277f. Cf. the ambivalence of the Erinyes at the end of Aesch. *Eum.*

[108] So Winnington-Ingram 267. Cf. also Brown, *Eumenides* 277.

[109] 'Curses' (*'Aραί*) is another name for the Erinyes (Aesch. *Eum.* 417; cf. Soph. *El.* 111).

[110] The claim that he is not 'lawless' (142) suggests a special right to enter the shrine of the Eumenides. But he also bridges the gap with conventional piety by having Ismene perform the proper apotropaic rites.

[111] For the resemblance between them cf. Winnington-Ingram 267f., 275; Segal 375; Kirkwood, *Melos* 110–15. For their association in cult see Edmunds, *Oedipus* 225–9.

[112] One also passed by a hero's shrine in silence (Burkert 208).

[113] Cf. Seale 116f.

[114] On this phrase and its implications see Henrichs.

eumeneia, 'good will' (631), the very word from which the
Eumenides get their name, as the dramatist carefully reminds us
(486).[115] With this blessing is bound up the destruction of his
enemies through his curse. This curse, which Polyneices calls
Oedipus' 'Erinys' (1299, 1434),[116] represents the goddesses' dark
side, their role as avenging Erinyes, which complements their benevolent aspect as Eumenides. Their destructive potential, emphasised
at the beginning of the play, is realised in the course of it through the
person of Oedipus, their suppliant, who will soon join them as a
chthonian power, sharing their dual power for vengeance and blessing.

If Oedipus is heroised as the incarnation of Help Friends/Harm
Enemies, does this mean the code is being held up for our approval?
Virtue is by no means a necessary qualification for cult status,[117] but
Oedipus abides by conventional moral norms, is condemned by no
one in the play, and maintains his moral consistency. His enemies are
shown to deserve punishment and his friends assistance. Moreover
this play comes closer than any we have looked at to presenting Help
Friends/Harm Enemies in its best possible light as a coherent code. A
single action instantiates both principles, making them properly
complementary, and Oedipus' justice is not merely the product of
human indignation, but sanctioned by Theseus and evidently by the
gods themselves.

Nevertheless, the play does not provide a straightforward vindication of Help Friends/Harm Enemies. Creon, an indisputable villain, reveals the incoherence that threatens the code when it is

---

[115] Knox (154 and n. 19) notes that this word is especially used of gods, and compares *Ant.* 1200. Similarly Long 50, comparing *h. Hom.* 22.7.

[116] Line 1299 has caused some difficulty, since Oedipus has not yet formally cursed
his sons, or uttered any curses in Polyneices' presence. The problem is compounded by Oedipus' own mention of an earlier curse (1375). These passages
have been taken by some to show that Oedipus cursed his sons before leaving
Thebes. Others have argued that the curse is postponed to achieve the maximum dramatic effect, and to strengthen the justice of Oedipus' case (so Jebb,
Introduction §6, who suggests that 1375 refers to 421–7 and 1299 to the family
curse). But the fact that we witness the decisive curse does not rule out previous
imprecations, alluded to at 1375 (cf. Kitto, *GT*[3] 391 n. 1; Brown, *Eumenides*
281). At the same time, 'Erinys' in 1299 could simply refer to Oedipus' presumed wrath against his sons, confirmed for Polyneices by the seers he con-
sulted (1300).

[117] See Burkert 207.

applied out of self-interest or passion without the constraint of an
impartial standard of justice. Polyneices' final scene sketches the
potential conflict between Help Friends and Harm Enemies and the
destructive futility of sacrificing friendship to enmity. Antigone
pleads for a modification of the code in favour of family *philia*, and
Theseus deprecates its implementation through mere wrath. And
even this, the most coherent application of the code that we have
encountered, is carried through only at enormous cost. Its success
depends on an irreconcilable breach of natural family *philia*. Despite
the justice of Oedipus' revenge, this heavy price is emphasised not
only by the pathetic figure of Polyneices, but by Antigone's moving
plea on his behalf and the predicament in which she is left as a result
of loyalty to her brother.

Both Oedipus' revenge and his benefaction to Athens are carefully represented as just. But they are not justified simply by the
talio, which is also the justice of Creon and Polyneices. The justice of
Oedipus' revenge is not merely assured by his own sense of injury
but guaranteed by Theseus, the rational, restrained representative of
impartial human justice. In this instance justice is done, but retaliation per se, and the emotions that provoke it, are not condoned.
Creon shows the evil consequences of unrestrained self-interested
passion, while Theseus provides a touchstone of rational justice,
approving strict retaliation but eschewing revenge. Oedipus is
linked with both: his implementation of justice is prompted by passion, but requires – and receives – the independent confirmation of
Theseus.

8

Conclusion

The soil of the reactive emotions is the very last to be conquered by the spirit of justice. Should it actually come to pass
that the just man remains just even toward his despoiler ... and
that even under the stress of hurt, contumely, denigration the
noble, penetrating yet mild objectivity of the just (the *judging*)
eye does not become clouded, then we have before us an instance of the rarest accomplishment, something that, if we are
wise, we will neither expect nor be too easily convinced of.

Nietzsche, *The Genealogy of Morals*

I have tried to bring out the richness and complexity of the ethical
fabric of Sophocles' plays. Moral issues are not merely motifs, but
inform the dramatic structure, and are developed with care and
subtlety on the linguistic level. A multiplicity of ethical standpoints
is presented in such a way that their implications and practical results
are dramatised through choice and argument. Although our sympathies are used to guide us towards approval of some characters and
condemnation of others, there is no simple correlation between sympathy and approval. While it may be true that an obviously unpleasant character tends to express sentiments contrary to
conventional Athenian values, these plays are not melodramas in
which only the virtuous command our sympathy and the villains
our distaste.[1] The tragic force of a character such as Polyneices in
Oedipus at Colonus is generated precisely by our complex response of
pity and disapproval. Conversely, the arguments of Odysseus at the
beginning of *Philoctetes* deserve our attention, even though he repels
us more and more as the play proceeds and the structure of the play
decisively rejects his values by excluding him from the final scenes.[2]
OC contains two of Sophocles' most clear-cut characters, Theseus
and Creon. Yet the interest of the play centres on neither, but on
Oedipus himself, a far more complex character both ethically and

---

[1] Cf. Dover 16f.

[2] It is worth remembering that not everyone finds him equally repulsive. He is
defended by Ronnet 258–61; Gellie 132; Lesky, *GTP* 175; Strohm 112–15.

emotionally. The chief significance of these black and white characters lies in their relationship to him.

Even when a play contains such clear-cut figures, the work as a whole dramatises the interplay of a whole range of emotions, attitudes, principles and actions, which may prompt tensions between our various sympathies and moral judgements. We approve of Theseus, but few have dared positively to disapprove of Oedipus, despite his harshness and the uneasiness it generates,[3] and fewer still could disapprove of Antigone.[4] Odysseus may be the villain of *Philoctetes*, but he is condemned only after his views have received an airing, been seen in action and found wanting. Philoctetes himself has our complete sympathy, yet we regret his final intransigence and also sympathise with Neoptolemus, whose values, though overlapping with those of Philoctetes, remain distinct. Similarly we respond to Ajax with horrified admiration while sympathising deeply with the sufferings of his dependants and applauding the sentiments and behaviour of Odysseus. In *Antigone* we sympathise with all the principal characters, if not simultaneously at least in turn, despite the passionate differences that divide them. Our increasing moral disapproval of Creon is not dissolved by the intense pity engendered at his fall. On the contrary, this disapproval remains an essential ingredient in the particular emotional response that he evokes. Likewise our sympathy with Electra's predicament and our distaste for Clytemnestra are essential to the sense of uneasiness aroused by the similarity in their characters and modes of argument.

There is thus no simple way to extract a moral 'message' from these plays. But as I have tried to show, Sophocles handles the ethical issues that centre round the talio and Help Friends/Harm Enemies in such a way as to provoke critical questioning of conventional moral assumptions. Yet although this treatment suggests that the code is seriously flawed as a guide to action, it also points towards some solutions.

One of the most obvious difficulties with an ethic based on *philia* is the problem of reconciling the claims of different *philoi*. Conflict of loyalties arises most readily between the three main classes of *philoi* – familial, civic and personal – whose *philia* is deter-

---

[3] Exceptions are Ronnet 304–6; Rosenmeyer, *Wrath* 97f. (who even defends Creon, 101).

[4] Bowra 331 does his best.

mined by different criteria, and who therefore embody competing types of claim. Such conflicts are a feature of Greek life which often appears in intensified form in tragedy. The rival claims of family and state are central to *Antigone*. The same theme is touched on in *Electra*, where Clytemnestra's unwillingness to consider any obligation outside the immediate family contributes to the weakness of her case. Competing loyalties of a different kind are integral to *OC*. Oedipus must choose between the presumptive *philia* of his family and Thebes, and the emerging friendship with Theseus and Athens based on reciprocal *charis*. He spurns first the hypocritical overtures of Creon, and then the more emotive claim of his son, preferring the new *philoi* who have shown some active concern for his wishes and interests. Polyneices likewise, in attacking his own brother, relies on the assumption that any *philos* can lose the rights of *philia*, but this produces a fatal weakness in his appeal to Oedipus. The third side of the triangle is illustrated in *Philoctetes*. This time the dilemma is that of Neoptolemus, who must choose between his obligations to the state (represented by Odysseus and the army) and his developing personal friendship with Philoctetes. *Antigone* offers us a passionate adherent of each kind of *philia*. Antigone focusses on the family and Creon on the *polis*, while Haemon, though he has an allegiance to both, sacrifices his life to the ties of personal love. Each pursues one kind of *philia* to the eventual exclusion of the others. This leads in each case to alienation or outright enmity with other presumptive *philoi*, showing the futility of trying to circumvent conflict by 'simplifying commitments'.[5]

Conflict of loyalties may also arise within one class of *philoi*, especially the family, owing to the strong presumptive tie of kinship-*philia*. This theme is fundamental to *Electra*, where Agamemnon's decision to sacrifice private to public obligations has caused Clytemnestra in turn to disrupt the kinship bond, thus splitting the entire family into two warring factions. Almost any kind of *philia* may be terminated on grounds of hostile behaviour, but Electra undermines her position by her refusal to allow her mother this argument while relying on it herself. A similar inconsistency undermines the claims of both Creon and Polyneices in *OC*. Only Oedipus manages to avoid it, by the ruthless consistency with which he rejects all who have willfully offended against kinship.

[5] The expression is Nussbaum's (51).

Conflicting loyalties may force one to pursue the interests of one friend rather than another. Worse still, they may oblige one to help one friend at another friend's expense. Help Friends forbids one to deceive friends, to thwart their desires by either treachery or violence, leaving persuasion as the only legitimate means of influence. But such strictures interfere with Creon's, Neoptolemus' or Odysseus' ability to help a much larger group of friends. Can they therefore disregard their specific obligations towards an individual friend? The answer, as it appears in Sophocles, is clearly no. The plays unequivocally discredit those who try to violate such norms. One might expect the interests of a majority of friends to outweigh the desires of one, especially when, as in both *Philoctetes* and *OC*, the single friend will arguably benefit from having his wishes disregarded in this way. This kind of utilitarian argument is available to both Odysseus in *Philoctetes* and Creon in *OC*, but is adopted by neither. It is touched on by the Atreidae in *Ajax* and Creon in *Antigone*, who claim that the pleasure of the individual must be subordinated to the interests of the larger social group, but in both cases it is discredited by the outcome. Yet without some such criterion, Help Friends/Harm Enemies is incapable of dealing with conflicts between its own injunctions.

There is also a permanent risk of internal inconsistency between Help Friends and Harm Enemies. Ideally the two principles are complementary. When my friend's interests are contrary to my enemy's, I can help the one by harming the other and the code will operate smoothly, as it does most clearly in warfare. *OC* provides us with a much more complex case of this kind. But the situation is not always so clear-cut. It is always possible that in helping a friend I may also be benefiting an enemy, or that Harm Enemies may involve harming a friend. This risk is exacerbated by the transitive character of friendship and enmity. If in acquiring new friends I also acquire all their friends and enemies, then the more friends and enemies I already have, the greater the chance that some of these new friendships and enmities will clash with some of the old. When this happens, or if for any other reason the interests of my friends and enemies coincide, then Help Friends and Harm Enemies turn from harmonious complementary principles into competitors. This is the final dilemma of Philoctetes. His new friend Neoptolemus is allied with the Greek army in a cooperative endeavour. Philoctetes' plan to thwart their venture will therefore injure his friend Neoptolemus as much as his enemies. Conversely, if he agrees to help Neoptolemus he will be obliged to sacrifice his own passionate desire for revenge. Philoctetes chooses to let Harm Enemies outweigh Help Friends – a course that, if generally followed, would undermine trust and endanger all constructive human relationships. The futility of this attitude is indicated by the arrival of Heracles, who uses his friendship with Philoctetes to reverse the destructive decision. Similarly Ajax single-mindedly pursues revenge and then suicide without regard for the wishes of his dependants. Friendship can only prevail once the intransigent hero has been removed.

A simple principle of priority can resolve this particular kind of conflict. Philoctetes' dilemma seems insoluble, but a constructive alternative is proposed by Neoptolemus, who rejects the idea that revenge should interfere with their mutual benefit. He urges Philoctetes to forego his vengeance and come to Troy, and even prevents him from killing Odysseus, evidently on the grounds that such revenge for its own sake will achieve nothing and only hinder their common goal of victory. He risks enmity with his former friends, but does not welcome it, treating it rather as a necessary evil. Harm Enemies is confined to the Trojans, against whom it will bring not merely the satisfaction of revenge, but the positive benefits of glory, plunder and a return home. Neoptolemus thus subordinates Harm Enemies to Help Friends in pursuit of a cooperative enterprise. But this ordering of principles is useful only for the relatively limited and straightforward cases where the conflict arises from an ability to pursue Help Friends and Harm Enemies simultaneously. Some other criterion is needed for settling conflicts within either Help Friends or Harm Enemies.

The potential for inconsistency is present in any moral code, since (as Aristotle knew) no set of principles can provide for all the complex eventualities of practical human existence.[6] Not even 'love thy neighbour' is as it stands a foolproof guide for action, at least if we interpret it as an ancient Greek would have done, in terms of practical help rather than mere sentiment. Which neighbours should get the benefit of my limited resources? In helping one, am I not depriving another? But the internal difficulties of Help Friends/

---

[6] On Aristotle see Nussbaum ch. 10.

Harm Enemies, and the moral deadlock that tends to result, are symptoms of a more fundamental problem. This is the relativity of a code that tends to evaluate others by their relationship to oneself rather than some external assessment of their actions or character. The assumption that people often behave like this is undeniably realistic. The great strength of Help Friends/Harm Enemies is that it is grounded in the realities of human psychology and human life. There is also a good deal to be said for a code that acknowledges the many competing values of which our moral lives are composed. But when faced with such dilemmas we need not only to acknowledge their complexity, but to make choices and decisions, and here Help Friends/Harm Enemies is not always so useful. As Dover says of conflicts between personal friends and patriotism, 'whichever way an individual resolved the conflict for himself, he was likely to be blamed in one quarter and praised in another' (Dover 304).

In Nagel's terminology, Help Friends/Harm Enemies may be seen as 'agent-relative' rather than 'agent-neutral'.[7] 'The judgment ... that something has agent-neutral or impersonal value ... means anyone has reason to want it to happen ... [whereas] an objective judgment that some kind of thing has agent-relative value commits us only to believing that someone has reason to want and pursue it if it is related to him in the right way' (Nagel 153f.). An agent-relative code provides motives only for interested parties – it tells *me* how to treat *my* friends and enemies – and thus tends to exacerbate the natural human tendency to judge and act from a narrowly personal perspective. Any moral code faces the challenge of convincing us that we should at least sometimes step outside this perspective and adopt criteria for moral judgement that are independent of personal interest.[8] The difficulty of doing so is brought out clearly by the figure of Creon in *Antigone*. Even he, the overtly rational proponent of an agent-neutral value (the good of the *polis*),[9] is derailed by the passionately personal character of his underlying motives. But Help Friends/Harm Enemies positively encourages the formation of moral judgements on such personal grounds. In so far as these prin-

[7] See Nagel 152–4, 164–6; Parfit 142f.
[8] This follows from the nature of morality as I have been using the term (above, p. 3, n. 8).
[9] This is agent-neutral relative to the members of the *polis*, since it is something they all have an obligation to promote.

ciples are rooted in emotion, they provide little incentive to curtail the impulses of passion in the interests of the desires or needs of others. Principles that tend to validate personal emotions in this way make the need for an impartial standard of judgement all the more acute. Different personal perspectives are bound to clash, and when the beliefs to which they give rise are held with equally passionate conviction, the result is insoluble conflict.

This problem is compounded by the tendency to present one's own ethical judgements, including those based on Help Friends/ Harm Enemies, as if they were themselves impartial in this way. There is a general tendency to lay claim to various apparently neutral moral terms in support of one's pursuit of Help Friends/Harm Enemies. These claims may be reinforced in various ways. Assertions of divine approval may be used to suggest the sanction of a higher authority independent of merely human convictions (a good example is Antigone's appeal to the eternal and unchanging laws of the gods).[10] The personification of justice and other moral norms similarly suggests an impartial arbiter who guarantees the validity and independence of one's value judgements (Clytemnestra in *Electra* uses this device).[11]

The value of agent-relative principles may indeed be impartial or agent-neutral, in the sense that we may all have reason to approve or promote them. A disinterested person might agree, for example, that it is a good thing in general (not just for the agent) that someone should bury a brother, avenge a father, or harm an enemy. I myself may have no reason to bury Polyneices, but I may still have reason to approve of Antigone's doing so. I may thus make an agent-neutral judgement that everyone should act for such agent-relative reasons. In such a case the agent may legitimately expect outsiders to approve of his or her behaviour, and others in the same position to act the same way. Hence the expectation of glory expressed by both Antigone and Electra. Hence too their indignation when their sisters, who share the same kinship obligations, refuse to participate in their activities.

But the neutral presentation of Help Friends/Harm Enemies also creates difficulties. For one thing, it enables one to claim independent justification for all kinds of personal responses, however

[10] Cf. Nussbaum 401f.
[11] Cf. above, p. 162, n. 50.

dubious or partial their motivation. It allows even Creon in *OC* to claim the sanction of 'justice' for behaviour that is prompted (as he admits) by the immediate impulse of personal pain, and that any independent observer would be likely to judge most reprehensible. It thus conflates the legitimate pursuit of a neutrally desirable end with the indulgence of personal passion. It may also lead to serious inconsistency. If harming enemies, for example, is a neutral value, then one should approve when others act on it. Needless to say, this breaks down in cases of conflict. Characters tend to claim both neutral support for their own pursuit of agent-relative goals (by expecting the approval of others), and a correspondingly neutral condemnation of their antagonists (by expecting others to share their disapproval). When the personal motives of two people clash, each denies the neutrality of the other's principles. So Electra and Clytemnestra both claim that their own pursuit of vengeance is 'just', while each denying the validity of the other's application of the same 'justice'. Electra explicitly challenges the neutrality of her mother's defence by suggesting that the underlying motive was not justice, but passion. But if both rely on the same principle, while each denying it to the other, then both claims to neutrality are undermined. Each remains locked into her own partial perspective, stepping outside it only to claim neutral validity for it. This naturally contributes to the passionate and blindly self-righteous invective that typifies so many of the moral encounters of tragedy. The personal impulses of love and hatred are in themselves quite sufficient to generate conflict. But when they are used as a foundation for allegedly neutral values, such conflicts become even less amenable to solution.

The inconsistency of claiming neutrality for one's own applications of Help Friends/Harm Enemies while denying it to one's opponent can be avoided by basing the claim to neutrality on grounds external to the code. One candidate for this role is the talio itself. In its most general form, the impressive dictum 'the doer must suffer' may seem not only agent-neutral but fully independent of Help Friends/Harm Enemies. But it loses this independence as soon as it is used to justify personal revenge. The apparently neutral *dike* that Clytemnestra claims as her ally turns out to sanction an application of the talio based ultimately on the criteria of Help Friends/Harm Enemies. It is only because one of her *philoi* has been harmed that she claims the justice of the talio in killing Agamemnon. Such personal applications of the talio reduce it to a rationale for endless vendetta.[12] For as we saw in *Electra* and *OC*, if both parties to a dispute regard themselves as right and the other as an unjust aggressor, the process of retaliation, of 'repaying' wrong for wrong, will never be complete. Each act of retaliation will seem not justice but injury to its recipient, who will then feel entitled to retaliate with his or her own act of 'justice', which to the enemy is naturally a further injury requiring revenge, and so on. Under such conditions the talio suffers from an intrinsic lack of any built-in criterion for resolving disputes. One source of *Electra*'s cheerless atmosphere is the absence of any such impersonal procedure in a world where the talio remains unquestioned.[13] The characters remain entangled in their own perspectives, trapping themselves in self-contradictions and delusions of impartiality which exclude the possibility of an unequivocally just outcome.

Personal applications of Help Friends/Harm Enemies may be justified more indirectly, by labelling one's enemies as wicked and one's friends as virtuous, as we saw most clearly in *Philoctetes*. Philoctetes' judgements are agent-neutral, for he expects others (including the gods) to share his view of his enemies, and anyone in his position (as he falsely thinks Neoptolemus is) to react the same way. As often turns out to be the case, however, his terms of reproach are themselves based on agent-relative criteria. It is just because the Atreidae and Odysseus were faithless friends that they have earned these apparently independent epithets. That everyone should disapprove of faithless friends is indeed a possible neutral principle. But Philoctetes warmly praises Neoptolemus for his services, despite the fact that they require the young man's desertion from the Greek army.

Philoctetes presents his judgements not only as agent-neutral,

---

[12] Cf. MacIntyre 6–9, 16f. on the interminable character combined with the appearance of objectivity in modern ethical debates. He sees the root of the modern problem as the use of conceptually incommensurable moral claims involving different value terms (8). The distinctive feature of Greek moral disagreement, however, is the ascription of widely varying content to the *same* set of moral terms (a feature by no means absent from modern debate). But the justice of the talio is a special case. Even when both disputants agree on the meaning of the term, it is still liable to generate interminable arguments precisely because of its meaning.

[13] Contrast both Aeschylus' *Oresteia* and Euripides' *Orestes*.

but as independent of Help Friends/Harm Enemies, for he believes (or at least prays) that the external authority of the gods will punish his enemies on his behalf. We might theoretically expect someone with a real faith in divine justice to wait for the gods to act. (The Greek leaders did eventually suffer for their various misdeeds.) But the vengeance of Harm Enemies is essentially personal. Philoctetes may hope for the gods to strike down his enemies, but given the opportunity he sees no reason not to do so himself. Like Ajax, he draws no distinction between revenge and punishment. By making the victim into both judge and executioner, Harm Enemies leaves personal and independent criteria for moral judgement inextricably entwined.

Help Friends/Harm Enemies and the talio thus cry out for some truly independent criterion, to govern relations between people regardless of their private feuds and friendships. One obvious kind of solution is to entrust the decision to some impartial figure of authority, such as a ruler. But *Antigone* points to the dangers of a supposedly neutral justice imposed from above. Creon's illusory rationality leads to self-deception and a stubborn adherence to a narrow and one-sided view of justice. His justice is not purely personal, for he aims (or thinks he aims) at the welfare of the city as a whole. But he clings passionately to a limited perspective from which the best of intentions cannot save him. What could have saved him, the drama suggests, was attention to one of the many warning voices of friends, offering insight into alternative points of view in an attempt at reasoned persuasion. The failure of these influences leaves us with a deep pessimism about the possibility of rational human evaluation of competing moral claims, and hence of a stably ordered civilisation.

Legal arbitration is another theoretically impersonal means of solving disputes. But as we see in *Ajax*, this too may be undermined by the corruptibility or fallibility of the arbitrators, and the suspicions and intolerance of the disputants. It is left unclear whether the judgement against Ajax over the arms of Achilles was an honest one. But that is less important than the attitude shown by the characters towards such a judgement. It is seen, as in fifth-century Athens, as just another weapon in the constant struggle against enemies – a weapon especially suited, as it happens, to the pliant and persuasive Odysseus. Ajax himself is presented as an honest participant in democratic procedures, symbolised by the casting of lots for the duel with Hector. But the same passage suggests ways in which others less honourable than he can manipulate these supposedly impartial procedures to their own advantage. When by such a judgement Ajax loses the arms of Achilles, he turns at once to self-help of the most violent kind.[14] And when the Atreidae appear we see the grounds for his suspicions, together with the pressing need for a judge who is both impartial and honest and seen to be so. Despite their appeals to authority and the good of the army as a whole, the petty vindictiveness of the Atreidae is as personal as Ajax' grand self-righteousness. Odysseus, however, holds out hope. Despite his role as winner of the arms, he eschews enmity and sagely dispenses honour where it is due. An Ajax will never accept a verdict against him, no matter how honest, democratic and fair, but an Odysseus may convince more ordinary people – the Tecmessas and Teucers of the world – that a justice independent of personal interests is not always beyond our reach.

Odysseus or any other judge, however trustworthy, needs criteria for reaching such decisions. What is ultimately required is not simply a neutral standard that sanctions the pursuit of agent-relative goals, but one that defines the approved goal itself in agent-neutral terms: not that Antigone should bury her brother, or even that all should be buried by their next of kin, but that no one should be denied burial. This principle is incompatible with the attempts of Creon in *Antigone* and the Atreidae in *Ajax* to pursue enmity beyond the grave. When the code clashes with an independent principle of this kind, it must yield, as Creon learns to his cost. The Atreidae are saved from the same error only by the friendly persuasion of Odysseus.

Another such principle is the proper treatment of the helpless or innocent, the stranger or suppliant, who is initially neutral with respect to *philia* and enmity but is protected by religious sanction. Oedipus supplicates at the shrine of the Eumenides, and Creon may not violate this supplication to help his friends at Thebes. Theseus makes it clear that even in Oedipus' own case Help Friends/Harm Enemies must harmonise with the principles of piety and respect for suppliants, exerting a friend's influence to ensure that Oedipus does

---

[14] As do Orestes and Electra when the decision goes against them in Euripides' *Orestes*.

not violate them. He is supported by Antigone, who plays a mediating role between her father and brother, both of whom she loves. As with the intervention of Odysseus at the end of *Ajax*, friendship itself becomes a means for enforcing independent values and thus peacefully resolving the conflicts that threaten disruption to moral norms and social harmony.

Neoptolemus, when faced with a conflict of loyalties, chooses according to independent criteria to support Philoctetes over Odysseus. He indicates at the outset, before his friendship with Philoctetes develops, that for him deception is unacceptable per se. Although he temporarily abandons this position under pressure from Odysseus, he finally reasserts it and acts accordingly, even against his own best interests. It is this remarkable self-sacrificing altruism that guarantees the impartiality of his decision. Philoctetes has been unjustly treated by the Greeks, who betrayed his friendship. Odysseus has behaved unjustly in the past, and tried to do so again. By the end of the play Neoptolemus has an obligation of *philia* towards both, so we cannot say that his decision is prompted simply by Help Friends. A justice external to Help Friends/Harm Enemies and the talio requires that he take Philoctetes' part. As in *Ajax* and *OC*, personal friendship is instrumental in bringing him to this understanding. But although his action is an application of Help Friends, it also has the independent sanction of other principles.

In *OC* this idea is developed further in the person of Theseus. Unlike Neoptolemus he is acting in his own interests, but he is in a position to elevate his behaviour beyond Help Friends/Harm Enemies and claim the independent validation of external principles. Moreover in virtue of his status and character he is able to place a similar seal of approval on the behaviour of others. Creon's treatment of Oedipus may be right according to the principles of personal retaliation and vendetta, but it is wrong by a neutral and impersonal standard of justice. Oedipus' treatment of his son is not merely right from his own perspective, but an impartially just punishment. Theseus' approval of Oedipus means not that a relentless pursuit of Help Friends/Harm Enemies is always justified, but that this particular application does in fact correspond to the requirements of an impersonal justice.

It may seem disappointing to suggest that the ultimate solution to the bewildering dilemmas of morality lies in the judgement of a man whose instantiation of the traditional virtues is complemented by reason and the authority to enforce his judgements. Yet this conclusion foreshadows the spirit of Aristotle's *Ethics*. The role of Theseus in *OC* is analogous to that of the *phronimos*, the man of practical wisdom, to whom we should turn as a standard for judging the proper emotional or practical response in a given situation (*EN* 1107a1f. and passim). And the world of Sophocles' plays is in some ways an Aristotelian one. Reason and passion are not intrinsically at odds, for right decisions are motivated by emotion in harmony with reason, as we see with Neoptolemus in *Philoctetes* and Oedipus in *OC*.[15] The bloodless and calculated rationality of Odysseus in *Philoctetes* is not a cause for admiration, nor does the peculiar self-indulgence of Ajax, Electra or Antigone in itself undermine their decisions, for right action is properly a source of pleasure to a good person. As Aristotle puts it with reference to Neoptolemus, 'Not everyone who acts from pleasure is intemperate or base or incontinent, but only the one who acts from disgraceful pleasure' (*EN* 1151b17–22). But proper action does require correct rational judgement, and this is often threatened by emotion. Creon in *Antigone* sets admirable rational goals, but they are undermined by his self-serving passionate impulses. As Aristotle tells us in one of his few pieces of practical advice, we should strive to counteract our own natural tendencies if we are to strike the mean of correct action (*EN* 1109b1–7).

Yet Sophocles does not criticise the traditional code as Aristotle would, by enumerating its deficiencies (cf. the discussion of retaliation at *EN* 1132b21–34). Rather his plays illustrate human motives for acting on certain values and principles, together with their consequences, and their adequacy or otherwise in the face of various dilemmas. The structural function of this ethical material in so many dramas is evidence of the rich tragic potential of traditional morality. It is precisely the deficiencies of such principles as a practical moral guide that give them this potential. Thus in the process of exploring the tragic consequences of traditional ethics, an implicit critique of such values emerges. Yet Sophoclean drama does not preach. It articulates a whole spectrum of responses to moral problems which, though clothed in the grandeur of the heroic age, were living issues for the fifth-century Greeks who had inherited the values of that age.

---

[15] For the Aristotelian character of Neoptolemus' moral education see my *Phusis*.

Conflicting loyalties to friends, family and city, justice towards friend and enemy, expediency versus justice, retaliation or forgiveness – these were the stuff of moral life as well as tragedy. Through his plays, Sophocles articulates some of the confusions surrounding these issues and the ambiguous terms in which they are expressed, drawing out implications and pitting alternatives against each other. If the poet teaches, it is not by expounding answers, but, like the Socrates of Plato's early dialogues, by provoking questions.

BIBLIOGRAPHY OF
SHORT TITLES

Adams: S.M. Adams, *Sophocles the Playwright* (Toronto 1957)

Adkins: A.W.H. Adkins, *Merit and Responsibility: A Study in Greek Values* (Oxford 1960)

Adkins, *Friendship*: A.W.H. Adkins, '"Friendship" and "self-sufficiency" in Homer and Aristotle', *CQ* 13 (1963) 30–45

Adkins, *Gods*: A.W.H. Adkins, 'Homeric gods and the values of Homeric society', *JHS* 92 (1972) 1–19

Adkins, *Honour*: A.W.H. Adkins, '"Honour" and "punishment" in the Homeric poems', *BICS* 7 (1960) 23–32

Adkins, *Problems*: A.W.H. Adkins, 'Problems in *Greek Popular Morality*', *CP* 73 (1978) 143–58

Adkins, *Tragedy*: A.W.H. Adkins, 'Aristotle and the best kind of tragedy', *CQ* 16 (1966) 78–102

Alexanderson, *Antigone*: B. Alexanderson, 'Die Stellung des Chors in der Antigone', *Eranos* 64 (1966) 85–105

Alexanderson, *Electra*: B. Alexanderson, 'On Sophocles' *Electra*', *CM* 27 (1966) 79–98

Alexiou: M. Alexiou, *The Ritual Lament in Greek Tradition* (Cambridge 1974)

Alt: K. Alt, 'Schicksal und *ΦΥΣΙΣ* im *Philoktet* des Sophokles', *Hermes* 89 (1961) 141–74

Annas: J. Annas, *An Introduction to Plato's Republic* (Oxford 1981)

Annas, *Friendship*: J. Annas, 'Plato and Aristotle on friendship and altruism', *Mind* 86 (1977) 532–54

Austin: J.L. Austin, *How to Do Things with Words* (Oxford 1962)

Avery: H.C. Avery, 'Heracles, Philoctetes, Neoptolemus', *Hermes* 93 (1965) 279–97

Baldry: H.C. Baldry, *The Unity of Mankind in Greek Thought* (Cambridge 1965)

Barbour: J.D. Barbour, *Tragedy as a Critique of Virtue* (Chico, CA 1984)

Beare: W. Beare, 'Sophocles, *Electra*, 11.17–19', *CR* 41 (1927) 111–12

Beauchet: L. Beauchet, *Histoire du droit privé de la république athénienne*, vol. 1 (Paris 1897)

Beck: F. A. Beck, *Greek Education* (London 1964)

Benardete: S. Benardete, '*XPH* and *ΔEI* in Plato and others', *Glotta* 43 (1965) 285–98

Benardete (1), (2), (3): S. Benardete, 'A reading of Sophocles' *Antigone*', (1) *Interpretation* 4 (1975) 148–96; (2) *Interpretation* 5 (1975) 1–55; (3) *Interpretation* 5 (1975) 148–84

Benveniste: E. Benveniste, *Le Vocabulaire des institutions indo-européennes*, vol. 1, *Economie, parenté société* (Paris 1969)

Beye: C. R. Beye, 'Sophocles' *Philoctetes* and the Homeric embassy', *TAPA* 101 (1970) 63–75

Biggs: P. Biggs, 'The disease theme in Sophocles' *Ajax*, *Philoctetes* and *Trachiniae*', *CP* 61 (1966) 223–35

Black: M.H. Black, *Poetic Drama as Mirror of the Will* (London 1977)

Blumenthal: H.J. Blumenthal, 'Euripides, *Alcestis* 282ff., and the authenticity of *Antigone* 905ff.', *CR* 24 (1974) 174–5

Blundell, *Odysseus*: M.W. Blundell, 'The moral character of Odysseus in *Philoctetes*', *GRBS* 28 (1987) 307–29

Blundell, *Phusis*: M.W. Blundell, 'The *phusis* of Neoptolemus in Sophocles' *Philoctetes*', *GR* 1988 (forthcoming)

Bolkestein: H. Bolkestein, *Wohltätigkeit und Armenpflege im vorchristlichen Altertum* (Utrecht 1939)

Bond: G.W. Bond (ed.), *Euripides: Heracles* (Oxford 1981)

Bonner and Smith: R.J. Bonner and G. Smith, *The Administration of Justice from Homer to Aristotle*, vol. 1 (Chicago 1930)

Booth: N.B. Booth, 'Sophocles, *Electra* 610–11', *CQ* 27 (1977) 466–7

Booth, *Antigone*: N.B. Booth, 'Sophocles: *Antigone* 599–603: a positive argument for κόνις', *CQ* 9 (1959) 76–7

Bowra: C.M. Bowra, *Sophoclean Tragedy* (Oxford 1944)

Bradshaw: A.T. von S. Bradshaw, 'The watchman scenes in the *Antigone*', *CQ* 12 (1962) 200–11

Bremmer: J. Bremmer, *The Early Greek Concept of the Soul* (Princeton 1983)

Brickhouse and Smith: T.C. Brickhouse and N.D. Smith, 'Justice and dishonesty in Plato's *Republic*', *SJP* 21 (1983) 79–95

Brink: C.O. Brink, *Horace on Poetry*, vol. 2 (Cambridge 1971)

Brown: W.E. Brown, 'Sophocles' Ajax and Homer's Hector', *CJ* 61 (1965–6) 118–21

Brown, *Eumenides*: A.L. Brown, 'Eumenides in Greek tragedy', *CQ* 34 (1984) 260–81

Bultmann: R. Bultmann, 'Polis und Hades in der Antigone des Sophokles', *Sophokles*, ed. H. Diller (Darmstadt 1967) 311–24

Burian, *Ajax*: P. Burian, 'Supplication and hero cult in Sophocles' *Ajax*', *GRBS* 13 (1972) 151–6

Burian, *Suppliant*: P. Burian, 'Suppliant and saviour', *Phoenix* 28 (1974) 408–29

Burkert: W. Burkert, *Greek Religion* (Eng. trans., Cambridge, Mass. 1985)

Burnet: J. Burnet (ed.), *Plato: Euthyphro, Apology of Socrates, Crito* (Oxford 1924)

Burnett: A.P. Burnett, *Three Archaic Poets* (Cambridge, Mass. 1983)

Burton: R.W.B. Burton, *The Chorus in Sophocles' Tragedies* (Oxford 1980)

Buxton: R.G.A. Buxton, *Persuasion in Greek Tragedy* (Cambridge 1982)

Bywater: I. Bywater, *Aristotle on the Art of Poetry* (Oxford 1909)

Calder, *Antigone*: W.M. Calder III, 'Sophokles' political tragedy: *Antigone*', *GRBS* 9 (1968) 389–407

Calder, *Philoctetes*: W.M. Calder III, 'Sophoclean apologia: *Philoctetes*', *GRBS* 12 (1971) 153–74

Cameron: H.D. Cameron, *Studies on the Seven Against Thebes of Aeschylus* (The Hague 1971)

Campbell: L. Campbell (ed.), *Sophocles* (2 vols., 2nd ed. Oxford 1879–81)

Chamberlain: C. Chamberlain, 'The meaning of the word *ethos* in Aristotle's *Poetics* and its interpretation in three Renaissance commentators on the *Poetics*', (diss. Berkeley 1980)

Chantraine: P. Chantraine, *Dictionnaire étymologique de la langue grecque* (Paris 1980)

Classen: J. Classen (ed.), *Thukydides* (4th ed, Berlin 1897)

Cohen: D. Cohen, 'The imagery of Sophocles: a study of Ajax's suicide', *GR* 25 (1978) 24–36

Coleman: R. Coleman, 'The role of the chorus in Sophocles' Antigone', *PCPS* 18 (1972) 4–27

Connor: W.R. Connor, *The New Politicians of Fifth-Century Athens* (Princeton 1971)

Cook: A.B. Cook, *Zeus: A Study in Ancient Religion* (Cambridge 1914–40)

Cooper: J.M. Cooper, 'Aristotle on friendship', *Essays on Aristotle's Ethics*, ed. A.D. Rorty (Berkeley and Los Angeles 1980) 301–40

Cope and Sandys: E.M. Cope and J.E. Sandys (eds.), *The Rhetoric of Aristotle* (Cambridge 1877)

Creed: J.L. Creed, 'Moral values in Thucydides' time', *CQ* 23 (1973) 213–31

Dain: A. Dain and P. Mazon (eds.), *Sophocle* (3 vols., Paris 1955–60)

Dale: A.M. Dale (ed.), *Euripides: Alcestis* (Oxford 1954)

Dale, *Electra*: A.M. Dale, 'The *Electra* of Sophocles', *Collected Papers* (Cambridge 1969) 221–9

Dale, *Ethos*: A.M. Dale, '*Ethos* and *dianoia*: 'character' and 'thought' in Aristotle's *Poetics*', *AUMLA* 11 (1959) 3–16 = *Collected Papers* (Cambridge 1969) 139–55

Dalmeyda: G. Dalmeyda, 'Sophocle, *Ajax*', *REG* 46 (1933) 1–14

Daube: D. Daube, *Civil Disobedience in Antiquity* (Edinburgh 1972)

Davidson: J.F. Davidson, 'The parodos of Sophocles' *Ajax*', *BICS* 22 (1975) 163–77

Dawe: R.D. Dawe (ed.), *Sophocles: Tragoediae* (2 vols., Leipzig 1975–9)

Dawe, *Ate*: R.D. Dawe, 'Some reflections on ate and hamartia', *HSCP* 72 (1967) 89–123

Dawe, *Inconsistency*: R.D. Dawe, 'Inconsistency of plot and character in Aeschylus', *PCPS* 9 (1963) 21–62

Dawe, *Studies*: R.D. Dawe, *Studies on the Text of Sophocles* (3 vols., Leiden 1973–8)

De Lacy: P. De Lacy, 'The four Stoic personae', *ICS* 2 (1977) 163–72

Delcourt: M. Delcourt, 'Le Suicide par vengeance dans la grèce ancienne', *Rev. de l'hist. des rel.* 119 (1939) 154–71

Denniston: J.D. Denniston, *The Greek Particles* (2nd ed. Oxford 1954)

Denniston, *Aristophanes*: J.D. Denniston, 'Technical terms in Aristophanes', *CQ* 21 (1927) 113–21

Detienne and Vernant: M. Detienne and J.-P. Vernant, *Cunning Intelligence in Greek Culture and Society* (Eng. trans. Atlantic Highlands, NJ 1978)

Dihle: A. Dihle, *Die goldene Regel* (Göttingen 1962)

Dihle, *Will*: A. Dihle, *The Theory of the Will in Classical Antiquity* (Berkeley and Los Angeles 1982)

Diller, *Menschendarstellung*: H. Diller, 'Menschendarstellung und Handlungsführung bei Sophokles', *A&A* 6 (1957) 157–69 = *Kleine Schriften* (Munich 1971) 286–303

Diller, *Selbstbewusstsein*: H. Diller, 'Über das Selbstbewusstsein der sophokleischen Personen', *WS* 69 (1956) 70–85 = *Kleine Schriften* (Munich 1971) 272–85

Diller, *Wissen*: H. Diller, 'Göttliches und menschliches Wissen bei Sophokles', *Kieler Universitätsreden* 3,1 (1950) = *Kleine Schriften* (Munich 1971) 255–71

Dirlmeier: F. Dirlmeier, Φίλος *und* Φιλία *im vorhellenistischen Griechentum* (Munich 1931)

Dirlmeier, *Theophilia*: F. Dirlmeier, 'θεοφιλία–φιλοθεία', *Philologus* 44 (1934) 57–77, 176–93

Dodds: E.R. Dodds, *The Greeks and the Irrational* (Berkeley and Los Angeles 1951)

Dodds, *Bacchae*: E.R. Dodds (ed.), *Euripides: Bacchae* (2nd ed. Oxford 1960)

Dodds, *Gorgias*: E.R. Dodds (ed.), *Plato: Gorgias* (Oxford 1959)

Dodds, *Misunderstanding*: E.R. Dodds, 'On misunderstanding the *Oedipus Rex*', *GR* 13 (1966) 37–49 = *Progress* 64–77

Dodds, *Morals*: E.R. Dodds, 'Morals and politics in the *Oresteia*', *PCPS* 6 (1960) 19–31 = *Progress* 26–44

Dodds, *Progress*: E.R. Dodds, *The Ancient Concept of Progress* (Oxford 1973)

Dover: K.J. Dover, *Greek Popular Morality* (Berkeley and Los Angeles 1974)

Dover, *Aspects*: K.J. Dover, 'Some neglected aspects of Agamemnon's dilemma', *JHS* 93 (1973) 58–69

Dover, *Clouds*: K.J. Dover, *Aristophanes: Clouds* (Oxford 1968)

Dover, *Evaluation*: K. J. Dover, 'The portrayal of moral evaluation in Greek poetry', *JHS* 102 (1983) 35–48

Earp: F.R. Earp, *The Way of the Greeks* (Oxford 1929)

Easterling, *Antigone*: P.E. Easterling, 'The second stasimon of *Antigone*', *Dionysiaca*, ed. R.D. Dawe, J. Diggle and P.E. Easterling (Cambridge 1978) 141–58

Easterling, *Character*: P.E. Easterling, 'Character in Sophocles', *GR* 24 (1977) 121–9

Easterling, *Homer*: P.E. Easterling, 'The tragic Homer', *BICS* 31 (1984) 1–8

Easterling, *Notes*: P.E. Easterling, 'Notes on tragedy and epic', *Papers Given at a Colloquium on Greek Drama in Honour of R.P. Winnington-Ingram*, ed. L. Rodley (London 1987) 52–62

Easterling, *Oedipus*: P.E. Easterling, 'Oedipus and Polynices', *PCPS* 13 (1967) 1–13

Easterling, *Philoctetes*: P.E. Easterling, '*Philoctetes* and modern criticism', *ICS* 3 (1978) 27–39

Easterling, *Presentation*: P.E. Easterling, 'Presentation of character in Aeschylus', *GR* 20 (1973) 3–19

Easterling, *Repetition*: P.E. Easterling, 'Repetition in Sophocles', *Hermes* 101 (1973) 14–34

Edmunds, *Chance*: L. Edmunds, *Chance and Intelligence in Thucydides* (Cambridge, Mass. 1975)

Edmunds, *Oedipus*: L. Edmunds, 'The cults and the legend of Oedipus', *HSCP* 85 (1981) 221–38

Egermann: F. Egermann, *Vom attischen Menschenbild* (Munich 1952)

Ehrenberg: V. Ehrenberg, *Sophocles and Pericles* (Oxford 1954)

Ellendt: F. Ellendt, *Lexicon Sophocleum* (revised by H. Genthe, Berlin 1872)

Else: G.F. Else, *The Madness of Antigone* (Heidelberg 1976)

Else, *Poetics*: G.F. Else, *Aristotle's Poetics: The Argument* (Cambridge Mass. 1963)

Erbse: H. Erbse, 'Neoptolemos und Philoktet bei Sophokles', *Hermes* 94 (1966) 177–201

Errandonea: I. Errandonea, 'Les Quatre Monologues d'Ajax et leur signification dramatique', *LEC* 26 (1958) 21–40

Farnell: L.R. Farnell, *Greek Hero Cults and Ideas of Immortality* (Oxford 1921)

Ferguson: J. Ferguson, *Moral Values in the Ancient World* (London 1958)

Finley, *ES*: M.I. Finley, *Economy and Society in Ancient Greece* (London 1981)

Finley, *Odysseus*: M.I. Finley, *The World of Odysseus* (4th ed. New York 1978)

Finley, *Three*: J.H. Finley, *Three Essays on Thucydides* (Cambridge, Mass. 1967)

Fisher: N.R.E. Fisher, 'Hybris and dishonour: I', GR 23 (1976) 177–93

Fitton Brown: D. Fitton Brown, 'Four notes on Sophocles', PCPS 12 (1966) 18–23

Flashar: H. Flashar, Der Dialog Ion als Zeugnis platonischer Philosophie (Berlin 1958)

Foot: P. Foot, 'Moral realism and moral dilemma', JP 80 (1983) 379–98

Fraenkel: E. Fraenkel, Aeschylus: Agamemnon (Oxford 1950)

Fränkel, Ephemeros: H. Fränkel, 'Man's "ephemeros" nature according to Pindar and others', TAPA 77 (1946) 131–45

Fränkel, Parmenides: H. Fränkel, 'Studies in Parmenides', Studies in Presocratic Philosophy, vol. 2, ed. R.E. Allen and D.J. Furley (London 1975) 1–47

Freis: C.R. Freis, 'Goodness and justice in Sophocles' (diss. Berkeley 1981)

Friedländer: P. Freidländer, Plato (2nd ed. Eng. trans. Princeton 1969)

von Fritz: K. von Fritz, Antike und moderne Tragödie (Berlin 1962)

von Fritz, Aias: K. von Fritz, 'Zur Interpretation des Aias', Antike und moderne Tragödie (Berlin 1962) 241–55 = RM 83 (1934) 113–28

von Fritz, Liebe: K. von Fritz, 'Haimons Liebe zu Antigone', Antike und moderne Tragödie (Berlin 1962) 227–40 = Philologus 89 (1934) 19–33

Funke: H. Funke, 'ΚΡΕΩΝ ΑΠΟΛΙΣ', A&A 12 (1966) 29–56

Gardiner: C.P. Gardiner, The Sophoclean Chorus: A Study of Character and Function (Iowa City 1987)

Garland: R. Garland, The Greek Way of Death (London 1985)

Garton, Characterisation: C. Garton, 'Characterisation in Greek tragedy', JHS 77 (1957) 247–54

Garton, Chameleon: C. Garton, 'The "chameleon trail" in the criticism of Greek tragedy', Studies in Philology 69 (1972) 389–413

Garvie: A.F. Garvie, 'Deceit, violence and persuasion in the Philoctetes', Studi classici in onore di Quintino Cataudella, vol. 1 (Catania 1972) 213–26

Gellie: G.H. Gellie, Sophocles: A Reading (Melbourne 1972)

Gill, Bow: C. Gill, 'Bow, oracle and epiphany in Sophocles' Philoctetes', GR 27 (1980) 137–46

Gill, Character: C. Gill, 'The question of character and personality in Greek tragedy', Poetics Today 7 (1986) 251–73

Gill, Ethos: C. Gill, 'The êthos/pathos distinction in rhetorical and literary criticism', CQ 34 (1984) 149–66

Glotz: G. Glotz, La Solidarité de la famille dans le droit criminel en Grèce (Paris 1904)

Goheen: R.F. Goheen, The Imagery of Sophocles' Antigone (Princeton 1951)

Goldhill: S. Goldhill, Reading Greek Tragedy (Cambridge 1986)

Gomme: A.W. Gomme, The Greek Attitude to Poetry and History (Berkeley and Los Angeles 1954)

Gould: J. Gould, 'Dramatic character and "human intelligibility" in Greek tragedy', PCPS 24 (1978) 43–67

Gould, *Hiketeia*: J. Gould, 'Hiketeia', *JHS* 93 (1973) 74–103

Gowans: C.W. Gowans (ed.), *Moral Dilemmas* (Oxford 1987)

Griffin: J. Griffin, *Homer on Life and Death* (Oxford 1980)

Griffith: M. Griffith (ed.), *Aeschylus: Prometheus Bound* (Cambridge 1983)

Grossman: G. Grossman, 'Das Lachen des Aias', *MH* 25 (1968) 65–85

Gudeman: A. Gudeman, *Aristoteles Περὶ Ποιητικῆς* (Berlin 1934)

Guthrie, *Odysseus*: W.K.C. Guthrie, 'Odysseus in the *Ajax*', *GR* 16 (1947) 115–19

Guthrie, *Socrates*: W.K.C. Guthrie, *Socrates* (Cambridge 1971), reprinted from *A History of Greek Philosophy*, vol. 3 (Cambridge 1969)

Guthrie, *Sophists*: W.K.C. Guthrie, *The Sophists* (Cambridge 1971), reprinted from *A History of Greek Philosophy*, vol. 3 (Cambridge 1969)

Halliwell: S. Halliwell, *Aristotle's Poetics* (London 1986)

Halperin: D. Halperin, 'Platonic *erôs* and what men call love', *Ancient Philosophy* 5 (1985) 161–204

Hamilton: R. Hamilton, 'Neoptolemus' story in the *Philoctetes*', *AJP* 96 (1975) 131–7

Hands: A.R. Hands, *Charities and Social Aid in Greece and Rome* (London 1968)

Harding: D.W. Harding, 'Psychological processes in the reading of fiction', *British Journal of Aesthetics* 2 (1962) 133–47

Harrison: A.R.W. Harrison, *The Law of Athens*, vol. 1 (Oxford 1968)

Harsh: P.W. Harsh, 'The role of the bow in the *Philoctetes* of Sophocles', *AJP* 81 (1960) 408–14

Hart: H.L.A. Hart, 'Prolegomenon to the principles of punishment', *Punishment and Responsibility* (Oxford 1968) 1–27

Haslam: M. Haslam, 'The authenticity of Euripides, *Phoenissae* 1–2 and Sophocles, *Electra* 1', *GRBS* 16 (1975) 149–74

Hathorn: R.Y. Hathorn, 'Sophocles' *Antigone*: Eros in Politics', *CJ* 54 (1958–9) 109–15

Havelock, *Dikaiosune*: E.A. Havelock, '*Dikaiosune*: an essay in Greek intellectual history', *Phoenix* 23 (1969) 49–70

Havelock, *Justice*: E.A. Havelock, *The Greek Concept of Justice* (Cambridge, Mass. 1978)

Havelock, *Preface*: E.A. Havelock, *Preface to Plato* (Cambridge, Mass. 1963)

Heath: M. Heath, *The Poetics of Greek Tragedy* (London 1987)

Heath, *Hesiod*: M. Heath, 'Hesiod's didactic poetry', *CQ* 35 (1985) 245–63

Heinimann: F. Heinimann, *Nomos und Physis* (Basel 1965)

Henrichs: A. Henrichs, 'The "sobriety" of Oedipus: Sophocles *O.C.* 100 misunderstood', *HSCP* 87 (1983) 87–100

Hester, *Distemper*: D.A. Hester, 'The heroic distemper', *Prometheus* 5 (1979) 241–55

Hester, *Friends*: D.A. Hester, 'To help one's friends and harm one's enemies', *Antichthon* 11 (1977) 22–41

Hester, *Unphilosophical*: D.A. Hester, 'Sophocles the unphilosophical', *Mnemosyne* 24 (1971) 11–59

Hewitt: J.W. Hewitt, 'The terminology of "gratitude" in Greek', *CP* 22 (1927) 142–61

Hinds: A.E. Hinds, 'The prophecy of Helenus in Sophocles' *Philoctetes*', *CQ* 17 (1967) 169–80

Hirzel: R. Hirzel, 'Die Talion', *Philologus* supp. 11 (1907–10) 405–82

Hirzel, "Ἄγραφος Νόμος: R. Hirzel, "Ἄγραφος Νόμος (Leipzig 1900)

Hirzel, *Themis*: R. Hirzel, *Themis, Dike und Verwandtes* (Leipzig 1907)

Hoey: T.F. Hoey, 'Inversion in the *Antigone*', *Arion* 9 (1970) 337–45

Howald: E. Howald, *Die griechische Tragödie* (Munich 1930)

Howe: T.P. Howe, 'Taboo in the Oedipus theme', *TAPA* 93 (1962) 124–43

Humphreys: S.C. Humphreys, 'Family tombs and tomb cult in ancient Athens: tradition or traditionalism?', *JHS* 100 (1980) 96–126

Huxley: G. Huxley, 'Thersites in Sophokles, *Philoktetes* 445', *GRBS* 8 (1967) 33–4

Inoue: E. Inoue, 'Sight, sound and rhetoric: *Philoctetes* 29ff.', *AJP* 100 (1979) 217–27

Jacoby: S. Jacoby, *Wild Justice* (New York 1983)

Jaeger: W. Jaeger, *Paideia*, vol. 1 (Eng. trans. Oxford 1939)

Jebb: R.C. Jebb (ed.), *Sophocles: The Plays and Fragments* (7 vols., Cambridge 1883–1900)

Jebb, *Rhetoric*: R.C. Jebb, *The Rhetoric of Aristotle* (Cambridge 1909)

Jens: W. Jens, 'Antigone-Interpretationen', *Sophokles* ed. H. Diller (Darmstadt 1967) 295–310

Johansen: H. Friis Johansen, 'Sophocles, 1939–59', *Lustrum* 7 (1962) 94–288

Johansen, *Elektra*: H. Friis Johansen, 'Die *Elektra* des Sophokles', *CM* 25 (1964) 8–32

Jones: J. Jones, *On Aristotle and Greek Tragedy* (London 1962)

Kahn: C.H. Kahn, 'Drama and dialectic in Plato's *Gorgias*', *OSAP* 1 (1983) 75–121

Kaibel: G. Kaibel, *Sophokles: Elektra* (Leipzig 1896)

Kakridis: J.T. Kakridis, *Homeric Researches* (Lund 1949)

Kamerbeek: J.C. Kamerbeek (ed.), *The Plays of Sophocles: Commentaries* (7 vols., Leiden 1953–84)

Kells: J.H. Kells (ed.), *Sophocles: Electra* (Cambridge 1973)

Kells, *Antigone*: J. H. Kells, 'Problems of interpretation in the *Antigone*', *BICS* 10 (1963) 47–64

Kells, *Philoctetes*: J.H. Kells, 'Sophocles, *Philoctetes* 1140–5', *CR* 13 (1963) 7–9

Keuls: E. Keuls, *The Reign of the Phallus* (New York 1985)

Kieffer: J.S. Kieffer, 'Philoctetes and *arete*', *CP* 37 (1942) 38–50

King: K.C. King, *Achilles: Paradigms of the War Hero from Homer to the Middle Ages* (Berkeley and Los Angeles 1987)

Kirkwood: G.M. Kirkwood, *A Study of Sophoclean Drama* (Ithaca 1958)

Kirkwood, *Electra*: G.M. Kirkwood, 'Two structural features of Sophocles' *Electra*', *TAPA* 73 (1942) 86–95

Kirkwood, *Homer*: G.M. Kirkwood, 'Homer and Sophocles' "Ajax"', *Classical Drama and its Influence*, ed. M.J. Anderson (London 1965) 53–70

Kirkwood, *Melos*: G.M. Kirkwood, 'From Melos to Colonus: τίνας χώρους ἀφίγμεθ' . . .;', *TAPA* 116 (1986) 99–117

Kitto, *GT*: H.D.F. Kitto, *Greek Tragedy* (1st ed. London 1939; 3rd ed. 1961)

Kitto, *FMD*: H.D.F. Kitto, *Form and Meaning in Drama* (2nd ed. London 1964)

Kitto, *SDP*: H.D.F. Kitto, *Sophocles: Dramatist and Philosopher* (London 1958)

Knapp: C. Knapp, 'A point in the interpretation of the *Antigone* of Sophocles', *AJP* 37 (1916) 300–16

Knox: B.M.W. Knox, *The Heroic Temper* (Berkeley and Los Angeles 1964)

Knox, *Ajax*: B.M.W. Knox, 'The *Ajax* of Sophocles', *HSCP* 65 (1961) 1–37

Knox, *Polis*: B.M.W. Knox, 'Sophocles and the *polis*', *Fond. Hardt Entr.* 29 (1983) 1–27

Knox, *Tyrannos*: B.M.W. Knox, 'Why is Oedipus called *Tyrannos*?' *CJ* 50 (1954) 97–102

Knox, *WA*: B.M.W. Knox, *Word and Action: Essays on the Ancient Theatre* (Baltimore 1979)

Kott: J. Kott, *The Eating of the Gods* (New York 1973)

Kraut: R. Kraut, *Socrates and the State* (Princeton 1984)

Kuhn (1) and (2): H. Kuhn, 'The true tragedy', (1) *HSCP* 52 (1941) 1–40; (2) *HSCP* 53 (1942) 37–88

Lacey: W.K. Lacey, *The Family in Classical Greece* (London 1968)

Lanata: G. Lanata, *Poetica Pre-Platonica* (Florence 1963)

Lattimore, *Themes*: R. Lattimore, *Themes in Greek and Latin Epitaphs* (Urbana 1962)

Lattimore, *Patterns*: R. Lattimore, *Story Patterns in Greek Tragedy* (Ann Arbor 1969)

Lawall: S.N. Lawall, 'Sophocles' Ajax: *aristos* . . . after Achilles', *CJ* 54 (1958–9) 290–4

Lawson: J.C. Lawson, *Modern Greek Folklore and Ancient Greek Religion* (Cambridge 1909)

Lesky, *GT*: A. Lesky, *Greek Tragedy* (Eng. trans. London 1965)

Lesky, *GTP*: A. Lesky, *Greek Tragic Poetry* (Eng. trans. New Haven 1983)

Lesky, *Zwei*: A. Lesky, 'Zwei Sophokles-Interpretationen', *Hermes* 80 (1952) 91–105

Letters: F.J.H. Letters, *The Life and Works of Sophocles* (London 1953)

Levy: C.S. Levy, 'Antigone's motives: a suggested interpretation', *TAPA* 94 (1963) 137–44

Linforth, *Ajax*: I.M. Linforth, 'Three scenes in Sophocles' *Ajax*', *UCPCP* 15 (1954) 1–28

Linforth, *Antigone*: I.M. Linforth, 'Antigone and Creon', *UCPCP* 15 (1961) 183–259

Linforth, *Antigone 471*: I.M. Linforth, 'Sophocles *Antigone* 471', *CP* 26 (1931) 196–7

Linforth, *Electra*: I.M. Linforth, 'Electra's day in the tragedy of Sophocles', *UCPCP* 19 (1963) 89–125

Linforth, *OC*: I.M. Linforth, 'Religion and drama in *Oedipus at Colonus*', *UCPCP* 14 (1951) 75–191

Linforth, *Philoctetes*: I.M. Linforth, 'Philoctetes, the play and the man', *UCPCP* 15 (1956) 95–156

Lloyd-Jones: H. Lloyd-Jones, *The Justice of Zeus* (2nd ed. Berkeley and Los Angeles 1983)

Lloyd-Jones, *Antigone*: H. Lloyd-Jones, 'Notes on Sophocles' *Antigone*', *CQ* 51 (1957) 12–27

Lloyd-Jones, *Sophoclea*: H. Lloyd-Jones, 'Sophoclea', *CQ* 4 (1954) 91–5

Lloyd-Jones, *Wilamowitz*: H. Lloyd-Jones, 'Tycho von Wilamowitz-Moellendorff on the dramatic technique of Sophocles', *CQ* 22 (1972) 214–28

Long: A.A. Long, *Language and Thought in Sophocles* (London 1968)

Long, *Fratricide*: A.A. Long, 'Pro and contra fratricide: Aeschylus *Septem* 653–719', *Studies in Honour of T.B.L. Webster*, vol. 1, ed. J.H. Betts, J.T. Hooker and J.R. Green (Bristol, 1986) 179–89

Long, *Morals*: A.A. Long, 'Morals and values in Homer', *JHS* 90 (1970) 121–39

Lucas: D.W. Lucas (ed.), *Aristotle: Poetics* (Oxford 1968)

MacDowell, *AHL*: D.M. MacDowell, *Athenian Homicide Law* (Manchester 1963)

MacDowell, *Hybris*: D.M. MacDowell, '*Hybris* in Athens', *GR* 23 (1976) 14–31

MacDowell, *LCA*: D.M. MacDowell, *The Law in Classical Athens* (London 1978)

Machin: A. Machin, *Cohérence et continuité dans le théâtre de Sophocle* (Haute-Ville 1981)

MacIntyre: A. MacIntyre, *After Virtue* (London 1981)

MacKay: L.A. MacKay, 'Antigone, Coriolanus and Hegel', *TAPA* 93 (1962) 166–74

Mackenzie: M.M. Mackenzie, *Plato on Punishment* (Berkeley and Los Angeles 1981)

Marcus: R.B. Marcus, 'Moral dilemmas and consistency', *JP* 77 (1980) 121–36

Masaracchia: A. Masaracchia, 'La scena dell'emporos nel Filottete di Sofocle', *Maia* 16 (1964) 79–98

Mauss: M. Mauss, *The Gift* (Eng. trans. New York 1967)

Mazon: *see* Dain

Méautis: G. Méautis, *Sophocle: essai sur le héros tragique* (2nd ed. Paris 1957)

Méautis, *L'Œdipe*: G. Méautis, 'L'Œdipe à Colone et le culte des héros', *Univ. de Neuchâtel Recueil de Travaux* 19 (1940)

Merkelbach: R. Merkelbach, 'Die Heroen als Geber des Guten und Bösen', *ZPE* 1 (1967) 97–9

Minadeo: R.W. Minadeo, 'Plot, theme and meaning in Sophocles' *Electra*', *CM* 28 (1967) 114–42

Moore: J.A. Moore, *Sophocles and Arete* (Cambridge, Mass. 1938)

Moore, *Ajax*: J.A. Moore, 'The dissembling-speech of Ajax', *YCS* 25 (1977) 47–66

Morris: I. Morris, 'The use and abuse of Homer', *CA* 5 (1986) 81–138

Morrow: G. Morrow, 'Plato and the law of nature', *Essays in Political Theory*, ed. M.R. Konvitz and A.E. Murphy (Ithaca 1948) 17–44

Mühl: M. Mühl, 'Über die Herkunft des platonischen Versöhnungsgedankens Staat v 470e', *PhW* 61 (1941) 429–31

Müller: G.M. Müller (ed.), *Sophokles: Antigone* (Heidelberg 1967)

Musurillo: H. Musurillo, *The Light and the Darkness* (Leiden 1967)

Musurillo, *Fire-walking*: H. Musurillo, 'Fire-walking in Sophocles' *Antigone* 618–19', *TAPA* 94 (1963) 167–75

Nagel: T. Nagel, *The View from Nowhere* (Oxford 1986)

Nagy: G. Nagy, *The Best of the Achaians* (Baltimore 1979)

Nestle: W. Nestle, 'Sophokles und die Sophistik', *CP* 5 (1910) 129–57

Nestle, *Euripides*: W. Nestle, *Euripides, der Dichter der griechischen Aufklärung* (Stuttgart 1901)

Nietzsche, *Morals*: F. Nietzsche, *The Genealogy of Morals* (Eng. trans. by F. Golffing, New York 1956)

North: H. North, *Sophrosyne* (Ithaca 1966)

Norwood: G. Norwood, *Greek Tragedy* (4th ed. London 1948)

Nussbaum: M. Nussbaum, *The Fragility of Goodness* (Cambridge 1986)

Nussbaum, *Consequences*: M. Nussbaum, 'Consequences and character in Sophocles' *Philoctetes*', *Phil. & Lit.* 1 (1976–7) 25–53

O'Brien: M.J. O'Brien, *The Socratic Paradoxes and the Greek Mind* (Chapel Hill 1967)

Opstelten: J.C. Opstelten, *Sophocles and Greek Pessimism* (Eng. trans. Amsterdam 1952)

Ostwald, *Nomos*: M. Ostwald, *Nomos and the Beginnings of the Athenian Democracy* (Oxford 1969)

Ostwald, *Pindar*: M. Ostwald, 'Pindar, *nomos*, and Heracles', *HSCP* 69 (1965) 109–38

Owen: A.S. Owen, '*TA T'ONTA KAI MEΛΛONTA*', *CR* 41 (1927) 50–2

Page: D.L. Page (ed.), *Euripides: Medea* (Oxford 1938)

Paolucci: A. and H. Paolucci (eds.), *Hegel on Tragedy* (New York 1962)

Parfit: D. Parfit, *Reasons and Persons* (Oxford 1984)

Parke and Wormell: H.W. Parke and D.E.W. Wormell, *The Delphic Oracle*, vol. 1 (Oxford 1956)

Parker: R. Parker, *Miasma* (Oxford 1983)

Pearson: A.C. Pearson (ed.), *Sophoclis Fabulae* (Oxford 1924)

Pearson, *Ajax*: A.C. Pearson, 'Sophocles, *Ajax*, 961–973', *CQ* 16 (1922) 124–36

Pearson, *Fragments*: A.C. Pearson, *The Fragments of Sophocles* (Cambridge 1917)

Pearson, *Glosses*: A.C. Pearson, 'Some glosses in the text of Sophocles', *CQ* 13 (1919) 118–26

Pearson, *Notes*: A.C. Pearson, 'Critical notes on Sophocles and in particular on the *Ajax*', *PCPS* 148 (1922) 14–28

Pearson, *PE*: L. Pearson, *Popular Ethics in Ancient Greece* (Stanford 1962)

Pearson, *Poetics*: L. Pearson, 'Characterization in drama and oratory – *Poetics* 1450a20', *CQ* 18 (1968) 76–83

Pembroke: S.G. Pembroke, 'Oikeiosis', in *Problems in Stoicism*, ed. A.A. Long (London 1971) 114–49

Perrotta: G. Perrotta, *Sofocle* (Messina–Florence 1935)

Podlecki, *Creon*: A.J. Podlecki, 'Creon and Herodotus', *TAPA* 97 (1966) 359–71

Podlecki, *Word*: A.J. Podlecki, 'The power of the word in Sophocles' *Philoctetes*', *GRBS* 7 (1966) 233–50

Pohlenz: M. Pohlenz, *Die griechische Tragödie* (2nd ed. Göttingen 1954)

Pohlenz, *Erläuterungen*: M. Pohlenz, *Erläuterungen* to *Die griechische Tragödie* (2nd ed. Göttingen 1954)

Pohlenz, *Führertum*: M. Pohlenz, *Antikes Führertum* (Leipzig 1934)

Putnam: H. Putnam, 'Literature, science and reflection', *NLH* 7 (1976) 483–91

Radt: S. Radt (ed.), *Tragicorum Graecorum Fragmenta*, vol. 4 (Göttingen 1977)

Raphael, *Literature*: D.D. Raphael, 'Can literature be moral philosophy?', *NLH* 15 (1983) 1–12

Raphael, *Paradox*: D.D. Raphael, *The Paradox of Tragedy* (Bloomington 1960)

Redard: G. Redard, *Recherches sur χρή, χρῆσθαι* (Paris 1953)

Redfield: J.M. Redfield, *Nature and Culture in the Iliad* (Chicago 1975)

Redfield, *Notes*: J.M. Redfield, 'Notes on the Greek wedding', *Arethusa* 15 (1982) 181–201

Reinhardt: K. Reinhardt, *Sophocles* (Eng. trans. Oxford 1979)

Robinson: D.B. Robinson, 'Topics in Sophocles' *Philoctetes*', *CQ* 19 (1969) 34–56

Rohde: E. Rohde, *Psyche* (Eng. trans. London 1925)

Rohdich: H. Rodich, *Antigone: Beitrag zu einer Theorie des sophokleischen Helden* (Heidelberg 1980).

de Romilly: J. de Romilly, *La Crainte et l'angoisse dans le théâtre d'Eschyle* (Paris 1958)

Ronnet: G. Ronnet, *Sophocle poète tragique* (Paris 1969)

Roscher: W.H. Roscher, *Lexicon der griechischen und römischen Mythologie* (Leipzig 1884–1937)

Rose: P.W. Rose, 'Sophocles' *Philoctetes* and the teachings of the Sophists', *HSCP* 80 (1976) 49–105

Rosenmeyer, *Gorgias*: T. G. Rosenmeyer, 'Gorgias, Aeschylus and *apate*', *AJP* 76 (1955) 225–60

Rosenmeyer, *Masks*: T.G. Rosenmeyer, *The Masks of Tragedy* (Austin 1963)

Rosenmeyer, *Wrath*: T.G. Rosenmeyer, 'The wrath of Oedipus', *Phoenix* 6 (1952) 92–112

Roussel: P. Roussel, 'Les Fiançailles d'Haimon et d'Antigone', *REG* 25 (1922) 63–81

Rowe: C.J. Rowe, 'The nature of Homeric morality', *Approaches to Homer*, ed. C.A. Rubino and C.W. Shelmerdine (Austin 1983) 248–75

Saïd: S. Saïd, *La Faute tragique* (Paris 1978)

Sandbach: F.H. Sandbach, 'Sophocles, *Electra* 77–85', *PCPS* 23 (1977) 71–3

Santirocco: M. Santirocco, 'Justice in Sophocles' *Antigone*', *Phil. & Lit.* 4 (1980) 180–98

Schadewaldt: W. Schadewaldt, 'Sophokles, Aias und Antigone', *Neue Wege zur Antike* 8 (1929) 61–109

Schein: S.L. Schein, *The Mortal Hero* (Berkeley and Los Angeles 1984)

Schlesinger: E. Schlesinger, 'Die Intrige im Aufbau von Sophokles' Philoktet', *RM* 111 (1968) 97–156

Schlesinger, Δεινότηs: E. Schlesinger, 'ΔΕΙΝΟΤΗΣ', *Philologus* 91 (1936–7) 59–66

Schmid: W. Schmid, 'Probleme aus der sophokleïschen Antigone', *Philologus* 62 (1903) 1–34

Schmidt: J.-U. Schmidt, *Sophokles Philoctet: eine Strukturanalyse* (Heidelberg 1973)

Schneidewin–Nauck: F.W. Schneidewin and A. Nauck (eds.), *Sophokles*, revised by E. Bruhn and L. Radermacher (7 vols., Berlin 1909–14)

Schütrumpf: E. Schütrumpf, *Die Bedeutung des Wortes Ethos in der Poetik des Aristoteles* (Munich 1970)

Scodel: R. Scodel, *Sophocles* (Boston 1984)

Scodel, *Doublets*: R. Scodel, 'Epic doublets and Polyneices' two burials', *TAPA* 114 (1984) 49–58

Scully: S.E. Scully, '*Philia* and *charis* in Euripidean tragedy' (diss. Toronto 1973)

Seaford: R. Seaford, 'The destruction of limits in Sophokles' *Elektra*', *CQ* 35 (1985) 315–23

Seale: D. Seale, *Vision and Stagecraft in Sophocles* (London 1982)

Seale, *Surprise*: D. Seale, 'The element of surprise in Sophocles' *Philoctetes*', *BICS* 19 (1972) 94–102

Segal: C.P. Segal, *Tragedy and Civilization: An Interpretation of Sophocles* (Cambridge, Mass. 1981)

Segal, *Electra*: C.P. Segal, 'The *Electra* of Sophocles', *TAPA* 97 (1966) 473–545

Segal, *Piety*: C.P. Segal, 'Philoctetes and the imperishable piety', *Hermes* 105 (1977) 133–58

Segal, *Praise*: C.P. Segal, 'Sophocles' praise of man and the conflicts of the *Antigone*', *Arion* 3 (1964) 46–66

Seidensticker: B. Seidensticker, 'Die Wahl des Todes bei Sophokles', *Fond. Hardt Entr.* 29 (1983) 105–44

Sheppard (1): J.T. Sheppard, 'The tragedy of *Electra*, according to Sophocles', *CQ* 12 (1918) 80–8

Sheppard (2): J.T. Sheppard, '*Electra*: a defence of Sophocles', *CR* 41 (1927) 2–9

Sheppard (3): J.T. Sheppard, '*Electra* again', *CR* 41 (1927) 163–5

Shucard: S.C. Shucard, 'Some developments in Sophocles' late plays of intrigue', *CJ* 69 (1973–4) 133–8

Sicherl: M. Sicherl, 'The tragic issue in Sophocles' *Ajax*', *YCS* 25 (1977) 67–98

Siewart: P. Siewart, 'The ephebic oath in fifth-century Athens', *JHS* 97 (1977) 102–11

Simpson: M. Simpson, 'Sophocles' Ajax: his madness and transformation', *Arethusa* 2 (1969) 88–103

Snell: B. Snell, *The Discovery of the Mind* (Eng. trans. Oxford 1953)

Stanford: W.B. Stanford (ed.), *Sophocles: Ajax* (London 1963)

Stanford, *Emotions*: W.B. Stanford, *Greek Tragedy and the Emotions* (London 1983)

Stanford, *Frogs*: W.B. Stanford (ed.), *Aristophanes: The Frogs* (2nd ed. London 1963)

Stanford, *Lies*: W.B. Stanford, 'Studies in the characterisation of Ulysses – III. The lies of Odysseus', *Hermathena* 75 (1950) 35–48

Stanford, *Light*: W.B. Stanford, 'Light and darkness in Sophocles' *Ajax*', *GRBS* 19 (1978) 189–97

Stanford, *UT*: W.B. Stanford, *The Ulysses Theme* (2nd ed. Oxford 1963)

Steidle: W. Steidle, *Studien zum antiken Drama* (Munich 1968)

Steiner: G. Steiner, *Antigones* (Oxford 1984)

Stevens, *Aesch. and Soph.*: P.T. Stevens, 'Colloquial expressions in Aeschylus and Sophocles', *CQ* 39 (1945) 95–105

Stevens, *Electra*: P.T. Stevens, 'Sophocles: *Electra*, doom or triumph?', *GR* 25 (1978) 111–20

Stevens, *Euripides*: P.T. Stevens, 'Colloquial expressions in Euripides', *CQ* 31 (1937) 182–91

Stevenson: C.L. Stevenson, 'Persuasive definitions', *Mind* 47 (1938) 331–50

Stinton (1) and (2): T.C.W. Stinton, (1) 'Notes on Greek tragedy, I', *JHS*

96 (1976) 121–45; (2) 'Notes on Greek tragedy, II', *JHS* 97 (1977) 127–54

Stokes: M.C. Stokes, *Plato's Socratic Conversations: Drama and Dialectic in Three Dialogues* (London 1986)

Strohm: H. Strohm, 'Zum Trug- und Täuschungsmotiv im sophokleischen Philoktetes', *WS* 20 (1986) 109–22

Sutton: D.F. Sutton, *The Lost Sophocles* (Lanham, MD 1984)

Taillardat: J. Taillardat, 'φιλότης, πίστις et *foedus*', *REG* 95 (1982) 1–14

Taplin, *Forethought*: O. Taplin, 'Yielding to forethought: Sophocles' *Ajax*', *Arktouros*, ed. G. Bowersock, W. Burkert and M.C. Putnam (Berlin 1979) 122–9

Taplin, *GTA*: O. Taplin, *Greek Tragedy in Action* (London 1978)

Taplin, *Philoctetes*: O. Taplin, 'Significant actions in Sophocles' *Philoctetes*', *GRBS* 12 (1971) 25–44

Taplin, *Trugedy*: O. Taplin, 'Tragedy and trugedy', *CQ* 33 (1983) 331–3

Tarrant, *Plato*: D. Tarrant, 'Plato as dramatist', *JHS* 75 (1955) 82–9

Tarrant, *Philoctetes*: R.J. Tarrant, 'Sophocles, *Philoctetes* 676–720: direction and indirection', *Greek Tragedy and its Legacy*, ed. M. Cropp, E. Fantham and S.E. Scully (Calgary 1986) 121–34

Thomson: G. Thomson, *The Oresteia of Aeschylus* (1st ed. Cambridge 1938; 2nd ed. Amsterdam 1966)

Tod: M.N. Tod, *A Selection of Greek Historical Inscriptions* (reprinted with a new concordance, Chicago 1985)

Torrance: R.M. Torrance, 'Sophocles: some bearings', *HSCP* 69 (1965) 269–327

Trousson: R. Trousson, 'La Philosophie du pouvoir dans l'*Antigone* de Sophocle', *REG* 77 (1964) 23–33

Untersteiner: M. Untersteiner, *The Sophists* (Eng. trans. New York 1954)

Usher: S. Usher, 'Individual characterization in Lysias', *Eranos* 63 (1965) 99–119

Vahlen: J. Vahlen, *Beiträge zu Aristoteles Poetik* (Leipzig 1914)

Verdenius: W.J. Verdenius, 'Homer, the educator of the Greeks', *Mededelingen der Koninklijke Nederlandse Akademie van Wetenschappen* 33.5 (1970)

Vermeule: E. Vermeule, *Aspects of Death in Early Greek Art and Poetry* (Berkeley and Los Angeles 1979)

Vernant, *GT*: J.-P. Vernant, 'Greek tragedy: problems of interpretation', *The Language of Criticism and the Sciences of Man*, ed. R. Macksey and E. Donato (Baltimore 1970) 273–89

Vernant, *MP*: J.-P. Vernant, *Mythe et pensée chez les Grecs*, vol. 1 (Paris 1965)

Vernant, *Tensions*: J.-P. Vernant, 'Tensions et ambiguïtés dans la tragédie grecque', J.-P. Vernant and P. Vidal-Naquet, *Mythe et tragédie en Grèce ancienne* (Paris 1972) 19–40

Vickers: B. Vickers, *Towards Greek Tragedy* (London 1973)

Vidal-Naquet: P. Vidal-Naquet, 'Le *Philoctète* de Sophocle et l'éphébie', J.-P. Vernant and P. Vidal-Naquet, *Mythe et tragédie en Grèce ancienne* (Paris 1972) 159–84

Vlastos, *Elenchus*: G. Vlastos, 'The Socratic elenchus', *OSAP* 1 (1983) 27–58

Vlastos, *Happiness*: G. Vlastos, 'Happiness and virtue in Socrates' moral theory', *Topoi* 4 (1985) 3–22

Vlastos, *Justice*: G. Vlastos, 'Socrates' contribution to the Greek sense of justice', *Archaiognosia* 1, 2 (1980) 301–24

Vlastos, *Love*: G. Vlastos, 'The individual as an object of love in Plato', *Platonic Studies* (2nd ed. Princeton 1981) 3–34

Waldock: A.J.A. Waldock, *Sophocles the Dramatist* (Cambridge 1951)

Webster: T.B.L. Webster, *An Introduction to Sophocles* (Oxford 1936)

Webster, *Philoctetes*: T.B.L. Webster (ed.), *Sophocles: Philoctetes* (Cambridge 1970)

Weinstock: H. Weinstock, *Sophokles* (3rd ed. Wuppertal 1948)

Wheeler: E.L. Wheeler, 'Sophistic interpretations and Greek treaties', *GRBS* 25 (1984) 253–74

Whitman: C.H. Whitman, *Sophocles: A Study of Heroic Humanism* (Cambridge, Mass. 1951)

Wigodsky: M.M. Wigodsky, 'The "salvation" of Ajax', *Hermes* 90 (1962) 149–58

Wilamowitz: T. von. Wilamowitz, *Die dramatische Technik des Sophokles* (Berlin 1917)

Wilamowitz, *Elektren*: U. von Wilamowitz, 'Die beiden Elektren', *Hermes* 18 (1883) 214–63

Willcock: M.M. Willcock, 'The funeral games of Patroclus', *BICS* 20 (1973) 1–11

Williams: B. Williams, *Ethics and the Limits of Philosophy* (Cambridge, Mass. 1985)

Williams, *ML*: B. Williams, *Moral Luck* (Cambridge 1981)

Williams, *PS*: B. Williams, *Problems of the Self* (Cambridge 1973)

Winnington-Ingram: R.P. Winnington-Ingram, *Sophocles: An Interpretation* (Cambridge 1980)

Winnington-Ingram, *Septem*: R.P. Winnington-Ingram, 'Septem Contra Thebas', *YCS* 25 (1977) 1–45 = *Studies in Aeschylus* (Cambridge 1983) 16–54

Winnington-Ingram, *Sophoclea*: R.P. Winnington-Ingram, 'Sophoclea', *BICS* 26 (1979) 1–12

Winnington-Ingram, *Tragica*: R.P. Winnington-Ingram, 'Tragica', *BICS* 16 (1969) 44–54

Winnington-Ingram, *Women*: R.P. Winnington-Ingram, 'Sophocles and women', *Fond. Hardt Entr.* 29 (1982) 233–49

Wolf: E. Wolf, *Sentenz und Reflexion bei Sophokles* (Leipzig 1910)

Wolff: E. Wolff, *Platos Apologie* (Berlin 1929)

Woodard (1) and (2): T.M. Woodard, '*Electra* by Sophocles: the dialectical design', (1) *HSCP* 68 (1964) 163–205; (2) *HSCP* 70 (1965) 195–233

Wycherly: R.E. Wycherly, 'Sophocles *Antigone* 904–20', *CP* 42 (1947) 51–2

Wyse: W. Wyse, *The Speeches of Isaeus* (Cambridge 1904)

INDEX

Achilles: and Ajax, 66 n. 31, 69 n. 42, 70 n. 50, 71 n. 57, 77 n. 85, 82 n. 105, 83 n. 116, 88, 100; arms of, 33, 66, 69f., 88–90, 93, 94, 100, 195, 196, 208 n. 91, 216f., 269f.; and Help Friends/Harm Enemies, 27, 34, 35, 47, 52 n. 132, 53 n. 134, 55, 216 n. 109; as heroic paradigm, 9 n. 28, 12, 14, 83 nn. 116–17, 113, 184, 185, 196, 200; and Neoptolemus, 184f., 192, 195, 197, 214f., 217

Adkins, A.W.H., 4f., 71, 166f.

Aegisthus, 153–5, 157, 160, 168, 172, 175–8, 180, 181

Aeschylus, 13, 29, 175, 177 nn. 107–8, 179, 182, 257

affection, 39–41, 43, 44f., 65, 75, 77, 80, 108f., 111f., 120, 125, 137, 144f., 155, 174, 195f., 202, 213, 221, 232, 248, 267, 271; parental, 40f., 79, 109, 151, 165, 226, 227, 228f.

afterlife, *see* underworld

Agamemnon (*see also* Atreidae): in Homer, 34, 195; in *Aj.*, 86, 89, 93–9, 101–3, 105; in *El.*, 150–7, 158–60, 162, 164–8, 173f., 176f., 256, 262

aidos, 76f., 90f., 98, 125, 162, 168, 171, 230, 239, 241–3; *see also* shame and disgrace

Ajax: in *Aj.*, 60–105, 113, 235, 241, 253, 261, 264, 269f., 272; in Homer, 83 n. 116, 87, 93, 94, 114

Ajax, 60–105, 113, 114, 174, 177, 183, 231, 235, 241, 248, 251, 253, 261, 263, 264, 269f., 271, 272

alliances, 34, 42, 47, 48, 53, 230f.

altruism in friendship, 35f., 40f., 43 n. 90, 50, 61, 101, 102f., 120–2, 124f., 141, 206, 217f., 219f., 222, 224f., 228, 232, 234–6, 240f., 265f., 271

anger, 27, 53, 65, 69f., 85, 130, 131f., 135, 137–9, 141, 169f., 179f., 195f., 214, 234, 236, 239, 241, 247, 250, 253, 255 n. 97, 256, 259

animals, humans and, 40, 41 n. 73, 43 n. 86, 45, 69 n. 42, 109, 138, 141, 143, 150, 153, 155, 194, 203, 224

Antigone: in *Ant.*, 106–15, 120f., 126–48, 235, 239, 262, 266, 272; in *OC*, 230, 232, 233, 238–43, 246–8, 251, 252, 255, 259, 261, 271

Antigone, 106–48, 158, 176f., 183, 239, 251, 261, 262, 263, 265, 266, 269, 270, 272

Apollo, 150, 173, 175f., 182f., 226, 230, 253

arete (excellence), 2 n. 5, 4f., 14, 29 n. 17, 56, 70, 88, 94, 96–101, 103, 105, 114, 119, 123, 155f., 166, 188, 191–3, 196f., 200, 205, 222, 249

Aristotle, 24f., 48, 52f., 54, 71 n. 57, 209, 228 n. 5, 272; on friendship, 29 n. 17, 28, 33, 35, 38, 41, 43 n. 86, 44, 46, 67, 125 n. 80, 126; on literature, 1, 14f., 16–24, 59 n. 151, 134

mutability of friendship and enmity, 38,
82, 85f., 87f., 98–100, 101, 103, 242;
see also enmity, permanence of

Nagel, T., 265
natural friendship and enmity, 26f.,
40–3, 46, 48, 148, 150–2, 155, 169,
229, 254
nature (*phusis*): and birth, 79, 91, 157,
158, 169, 182, 185; of individual
characters, 113, 122, 140, 188, 189,
203, 206, 227; female, 111, 153, 160,
172, 175, *see also* women; *see also*
human nature; natural friendship and
enmity; animals, humans and
necessity and choice, 167, 170f., 188,
194, 207, 208f., 215, 238, 247
Neoptolemus, 18 n. 57, 184–225, 243,
251, 261, 262, 263f., 268, 271, 272
nobility, 71, 72, 75, 77, 86, 91, 95, 97,
98, 110, 111, 112, 152f., 157, 171,
185, 196, 199, 205, 212, 220, 249
noblesse oblige, 44, 87, 91, 202 n. 71
nurture, 41f., 43, 44, 77, 125, 150, 153,
240 n. 45, 247
Nussbaum, M.C., 108, 124

obedience, *see* authority, respect for
Odysseus: in *Aj.*, 60–64, 76, 82, 85f., 89,
94, 95–105, 231, 242, 251, 261, 269,
270, 271; in Homer, 12, 60, 83 n. 116,
114; in *Phil.*, 17f., 23f., 173 n. 84,
184–204, 205–14, 218, 221, 224, 233,
247, 260, 261, 262, 263, 268, 271, 272;
traditional persona of, 60, 61 n. 6, 63,
83, 90, 103, 184 n. 1, 185, 187 n. 13,
191
Oedipus, 226–59, 260f., 262, 270, 272
Oedipus at Colonus, 226–59, 260f., 262,
263, 267, 268, 270f., 272
Oedipus Tyrannus, 24f., 233 n. 29
old age, 41f., 43, 76, 233, 256; and
youth 115 n. 36, 131f., 255; *see also*
youth oracles and prophecies,
85 n. 127, 138, 139, 176, 177, 183,
184, 205 n. 82, 215, 224, 226, 227,
228 n, 6, 230, 233, 244, 246 n. 63, 253;
see also Apollo, Teiresias
Orestes, 149–55, 169, 172–7, 178f., 180,
181, 182f.

paedagogus (in *El.*), 153, 154, 173, 174,
175, 180
pain and grief, 179, 232, 255, 256, 267;
and enmity, 27, 28, 157, 177, 196,
228, 234, 238, 240; at death of friends,
74, 76, 78, 80, 130, 137, 139, 141f.,
154, 155, 180, 251; and friendship,
34f., 38, 43, 46, 57, 72–4, 104, 112,
125, 140, 185, 206, 229, 235, 240, 244;
moral, 110, 135, 157f., 159, 189,
201 n. 64, 206; and pleasure, 68, 125,
139–41, 234f., 240
panourgia (villainy), 54, 120 n. 54, 162,
188f., 196, 211
parents and children, 36, 38, 40–2, 48,
66, 68, 70, 75–7, 79, 81, 84, 86, 93,
107f., 120–2, 123, 131, 133f., 137f.,
142, 147, 150–77, 181–3, 226–9, 232,
233, 238–48; *see also philia*, kinship-
paternalism, 36f., 220 n. 119, 234–6, 263
payment model of justice, 29, 31, 32f.,
41f., 44, 54, 70, 130, 135, 162, 164,
168f., 222, 237, 239, 268
persuasion, 14, 167, 185, 190, 206, 223,
233, 245, 249; in drama, 12; by
friends, 37, 73f., 82, 95–9, 101, 214f.,
221f., 263, 270f.; openness to, 99,
121, 128, 131f., 160, 203, 211, 216,
241, 247, 252, 269; *see also* learning
from others
philanthropia, 43
philia, 31–49; benefits of, 31–3, 35f.,
41f., 43, 45–7, 49, 50, 58f.; civic, 38,
43f., 48, 50, 52f., 58f., 117–20, 121,
124–7, 138, 148, 154f., 226f., 229,
231f., 236, 261f., 265; *see also*
unanimity, political; *polis*; initiation
of, 45f., 49, 97, 99, 102, 105, 174, 196,
204, 229–32; kinship-, 37, 38, 39–43,
44f., 48, 50, 75–7, 79–81, 84, 86, 94f.,
102, 104, 105, 106–22, 124f.,
129 n. 98, 132–6, 137f., 141f., 146,
148, 150–61, 164–70, 174, 180, 181f.,
226–9, 232, 233f., 239, 241–8, 259,
261f., *see also* marriage; parents and
children; personal, 44–7, 48, 50, 52,
74f., 117f., 120f., 122, 134, 138, 213,
221, 224f., 230f., 252, 261f., 265, *see
also* affection, gods and friendship
and enmity, marriage; presumptive,